MATHEMATICS

A Basic Course

DAVID G. SALTEN

Former Superintendent of Schools
Long Beach, N. Y.

ROBERT W. DEVER

Baldwin High School
Baldwin, N. Y.

THE ADULT EDUCATION COMPANY
888 Seventh Avenue, New York, N.Y. 10106

CONTENTS

PREFACE

The use of numbers is essential to our daily living. Just recall how many times you used arithmetic today. In fact, hardly a day passes in which you have not used arithmetic in some way. The arithmetic you do each day is as important as the language you speak. Arithmetic is not difficult to master; it can even be fun.

The purpose of this book is to teach you to do everyday arithmetic problems in a simple, logical, step-by-step manner. In this book you will learn many useful ways to help you master the fundamentals of arithmetic. Master the Rules to Remember, practice the How to Do Examples, take the General Skills Exercises and Mastery Tests, go on to the Chapter Reviews and, finally, tackle the Skills Tests in the back of the book.

You'll succeed in mastering arithmetic if you work conscientiously at it. In mathematics, practice is the key to success. Learn the mathematical operations involved—study them until you know them well. Then go on to the tests. Check your score. If you discover areas of weakness, review the principles until you have overcome them. Then go on to the next topic.

Follow this plan and you will surely achieve success.

1

USING WHOLE NUMBERS

How the Use of Numbers Began

Many thousands of years ago this was a world without numbers. Nobody missed them because nobody needed them. Everyone knew just what belonged to him and what did not. If a cow was missing, the owner knew it was gone, not by counting the cows, but for the same reason a mother would know if one of her children did not come home for dinner.

But soon people acquired more and more property. They would count one cow, two cows, three cows; one vase, two vases, three vases; always one, two, three or more of something they owned or saw.

How far we have advanced from the time of our ancestors! Today, using numerals and mathematics, man builds bridges, skyscrapers . . . flies off the earth like a bird . . . even measures the distance to the moon and the brightness of the light given off by the firefly! But it is just as important, though not as exciting, that he can tell the time, pay the grocer, count the runs in a baseball game and use the same numbers in many different ways in everyday life.

So you see, mathematics and numbers, from simple arithmetic to complex algebraic and geometric calculations, are important to life in our times.

How We Read and Write Large Numbers

To make it easier to read large numbers, we separate the figures of the number by commas into groups of three, counting from right to left. Each group is called a *period* and has its own name.

The system of numbers we use, called the Hindu-Arabic system, is one of the world's greatest inventions. It is a *decimal* system; that is, it is based on *tens*. In this system, we need only ten symbols to write any number of any size. We can do this because we use a *place system*. The symbols we use are 0, 1, 2, 3, 4, 5, 6, 7, 8, 9. These symbols are called *digits*. The *value* a digit represents is determined by the *place* it has in the number; if a digit is moved to the left one place, the value it represents becomes ten times as great.

Zero in the decimal system is a "place-holder"; in the number **30**, the zero shows that 3 has been moved to the left one place, thus counting tens instead of ones. The place value in numbers are shown in the following table.

Hundred billions	Ten billions	Billions	Hundred millions	Ten millions	Millions	Hundred thousands	Ten thousands	Thousands	Hundreds	Tens	Ones
6	8	2,	8	4	7,	1	3	6,	5	9	2
	Billions			Millions			Thousands			Ones	

This number is read: six hundred eighty-two billion, eight hundred forty-seven million, one hundred thirty-six thousand, five hundred ninety-two. Notice that the word "and" is never used in reading a whole number.

682,	**847,**	**136,**	**592**
Billions	Millions	Thousands	Ones or Units
Period	Period	Period	Period

Rule to Remember

1. All periods of a number contain three digits, or places (the first period on the left may or may not).

2. Zero is used as a place-holder.

EXERCISES

Reading and Writing Numbers

1. *Read these numbers:*
   a. 846,732,184
   b. 1,384,926,123
   c. 11,123,456,789
   d. 732,846,123
   e. 7,846,810,926
   f. 127,737,246,821
   g. 1,004,002,001
   h. 101,120,320,140
   i. 126,000

2. *Place commas in their proper places in the following numbers:*
   a. 32231
   b. 1234
   c. 64357842
   d. 832164
   e. 4158932
   f. 124789914
   g. 9271324
   h. 18213762
   i. 1249874162

3. *Write the following numbers:*
   a. 3 million, 401 thousand, 127
   b. 51 million, 84 thousand, 10
   c. 67 million, 4 thousand, 3
   d. 140 million, 327 thousand, 420
   e. 106 million, 100 thousand, 100
   f. 237 million, 21 thousand, 54
   g. 8 billion, 142 million, 426 thousand, 321
   h. 97 billion, 26 million, 304 thousand, 100
   i. 146 billion, 8 million, 23 thousand, 54
   j. 349 billion, 327 million, 6 thousand, 5

4. a. How many hundreds are there in 746,132?
   b. How many thousands in 145,891,748?
   c. How many millions in 6,129,846?
   d. How many billions in 3,579,324,126?

5. *Write the following numbers in words:*
   a. 89
   b. 459
   c. 12,100
   d. 89,050
   e. 7,003
   f. 124,500
   g. 103,120
   h. 800,008
   i. 925,500
   j. 900,600
   k. 5,500,000
   l. 150,800,000

USING WHOLE NUMBERS

Roman Numerals

The Romans used seven capital letters to represent numbers. They put them together to form many different combinations. Roman numerals are used in some books in numbering chapters, on some watch and clock dials and on the cornerstones of some buildings. In writing numbers, the Romans could add and subtract.

The Roman system of numbers is based upon these number symbols: I, V, X, L, C, D and M. This is what each symbol represents:

Roman Numeral	I	V	X	L	C	D	M
Hindu-Arabic Numeral	1	5	10	50	100	500	1000

Rules to Remember

1. *If a symbol is repeated, its value is repeated. The symbols V, L and D are never repeated.*

2. *The same symbol is never written more than three times in succession.*

3. *A symbol written after a symbol of greater value increases the value of the larger number; the two values are added.*

4. *A symbol written before a symbol of greater value decreases the value of the larger number; the two values are subtracted. The symbols V, L and D are never subtracted. The symbols I, X and C are subtracted from the next two larger numerals, but from no others.*

TABLE OF ROMAN NUMBERS AND THEIR ARABIC EQUIVALENTS

Roman	Arabic	Roman	Arabic	Roman	Arabic
I	1	XI	11	XC	90
II	2	XV	15	C	100
III	3	XIX	19	CX	110
IV	4	XX	20	CC	200
V	5	XXV	25	CD	400
VI	6	XXX	30	D	500
VII	7	XL	40	DC	600
VIII	8	XLIX	49	CM	900
IX	9	L	50	M	1000
X	10	LXXX	80	MM	2000

EXERCISES

Roman and Arabic Numbers

1. *Write the following in Roman numerals:*
   a. 37   *g.* 68   *m.* 99
   b. 101   *h.* 117   *n.* 149
   c. 250   *i.* 375   *o.* 480
   d. 1100   *j.* 1666   *p.* 1860
   e. 1957   *k.* 2001   *q.* 2249
   f. 3310   *l.* 3370   *r.* 3399

2. *Write the following in Arabic numerals:*
   a. IX   *g.* XXXIX   *m.* XLIV
   b. XLV   *h.* LXVI   *n.* LXX
   c. CXXV   *i.* XCVII   *o.* CXVI
   d. CCIX   *j.* CDL   *p.* DCXL
   e. MXCIV   *k.* CMXXV   *q.* ML
   f. MMCLXXVI   *l.* MMMDXC   *r.* MCDXI

3. *Write in Hindu-Arabic symbols: three million, one thousand, sixty-two.*

Rounding Off Numbers

The American Baseball League had a record attendance of 6,976,249 people in one year. Of course, this number is hard to remember. So, to make remembering easier, we *round off* the number. We say that the record attendance is about 7,000,000.

However, not all numbers are rounded off. Sometimes we must be exact. If a team's uniforms cost $299, would you pay the outfitter $300? If 103 people are coming into a theater, we are not satisfied with "about" 100 seats.

Whether or not we round off a number and how much we round it off depends upon how the number is to be used.

How to Round Off Numbers

In rounding off a number to a required number of places, keep as many figures to the left as are needed. Drop the other figures and replace them with zeros. Examine the digit that is one place to the right of the last figure required. If this digit is 5 or greater, add 1 to the last figure kept. If the numeral is less than 5, do not change the round number.

HOW TO DO THE EXAMPLE

"More than 5"

4,872,156 rounded to the nearest million is **5,000,000**

"Less than 5"

361,271 rounded to the nearest thousand is **361,000.**

"Number is 5"

85 rounded to the nearest ten is **90.**

EXERCISES
Rounding Off Numbers

1. *Round off each of the following numbers to the nearest ten:*

a. 11	*e.* 99	*h.* 291
b. 17	*f.* 122	*i.* 1,488
c. 58	*g.* 178	*j.* 2,111
d. 72		

2. *Round off the following numbers to the nearest hundred:*

a. 621	*d.* 1009	*g.* 5101
b. 868	*e.* 1453	*h.* 7249
c. 951	*f.* 2309	*i.* 10,163

3. *Round off each of the following to the nearest thousand:*
   - *a.* 4,126
   - *b.* 5,555
   - *c.* 12,126
   - *d.* 15,742
   - *e.* 37,500
   - *f.* 98,832
4. *Round off each of the following numbers to the nearest million:*
   - *a.* 2,146,528
   - *b.* 3,498.461
   - *c.* 8,500,000
   - *d.* 11,126,101
   - *e.* 14,876,002
   - *f.* 29,589,320
5. *a.* The centerfield distance from home plate to the fence in a baseball stadium is 475 feet. Expressed to the nearest hundred feet, the distance is ....

   b. The N.Y. Mets won the National League and World Series Championships. Each player received $18,338. This sum, rounded to the nearest thousand, is (*a*) $18,500, (*b*) $19,000, (*c*) $18,000.

   c. According to the Bureau of Census, there are 22,354,000 blacks in the U.S. Expressed to the nearest million the population is (*a*) 22,000,000, (*b*) 23,000,000, (*c*) 22,500,000.

   d. The population of Puerto Rico is 2,741,800. To the nearest million, this is ....

   e. In the election of 1964, Richard M. Nixon received 31,770,237 votes. To the nearest million, this is ....

6. *Round off each of the numbers in problem 4 above, to the nearest hundred thousand.*
7. *Round off each of the numbers in problem 4 above, to the nearest ten thousand.*
8. Round off each of the following amounts to the nearest dollar: (*a*) $5.40, (*b*) $16.66, (*c*) $113.78.

Adding Whole Numbers

When we add a group of numbers, the result of adding groups of numbers is called the *sum*. The separate numbers to be added are called the *addends*. Numbers can be added in any order.

In adding a series of numbers, begin with the column at the right. If the sum of a column of digits is ten or larger, carry the tens digit and add it to the sum of the digits in the next column to the left.

Always check your work! It takes a little more time, but the effort is worth it. It will guarantee the accuracy of your work.

Essentials to Remember

Checking. Careless mistakes are sometimes made because the work was not checked. It is always wise to check your answer. If, when you first added the numbers, you added *up* the columns, check by adding *down* each column. If the addition is correct, you will get the same sum both times.

HOW TO DO THE EXAMPLE

Add upward:

2861	⎫
9734	⎬ Addends
1258	⎱
7936	⎭
Think: 2 1 1	Carry
21,789	Sum

Check: Reverse addition by adding columns downward.

Think: 2 1 1   Carry
2861
9734
1258
7936
21,789 √

EXERCISES

Adding Whole Numbers

1. *Add the following columns of numbers and check each answer.*

a. 53	*b.* 11	*c.* 33	*d.* 427	*e.* 3631
78	19	27	784	4210
29	24	14	962	9641
14	99	17	1042	7589
65	88	18		
		19		
		22		

2. *Add the following numbers and check:*

a. 45,067; 8853; 633; 12,357

b. 1284; 33,196; 8654; 321,157

3. *Find the sum of:*
  a. 864; 9261; 10001; 83691
  b. 15326; 17000; 29105; 121636

4. *Add the following numbers and check:*

a.	b.	c.
86421	12468	846297
97635	97321	124581
10421	46529	297642
56890	84111	413789
	93123	

5. *Rewrite, add the following numbers and check:*
  a. $2746 $1896 $2145 $976
  b. $13589 $29462 $94001 $87503
  c. $29754 $18964 $98423 $74349
  d. $37917 $42560 $80401 $90123 $246 $10

6. In one year, attendance figures for National League ball clubs were: Atlanta, 1,458,320; Chicago, 1,664,859; Houston, 1,442,995; Los Angeles, 1,784,527; New York, 2,175,373; San Francisco, 873,000. What was the total attendance?

7. The purchase order for office supplies was as follows: $3.50 for paper; 79 cents for a note pad; 86 cents for pencils; 25 cents for a ruler; 89 cents for ball point pens. What was the total bill?

8. Four men decide to go into business. The money invested is as follows: $4638, $3562, $4000, and $6250. How much did they all invest together?

9. The area in square miles of the following countries is: Soviet Union, 8,647,749; Canada, 3,850,790; China, 3,690,546; United States, 3,614,254. Find the total number of square miles.

10. The five cities with the largest populations are: Tokyo, 8,907,000; New York, 7,969,000; Shanghai, 6,900,000; Moscow, 6,422,000. Find the total population for these cities.

11. Harry Jones works in a factory where he makes airplane parts. During one week he made the following number of articles: 498, 564, 684, 582, 491. How many articles did he produce?

12. The ratings of the engines of a four-motor plane are as follows: 3,600 horsepower, 3,500 horsepower, 3,000 horsepower, and 3,800 horsepower. What is their total horsepower?

Subtracting Whole Numbers

Subtraction is the opposite of addition. When we add, we put two groups together to form a larger group. When we subtract, we take part of a group away and find the size of the group that is left.

In subtracting numbers, the number which is to be made smaller is called the *minuend;* the number to be "taken away" or subtracted is called the *subtrahend.* The answer is called the *remainder,* or *difference.*

In a mid-western town, there were 1465 accidents in one year due to household carelessness. As a result of an Accident Prevention Drive, the number of accidents was cut down to 891 the following year. How many fewer accidents were there after the drive? Let's work out the problem.

Essential to Remember

In checking a subtraction example, add the remainder and the subtrahend. If your answer is correct, the result obtained by the addition equals the minuend.

HOW TO DO THE EXAMPLE

Problem: Subtract 891 from 1465 and check.

		Check	
1465	Minuend	1465	
891	Subtrahend	891	◄ Add these
574	Remainder	574	◄ two numbers
		1465 √	

EXERCISES

Subtracting Whole Numbers

1. *Subtract, then check your answers:*

   a. 463   *b.* 976   *c.* 847   *d.* 746
     221   482   101   213

2. *Subtract and check:*

   a. 1742   *b.* 2478   *c.* 10,421   *d.* 11,643
     104   1096   1,748   7,921

3. *Subtract and check:*

   a. 204,623   *b.* 743,196   *c.* 987,211   *d.* 1,123,406
     21,004   99,999   104,320   743,921

4. John went to the supermarket with a $20 bill. He bought the following items: meats, $8.27; dairy products, $2.34; bread, $.47; fruits and vegetables, $2.25. How much change did he bring home?

5. In the 1968 presidential election, the total popular vote cast was 73,211,562. Of this total, Nixon received 31,785,480; Humphrey received 31,275,165 and Wallace received 9,906,473. How many more votes did Nixon get than did Humphrey? How many more votes did Humphrey get than Wallace?

6. The President of the United States receives a salary of $200,000 per year. The Vice President gets $62,500. How much more money does the President get than does the Vice President?

7. At the beginning of one day Mr. Henry had $398.47 in his special checking account. At the end of the day he had a balance of $127.29 left in his account. How much money did he pay out by check?

8. In one year in the United States, 410,000 television sets were made having a value of $120,000,000. Five years later, 9,000,000 sets were made having a value of $1,600,000,000. What was the increase in the number of sets produced? What was the increase in value?

9. A man has $12,500 with which to build a house. The house plot costs $2500; the house costs $15,500; the garage costs $1275. Other expenses amount to $2525. How much money must he borrow to complete his home?

10. A man can buy a car for $3275 if he pays cash. If he takes 12 months to pay for the car, it will cost him $3749. How much does he save by paying cash?

11. The attendance at a professional basketball game totaled 9,329. 7,129 seats were reserved. How many people did not have reserved seats?

12. The population of Ourtown was 72,340 in 1960, and 83,286 in 1970. What was the growth in population in this 10-year period? Give the answer to the nearest hundred, and to the nearest thousand.

13. During one year an airline serving the West was scheduled to fly 683,926 miles. However, bad weather caused some flights to be cancelled so that only 613,110 miles were flown. How many miles of flight were cancelled?

14. On January 1, a water meter read 26,124 gallons. At the end of the month the reading was 48,901 gallons. How many gallons were used?

15. During a six-month interval a manufacturing company earned $5,126,423. During the next six-month period the earnings amounted to $6,374,910. How much of an increase was there in the earnings?

GENERAL SKILLS EXERCISE

Try the following test of your skill. If you get any wrong, turn to the pages shown after each question, and learn the correct answer.

1. Our system of numbers is called the .... (page 2).

2. Numbers greater than thousands are arranged in groups of three numbers called .... (page 2).

3. Our number system is a place system based on .... (page 2).

4. The largest possible number that can be written with the numbers 6, 3, 5 is .... (page 2).

5. In rounding off a number to the nearest hundred when the number in the tens place is 5, we .... (*increase, decrease*) the hundreds number (page 6).

6. The order in which numbers are added .... (*does, does not*) change the sum (page 7).

7. If you added a column of numbers upwards, you check the addition by adding the columns .... (page 8).

8. The larger number from which another number is subtracted is called the .... (page 10).

9. When one number is subtracted from another, the result is called the .... (page 10).

10. The numbers being added are called the .... (page 8).

My Score ——————

Multiplying Whole Numbers

John Willitt, quizmaster of the television program "We Challenge You This Week!" was preparing a list of questions for the coming week's program. There were to be 35 contestants and he decided that he would judge the length of the list of questions by allowing an average of 12 questions for each contestant. To find the number of questions he needed, he multiplied 35 by 12.

The quizmaster now knew that he had to make up 420 questions for the coming week's program. Here's how he worked out the problem:

First, he kept like places in columns, units under units, tens under tens, and so on.

35	Multiplicand
×12	Multiplier
70	Partial product
35	Partial product
420	Product

To find the total of a given number of *equal* groups, we can multiply. In multiplication, the number by which you multiply is called the *multiplier;* the number being multiplied is called the *multiplicand.* The number resulting from the multiplication is called the *product.* The numbers obtained by the multiplication which are added to obtain the product are called the *partial products.*

In writing the partial products make sure that you write the last digit of the partial product under the digit of the multiplier by which you have multiplied.

Essentials to Remember

Multiplication can be checked by interchanging the multiplier and multiplicand and multiplying again. If the multiplication is correct, the same product is obtained. The multiplication may also be checked by dividing the product by the multiplier. The answer obtained should be the same as the multiplicand.

HOW TO DO THE EXAMPLE

Problem: Multiply 537 by 46 and check.

		Check	or	Check
537	Multiplicand	46		537 ✓
×46	Multiplier	×537		46) 24702
3222	Partial product	322		230
2148	Partial product	138		170
24,702	Product	230		138
		24,702 ✓		322
				322

Rules to Remember

The product of any number multiplied by zero is zero.

$$0 \times 9 = 0$$

The product of any number multiplied by one is the same number.

$$1 \times 9 = 9$$

The order in which numbers are multiplied does not change the product.

$$9 \times 1 = 9; \ 1 \times 9 = 9$$

EXERCISES

Multiplying Whole Numbers

1. *Multiply each of the following and check your answer:*

   a. 517   b. 697   c. 843   d. 709
      42   57   90   86
   ──   ──   ──   ──

2. *Find the product in each of the following and check your results:*

   a. 8,927   b. 12,009   c. 28,400   d. 20,003
      504   420   202   209
   ──   ──   ──   ──

3. *Obtain the product of each and check your results:*

   a. 948×15 b. 1123×49 c. 26098×409

4. *Multiply and check:*

   a. 7598   b. 85432   c. 38540
      37   76   85
   ──   ──   ──

5. *Obtain the products and check each answer:*

   a. 3786   b. 9573   c. 1426
      587   9348   876
   ──   ──   ──

6. The product obtained when a number is multiplied by **zero**
is ....

7. *Multiply and check:*

   a. 4126   b. 32745   c. 29641
      913   192   121
   ──   ──   ──

8. *Multiply and check:*

   a. 3960   b. 2160   c. 3841
      120   101   210
   ──   ──   ──

9. *Multiply and check:*

   a. 2320   b. 4001   c. 9007
      320   401   620
   ──   ──   ──

10. *Obtain the product of:*

    a. 8,927 and 504   b. 12,009 and 420

11. *Find the product of:*

    a. 7643 and 101   c. 106,896 and 1105
    b. 96,121 and 804   d. 208,641 and 11,364

12. A man buys 150 shares of stock at the market price of $125 each share. In addition, he pays a broker's commission of $160. How much did the shares cost?

13. A gasoline company owned a fleet of 160 trucks each with a capacity of 3,175 gallons. If each of these trucks made two trips one day, each time completely filled, how many gallons of gas were delivered that day?

14. A bushel of potatoes weighs about 70 pounds. A grower has 500 bushels of potatoes. How many 100 pound bags can the grower fill?

15. A farmer owns 169 acres of orchard land which he wishes to plant. In each acre he plants 20 rows of apple trees, with 30 in each row. How many apple trees does he plant?

Dividing Whole Numbers

Division is the opposite of multiplication. Division can be used to solve two kinds of problems: (1) When we know the number of equal groups and want to find the size of each group, and (2) when we know the size of each group and want to find the number of groups.

In a bowling club there were 40 bowlers. The captain wanted to form teams of 4 bowlers each. How many teams could he form?

To find the number of equal teams, he divided 40 by 4 and found he could form 10 teams.

In this problem we knew the total in the large group and, by division divided this group into equal smaller groups.

If the captain had known he wanted 10 equal teams, division could be used to find the *size* of each squad.

In division, the number that is to be divided is called the *dividend*. The number by which the dividend is to be divided is called the *divisor*. The answer is called the *quotient*. The *remainder* is what is left over after the dividend has been divided into equal parts. If there is a remainder, it may be written over the divisor and expressed as a fraction in the quotient.

The same division example can be indicated in three different ways: $84\overline{)7321}$ $\frac{7321}{84}$ or $7321 \div 84.$

In all three cases, the divisor is 84 and the dividend is 7321.

Rules to Remember

The division sign (÷) is read "divided by."

Division can be checked by multiplying the quotient and the divisor and adding the remainder to their product.

HOW TO DO THE EXAMPLE

Problem: Divide 7321 by 84 and check.

1. *Divide.* How many 84's are there in 73? in 732? Try 9; that is, multiply 84 by 9. Since the result, 756, is larger than 732, try 8. Write the 8 over the 2.

2. *Multiply.* Multiply 84 by the partial quotient 8. Place the product 672 under 732.

3. *Subtract.* Subtract 672 from 732. The remainder must be smaller than 84, the divisor.

4. *Bring down* the next number, 1, and place it next to the 0 of 60. The new dividend is 601.

5. *Continue.* Divide the 84 into 601, write the 7 over the 1, and repeat the process. The remainder is 13. Write the remainder as a fraction of 84 in the quotient.

Quotient $87\frac{13}{84}$

Divisor 84) 7321 Dividend

672

601

588

13 Remainder

Check

Multiply the divisor 84 by the quotient 87. When you have completed the multiplication, add the remainder to the product.

$$
\begin{array}{r}
84 \\
\times 87 \\
\hline
588 \\
672 \\
\hline
7308 \\
+13 \\
\hline
7321 \;\checkmark
\end{array}
$$

Estimating Quotients

In solving a division problem it is often best to save time by estimating the quotient. This means that you make a rough estimate of the answer before you start the work. When the estimate is made, you know the approximate size of the answer.

For example, let us suppose that you are given the problem $39\overline{)158}$. To estimate the answer, round off both numbers, changing the problem to $40\overline{)160}$. To make the problem even simpler, you drop the zero at the end of each number, and then divide 16 by 4. Your estimated answer is 4. You know that the actual answer is very near that.

Estimating quotients helps you in two ways: you can use the estimate as a guide in finding your answer, and you can use it as a rough check after you have found your answer. It will tell you if your answer is approximately correct, and it will help you to judge more easily what numbers must be in the quotient.

EXERCISES
Dividing and Multiplying Whole Numbers

1. *Divide the following and check your answers.*

   a. $47\overline{)6532}$ c. $68\overline{)9432}$ e. $98\overline{)10684}$

   b. $62\overline{)12403}$ d. $26\overline{)20904}$ f. $79\overline{)36547}$

2. *Do the division and check your results.*

   a. $6896 \div 142$ c. $2700 \div 269$ e. $7426 \div 429$

   b. $9125 \div 125$ d. $555556 \div 567$ f. $88275 \div 825$

3. *Divide and check:*

   a. $327\overline{)14268}$ b. $498\overline{)21264}$ c. $586\overline{)984321}$

4. *Estimate the quotients of each of the following and then find the more accurate answers.*

   a. $21\overline{)659}$ c. $62\overline{)401}$ e. $59\overline{)5555}$

   b. $198\overline{)8629}$ d. $364\overline{)3730}$ f. $480\overline{)3522}$

5. Each bus can carry 40 passengers. How many buses are required to transport 840 passengers?

6. A trucking company owns 68 trucks, each capable of delivering 28,642 pounds per day. How many pounds of material can be delivered each day?

7. One state has 17 counties each having an average population of 39,142 people. Approximately how many people live in the state?

8. A man buys 40 books and pays $160. How much does each

9. *Divide and check:*

    a. 871)$\overline{32167}$ *b.* 196)$\overline{81302}$ *c.* 251)$\overline{81229}$

10. *Divide and check:*

    a. 828543÷425   *b.* 62973÷576   *c.* 631031÷341

11. How many 15's are there in 2595?

12. Mr. Perez spent $32 for baseball bats for his Little League team. Each bat cost $4. How many bats did he buy?

13. Mr. Jones is taking his family on a vacation trip covering 3,200 miles. He can go 20 miles on each gallon of gasoline. If gasoline cost 40 cents a gallon, how much will the gasoline cost for the trip?

14. A man bought a house for 16,000. He is to pay this amount at the rate of $200 per month. How long will it take him to pay for the house.

Comparing Numbers by Division

Division can also be used to show that one number is a certain number of times as large as another number.

Rule to Remember

To find what multiple a larger number is of a smaller, divide the larger number by the smaller number.

HOW TO DO THE EXAMPLE

Problem: Mr. Michaels has $400 in the bank. His son, Martin, has $80 in the bank. Mr. Michaels' deposit is how many times as large as Martin's?

To solve this problem we divide $400 by $80.

$$\$400 \div \$80 = 5.$$

The quotient, 5, tells us that Mr. Michaels' deposit, $400, is 5 times as large as Martin's $80 deposit.

EXERCISES

Comparing Numbers by Division

1. *The larger number is how many times as large as the smaller?*
   a. 200 than 5?   *c.* 100 than 35?   *e.* 19 than 17?
   b. 36 than 18?   *d.* 13 than 5?   *f.* 150 than 30?

2. Last week Henry worked 14 hours on his part-time job. Al worked 6 hours. How many times as great is the number of hours Henry worked compared to the number Al worked?

Averages

When we want to find a single number that will represent all the numbers in a group of unequal sums or quantities we find the *average* (or *arithmetic mean*). In the example below the kind of average that is found is called the *arithmetic mean*.

Rule to Remember

To find the average of a group of unequal numbers, we add the numbers and then divide their sum by the number of addends.

HOW TO DO THE EXAMPLE

Problem: John made the following number of radio sets in one week: 82, 70, 98, 86 and 90. What was his average production for the week?

82 **Step 1.** Add the sets.   **Step 2.** Divide the sum by the
70   number of addends (5)
98 $85\frac{1}{5}$
86   5) 426
90
426 Sum

John's average production was 85 radio sets for the week

EXERCISES

Finding Averages

1. Find the average of 76, 58, 75, 90 and 82.

2. What is the average of 28, 36, 40, 32, 50, 60 and 80?

3. A new play was given on 5 different days. The play was attended by 1,560 people. What was the average number of people attending each performance?

4. A plane leaves New York City at 1 a.m. and travels 2,650 miles. It arrives at its destination at 12 noon. What was the average speed of the plane?

5. In a magazine sales contest, 6 salesmen sold the following number of magazine subscriptions: 42, 36, 28, 30, 25, 27. What was the average number of subscriptions sold by each salesman?

6. Last year Mr. Henry drove his car for 8,720 miles. What was his average mileage per month?

7. A salesman works on a commission basis. His commissions for each of the last 6 months were as follows: $650, $612, $718, $812, $672, and $723. What was his average monthly commission?

8. During one week the temperatures at 6 a.m. were as follows: 56°, 58°, 48°, 60°, 58°, 59°, 62°. What was the average temperature at 6 o'clock in the morning?

9. Mr. Martin's salary for the last five years has been $8590, $9020, $3900, $4600, and $4200. What was his average yearly earnings?

10. A train covered 630 miles in 17 hours. What was the train's average speed?

GENERAL SKILL EXERCISE

How are you doing? Try the following test. If you get any wrong, turn to the pages shown after each question. Practice those problems until you have mastered them.

1. The number being multiplied in multiplication is known as the .... (page 13).

2. The number resulting from a multiplication example is the .... (page 13).

3. To check multiplication, before multiplying again we interchange the .... with the .... (page 14).

4. Any number multiplied by zero gives the product ...... (page 14).

5. The number obtained as a result of division is called the .... (page 16).

6. To check division, multiply the .... by the divisor and add .... to the product (page 17).

7. To find out how many times one number is as large as another. .... the larger number by the smaller number (page 19),

8. John has $3 and Henry has $.50. How many times as great is John's sum of money? .... (page 19).

9. Adding several numbers and then dividing their sum by the number of numbers gives the .... of the numbers (page 20).

10. What is the average of 8, 10, 12 and 11 .... (page 20).

——————— *My Score*

PRINCIPLES TO REMEMBER

1. The Hindu-Arabic system of numbers, which we use, is based on tens. Each place in a number has a value. Large numbers are divided into groups of three numbers by the use of commas.

2. The Roman system uses seven capital letters to represent numbers: I, V, X, C, D, L, M.

3. Numbers may be added in any order without changing the sum. Check all additions.

4. In subtracting numbers, the sum of the subtrahend and the difference equals the minuend.

5. When numbers are multiplied, the order in which the numbers are multiplied does not change the product. To check multiplication, interchange the multiplier and the multiplicand and remultiply.

6. Four numbers are involved in division: divisor, dividend, quotient and remainder (which is zero when the division is exact). To check division, multiply the divisor and the quotient and add the remainder to obtain the dividend.

7. Dividing a larger number by a smaller number tells us how many times as great the larger number is, as compared with the smaller.

8. The average of a group of numbers is obtained by adding the numbers and dividing their sum by the number of addends.

MASTERY TEST

1. *Round each of the following numbers to the nearest hundred thousand:*

    a. 946,853   *b.* 555,000   *c.* 1,846,734

2. *Round each of the following to the nearest million:*

    a. 3,046,139   *b.* 8,847,921   *c.* 9,999,133

3. *Add each of the following columns:*

a. 4827	*b.* 9648	*c.* 9003
9731	372	7302
8461	21	6411
3842	5869	3972

4. *Add each of the following columns:*

a. 59842	*b.* 61320	*c.* 10496
64112	74918	21341
32918	32146	46932
2760	58932	18739
	18410	26410
		57655

5. *Subtract each of the following:*

a. 79383	*b.* 91103	*c.* 89325
15489	4063	10910

6. *Subtract each of the following:*

a. 1,393,469	*b.* 6,841,107	*c.* 109,839,425
998,043	1,526,988	86,123,101

7. *Multiply and check:*

a. 821	*b.* 568	*c.* 1039
325	927	846

8. *Multiply and check:*

a. 1826	*b.* 5986	*c.* 8973
1039	2132	4896

9. *Divide each of the following and check:*
   a. $47\overline{)51246}$ b. $75\overline{)89642}$ c. $96\overline{)329641}$

10. *Divide each of the following and check:*
    a. $365\overline{)85983}$ b. $493\overline{)65312}$ c. $819\overline{)497381}$

11. *Perform the following operations and check:*
    a. 352×461 b. 972×1604 c. 8301×4910

12. *Perform the following and check:*
    a. $32612\div96$ b. $459,621\div642$ c. $2,876,924\div3504$

13. *Find the average of the following numbers:*
    a. 896, 421, 635, 146, 975   b. 428, 625, 918, 133

14. *Find the average of:*
    a. 1263, 1838, 1429, 2130, 2608   b. 3129, 8243, 6280, 4136

15. Mrs. Smith bought 22 yards of fabric at $2 per yard. She gave the clerk two $20 bills and a $10 bill. How much change did she receive?

16. James needs $35 to buy a bicycle for his paper delivery route. He has a part-time job in a grocery store where he works 2 hours a day at $1 an hour. How many days will he have to work to earn enough money to buy the bicycle?

17. A large bomber uses about ten gallons of gasoline for each mile. If it has been fueled with 9000 gallons, approximately how far can it fly?

18. On January 1 the gauge on Mr. Castle's fuel oil tank read 704 gallons. January 31 the gauge read 516 gallons. What was the average number of gallons of oil used daily?

19. The citizens of the town of Hempstead collected $12,456 as a result of dances and parties. Of this they distributed $250 to the Red Cross, $500 to the Salvation Army and $400 to the Soldiers' Aid Fund. The remainder of the money was distributed equally among 4 hospitals. How much did each hospital receive?

20. A plane leaves New York City at 3:15 p.m. and flies at an average speed of 310 miles per hour. It arrives at its destination at 6:45 p.m. How many miles does the plane fly?

————— *My Score*

2 | COMMON FRACTIONS

We use fractions whenever we use measures, whether in measuring lengths, baking or cooking. A fraction represents a part of one whole thing. A fraction indicates that something has been cut or divided into a number of equal parts. For example, suppose a pie has been divided into 4 equal parts. If you eat 1 piece of the pie, you have taken 1 part of 4 parts. This part of the pie can be represented by the fraction $\frac{1}{4}$. The remaining portion of the pie, which consists of three of the four equal parts of the pie, is represented by the fraction $\frac{3}{4}$.

In a fraction, the upper and lower numbers are called the *terms* of the fraction. The top term of a fraction, or the term above the fraction sign, is called the *numerator;* the bottom term, or the term below the fraction sign, is called the *denominator.*

$$\frac{1 \quad \text{Numerator}}{4 \quad \text{Denominator}}$$

Principles to Remember

The numerator (top part) of a fraction tells us the number of parts of a divided object.

The denominator (lower part) of a fraction indicates the name of the equal parts and indicates how many equal parts were made from the whole.

$$\frac{3}{5} \qquad\qquad\qquad\qquad \frac{2}{5}$$

A fraction may stand for part of a group. Here is a group of 5 apples. Each apple is $\frac{1}{5}$ (one fifth) of the group. If we take away 2 apples, we say that we are removing $\frac{2}{5}$ of the number of apples present. If we take away 3 apples, we are removing $\frac{3}{5}$ of the number of apples present. In this instance, a fraction is being used to stand for a part of a group.

A fraction also indicates division. For example, the fraction $\frac{3}{4}$ means $3 \times \frac{1}{4}$, or $\frac{1}{4} \times 3$, or $4\overline{)3}$, or $3 \div 4$; similarly, $\frac{8}{9}$ means $8 \div 9$. In this meaning of the fraction, the denominator is to be divided into the numerator.

Let us go back to the picture of the pie. If you take the four equal parts, you would have the whole thing, represented as 1. Since you have taken four parts out of four, we see that this fact, written as a fraction, $\frac{4}{4}$, is equal to 1. Similarly, $\frac{5}{5}$ of the group of apples above would be the *whole* group: $\frac{5}{5} = 1$ whole group. Likewise, $\frac{7}{7}$, as division, means $7 \div 7$, or 1.

Principle to Remember

If in any fraction the numerator and denominator are equal, the fraction is equal to 1.

EXERCISES

Fractions

1. *a.* What fractional part of
   square A is shaded?
   b. What fractional part of
   square B is shaded?
   What part is not shaded?

A   B

2. *a.* What part of the circle is not shaded?
   b. If one of the unshaded portions were
   to be cut in half, what part of the circle
   would each of the two new pieces be?

3. Shade the portion of each figure as indicated.
   figure *a*—shade $\frac{5}{6}$ figure *c*—shade $\frac{3}{6}$
   figure *b*—shade $\frac{1}{8}$ figure *d*—shade $\frac{3}{8}$

C

a   b   c   d

4. *a.* What part of group *a*, below, has been shaded?
   b. What part of group *b* has been shaded?
   c. What part of the squares in group *c* is empty?
   d. The freighters in *d* were in the harbor waiting to receive
   cargo. The black ships have taken on their cargoes and the
   white ships have not. What part of the ships have not yet
   been loaded?

a   b   c   d

5. *a.* The upper term of a fraction is called the ....
   b. The lower term of a fraction is called the ....

c. The upper term indicates the .... of parts being discussed.

d. The lower term indicates the .... of these parts.

6. *Underline the largest fraction of each group.*

a. $\frac{1}{3}$ $\frac{1}{2}$ $\frac{1}{4}$ b. $\frac{1}{6}$ $\frac{1}{7}$ $\frac{1}{8}$ c. $\frac{3}{6}$ $\frac{3}{8}$ $\frac{3}{7}$

7. *Underline the smallest fraction in each group.*

a. $\frac{1}{16}$ $\frac{1}{8}$ $\frac{1}{4}$ b. $\frac{1}{6}$ $\frac{1}{5}$ $\frac{1}{4}$ c. $\frac{2}{3}$ $\frac{2}{5}$ $\frac{2}{9}$

8. *Refer to the figures and fill in the blanks.*

$\frac{?}{4} = 1$ $\frac{?}{6} = 1$ $\frac{?}{6} = \frac{1}{3}$ $\frac{?}{10} = 1$ $\frac{?}{5} = 1$

$\frac{?}{4} = \frac{1}{2}$ $\frac{?}{6} = \frac{1}{2}$ $\frac{?}{3} = 1$ $\frac{?}{10} = \frac{1}{2}$ $\frac{?}{10} = \frac{1}{5}$

Types of Fractions

Before we can work with fractions we must know the different kinds of fractions that exist.

Common Fraction. A common fraction is a number that has a numerator and a denominator represented by numbers placed the one above, and the other below, a horizontal line.

$\frac{3}{7}$ **is a common fraction**

$$\frac{1}{2}$$

PROPER FRACTION

$$\frac{2}{1}$$

IMPROPER FRACTION

1. Proper Fraction. If the numerator of a fraction is less than the denominator, the fraction is called a *proper fraction.* The value of a proper fraction is always less than 1. $\frac{6}{7}, \frac{1}{5}$ and $\frac{9}{10}$ are proper fractions

2. Improper Fractions. If the numerator of a fraction is equal to or larger than the denominator, the fraction is called an *improper fraction.*

The value of an improper fraction is equal to or larger than 1.

$\frac{5}{3}, \frac{3}{2}, \frac{6}{6}$ are improper fractions

Mixed Numbers. A number which consists of a whole number and a fraction is called a *mixed number*.

$3\frac{1}{2}, 5\frac{1}{4}, 9\frac{7}{8}$ are mixed numbers

EXERCISES

Types of Fractions

1. *From the following fractions, choose the proper fractions.*
   a. $\frac{9}{4}$ $\frac{7}{8}$ $\frac{6}{5}$ b. $\frac{3}{5}$ $\frac{7}{6}$ $\frac{8}{7}$ c. $\frac{3}{3}$ $\frac{4}{3}$ $\frac{1}{2}$

2. *Choose the improper fractions from each of the following groups.*
   a. $\frac{8}{7}$ $\frac{3}{5}$ $\frac{2}{3}$ b. $\frac{9}{8}$ $\frac{4}{5}$ $\frac{1}{3}$ c. $\frac{6}{5}$ $\frac{1}{6}$ $\frac{5}{6}$

3. *Using the numbers 4, 3, and 7, or any two of them, write:*
   a. an improper fraction ....
   b. a proper fraction ....
   c. a mixed number ....

4. *Express:*
   a. A quarter as a fractional part of a dollar ....
   b. A dime as a fractional part of a dollar ....
   c. A nickel as a fractional part of a dollar ....

5. a. Express a dollar and twenty-five cents as a mixed number.
   b. Express three dollars and fifty cents as a mixed number.
   c. Express fifteen dollars and seventy-five cents as a mixed number.

How to Work With Fractions

In order to work with fractions we must learn how to:

1. Change a fraction to lower terms.
2. Change a fraction to higher terms.
3. Change an improper fraction to a whole or a mixed number.
4. Change a whole number to an improper fraction.
5. Change a mixed number to an improper fraction.

Reducing a Fraction to Lowest Terms

Mary and Dick were trading foreign stamps. Together they had 76 stamps. Dick took 38. "Now," he said, "I have $\frac{38}{76}$ of all the stamps."

This was a true, but a rather awkward way for Dick to express himself. Actually, Dick had $\frac{1}{2}$ of all the stamps.

Principles to Remember

1. The numerator and the denominator of a fraction may be divided by the same number without changing the value of the fraction.

2. A proper fraction is in its simplest form when the only number that divides into both the numerator and denominator without a remainder is 1.

HOW TO DO THE EXAMPLE

To reduce a fraction to its simplest form, divide the numerator and denominator by the largest number that will divide into both of them exactly.

$\frac{8}{12} = \frac{8 \div 4}{12 \div 4} = \frac{2}{3}$ Divide both terms by 4.

$\frac{24}{64} = \frac{24 \div 8}{64 \div 8} = \frac{3}{8}$ Divide both terms by 8.

$$\frac{4}{8} = \frac{1}{2}$$

For convenience and clarity a fraction must always be expressed in its simplest form. That is, it must be reduced to its lowest terms. To reduce a fraction to its lowest terms, divide the numerator and the denominator by the largest number that will divide into both of them evenly.

1. What is the simplest form of $\frac{3}{6}$?
2. Reduce $\frac{14}{21}$ to its lowest terms.

Changing a Fraction to Higher Terms

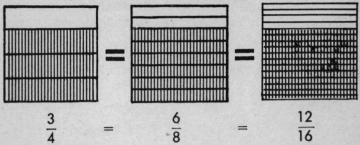

$$\frac{3}{4} \quad = \quad \frac{6}{8} \quad = \quad \frac{12}{16}$$

In these figures, we see that $\frac{3}{4}$ of a square inch represents the same amount as $\frac{6}{8}$ or $\frac{12}{16}$ of a square inch. Therefore, we can say that $\frac{3}{4} = \frac{6}{8} = \frac{12}{16}$. We call these fractions *equal* or *equivalent* fractions.

Equivalent fractions are fractions that have different forms but the same value.

Rule to Remember

The numerator and denominator of a fraction may be multiplied by the same number without changing the value of the fraction. The resulting equivalent fraction is actually the same fraction expressed in higher terms.

HOW TO DO THE EXAMPLE

Problem 1. Change $\frac{2}{3}$ to an equivalent fraction having 9 as the denominator. $\frac{2}{3} = \frac{?}{9}$.

We must first find by what number the 3 should be multiplied to get 9. Divide 9 by 3. The result is 3. To obtain the equivalent fraction, multiply both numerator and denominator by 3.

$$\frac{2}{3} = \frac{2 \times 3}{3 \times 3} = \frac{6}{9}. \quad \text{Multiplying both terms by 3.}$$

Problem 2. Change $\frac{3}{8}$ to an equivalent fraction having 16 as the denominator. $\frac{3}{8} = \frac{?}{16}$. $\quad 16 \div 8 = 2$.

$$\frac{3}{8} = \frac{3 \times 2}{8 \times 2} = \frac{6}{16}$$

EXERCISES

Working With Fractions

1. *Reduce each of the fractions to simplest terms.*

a. $\frac{9}{12}=$ g. $\frac{7}{28}=$ m. $\frac{22}{24}=$ s. $\frac{16}{26}=$

b. $\frac{36}{64}=$ h. $\frac{18}{36}=$ n. $\frac{30}{40}=$ t. $\frac{12}{18}=$

c. $\frac{35}{45}=$ i. $\frac{9}{270}=$ o. $\frac{8}{128}=$ u. $\frac{45}{54}=$

d. $\frac{125}{200}=$ j. $\frac{64}{192}=$ p. $\frac{44}{132}=$ v. $\frac{8}{120}=$

e. $\frac{19}{76}=$ k. $\frac{23}{92}=$ q. $\frac{17}{136}=$ w. $\frac{22}{120}=$

f. $\frac{30}{60}=$ l. $\frac{18}{24}=$ r. $\frac{98}{196}=$ x. $\frac{90}{360}=$

2. *Change each of the following fractions to higher terms.*

a. $\frac{1}{2}=\frac{}{8}$ e. $\frac{1}{4}=\frac{}{16}$ i. $\frac{1}{6}=\frac{}{18}$ m. $\frac{1}{3}=\frac{}{12}$ q. $\frac{1}{7}=\frac{}{14}$

b. $\frac{2}{3}=\frac{}{8}$ f. $\frac{3}{5}=\frac{}{10}$ j. $\frac{5}{6}=\frac{}{18}$ n. $\frac{4}{3}=\frac{}{12}$ r. $\frac{5}{7}=\frac{}{21}$

c. $\frac{5}{12}=\frac{}{24}$ g. $\frac{4}{9}=\frac{}{36}$ k. $\frac{7}{8}=\frac{}{32}$ o. $\frac{3}{4}=\frac{}{16}$ s. $\frac{4}{2}=\frac{}{10}$

d. $\frac{7}{10}=\frac{}{50}$ h. $\frac{5}{12}=\frac{}{36}$ l. $\frac{3}{16}=\frac{}{64}$ p. $\frac{11}{12}=\frac{}{60}$ t. $\frac{4}{15}=\frac{}{60}$

Changing a Mixed Number to an Improper Fraction

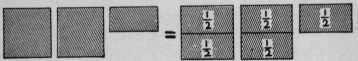

The above diagram shows $2\frac{1}{2}$ shaded squares. On the right we have divided the squares into halves. We see that there are 5 halves, $\frac{5}{2}$, in the $2\frac{1}{2}$ squares. This means that the mixed number $2\frac{1}{2}$ is equal to the improper fraction $\frac{5}{2}$.

Essentials to Remember

To change a mixed number to an improper fraction:

1. Multiply the denominator of the fraction by the whole number.

2. Add the numerator of the fraction to the product of the multiplication.

3. Write the result over the denominator.

[Continued on top of opposite page]

HOW TO DO THE EXAMPLE

Problem 1. Change $3\frac{2}{5}$ to an improper fraction.

$$3\frac{2}{5} = \frac{3 \times 5 + 2}{5} = \frac{17}{5}$$

Multiply the whole number 3 by the denominator 5. Add the numerator of the fraction to the product. Write the sum, 17, over the denominator, 5.

Problem 2. Change $3\frac{1}{16}$ to an improper fraction.

$$3\frac{1}{16} = \frac{3 \times 16 + 1}{16} = \frac{49}{16}$$

Changing an Improper Fraction to a Whole or Mixed Number

The Women's Community Club wanted to buy cakes for a party. They asked the bakery clerk for 8 chocolate cup cakes, 8 vanilla, 8 lemon and 9 vanilla with chocolate icing.

This, said the clerk, made $2\frac{3}{4}$ dozen. The clerk knew that 33 cakes were equal to $2\frac{3}{4}$ dozen by changing an improper fraction to a mixed number. Since there are 12 cakes in a dozen, *one* cake is $\frac{1}{12}$ of a dozen and 33 cakes equal $\frac{33}{12}$ dozen. The quotient of $33 \div 12$ is 2, with a remainder of 9. $\frac{33}{12} = 2\frac{9}{12} = 2\frac{3}{4}$.

Rule to Remember

To change an improper fraction to a whole or a mixed number, divide the numerator by the denominator. If there should be a remainder, write it over the denominator. The resulting fraction should then be reduced to its simplest terms.

HOW TO DO THE EXAMPLE

Problem 1. Change $\frac{27}{3}$ to a whole number.

$\frac{27}{3} = 9$ Divide 27 by 3.

Problem 2. Change $\frac{18}{4}$ to a mixed number.

$\frac{18}{4} = 4\frac{2}{4} = 4\frac{1}{2}$ Divide 18 by 4. Write remainder, 2, over denominator, 4. Reduce to simplest terms.

Changing a Whole Number to an Improper Fraction

In working with fractions we must frequently write a whole number as an equal improper fraction with a specific denominator.

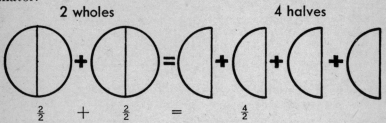

2 wholes   4 halves

$$\frac{2}{2} \quad + \quad \frac{2}{2} \quad = \quad \frac{4}{2}$$

Essentials to Remember

To change a whole number to an improper fraction with a specific denominator:

1. Multiply the denominator of the whole fraction by the whole number.

2. Write the result over the denominator.

HOW TO DO THE EXAMPLE

Problem: Change 8 into an equivalent fraction having 7 as the denominator.

$$8 = \frac{?}{7}$$

Multiply the denominator 7 by the whole number 8. Write the product, 56, as the numerator of the new fraction.

$$8 = \frac{8 \times 7}{7} = \frac{56}{7}$$

EXERCISES

Changing Fractions

1. *Change the following numbers into improper fractions as indicated.*

a. $7 = \frac{}{2}$ *c.* $1 = \frac{}{8}$ *e.* $8 = \frac{}{3}$ *g.* $14 = \frac{}{14}$ *i.* $3 = \frac{}{5}$ *k.* $17 = \frac{}{4}$

b. $15 = \frac{}{4}$ *d.* $8 = \frac{}{8}$ *f.* $19 = \frac{}{8}$ *h.* $29 = \frac{}{4}$ *j.* $23 = \frac{}{4}$ *l.* $13 = \frac{}{5}$

m. $4 = \frac{}{3}$	o. $2 = \frac{}{10}$	q. $9 = \frac{}{3}$	s. $5 = \frac{}{16}$
n. $18 = \frac{}{5}$	p. $6 = \frac{}{5}$	r. $12 = \frac{}{10}$	t. $28 = \frac{}{7}$

2. *Write each of the following as a whole number or as a mixed number.*

a. $\frac{8}{3} =$	f. $\frac{11}{2} =$	k. $\frac{13}{3} =$	p. $\frac{12}{6} =$	u. $\frac{36}{16} =$
b. $\frac{54}{6} =$	g. $\frac{39}{12} =$	l. $\frac{53}{6} =$	q. $\frac{35}{10} =$	v. $\frac{12}{9} =$
c. $\frac{30}{12} =$	h. $\frac{13}{13} =$	m. $\frac{43}{6} =$	r. $\frac{29}{12} =$	w. $\frac{15}{15} =$
d. $\frac{7}{4} =$	i. $\frac{42}{10} =$	n. $\frac{89}{12} =$	s. $\frac{99}{11} =$	x. $\frac{23}{23} =$
e. $\frac{7}{5} =$	j. $\frac{8}{6} =$	o. $\frac{9}{8} =$	t. $\frac{11}{4} =$	y. $\frac{10}{10} =$

3. *Write each of the following mixed numbers as improper fractions.*

a. $7\frac{1}{2} =$	f. $8\frac{3}{4} =$	k. $4\frac{1}{2} =$	p. $7\frac{2}{7} =$	u. $8\frac{1}{3} =$
b. $5\frac{1}{2} =$	g. $2\frac{5}{16} =$	l. $10\frac{2}{3} =$	q. $2\frac{5}{8} =$	v. $9\frac{1}{8} =$
c. $8\frac{1}{5} =$	h. $12\frac{1}{7} =$	m. $18\frac{1}{6} =$	r. $21\frac{1}{10} =$	w. $16\frac{2}{3} =$
d. $33\frac{1}{3} =$	i. $66\frac{2}{3} =$	n. $87\frac{1}{2} =$	s. $22\frac{3}{8} =$	x $2\frac{7}{13} =$
e. $1\frac{1}{14} =$	j. $9\frac{4}{9} =$	o. $8\frac{7}{8} =$	t. $3\frac{7}{21} =$	y. $46\frac{1}{2} =$

GENERAL SKILL EXERCISE

Try the following practice examples. If you need help, turn to the pages listed at the end of the example and learn how to do the exercise.

1. A piece of wood is 3 inches long. This, expressed as a fraction of a foot, is .... (page 25).

2. Three men shared two sandwiches. What part of a sandwich did each man receive? .... (page 26).

3. In the fraction $\frac{2}{7}$, into how many parts is the whole divided? .... (page 26).

4. In the fraction $\frac{3}{8}$, how many parts are being taken? .... (page 26).

5. The largest fraction of $\frac{1}{6}$, $\frac{1}{7}$, $\frac{1}{5}$, is .... (page 26).

6. How many tenths are there in $\frac{1}{2}$? .... (page 31).

7. The improper fraction found in the following group is .... $\frac{1}{2}$, $\frac{3}{8}$, $\frac{2}{2}$ (page 29).

8. Expressed in lowest terms, $\frac{36}{108}$ is .... (page 30).

9. The fraction $\frac{22}{5}$ expressed as a mixed number is .... (page 33).

10. The fraction $\frac{45}{180}$ expressed in its simplest terms is .... (page 30).

11. $\frac{7}{12}$ expressed as 36ths is .... (page 30).

12. 8 expressed as an improper fraction whose denominator is 5 is .... (page 34).

13. $\frac{49}{5}$ expressed as a mixed number is .... (page 32).

14. $17\frac{2}{3}$ expressed as an improper fraction is .... (page 32).

15. Express $\frac{17}{17}$ as a whole number .... (page 26).

─────── *My Score*

Addition of Fractions

Adding Fractions Having the Same Denominator

If we add the $\frac{1}{4}$'s of the square, we have the complete square, or 1 square. This means that $\frac{1}{4}+\frac{1}{4}+\frac{1}{4}+\frac{1}{4}=\frac{4}{4}=1$. When we add fractions that have the same denominator, we are adding *like* fractions; that is, fractions with a *common denominator*.

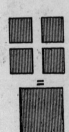

Essentials to Remember

To add fractions having the same denominator (*like* fractions), add their numerators and write the sum over the common denominator. (*Do not add the denominators.*) Reduce the resulting fraction to lowest terms.

[Continued on top of page 37]

HOW TO DO THE EXAMPLE

Problem 1. Add $\frac{1}{5}$ and $\frac{3}{5}$

$$\frac{1}{5}$$

$$\frac{3}{5}$$

$$\overline{\frac{4}{5}}$$ ← Result of adding the numerators.
← Common Denominator.

Problem 2. Add $\frac{2}{15}$, $\frac{4}{15}$ and $\frac{8}{15}$

$$\frac{2}{15}$$

$$\frac{4}{15}$$

$$\frac{8}{15}$$

$$\overline{\frac{14}{15}}$$ ← Sum of the numerators
← Common denominator

Problem 3. Add $3\frac{1}{12}$, $6\frac{5}{12}$ and $4\frac{11}{12}$

$$3\frac{1}{12}$$

$$6\frac{5}{12}$$

$$4\frac{11}{12}$$

Sum of the whole numbers → $13\frac{17}{12}$ Sum of the fractions
$= 14\frac{5}{12}$ Answer in simplest form.

EXERCISES

Adding Fractions with Like Denominators

Add the following fractions. Reduce all sums to lowest terms.

a. $\frac{1}{2}$ $\frac{1}{2}$	d. $\frac{1}{4}$ $\frac{1}{4}$	g. $\frac{2}{6}$ $\frac{1}{6}$	j. $3\frac{4}{10}$ $5\frac{2}{10}$	m. $\frac{7}{12}$ $\frac{3}{12}$
b. $\frac{5}{8}$ $\frac{3}{8}$	e. $\frac{3}{10}$ $\frac{2}{10}$	h. $\frac{5}{16}$ $\frac{3}{16}$	k. $7\frac{2}{6}$ $5\frac{4}{6}$	n. $\frac{8}{8}$ $2\frac{2}{8}$
c. $\frac{3}{7}$ $\frac{1}{7}$	f. $\frac{8}{12}$ $\frac{9}{12}$	i. $\frac{1}{9}$ $\frac{1}{9}$	l. $9\frac{1}{11}$ $4\frac{10}{11}$	o. $8\frac{7}{14}$ $5\frac{8}{14}$

$p.\ \frac{1}{13}$	$q.\ \frac{3}{8}$	$r.\ \frac{1}{10}$	$s.\ 1\frac{2}{21}$	$t.\ 2\frac{7}{30}$
$\frac{3}{13}$	$\frac{2}{8}$	$\frac{7}{10}$	$7\frac{4}{21}$	$5\frac{11}{30}$
$\frac{7}{13}$	$\frac{4}{8}$	$\frac{9}{10}$	$8\frac{9}{21}$	$7\frac{11}{30}$

Fractions Having Different Denominators

Joe tried to find the total thickness of a board $\frac{5}{8}$ of an inch thick covered with a layer of formica $\frac{1}{16}$ of an inch thick. In solving the problem, James had to add unlike fractions; that is, fractions having different denominators.

He decided that $\frac{5}{8}$ of an inch is equivalent to $\frac{10}{16}$ of an inch, and that $\frac{10}{16}''$ and $\frac{1}{16}''$ are *like* fractions and can be added.

First change $\frac{5}{8}''$ to an equivalent fraction.　　$\frac{10}{16}''$

Then add $\frac{1}{16}''$:　　$+\frac{1}{16}''$

Total thickness　　$\frac{11}{16}''$

Rule to Remember

To add fractions having different denominators (unlike fractions), the fractions must be changed to equivalent fractions which have the same or a *common denominator*.

Sometimes the sum is an improper fraction which must be simplified:

The least or lowest common denominator is the smallest number into which the denominators of all the fractions will divide without any remainder. Thus, the least or lowest common denominator (L.C.D.) of the fractions $\frac{5}{8}$ and $\frac{1}{16}$ is 16; the L.C.D. of $\frac{3}{4}$ and $\frac{1}{2}$ is 4; the L.C.D. of $\frac{2}{3}$ and $\frac{1}{2}$ is 6.

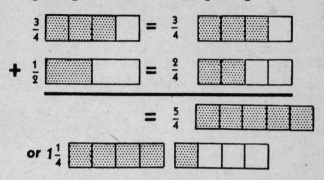

Hints to Find the Least Common Denominator

1. First try the largest of the denominators.
2. Multiply the largest denominator by 2, by 3, and so on until you find the least common denominator.
3. If all lower numbers fail to provide a common denominator, use the product of the two denominators.

HOW TO DO THE EXAMPLE

Problem 1. Add $\frac{1}{2}$ and $\frac{1}{8}$

$\frac{1}{2} = \frac{4}{8}$ ← Least common denominator

$\frac{1}{8} = \frac{1}{8}$

$\frac{5}{8}$ ← Sum of numerators

Problem 2. Add $\frac{1}{5}$, $\frac{1}{4}$ and $\frac{3}{10}$

$\frac{1}{5} = \frac{4}{20}$

$\frac{1}{4} = \frac{5}{20}$ — Least common denominator

$\frac{3}{10} = \frac{6}{20}$

$\frac{15}{20} = \frac{3}{4}$ Answer in simplest form

EXERCISES

Adding Fractions

1. *Add the following fractions. Write the answer in the simplest form.*

a. $\dfrac{1}{2} + \dfrac{1}{6}$ c. $\dfrac{7}{8} + \dfrac{1}{3}$ e. $\dfrac{1}{4} + \dfrac{2}{5}$ g. $\dfrac{3}{4} + \dfrac{7}{10}$ i. $\dfrac{3}{8} + \dfrac{1}{6}$

b. $\dfrac{3}{7} + \dfrac{2}{3}$ d. $\dfrac{2}{5} + \dfrac{3}{7}$ f. $\dfrac{5}{6} + \dfrac{1}{5}$ h. $\dfrac{5}{8} + \dfrac{1}{6}$ j. $\dfrac{3}{16} + \dfrac{1}{32}$

2. *Add. Write the answer in the simplest form.*

a. $\dfrac{1}{2} + \dfrac{1}{4} + \dfrac{1}{8}$ c. $\dfrac{2}{3} + \dfrac{5}{6} + \dfrac{1}{12}$ e. $\dfrac{2}{3} + \dfrac{3}{4} + \dfrac{5}{2}$ g. $\dfrac{3}{5} + \dfrac{1}{10} + \dfrac{1}{2}$ i. $\dfrac{3}{8} + \dfrac{5}{6} + \dfrac{3}{4}$

b. $\dfrac{5}{12} + \dfrac{7}{8} + \dfrac{3}{4}$ d. $\dfrac{3}{4} + \dfrac{5}{6} + \dfrac{1}{4}$ f. $\dfrac{1}{3} + \dfrac{2}{9} + \dfrac{5}{6}$ h. $\dfrac{5}{8} + \dfrac{1}{3} + \dfrac{3}{4}$ j. $\dfrac{7}{8} + \dfrac{8}{9} + \dfrac{1}{4}$

3. *Find the sum. Write the answer in the simplest form.*

a. $2\frac{1}{4} + 2\frac{1}{2}$ g. $3\frac{1}{6} + 2\frac{2}{3}$ m. $5\frac{3}{10} + 2\frac{4}{5}$ s. $8\frac{4}{5} + 1\frac{3}{10}$ y. $7\frac{2}{5} + 3\frac{8}{10}$

b. $6\frac{9}{10} + 7\frac{1}{2}$ h. $12\frac{3}{4} + 22\frac{4}{5}$ n. $18\frac{9}{10} + \frac{1}{3}$ t. $15\frac{3}{5} + 18\frac{3}{10}$ z. $24\frac{3}{16} + 18\frac{3}{8}$

c. $\frac{8}{9} + 5\frac{3}{9}$ i. $4\frac{3}{4} + \frac{1}{4}$ o. $2\frac{5}{8} + \frac{3}{8}$ u. $\frac{3}{4} + 5\frac{2}{4}$ aa. $5\frac{5}{8} + \frac{7}{8}$

d. $14\frac{3}{8} + 5\frac{2}{8}$ j. $15\frac{1}{4} + 9\frac{3}{8}$ p. $2\frac{5}{8} + 6\frac{7}{8}$ v. $8\frac{3}{5} + 7\frac{4}{5}$ bb. $12 + \frac{5}{8}$

e. $\frac{1}{4} + \frac{3}{4} + \frac{2}{4}$ k. $\frac{2}{9} + \frac{4}{9} + \frac{5}{9}$ q. $2\frac{1}{8} + \frac{5}{8} + 9\frac{3}{8}$ w. $15\frac{3}{7} + 8\frac{4}{7} + 19\frac{5}{7}$ cc. $23\frac{3}{11} + 19\frac{8}{11} + 36\frac{10}{11}$

f. $8\frac{1}{8} + 9\frac{3}{4} + 7\frac{5}{12}$ l. $5\frac{3}{4} + 12\frac{1}{2} + 9\frac{7}{8}$ r. $11\frac{1}{2} + 19\frac{3}{10} + \frac{3}{8}$ x. $22\frac{1}{4} + 18\frac{2}{3} + 31\frac{1}{2}$ dd. $22\frac{7}{8} + 16\frac{1}{8} + 15\frac{5}{12}$

Subtraction of Fractions Having the Same Denominator

Don had just finished painting 10 of 16 rooms. He said, "Each room is $\frac{1}{16}$ of the total rooms I must paint. Since I have done $\frac{10}{16}$ of the job, which is $\frac{16}{16}$, I have $\frac{6}{16}$ or $\frac{3}{8}$ left to do." Was he right?

This is the rule that Don followed:

Rule to Remember

To subtract fractions having the same denominator, subtract the numerators and write the difference over the common denominator. *Do not subtract the denominators!*

HOW TO DO THE EXAMPLE

Problem **1.** Subtract $\frac{2}{9}$ from $\frac{7}{9}$

$$\frac{7}{9}$$

$$\frac{2}{9}$$

$$\frac{5}{9} \leftarrow \text{Difference of numerators}$$

Problem **2.** Subtract: $3\frac{7}{12} - 1\frac{5}{12}$

$$3\frac{7}{12}$$

$$1\frac{5}{12}$$

Difference of → $2\frac{2}{12}$ ← Difference of numerators

whole numbers $= 2\frac{1}{6}$ Answer in simplest form

Problem **3.** Subtract $2\frac{5}{6}$ from 4

$4 = 3\frac{6}{6}$ Since $\frac{5}{6}$ must be subtracted from a *like* fraction, change one *whole* of the minuend 4 to $\frac{6}{6}$, so that the new minu-

$2\frac{5}{6} = 2\frac{5}{6}$ end is $3\frac{6}{6}$.

$$1\frac{1}{6} \leftarrow \text{Difference of numerators}$$

Problem **4.** From $5\frac{1}{8}$ take $3\frac{5}{8}$

Since $\frac{5}{8}$ cannot be subtracted from $\frac{1}{8}$ we

$5\frac{1}{8} = 4\frac{9}{8}$ take one whole, or $\frac{8}{8}$ from 5, making the 5

$3\frac{5}{8} = 3\frac{5}{8}$ become 4, and then add the $\frac{8}{8}$ to the $\frac{1}{8}$ to

have $\frac{9}{8}$.

$$1\frac{4}{8} \leftarrow \text{Difference of numerators}$$

$$1\frac{4}{8} = 1\frac{1}{2} \quad \text{Answer in simplest form}$$

EXERCISES

Subtracting Fractions

1. *Subtract the following fractions. Reduce all answers to simplest terms.*

a. $\frac{7}{12}$
$\frac{5}{12}$

f. $\frac{5}{8}$
$\frac{3}{8}$

k. $\frac{3}{10}$
$\frac{2}{10}$

p. $\frac{5}{16}$
$\frac{3}{16}$

u. $\frac{1}{4}$
$\frac{1}{4}$

b. $8\frac{3}{4}$
$5\frac{3}{4}$

g. $6\frac{2}{3}$
$5\frac{1}{3}$

l. $7\frac{2}{6}$
$5\frac{1}{6}$

q. $5\frac{7}{8}$
$\frac{5}{8}$

v. $6\frac{2}{3}$
$5\frac{1}{3}$

c. $5\frac{7}{9}$
$2\frac{2}{9}$

h. $15\frac{3}{5}$
$12\frac{1}{5}$

m. $8\frac{3}{4}$
$\frac{1}{4}$

r. $\frac{7}{9}$
$\frac{7}{9}$

w. $8\frac{9}{16}$
7

d. $8\frac{3}{5}$
$7\frac{4}{5}$

i. $6\frac{3}{8}$
$5\frac{5}{8}$

n. $3\frac{3}{5}$
$1\frac{4}{5}$

s. $15\frac{1}{8}$
$9\frac{3}{8}$

x. $23\frac{2}{7}$
$15\frac{4}{7}$

e. 5
$3\frac{1}{6}$

j. 7
$5\frac{3}{8}$

o. 14
$11\frac{1}{5}$

t. 26
$19\frac{4}{7}$

y. 35
$29\frac{11}{16}$

2. *Do the following examples.*

a. $\frac{2}{3}-\frac{1}{3}=$

d. $1\frac{5}{6}-\frac{1}{6}=$

g. $\frac{5}{8}-\frac{3}{8}=$

j. $1\frac{1}{7}-\frac{2}{7}=$

b. $\frac{5}{6}-\frac{1}{6}=$

e. $\frac{4}{7}-\frac{1}{7}=$

h. $\frac{3}{5}-\frac{2}{5}=$

k. $1\frac{1}{8}-\frac{4}{8}=$

c. $7\frac{3}{8}-2\frac{5}{8}=$

f. $4-3\frac{1}{8}=$

i. $5\frac{11}{16}-3\frac{13}{16}=$

l. $3\frac{1}{8}-2=$

Subtraction of Fractions Having Different Denominators

In a book on world geography, Fred found statistics on coal production in various parts of the world. He read that the United States produces $\frac{39}{100}$ of the world's coal. The United Kingdom, he read, produces $\frac{1}{5}$.

Fred was puzzled. "Which country produces more coal?" he wondered. "And how much more does that country produce?"

First Fred set about finding a common denominator. This was easy, for he could use the denominator of one of his fractions—100. He changed $\frac{1}{5}$ to $\frac{20}{100}$. Then he knew which country produced more coal, for 39 is greater than 20.

To find the difference, Fred subtracted $\frac{20}{100}$ from $\frac{39}{100}$. He found this answer:

The United States produces $\frac{19}{100}$ more of the world's coal than the United Kingdom produces.

Sometimes *both* fractions must be changed to obtain like fractions:

Rule to Remember

To subtract fractions having different denominators, first change the fractions to equivalent fractions having a common denominator. (Follow the hints given on page 39 to find the least common denominator.) To subtract the fractions when they have a common denominator, subtract the numerators and write the difference over the denominator. *Do not subtract the denominators!*

HOW TO DO THE EXAMPLE

Problem 1. Subtract $\frac{1}{4}$ from $\frac{7}{8}$.

$$\frac{7}{8} = \frac{7}{8} \leftarrow \text{Least common denominator}$$
$$\frac{1}{4} = \frac{2}{8}$$
$$\overline{\phantom{\frac{1}{4}=} \frac{5}{8}} \leftarrow \text{Difference of numerators}$$

[Continued on top of page 44]

Problem 2. Find the difference between $4\frac{2}{3}$ and $1\frac{1}{5}$.

$$4\frac{2}{3} = 4\frac{10}{15}$$
$$1\frac{1}{5} = 1\frac{3}{15}$$

Difference of whole numbers → $3\frac{7}{15}$

Problem 3. Subtract $3\frac{3}{4}$ from $9\frac{1}{3}$.

$$9\frac{1}{3} = 9\frac{4}{12} = 8\frac{16}{12}$$
$$3\frac{3}{4} = 3\frac{9}{12} = 3\frac{9}{12}$$

Difference of → $5\frac{7}{12}$ ← Difference of
whole numbers   numerators

Since we cannot subtract $\frac{9}{12}$ from $\frac{4}{12}$, we borrow 1 or $\frac{12}{12}$ from 9, making 9 become 8 and then add the $\frac{12}{12}$ to $\frac{4}{12}$ which gives $\frac{16}{12}$.

EXERCISES

Subtracting Fractions

1. *Subtract the following fractions. Write the answer in simplest form.*

a. $\frac{5}{6}$	c. $\frac{1}{2}$	e. $\frac{7}{8}$	g. $\frac{9}{10}$	i. $\frac{3}{4}$
$\frac{1}{3}$	$\frac{1}{6}$	$\frac{3}{4}$	$\frac{4}{5}$	$\frac{5}{12}$

b. $\frac{7}{12}$	d. $\frac{5}{6}$	f. $\frac{7}{8}$	h. $\frac{4}{5}$	j. $\frac{7}{12}$
$\frac{1}{3}$	$\frac{3}{4}$	$\frac{3}{16}$	$\frac{1}{4}$	$\frac{1}{4}$

2. *Subtract. Write the answer in simplest form.*

a. $8\frac{13}{14}$	e. $5\frac{1}{2}$	i. $9\frac{2}{3}$	m. $5\frac{3}{4}$	q. $8\frac{1}{12}$
$4\frac{5}{7}$	$3\frac{2}{3}$	$6\frac{11}{12}$	$1\frac{1}{2}$	$2\frac{5}{8}$

b. $3\frac{1}{2}$	f. $7\frac{1}{3}$	j. $6\frac{1}{4}$	n. $4\frac{1}{4}$	r. $8\frac{2}{8}$
$1\frac{7}{8}$	$3\frac{5}{6}$	$4\frac{2}{3}$	$2\frac{5}{16}$	$4\frac{1}{2}$

c. $3\frac{1}{6}$	g. $6\frac{1}{5}$	k. $6\frac{3}{4}$	o. $8\frac{1}{10}$	s. $5\frac{1}{12}$
$1\frac{5}{12}$	$3\frac{3}{10}$	$4\frac{13}{16}$	$4\frac{3}{5}$	$3\frac{1}{3}$

d. $24\frac{1}{3}$	h. $32\frac{5}{8}$	l. $12\frac{1}{8}$	p. $26\frac{1}{10}$	t. $33\frac{11}{12}$
$13\frac{2}{3}$	$10\frac{1}{2}$	$8\frac{2}{3}$	$15\frac{3}{4}$	$21\frac{7}{8}$

$u.\ 14\frac{3}{6}$	$v.\ 17\frac{5}{6}$	$w.\ 13$	$x.\ 24$	$y.\ 21\frac{3}{8}$
9	6	$8\frac{3}{8}$	$17\frac{5}{8}$	$21\frac{3}{4}$

3. *Do each of the following and express each answer in the simplest form.*

a. $\frac{1}{12}+\frac{3}{8}-\frac{3}{16}=$

b. $\frac{3}{5}+\frac{3}{20}-\frac{3}{10}$

c. $\frac{2}{3}+\frac{4}{9}-\frac{5}{6}$

d. $\frac{3}{16}-\frac{3}{8}+\frac{5}{4}$

e. $4\frac{8}{10}+6\frac{1}{2}-3\frac{1}{5}$

f. $7-3\frac{1}{4}+8\frac{1}{16}$

g. $\frac{1}{4}+\frac{5}{14}-\frac{3}{7}$

h. $3\frac{1}{2}+6\frac{1}{4}-2\frac{3}{4}$

i. $\frac{3}{7}+\frac{4}{14}-\frac{1}{4}$

j. $\frac{2}{9}+\frac{5}{6}-1\frac{5}{18}$

k. $\frac{5}{12}-\frac{1}{4}+\frac{3}{8}$

l. $\frac{3}{4}-\frac{3}{32}+\frac{1}{8}$

m. $11\frac{1}{2}+4\frac{3}{5}-8\frac{4}{15}$

n. $2+\frac{4}{9}-\frac{5}{6}$

o. $\frac{5}{12}+7\frac{1}{4}-\frac{5}{8}$

Comparing Fractions

Suppose that a pie is cut into four equal parts, and then each of these parts is cut in half. The smaller pieces are $\frac{1}{2}$ of the portion that was cut, but, these new pieces are each $\frac{1}{8}$ of the entire pie. We can see that $\frac{1}{8}$ of an object is smaller than $\frac{1}{4}$ of the same object; $\frac{2}{8}$ is smaller than $\frac{2}{4}$, and $\frac{3}{8}$ is less than $\frac{3}{4}$. In dividing, the quotient of $\frac{12}{4}$ is less than the quotient of $\frac{12}{3}$ or $\frac{12}{2}$.

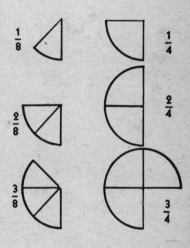

If fractions have *like numerators*, the fraction which has the *largest denominator* has the *smallest value*.

If we compare fractions which have *like denominators*, it is easy to see that the fraction which has the *largest numerator* has the *greatest value*: $\frac{3}{4}$ is larger than $\frac{2}{4}$ or $\frac{1}{4}$; $\frac{17}{25}$ is larger than $\frac{16}{25}$.

Sometimes we wish to compare two fractions in which neither denominators nor numerators are alike. For example:

Steve, the captain of the YMCA basketball team, made $\frac{1}{3}$ of all the baskets in one game. His teammate, Marty, made $\frac{3}{8}$ of all the baskets. Which of the two scored more points?

To compare $\frac{3}{8}$ with $\frac{1}{3}$, first find the common denominator. Multiplying both denominators, 8 and 3, gives 24. This is the lowest common denominator.

Now change both fractions to 24ths. $\frac{3}{8} = \frac{9}{24}$, $\frac{1}{3} = \frac{8}{24}$. Therefore, because 9 (24ths) is larger than 8 (24ths), Marty had scored the most baskets.

When we are given a group of fractions and must choose the one having the greatest value, we follow this rule:

Rule to Remember

Fractions can be compared only when they have like numerators or denominators. Therefore, to compare unlike fractions, change one or both to equivalent fractions so that all have like denominators.

HOW TO DO THE EXAMPLE

Problem 1. Which of the following fractions is the largest? The smallest? $\frac{2}{3}$, $\frac{3}{4}$, $\frac{1}{2}$?

Change the fractions to the same denominator. The least common denominator of these fractions is 12. Therefore,

$$\frac{2}{3} = \frac{8}{12} \qquad \frac{3}{4} = \frac{9}{12} \qquad \frac{1}{2} = \frac{6}{12}$$

Comparing these like fractions, we see that $\frac{6}{12}$ or $\frac{1}{2}$ is the smallest fraction and $\frac{9}{12}$ or $\frac{3}{4}$ is the largest fraction.

Problem 2. Which of the following has the greatest value? The least value?

$$\frac{1}{3}, \quad \frac{1}{4}, \quad \frac{1}{2}$$

Since the numerators are alike, the fraction $\frac{1}{4}$, which has the greatest denominator, has the smallest value, and the fraction $\frac{1}{2}$, with the smallest denominator, has the greatest value.

General Rules to Remember

1. When fractions have the same denominator but different numerators, the fraction having the largest numerator has the greatest value.

2. When fractions have different denominators but the same numerator, the fraction having the smallest denominator has the greatest value.

EXERCISES

Fractions

1. *In each of the following groups of fractions select the largest fraction.*
   - *a.* $\frac{1}{2}$ or $\frac{1}{3}$
   - *c.* $\frac{7}{10}$ or $\frac{3}{5}$
   - *e.* $\frac{3}{4}$ or $\frac{5}{8}$
   - *g.* $\frac{13}{32}$ or $\frac{5}{8}$
   - *b.* $\frac{2}{3}$ or $\frac{3}{4}$
   - *d.* $\frac{9}{64}$ or $\frac{1}{8}$
   - *f.* $\frac{7}{32}$ or $\frac{1}{4}$
   - *h.* $\frac{5}{8}$ or $\frac{1}{2}$

2. *Select the smallest fraction in each group.*
   - *a.* $\frac{4}{5}$ or $\frac{3}{4}$
   - *c.* $\frac{5}{8}$ or $\frac{2}{3}$
   - *e.* $\frac{3}{8}$ or $\frac{7}{16}$
   - *g.* $\frac{3}{4}$ or $\frac{5}{8}$
   - *b.* $\frac{8}{10}$ or $\frac{1}{2}$
   - *d.* $\frac{4}{9}$ or $\frac{3}{8}$
   - *f.* $\frac{9}{16}$ or $\frac{3}{4}$
   - *h.* $\frac{4}{5}, \frac{3}{4}, \frac{11}{16}$

3. *Select the equal fractions in each group.*
   - *a.* $\frac{3}{4}$ $\frac{7}{8}$ $\frac{15}{20}$ $\frac{9}{12}$
   - *c.* $\frac{4}{8}$ $\frac{4}{9}$ $\frac{5}{16}$ $\frac{1}{6}$
   - *b.* $\frac{1}{2}$ $\frac{5}{8}$ $\frac{32}{64}$ $\frac{4}{9}$
   - *d.* $\frac{3}{5}$ $\frac{8}{10}$ $\frac{27}{45}$ $\frac{1}{2}$

4. *Which is the largest fraction in each group?*
   - *a.* $\frac{9}{16}$ $\frac{3}{4}$ $\frac{1}{2}$
   - *b.* $\frac{2}{5}$ $\frac{3}{4}$ $\frac{9}{16}$
   - *c.* $\frac{3}{8}$ $\frac{1}{2}$ $\frac{7}{8}$

5. A pile of books is made up of four books whose thicknesses are $1\frac{1}{2}$ inch, $1\frac{1}{8}$ inch, $\frac{7}{8}$ inch and $2\frac{1}{4}$ inches, respectively. How high was the pile of books?

6. A container with its contents weighs $189\frac{3}{4}$ pounds. The container itself weighs $15\frac{3}{8}$ pounds. How much do the contents weigh?

7. Harry weighed $112\frac{1}{2}$ pounds two months ago. He lost $3\frac{1}{8}$ pounds because of an illness. John weighs $103\frac{3}{4}$ pounds. Who weighs more? By how much?

8. A fruit store has $26\frac{3}{4}$ pounds of tomatoes. The following amounts were sold: $1\frac{1}{2}$ pounds, $3\frac{1}{4}$ pounds, $4\frac{1}{8}$ pounds, and $5\frac{3}{8}$ pounds. How many pounds were left?

9. Mark spent the following time one week building a bookcase: $2\frac{1}{4}$ hours, 1 hour and 20 minutes, 2 hours and 15 minutes, 1 hour and 15 minutes, 3 hours. How many hours did he spend that week?

GENERAL SKILL EXERCISE

How are you doing? Try the following test. If you get any wrong, turn to the pages shown after each question. Practice those problems until you have mastered them.

1. The sum of $\frac{3}{2}$ and $\frac{5}{2}$ is .... (page 36).

2. Does the sum of $\frac{2}{3}$ and $\frac{4}{3}$ equal $\frac{6}{6}$? .... (page 36).

3. To add $\frac{1}{6}$ and $\frac{3}{4}$, the least common denominators you must use are .... (page 38).

4. To add eighths and sixths, change both of them to.... (page 39).

5. One part of an object is $\frac{5}{6}$. What is the other part of the object? .... (page 41).

6. In subtracting mixed numbers, if a larger fraction is being subtracted, you must take 1 from the whole number in the .... (page 41).

7. If you cannot obtain the least common denominator easily, you can use the .... of the denominators (page 39).

8. In subtracting like fractions, subtract only the .... of the fractions (page 41).

9. If the lower term of a fraction is made larger, the value of the fraction is (increased or decreased) .... (page 47).

10. If two fractions have the same denominator, the one with the largest numerator is .... (page 47).

_____*My Score*

Multiplying a Fraction and a Whole Number

A customer in a supermarket bought 5 packages of hamburger patties, each of which contained $\frac{1}{2}$ pound. What was the total weight of her purchase?

One way of finding the answer is by adding the fractions: $\frac{1}{2}+\frac{1}{2}+\frac{1}{2}+\frac{1}{2}+\frac{1}{2}=2\frac{1}{2}$ pounds.

A shorter way of solving the problem is by multiplying the fraction $\frac{1}{2}$ by the whole number 5.

$$5\times\frac{1}{2}=\frac{5}{2}=2\frac{1}{2} \text{ pounds}$$

Essentials to Remember

To multiply a whole number and a fraction:

1. Reduce the fraction to its lowest terms.

2. Change the whole number to an improper fraction by placing it over the denominator 1.

3. Multiply the two numerators to obtain the numerator of the answer.

4. Multiply the denominators to obtain the denominator of the answer.

5. Reduce fractions when possible. Reduction can be done by dividing a numerator and a denominator by the same number. The numbers that are divided are crossed out, and the quotients are written as the new numerator and the new denominator.

HOW TO DO THE EXAMPLE

Problem 1. Multiply $4 \times \frac{2}{3}$

Change 4 to an improper fraction with a denominator of 1. Then multiply the fractions.

$$\frac{4}{1} \times \frac{2}{3} = \frac{4 \times 2}{1 \times 3} = \frac{8}{3} = 2\frac{2}{3}$$

Problem 2. Find $\frac{7}{8}$ of 40.

$$\frac{7}{8} \times 40 = \frac{7}{\cancel{8}_1} \times \frac{\cancel{40}^5}{1} = 35$$

Problem 3. What is $\frac{2}{3}$ of 21?

$$\frac{2}{\cancel{3}_1} \times \frac{\cancel{21}^7}{1} = 14$$

EXERCISES
Multiplying a Fraction and a Whole Number

1. *Multiply each of the following:*

a. $\frac{2}{8} \times 21$	g. $\frac{1}{2} \times 23$	m. $7 \times \frac{4}{5}$	s. $3 \times \frac{3}{16}$
b. $24 \times \frac{5}{8}$	h. $10 \times \frac{1}{4}$	n. $16 \times \frac{3}{8}$	t. $9 \times \frac{5}{12}$
c. $\frac{4}{7} \times 28$	i. $16 \times \frac{3}{8}$	o. $36 \times \frac{7}{12}$	u. $\frac{5}{16} \times 28$
d. $3 \times \frac{3}{16}$	j. $\frac{1}{8} \times 32$	p. $5 \times \frac{7}{10}$	v. $\frac{5}{16} \times 18$
e. $\frac{4}{5} \times 25$	k. $25 \times \frac{3}{5}$	q. $2 \times \frac{7}{10}$	w. $4 \times \frac{5}{12}$
f. $\frac{1}{5} \times 20$	l. $5 \times \frac{3}{10}$	r. $\frac{5}{16} \times 18$	x. $12 \times \frac{2}{3}$
			y. $32 \times \frac{1}{8}$

2. *Find:*

a. $\frac{3}{4}$ of 18		*e.* $\frac{15}{16}$ of 32		*h.* $\frac{3}{8}$ of 13
b. $\frac{1}{2}$ of 5		*f.* $\frac{3}{8}$ of 72		*i.* $\frac{3}{7}$ of 15
c. $\frac{1}{8}$ of 29		*g.* $\frac{9}{32}$ of 72		*j.* $\frac{12}{17}$ of 69
d. $\frac{3}{8}$ of 45				

3. *What is*

a. $\frac{1}{8}$ of 4?		*e.* $\frac{15}{16}$ of 16?		*h.* $\frac{3}{5}$ of 47?
b. $\frac{5}{8}$ of 14?		*f.* $\frac{5}{4}$ of 36?		*i.* $\frac{1}{2}$ of 1?
c. $\frac{7}{10}$ of 38?		*g.* $\frac{2}{8}$ of 24?		*j.* $\frac{2}{3}$ of 3?
d. $\frac{8}{9}$ of 54?				

Multiplying a Fraction by a Fraction

Frank had one-half of a candy bar left. He gave $\frac{1}{3}$ of the half bar to his friend. What part of the whole bar did his friend receive?

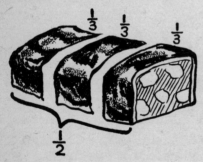

Frank is actually trying to find how much $\frac{1}{3}$ of $\frac{1}{2}$ is. To do this, he must first multiply the numerators and place this product over the product of the denominators.

$$\frac{1}{3} \times \frac{1}{2} = \frac{1 \times 1}{3 \times 2} = \frac{1}{6}$$

Sometimes the fractions to be multiplied are not unit fractions, but have numerators larger than one. If Frank had $\frac{3}{4}$ of the candy bar left, and gave $\frac{2}{3}$ of this to two friends, how much did he give away?

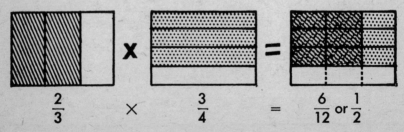

$$\frac{2}{3} \qquad \times \qquad \frac{3}{4} \qquad = \qquad \frac{6}{12} \text{ or } \frac{1}{2}$$

Rule to Remember

The product of two fractions is the product of the numerators divided by the product of the denominators; these products are written as a fraction.

HOW TO DO THE EXAMPLE

1. Multiply the numerators to obtain the numerator of the product.

2. Multiply the denominators to obtain the denominator of the product.

3. If there is a common factor by which both the numerator and denominator may be divided evenly, reduce before multiplying.

Problem 1. Multiply $\frac{1}{2}$ by $\frac{1}{2}$.

$$\frac{1}{2} \times \frac{1}{2} = \frac{1 \times 1}{2 \times 2} = \frac{1}{4} \leftarrow \text{Product of numerators}$$
$$\leftarrow \text{Product of denominators}$$

Problem 2. Multiply $\frac{7}{9}$ by $\frac{5}{8}$ *Problem 3.* Multiply $\frac{5}{12}$ by $\frac{3}{4}$

$$\frac{5}{8} \times \frac{7}{9} = \frac{5 \times 7}{8 \times 9} = \frac{35}{72}$$

$$\overset{1}{\frac{3}{4}} \times \frac{5}{\underset{4}{12}} = \frac{1 \times 5}{4 \times 4} = \frac{5}{16}$$

Multiplying More than Two Fractions

Rule to Remember

In multiplying three or more fractions, follow the same method that applies to the multiplication of two fractions.

HOW TO DO THE EXAMPLE

1. Multiply numerators to obtain the numerator of the product.

2. Multiply denominators to obtain the denominator of the product.

3. Reduce before multiplying

Problem: Find the product of $\frac{5}{6}$, $\frac{3}{10}$ and $\frac{8}{15}$.

$$\overset{1}{\underset{2}{\frac{5}{6}}} \times \overset{1}{\underset{5}{\frac{3}{10}}} \times \overset{4}{\underset{3}{\frac{8}{15}}} = \frac{1 \times 1 \times \overset{2}{4}}{2 \times 5 \times 3} = \frac{2}{15} \quad \text{Answer}$$

EXERCISES
Multiplying Fractions

1. *Multiply each of the following.*

   a. $\frac{1}{8} \times \frac{3}{4}$ f. $\frac{3}{4} \times \frac{2}{5}$ k. $\frac{3}{8} \times \frac{3}{9}$ p. $\frac{5}{12} \times \frac{6}{25}$

   b. $\frac{1}{8} \times \frac{5}{6}$ g. $\frac{9}{10} \times \frac{5}{6}$ l. $\frac{2}{3} \times \frac{1}{5}$ q. $\frac{9}{10} \times \frac{5}{12}$

   c. $\frac{1}{8} \times \frac{3}{10}$ h. $\frac{5}{12} \times \frac{3}{10}$ m. $\frac{3}{5} \times \frac{5}{8}$ r. $\frac{3}{4} \times \frac{5}{9}$

   d. $\frac{13}{15} \times \frac{3}{26}$ i. $\frac{7}{8} \times \frac{4}{35}$ n. $\frac{9}{28} \times \frac{14}{56}$ s. $\frac{5}{32} \times \frac{4}{25}$

   e. $\frac{3}{8} \times \frac{12}{45}$ j. $\frac{18}{27} \times \frac{81}{90}$ o. $\frac{7}{60} \times \frac{180}{287}$ t. $\frac{3}{35} \times \frac{105}{188}$

2. *Multiply.*

   a. $\frac{2}{3} \times \frac{3}{8}$ i. $\frac{5}{6} \times \frac{1}{2}$ q. $\frac{7}{16} \times \frac{2}{3}$ y. $\frac{7}{8} \times \frac{4}{7}$

   b. $\frac{15}{16} \times \frac{28}{25}$ j. $\frac{4}{9} \times \frac{6}{11}$ r. $\frac{3}{4} \times \frac{3}{4}$ z. $\frac{2}{9} \times \frac{27}{28}$

   c. $\frac{2}{3} \times \frac{7}{8}$ k. $\frac{21}{25} \times \frac{10}{21}$ s. $\frac{4}{9} \times \frac{6}{7}$

   d. $\frac{2}{3} \times \frac{6}{8} \times \frac{7}{8}$ l. $\frac{2}{3} \times \frac{1}{5} \times \frac{9}{10}$ t. $\frac{2}{3} \times \frac{3}{5} \times \frac{1}{2}$

   e. $\frac{17}{18} \times \frac{4}{5} \times \frac{20}{21}$ m. $\frac{5}{8} \times \frac{4}{25} \times \frac{1}{2}$ u. $\frac{9}{8} \times \frac{1}{5} \times \frac{1}{10}$

   f. $\frac{4}{9} \times \frac{3}{8} \times \frac{1}{12}$ n. $\frac{6}{13} \times \frac{26}{39} \times \frac{3}{10}$ v. $\frac{8}{11} \times \frac{33}{46} \times \frac{3}{16}$

   g. $\frac{15}{32} \times \frac{8}{9} \times \frac{11}{24}$ o. $\frac{9}{16} \times \frac{8}{21} \times \frac{7}{45}$ w. $\frac{8}{27} \times \frac{36}{45} \times \frac{15}{21}$

   h. $\frac{9}{50} \times \frac{10}{63} \times \frac{7}{18}$ p. $\frac{11}{15} \times \frac{27}{66} \times \frac{9}{19}$ x. $\frac{21}{34} \times \frac{17}{22} \times \frac{11}{18}$

Multiplying a Fraction and a Mixed Number

Essentials to Remember

1. Change the mixed number to an improper fraction.

2. Multiply, following the method for the multiplication of fractions.

HOW TO DO THE EXAMPLE

Problem 1. Multiply $\frac{2}{3} \times 4\frac{1}{2}$

Change the mixed number $4\frac{1}{2}$ to the improper fraction $\frac{9}{2}$.

$$\frac{2}{3} \times \frac{9}{2} = 3$$

Problem 2. Multiply $8\frac{4}{5} \times \frac{15}{16}$

Change $8\frac{4}{5}$ to $\frac{44}{5}$. Multiply.

$$\frac{44}{5} \times \frac{15}{16} = \frac{33}{4} = 8\frac{1}{4}$$

EXERCISES
Multiplying a Fraction and a Mixed Number

1. *Multiply each of the following:*

   a. $1\frac{1}{5} \times \frac{7}{10}$ f. $\frac{15}{16} \times 1\frac{1}{8}$ k. $\frac{1}{8} \times 6\frac{3}{4}$

   b. $6\frac{2}{8} \times \frac{15}{16}$ g. $\frac{3}{5} \times 2\frac{9}{10}$ l. $\frac{5}{8} \times 3\frac{1}{3}$

   c. $1\frac{3}{8} \times \frac{2}{3}$ h. $5\frac{1}{6} \times \frac{1}{4}$ m. $4\frac{2}{8} \times \frac{1}{2}$

   d. $\frac{4}{5} \times 1\frac{1}{10}$ i. $\frac{3}{4} \times 5\frac{1}{3}$ n. $\frac{9}{16} \times 2\frac{2}{3}$

   e. $5\frac{1}{2} \times \frac{2}{3}$ j. $3\frac{3}{5} \times \frac{3}{8}$ o. $4\frac{2}{8} \times \frac{1}{6}$

2. *Obtain the product of each of the following:*

   a. $6\frac{2}{3} \times \frac{3}{4}$ f. $3\frac{1}{3} \times \frac{4}{5}$ k. $2\frac{3}{4} \times \frac{6}{11}$

   b. $\frac{2}{3} \times 5\frac{2}{5}$ g. $\frac{3}{5} \times 2\frac{1}{7}$ l. $8\frac{1}{3} \times \frac{3}{5}$

   c. $\frac{3}{2} \times 2\frac{3}{8}$ h. $\frac{2}{3} \times 1\frac{1}{2}$ m. $\frac{3}{4} \times 7\frac{1}{5}$

   d. $5\frac{1}{4} \times \frac{2}{8}$ i. $9\frac{1}{4} \times \frac{4}{6}$ n. $4\frac{4}{5} \times \frac{5}{6}$

   e. $9\frac{1}{2} \times \frac{3}{5}$ j. $3\frac{3}{5} \times \frac{2}{3}$ o. $4\frac{1}{8} \times \frac{3}{11}$

3. *Multiply each of the following:*

   a. $1\frac{3}{8} \times 1\frac{1}{3}$ f. $5\frac{1}{4} \times 2\frac{1}{3}$ k. $3\frac{1}{3} \times 5\frac{1}{10}$

   b. $4\frac{2}{5} \times 3\frac{3}{8}$ g. $3\frac{1}{7} \times 5\frac{1}{4}$ l. $3\frac{3}{4} \times 5\frac{1}{3}$

   c. $5\frac{5}{6} \times 2\frac{4}{5}$ h. $8\frac{3}{4} \times 2\frac{1}{7}$ m. $5\frac{1}{3} \times 5\frac{1}{3}$

   d. $14\frac{2}{3} \times 5\frac{3}{8}$ i. $16\frac{3}{4} \times 4\frac{2}{3}$ n. $2\frac{3}{8} \times 1\frac{4}{7}$

   e. $2\frac{4}{5} \times 1\frac{1}{2}$ j. $10\frac{1}{2} \times 14\frac{1}{2}$ o. $9\frac{1}{2} \times 9\frac{1}{2}$

Multiplying Mixed Numbers

Essentials to Remember

1. Change the mixed numbers to improper fractions.

2. Multiply, using the rules for multiplication of fractions.

HOW TO DO THE EXAMPLE

Problem 1. Multiply $6\frac{1}{4} \times 1\frac{1}{5}$

$6\frac{1}{4} \times 1\frac{1}{5} = \frac{\overset{5}{\cancel{25}}}{\cancel{4}_2} \times \frac{\overset{3}{\cancel{6}}}{\cancel{5}_1}$ Mixed numbers changed to improper fractions

$= \frac{15}{2} = 7\frac{1}{2}$ Answer

Problem 2. Multiply $3\frac{1}{3} \times 1\frac{1}{5}$

$3\frac{1}{3} \times 1\frac{1}{5} = \frac{\overset{2}{\cancel{10}}}{\cancel{3}_1} \times \frac{\overset{2}{\cancel{6}}}{\cancel{5}_1} = 4$

Multiplying Mixed Numbers and Whole Numbers

In multiplying a mixed number by a whole number, it is sometimes better to arrange the work in a vertical column.

HOW TO DO THE EXAMPLE ────────────────

Problem 1. Multiply 64 by $7\frac{3}{8}$.

$$
\begin{array}{r}
64 \\
7\frac{3}{8} \\
\hline
24 \\
448 \\
\hline
472
\end{array}
$$

24   ← Fraction times whole number ($\frac{3}{8} \times 64 = 24$)

448   ← Whole number times whole number ($7 \times 64 = 448$)

472   Answer

Problem 2. Multiply 69 by $23\frac{2}{3}$.

$$
\begin{array}{r}
69 \\
23\frac{2}{3} \\
\hline
46 \\
207 \\
138 \\
\hline
1633
\end{array}
$$

1633   Answer

────────────────────────────────────

EXERCISES

Multiplying Mixed Numbers and Whole Numbers

1. *Multiply:*
   a. $6 \times 3\frac{1}{8}$
   b. $45 \times 3\frac{1}{8}$
   c. $22 \times 2\frac{1}{4}$
   d. $2\frac{5}{8} \times 32$
   e. $28 \times 9\frac{6}{11}$
   f. $5 \times 6\frac{1}{8}$
   g. $1\frac{3}{8} \times 24$
   h. $7\frac{3}{4} \times 15$
   i. $36 \times 2\frac{5}{8}$
   j. $54 \times 6\frac{1}{18}$
   k. $8 \times 2\frac{1}{2}$
   l. $3\frac{1}{8} \times 11$
   m. $1\frac{3}{8} \times 16$
   n. $12 \times 3\frac{5}{8}$
   o. $96 \times 5\frac{5}{16}$

2. *Multiply each of the following vertically.*
   a. $44 \times 18\frac{3}{4}$
   b. $55 \times 13\frac{3}{11}$
   c. $65 \times 19\frac{5}{8}$
   d. $36 \times 9\frac{1}{2}$
   e. $54 \times 26\frac{5}{8}$
   f. $76 \times 32\frac{3}{4}$

3. *Find the products of each of the following:*
   a. $5 \times 3\frac{3}{4}$
   b. $\frac{3}{8} \times 4\frac{4}{5}$
   c. $\frac{1}{3} \times 9$
   d. $\frac{1}{8} \times \frac{3}{10} \times \frac{1}{21}$
   e. $7\frac{3}{8} \times 1\frac{9}{10}$
   f. $5\frac{2}{8} \times 4$
   g. $10 \times 3\frac{3}{8}$
   h. $7\frac{3}{8} \times 1\frac{2}{19}$
   i. $\frac{5}{8} \times \frac{3}{7}$
   j. $\frac{1}{8} \times \frac{5}{16}$
   k. $3\frac{1}{2} \times \frac{1}{8}$
   l. $6\frac{1}{8} \times 2\frac{3}{7} \times 5\frac{1}{4}$

m. $12\frac{1}{2} \times 3\frac{2}{5}$ p. $\frac{5}{8} \times 3\frac{1}{4} \times 2\frac{1}{2}$ s. $3\frac{3}{8} \times 6\frac{1}{2}$

n. $\frac{6}{7} \times \frac{14}{21} \times \frac{2}{3}$ q. $5 \times \frac{3}{10}$ t. $8 \times \frac{1}{8}$

o. $16\frac{1}{2} \times 2\frac{1}{11}$ r. $18\frac{1}{2} \times 3\frac{1}{8}$ u. $12\frac{1}{2} \times 6\frac{1}{4}$

GENERAL SKILL EXERCISE

How are you doing? Try the following test. If you get any wrong, turn to the pages shown after each question. Practice those problems until you have mastered them.

1. Instead of adding 6 equal fractions, the answer can be obtained by .... the fraction by 6 (page 48).

2. A whole number may be changed into a fraction by writing the number over a denominator of .... (page 49).

3. Dividing a numerator and a denominator in a multiplication problem by the same number is called .... (page 49).

4. A loaf of bread weighs $2\frac{1}{8}$ pounds. How many pounds do 3 loaves of bread weigh? .... (page 54).

5. Before mixed numbers are multiplied, they are usually changed to .... (page 53).

6. A boy walks at the rate of $1\frac{1}{2}$ miles an hour. How far does he travel in 3 hours? .... (page 54).

7. The product of two fractions is the product of the numerators .... by the product of the denominators (page 51).

8. $\frac{7}{12} \times \frac{12}{7}$ .... (page 51).

9. $\frac{1}{2}$ of 16 .... (page 49).

10. $\frac{2}{3}$ of 96 .... (page 49).

My Score ————

PROBLEMS

1. Henry rides his bicycle at a speed of about $5\frac{1}{2}$ miles per hour. How far can he ride in $2\frac{1}{2}$ hours? 3 hours? $3\frac{1}{2}$ hours?

2. A cardboard box weighs $19\frac{3}{4}$ ounces. What is the weight of 17 boxes?

3. A quart of water weighs about $2\frac{1}{12}$ pounds. How much do the 22 quarts in a tank weigh?

4. Each cubic foot of water contains $7\frac{1}{2}$ gallons. How many gallons are there in $3\frac{1}{2}$ cubic feet of water?

5. In a certain town the cost of the electricity is 6 cents per kilowatt hour. If Henry left a bulb burning for $5\frac{3}{4}$ hours, how much did it cost? for $8\frac{1}{4}$ hours? $7\frac{1}{4}$ hours? $12\frac{1}{2}$ hours?

6. How much ribbon must be bought to put on 18 hats if each hat requires $\frac{7}{18}$ of a yard of ribbon?

7. The weights of three boys are as follows: $94\frac{1}{8}$ pounds, $89\frac{3}{4}$ pounds, and $87\frac{1}{4}$ pounds. What is the total weight of these boys?

8. After working $3\frac{1}{2}$ hours at a job, a man is joined at work by two other men. It takes $2\frac{1}{4}$ hours for all three men to complete the job. What is the total number of man-hours spent on the job?

9. The price of grapes is $22\frac{1}{2}$ cents a pound. How much do $5\frac{1}{4}$ pounds cost?

10. James uses his allowance in the following way: $\frac{1}{8}$ for carfare, $\frac{1}{4}$ for lunches and $\frac{7}{16}$ for the movies. The remainder he saves. What part of his allowance does he save?

Division with Fractions

James has two sandwiches, each of which he divides into 4 pieces. To how many friends can he give a part of the sandwiches?

Since each sandwich has 4 quarters, there are 2×4 or 8 quarters.

$$2 \qquad \div \qquad \frac{1}{4} \qquad = \qquad 8$$

Thus, when we ask "How many quarters or fourths are there in two wholes?" we really indicate division, written as $2\div\frac{1}{4}$. We have seen that when 2 wholes were divided into fourths, we would have 8 fourths, or that $2\div\frac{1}{4}=8$. Now let us see how to divide by a fraction.

Rule to Remember

When a whole number is divided by a proper fraction, the quotient is larger than the original whole number, because the result is more but smaller parts.

HOW TO DO THE EXAMPLE

Problem: Divide 2 by $\frac{1}{4}$. $2 \div \frac{1}{4}$

Rewrite the problem, making the following changes:

1. Invert the *divisor*, the number which follows the division sign ($\div$). A fraction is inverted by turning it upside down. Thus, when the fraction $\frac{2}{3}$ is inverted it becomes $\frac{3}{2}$; $\frac{1}{4}$ inverted becomes $\frac{4}{1}$. If the divisor is a whole number, first write it over a denominator of 1 and then invert. For example, if the divisor is 3, first write it as $\frac{3}{1}$, then invert this fraction to $\frac{1}{3}$. The inverted fraction is called the *reciprocal* of the original fraction.

2. Change the division sign to a multiplication sign.

3. Now multiply, following the rules for the multiplication of fractions.

$$2 \div \tfrac{1}{4} = 2 \times \tfrac{4}{1} = 8$$

Dividing a Whole Number by a Fraction

The gym class was divided into 3 squads of 12 boys each. When the class decided to play baseball, the instructor had to reorganize the squads to make them $\frac{3}{4}$ of their former size.

The instructor found that if he reduced each of the three squads to $\frac{3}{4}$ of their size, he would get squads of 9 boys each. How many baseball teams could he form?

This is what he did:

$$3 \div \tfrac{3}{4} =$$
$$3 \times \tfrac{4}{3} = \tfrac{1\,2}{3} = 4$$

The instructor left 9 boys in each squad, took three boys away from each of the three squads, and made a fourth squad from the three groups of three. Then the class had 4 baseball teams.

Rule to Remember

To divide a whole number by a fraction, multiply the whole number by the denominator of the fraction and divide the result by the numerator of the fraction.

HOW TO DO THE EXAMPLE

1. Invert divisor
2. Change division sign to multiplication sign.
3. Multiply

Problem 1. Divide 15 by $\tfrac{3}{4}$

$$15 \div \tfrac{3}{4} =$$

$$\overset{5}{\cancel{15}} \times \tfrac{4}{\underset{1}{\cancel{3}}} \quad \text{Divisor inverted}$$
Sign
Changed

$$\overset{5}{\cancel{15}} \times \tfrac{4}{\underset{1}{\cancel{3}}} = 20 \text{ Answer}$$

Problem 2. Divide 12 by $\tfrac{2}{3}$

$$12 \div \tfrac{2}{3} =$$

$$\overset{6}{\cancel{12}} \times \tfrac{3}{\underset{1}{\cancel{2}}} = 18 \text{ Answer}$$

EXERCISES

Dividing a Whole Number by a Fraction

1. *Divide each of the following:*

a. 15 by $\tfrac{1}{5}$	f. 28 by $\tfrac{4}{7}$	k. 3 by $\tfrac{1}{7}$
b. 8 by $\tfrac{1}{2}$	g. 4 by $\tfrac{2}{3}$	l. 6 by $\tfrac{4}{5}$
c. 2 by $\tfrac{1}{6}$	h. 8 by $\tfrac{3}{4}$	m. 4 by $\tfrac{1}{10}$
d. 6 by $\tfrac{3}{8}$	i. 9 by $\tfrac{9}{16}$	n. 12 by $\tfrac{9}{14}$
e. 16 by $\tfrac{8}{9}$	j. 20 by $\tfrac{4}{5}$	o. 18 by $\tfrac{3}{8}$

Division of a Fraction by a Fraction

The diagram at the right shows $\frac{3}{4}$ of a pie. How many fourths or quarters are there? By actual count, we find there are 3 quarters. Let us see how to do the following examples by division:

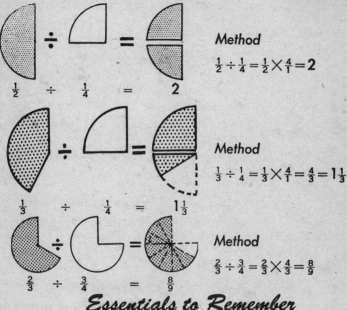

Method

$$\frac{1}{2} \div \frac{1}{4} = \frac{1}{2} \times \frac{4}{1} = 2$$

$\frac{1}{2} \quad \div \quad \frac{1}{4} \quad = \quad 2$

Method

$$\frac{1}{3} \div \frac{1}{4} = \frac{1}{3} \times \frac{4}{1} = \frac{4}{3} = 1\frac{1}{3}$$

$\frac{1}{3} \quad \div \quad \frac{1}{4} \quad = \quad 1\frac{1}{3}$

Method

$$\frac{2}{3} \div \frac{3}{4} = \frac{2}{3} \times \frac{4}{3} = \frac{8}{9}$$

$\frac{2}{3} \quad \div \quad \frac{3}{4} \quad = \quad \frac{8}{9}$

Essentials to Remember

1. Invert the divisor.

2. Change the division sign to a multiplication sign.

3. Multiply following the rules of multiplication.

HOW TO DO THE EXAMPLE

Problem 1. Divide $\frac{3}{4}$ by $\frac{1}{4}$.

$$\frac{3}{4} \div \frac{1}{4} =$$

$$\frac{3}{\underset{1}{4}} \times \frac{4}{1} = 3 \text{ Answer}$$

Problem 2. Divide $\frac{4}{9}$ by $\frac{16}{3}$

$$\frac{4}{9} \div \frac{16}{3} =$$

$$\frac{4}{\underset{3}{9}} \times \frac{3}{\underset{4}{16}} = \frac{1}{12} \text{ Answer}$$

EXERCISES

Dividing a Fraction by a Fraction

1. *Divide each of the following:*

   a. $\frac{1}{4} \div \frac{3}{8}$ f. $\frac{3}{5} \div \frac{2}{5}$ k. $\frac{4}{9} \div \frac{2}{3}$

   b. $\frac{3}{8} \div \frac{1}{2}$ g. $\frac{2}{7} \div \frac{4}{5}$ l. $\frac{1}{4} \div \frac{1}{2}$

   c. $\frac{3}{8} \div \frac{3}{5}$ h. $\frac{3}{5} \div \frac{2}{3}$ m. $\frac{9}{10} \div \frac{3}{5}$

   d. $\frac{5}{8} \div \frac{1}{2}$ i. $\frac{1}{4} \div \frac{3}{16}$ n. $\frac{7}{12} \div \frac{5}{8}$

   e. $\frac{1}{3} \div \frac{1}{8}$ j. $\frac{1}{4} \div \frac{7}{16}$ o. $\frac{5}{12} \div \frac{1}{3}$

2. *Complete each of the following:*

   a. $6 \div \frac{3}{5}$ f. $\frac{3}{8} \div \frac{1}{4}$ k. $9 \div \frac{3}{8}$

   b. $\frac{1}{8} \div \frac{3}{10}$ g. $\frac{1}{6} \div \frac{9}{16}$ l. $8 \div \frac{3}{12}$

   c. $\frac{1}{8} \div \frac{1}{6}$ h. $8 \div \frac{5}{6}$ m. $\frac{1}{8} \div \frac{11}{16}$

   d. $7 \div \frac{3}{14}$ i. $\frac{1}{8} \div \frac{3}{6}$ n. $\frac{3}{4} \div \frac{11}{16}$

   e. $9 \div \frac{2}{3}$ j. $11 \div \frac{3}{22}$ o. $\frac{1}{8} \div \frac{1}{24}$

Dividing a Fraction by a Whole Number

If the $\frac{3}{8}$ of the pie at the left is to be divided into 6 parts, what part of the original pie will each of the newly cut pieces be? Here, we are actually dividing the fraction $\frac{3}{8}$ by the whole number 6.

Essentials to Remember

1. If the divisor is a whole number, write it over a denominator of 1.

2. Invert the divisor.

3. Change the division sign to a multiplication sign and multiply.

HOW TO DO THE EXAMPLE

Problem 1. Divide $\frac{3}{8}$ by 6.

$$\frac{3}{8} \div 6 =$$

$$\frac{3}{8} \div \frac{6}{1} =$$

$$\frac{3}{8} \times \frac{1}{\cancel{6}_2} = \frac{1}{16} \quad \text{Answer}$$

Problem 2. Divide $\frac{8}{9}$ by 16.

$$\frac{8}{9} \div 16 =$$

$$\frac{8}{9} \div \frac{16}{1}$$

$$\frac{\cancel{8}}{9} \times \frac{1}{\cancel{16}_2} = \frac{1}{18} \quad \text{Answer}$$

EXERCISES
Dividing a Fraction by a Whole Number

1. *Divide.*

a. $\frac{2}{3} \div 8$	f. $\frac{3}{4} \div 6$	k. $\frac{3}{8} \div 12$	p. $\frac{5}{6} \div 10$
b. $\frac{5}{9} \div 15$	g. $\frac{3}{10} \div 21$	l. $\frac{1}{8} \div 2$	q. $\frac{11}{20} \div 22$
c. $\frac{1}{4} \div 3$	h. $\frac{1}{8} \div 10$	m. $\frac{2}{3} \div 4$	r. $\frac{3}{4} \div 6$
d. $\frac{3}{8} \div 6$	i. $\frac{2}{5} \div 12$	n. $\frac{5}{9} \div 8$	s. $\frac{11}{12} \div 5$
e. $\frac{9}{10} \div 12$	j. $\frac{3}{14} \div 21$	o. $\frac{15}{16} \div 10$	t. $\frac{8}{9} \div 22$

Division of Mixed Numbers and Whole Numbers

A farmer sold $2\frac{1}{4}$ acres of land to a builder. The land was divided into four equal lots, and a house was built on each lot. How much land was included with each house?

In this problem we must divide $2\frac{1}{4}$ by 4.

Essentials to Remember

1. Change both the mixed number and the whole number to improper fractions.

2. Invert the divisor.

3. Change the division sign to a multiplication sign.

4. Multiply.

HOW TO DO THE EXAMPLE

Problem 1: $2\frac{1}{4} \div 4$

Numbers changed to improper fractions $\frac{9}{4} \div \frac{4}{1}$

Sign changed, divisor inverted $\frac{9}{4} \times \frac{1}{4} = \frac{9}{16}$ **of an acre**

Problem 2: Divide 2 by $1\frac{1}{3}$.

$2 \div 1\frac{1}{3}$

$\frac{2}{1} \div \frac{4}{3} =$ Numbers changed to improper fractions.

$\frac{\overset{1}{2}}{1} \times \frac{3}{\underset{2}{4}} =$ Divisor inverted, sign changed

$\frac{3}{2}$ or $1\frac{1}{2}$ Answer

Problem 3: Divide $4\frac{2}{3}$ by $1\frac{1}{6}$

$4\frac{2}{3} \div 1\frac{1}{6} =$

$\frac{14}{3} \div \frac{7}{6} =$

$\frac{\overset{2}{14}}{\underset{1}{3}} \times \frac{\overset{2}{6}}{\underset{1}{7}} = 4$ **Answer**

EXERCISES

Dividing Mixed Numbers and Whole Numbers

1. *Divide.*

a. $6 \div 2\frac{1}{2}$	*i.* $10 \div 2\frac{2}{5}$	*q.* $7 \div 4\frac{2}{3}$
b. $8 \div 3\frac{1}{4}$	*j.* $3 \div 2\frac{1}{10}$	*r.* $4 \div 2\frac{2}{3}$
c. $3\frac{1}{8} \div 2$	*k.* $2\frac{1}{2} \div 5$	*s.* $3\frac{1}{2} \div 7$
d. $5\frac{5}{6} \div 15$	*l.* $2\frac{4}{5} \div 10$	*t.* $3\frac{1}{5} \div 16$
e. $1\frac{1}{3} \div 2$	*m.* $2\frac{5}{8} \div 7$	*u.* $6 \div 1\frac{2}{3}$
f. $3 \div 1\frac{1}{2}$	*n.* $1\frac{2}{3} \div 12$	*v.* $5\frac{1}{2} \div 5$
g. $11 \div 4\frac{1}{2}$	*o.* $16 \div 3\frac{1}{5}$	*w.* $9\frac{1}{2} \div 3$
h. $4 \div 6\frac{2}{3}$	*p.* $11\frac{1}{3} \div 3$	*x.* $15 \div 3\frac{1}{8}$

2. *Divide.*

a. $2\frac{1}{16} \div 1\frac{5}{6}$	*j.* $5\frac{1}{2} \div 3\frac{2}{3}$	*s.* $7\frac{1}{4} \div 1\frac{1}{8}$
b. $3\frac{1}{7} \div 1\frac{4}{7}$	*k.* $1\frac{1}{6} \div 1\frac{1}{3}$	*t.* $12\frac{4}{5} \div 2\frac{1}{8}$
c. $4\frac{4}{7} \div 1\frac{5}{16}$	*l.* $15\frac{2}{5} \div 1\frac{1}{10}$	*u.* $3\frac{1}{9} \div 1\frac{1}{2}$
d. $2\frac{7}{10} \div 7\frac{1}{5}$	*m.* $8\frac{1}{5} \div 4\frac{1}{6}$	*v.* $10\frac{1}{6} \div 8\frac{2}{3}$
e. $5\frac{1}{8} \div 2\frac{1}{4}$	*n.* $6\frac{1}{8} \div 4\frac{1}{4}$	*w.* $2\frac{1}{6} \div 8\frac{1}{3}$
f. $2\frac{5}{8} \div 2\frac{1}{4}$	*o.* $7\frac{2}{5} \div 3\frac{7}{10}$	*x.* $1\frac{2}{3} \div 8\frac{1}{8}$
g. $7\frac{2}{5} \div 4\frac{7}{10}$	*p.* $4\frac{1}{6} \div 4\frac{1}{3}$	*y.* $5\frac{5}{6} \div 2\frac{1}{12}$
h. $8\frac{1}{4} \div 1\frac{5}{6}$	*q.* $2\frac{2}{3} \div 4\frac{1}{3}$	*z.* $1\frac{3}{4} \div 2\frac{3}{16}$
i. $2\frac{4}{5} \div 3\frac{1}{5}$	*r.* $4\frac{7}{12} \div 2\frac{1}{8}$	

To Find Fractional Parts

Tom has a small bread route. He earns \$12 a day in commissions. He saves \$7 each week. What part of his earnings does he save?

In this example we are trying to find what fractional part one number is of another.

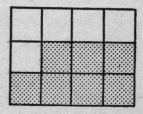

In this diagram, we see that the rectangle has been divided into 12 squares, 7 of which have been shaded. Thus, we can see that 7 out of 12 squares are shaded, or $\frac{7}{12}$ of the whole rectangle.

Rule to Remember

To find what fractional part one number is of another, write a fraction in which the smaller number is the numerator and the larger number is the denominator, and reduce the fraction to its lowest terms. In other words, the smaller number is divided by the larger number.

$\frac{7}{12}$ is the fractional part of his earnings Tom saves.

EXERCISES

Finding Fractional Parts

1. *Give the answer to each of the following questions in lowest terms:*

   a. 7 is what part of 21?
   b. 5 is what part of 25?
   c. 9 is what part of 27?
   d. 14 is what part of 21?
   e. What part of 75 is 25?

   f. What part of 36 is 18?
   g. What part of 49 is 21?
   h. What part of 100 is 35?
   i. What part of 13 is 5?
   j. What part of 19 is 17?

2. Maria was given 35 boxes of candy to sell for the muscular disease drive. She sold 30 boxes. What fractional part of the boxes she was given to sell did she sell?

To Find a Number, Given a Fractional Part of the Number

Problem: The audience at a movie occupies $\frac{9}{10}$ of the seats in the theater. If there are 630 people present, how many seats are there in the theater?

In this problem we know a fractional part of a number and we are trying to find the whole number.

Rule to Remember

To find a number when a fractional part of the number is known, *divide* the known number *by the numerator* of the fraction and then *multiply* the result *by the denominator* of the fraction.

There are two ways in which we can do this.

HOW TO DO THE EXAMPLE

Method 1. Since we know that $\frac{9}{10}$ of the number of seats amounts to 630, then $\frac{1}{10}$ of the seats would amount to $630 \div 9$, or 70 seats. The full number of seats, or $\frac{10}{10}$, would be equal to 10×70 or 700 seats.

$$630 \div 9 = 70$$
$$70 \times 10 = 700 \text{ seats}$$

Method 2. Another way of doing this example is by dividing the given number by the fraction.

$$630 \div \frac{9}{10} =$$
$$\overset{70}{\cancel{630}} \times \frac{10}{\cancel{9}_1} = 700 \text{ seats}$$

EXERCISES

Finding a Number

1. *Find the missing numbers:*

    a. The number of which 5 is $\frac{1}{3}$ is............................

    b. The number of which 9 is $\frac{1}{2}$ is............................

    c. The number of which 6 is $\frac{1}{4}$ is............................

2. *Complete each of the following:*

    a. 20 is $\frac{1}{2}$ of ....

    b. 24 is $\frac{2}{3}$ of ....

    c. 18 is $\frac{1}{6}$ of ....

    d. $2\frac{1}{4}$ is $\frac{3}{2}$ of ....

    e. $14\frac{1}{2}$ is $\frac{3}{8}$ of ....

    f. $2\frac{1}{4}$ is $\frac{2}{3}$ of ....

3. A delivery truck was loaded with materials. The driver had delivered 1575 pounds when his truck broke down. By this time he had delivered $\frac{3}{4}$ of the load. How many pounds had he started out with?

4. Harry delivered 48 newspapers after school one day. This was $\frac{8}{8}$ of the number of papers delivered by Martin. How many papers did Martin deliver?

5. John saw a bicycle at a sale. It was marked $15 for clearance. The price tag stated that this clearance price was $\frac{2}{8}$ of the original price. What was the original price?

6. Mrs. Smith's electric bill for this month was $8. This bill was $\frac{8}{8}$ of her bill for the previous month. How much was her previous bill?

PROBLEMS

1. An express train covers a distance of 135 miles in $2\frac{1}{4}$ hours. What is the average speed of the train?

2. Alan wishes to build an embankment for his railroad trains to run on. He wants the height to be $8\frac{1}{4}$ inches. If he uses strips of plywood $\frac{3}{8}$ inch thick, how many strips does he need?

3. Mr. Jones has two boards, each of which is 14 feet in length. How many shelves, each $4\frac{2}{3}$ feet long, can he make from the boards?

4. John's mother paid $2\frac{1}{2}$ for a $2\frac{1}{2}$-pound steak. How much does one pound of steak cost?

5. During the five days of a school week, Edward spent $12\frac{1}{2}$ hours studying. What is the average number of hours he spent studying each day?

GENERAL SKILL EXERCISE

How are you doing? Try the following test. If you get any wrong, turn to the pages shown after each question. Practice those problems until you have mastered them.

1. If you know $\frac{2}{8}$ of a number, you find the whole number by .... (page 64).

2. Inverting a fraction results in a new fraction called the .... of the original fraction (page 57).

3. In dividing by a fraction, invert the divisor and then .... the dividend by the resulting fraction (page 57).

4. In dividing a fraction by a whole number, after inverting the divisor, the numerator of the divisor is always .... (page 60).

5. When dividing by a mixed number, the mixed number must first be changed to a (an) .... (page 61).

6. The result of dividing $3\frac{1}{8}$ by $1\frac{1}{2}$ is .... (page 61).

7. If you have $7 and spend $3, what fractional part of your money did you spend? .... (page 63).

8. Before mixed numbers can be divided, they must first be changed to .... (page 61).

9. To find a number if we know a fractional part of it, we can divide the given number by the .... and multiply the result by the .... (page 64).

10. The number of which 12 is $\frac{2}{3}$ is .... (page 64).

_____ *My Score*

PRINCIPLES TO REMEMBER

1. A fraction may represent a part of a whole thing or a part of a group, or it may indicate division.

2. If the numerator and denominator of a fraction are equal, the value of the fraction is 1.

3. The numerator and denominator of a fraction may be multiplied or divided by the same number without changing the value of the fraction.

4. A fraction is in its simplest terms when the numerator and denominator have no common divisor other than 1.

5. To add like fractions, add their numerators and write the sum over the common denominator.

6. To subtract like fractions, subtract the numerators and write the difference over the common denominator.

7. To add or subtract unlike fractions, first change the fractions to equivalent like fractions having the least common denominator and then add or subtract the numerators, writing the result over the common denominator.

8. Fractions can be compared only when they have the same numerator or the same denominator.

9. To multiply fractions, first multiply the numerators and then multiply the denominators. Write the product of the numerators

over the product of the denominators and reduce this fraction to lowest terms.

10. To divide by a fraction, invert the divisor and then multiply the dividend by the new fraction.

11. To find what fractional part one number is of another, place the smaller number over the larger number and reduce the fraction if possible.

12. To find a number when a fractional part of the number is known, divide the known number by the fraction.

MASTERY TEST

Complete each of the following statements:

1. The lower term of a fraction is called the ....

2. A mixed number is made up of a .... and a
....

3. To invert a fraction means to ....

4. A fraction in which the numerator is equal to or larger than the denominator is called a (an) .... fraction.

5. To change a fraction to an equivalent fraction having higher terms we .... both the numerator and denominator by the .... number.

6. To reduce a fraction to an equivalent fraction with lowest terms we .... the numerator and the denominator by the largest whole number which is a factor of both.

7. To change a mixed number to an improper fraction .... the denominator by the whole number, ... the numerator and place the result over the ....

8. In order to add or subtract fractions, the fractions must have a .... denominator.

9. The product of a proper fraction multiplied by a proper fraction is .... (greater than, less than) 1.

10. If a proper fraction is divided by a whole number, the answer is .... (greater than, less than) 1.

11. If a number is divided by a proper fraction, the answer is .... (greater, less than) the original number.

12. Dividing a numerator and a denominator by the same number is called ....

13. In dividing by a fraction, first .... the divisor, and then ....

14. The product is smaller than the multiplier when we multiply a .... by a ....

15. A quotient is larger than its dividend when we ....

16. An example of a mixed number is ....

17. An example of a proper fraction that can be reduced is ....

18. An example of a proper fraction that cannot be reduced is ....

19. An example of an improper fraction that can be reduced to a mixed number is ....

20. An example of an improper fraction that cannot be reduced to a mixed number is ....

21. The fraction $\frac{48}{64}$ expressed in lowest terms is ....

22. Changed to a mixed number, $\frac{19}{3}$ equals ....

23. The fraction $\frac{3}{5}$ is larger than $\frac{1}{10}$ by ....

24. A fraction equal to $\frac{3}{4}$ is ....

25. When the fractions $\frac{1}{2}$ and $\frac{2}{3}$ are changed to 6ths, 6 is called the ....

26. Subtract $8\frac{2}{3}$ from $16\frac{1}{2}$.

27. Divide 36 by $2\frac{1}{4}$.

28. Find the sum of $6\frac{1}{4}$, $3\frac{2}{3}$, $\frac{1}{2}$.

29. At the rate of $2\frac{2}{3}$ bushels of seed per acre, how many bushels of seed will it take to plant 28 acres?

30. If 12 is $\frac{2}{5}$ of a number, what is the number?

31. How many $\frac{1}{4}$ pound bags can be filled from 12 pounds of peanuts?

32. A baseball team lost 2 games, which was $\frac{2}{7}$ of the total number of games played. How many games did the team play?

33. Multiply 40 by $6\frac{1}{4}$.

34. How much does $4\frac{2}{3} + 1\frac{1}{2} - 3\frac{1}{4}$ equal?

35. What fractional part of 120 is 45?

36. Multiply $8\frac{2}{5}$ by $6\frac{2}{3}$.

37. What is the product of $2\frac{1}{3}$, $5\frac{1}{10}$ and $5\frac{1}{2}$?

38. How many $4\frac{1}{2}$'s are there in 72?

39. Which is smaller, $2\frac{3}{4} \times 74$ or $11\frac{7}{8} \times 14$?

40. Find the average of $8\frac{3}{4}$, $6\frac{5}{8}$, $12\frac{7}{8}$, $9\frac{1}{2}$, $5\frac{7}{8}$.

41. 55 is $\frac{5}{8}$ of what number?

42. 9 is what part of 11?

43. 6 is $\frac{3}{4}$ of what number?

44. How much is $\frac{1}{3}$ of $\frac{1}{2}$?

45. The fraction $\frac{7}{8}$ indicates that something has been divided into .... equal parts and that .... are being taken.

46. Which of the following is the largest: $\frac{5}{12}$, $\frac{1}{2}$, $\frac{3}{8}$?

47. James takes $1\frac{3}{4}$ hours to make one model car. How long does it take him to build 6 models?

PROBLEMS

1. Mrs. Jones has $4\frac{1}{2}$ grapefruit. To how many people can she serve $\frac{1}{2}$ grapefruit each?

2. John is $58\frac{1}{4}$ inches tall. Alfred is $55\frac{3}{4}$ inches tall. How much taller is John?

3. An electrician had $63\frac{1}{4}$ inches of wire. He used $16\frac{3}{4}$ inches. How much wire did he have left?

4. Mr. Adams is a traveling salesman. During one week he traveled the following distances: $88\frac{1}{10}$, $196\frac{3}{10}$, 203, $178\frac{1}{10}$ and 168 miles. What was his total mileage?

5. A builder bought the following amounts of linoleum: $126\frac{1}{2}$ yards, 138 yards, $218\frac{3}{8}$ yards, $196\frac{1}{8}$ yards and 206 yards. He used 61 yards on one job, and on another $37\frac{3}{8}$ yards. How many yards did he have left?

6. James bought $41\frac{1}{2}$ feet of lumber to do some repair work around the house. On the door he used $6\frac{1}{2}$ feet, on the cellar windows he used 3 feet. How many feet did he have left?

7. In order to go home from the movies, James had to ride $2\frac{9}{10}$ miles by bus and then walk $\frac{3}{10}$ of a mile. How far does James live from the movies?

8. In making a bookcase, Henry used the following amount of lumber for the shelves: $9\frac{1}{16}$ feet, $6\frac{5}{16}$ feet, and $8\frac{11}{16}$ feet. He had originally bought 26 feet of lumber. How many feet does he have left?

9. From a farm containing 680 acres, $455\frac{1}{2}$ acres were sold. How many acres were left?

10. John was 15 years and 3 months old when Adam was born. Adam is now 14 years and 9 months old. How old is John now?

3 | DECIMAL FRACTIONS

What Are Decimal Fractions?

In an inter-class running meet, Henry won the 100-yard dash by running this distance in 13.4 seconds. In this statement, the time is read as 13 and four tenths seconds. The four tenths of a second, when written as .4, is called a *decimal fraction*.

We have already learned that a fraction represents a part of something. We also have seen one way of writing a fractional part: the common fraction. Another form which expresses a part of something is the decimal fraction. A *decimal fraction* is a special kind of fraction whose denominator is 10, 100, 1000, 10,000 or any higher power of 10. (See table on page 71.)

Writing Decimals

A decimal fraction is written without a denominator. The number at the right of the decimal point is the numerator of the decimal fraction. The decimal point is used to show whether the denominator is 10, 100, 1000, and so on. The denominator is indicated as follows:

If there is one figure after the decimal point, the fraction is expressed in tenths. It has a denominator of 10, which has *one* zero. $.9$ means $\frac{9}{10}$

If there are two figures after the decimal point, the fraction is expressed in hundredths; its denominator is 100, which has *two* zeros. $.02$ means $\frac{2}{100}$

If there are three figures after the decimal point, the fraction is expressed in thousandths; its denominator is 1000, which has *three* zeros. $.324$ means $\frac{324}{1000}$

Rule to Remember

When a fraction is written as a decimal fraction, the decimal fraction must have as many places to the right of the decimal point as there are zeros in the denominator.

For example, to write $\frac{8}{10}$ as a decimal fraction we place the decimal point in front of the 8 so that it becomes $.8$; to write $\frac{8}{100}$ as a decimal fraction we must place one zero in front of the 8 to give it two places, thus $\frac{8}{100}$ written as a decimal fraction is $.08$. Similarly, $\frac{8}{1000}$ requires two zeros in front of the 8 to give it three places. Thus $\frac{8}{1000}$ becomes $.008$ as a decimal fraction.

Reading Decimals

Each decimal place in a decimal fraction is given a name.

Tenths	Hundredths	Thousandths	Ten-thousandths	Hundred-thousandths	Millionths
.3	7	6	8	5	4

A number like 8.73, which consists of both a whole number and a decimal, is a decimal *mixed number*, and is called a *mixed decimal*.

In reading a mixed decimal the decimal point is read *and*.

A decimal fraction is read as a whole number and then given the name of the last place. For example, .5 is read 5 tenths; .24 is read 24 hundredths; .083 is read 83 thousandths (because the 3 is in the thousandths place); .000406 is read 406 millionths. The number in the table on page 71 is read 376,854 millionths. The mixed decimal 32.384 is read 32 and 3 hundred 84 thousandths.

Place Value

In the decimal fraction .5555 each number stands in a different place. The last 5 is in the ten-thousandths place and means $\frac{5}{10000}$. The 5 in the next place to the left is $\frac{5}{1000}$; the 5 next to this is $\frac{5}{100}$ and the first 5 to the right of the decimal point is $\frac{5}{10}$. As we move to the left in this decimal fraction, each new 5 represents 10 times the 5 to the right of it. Thus, we see that in our number system each number has *place value*, since the value of the number depends on the place where it exists.

Rule to Remember

If any figure of a number is moved one place to the left, the value of that figure is multiplied by 10.

EXERCISES

Decimal Fractions

1. *Write the numerator and denominator of each of the following decimal fractions:*

    a.　.3　　denominator .... numerator ....

    b.　.05　　denominator .... numerator ....

    c.　.175　　denominator .... numerator ....

    d.　.0871　denominator .... numerator ....

2. *Write each of the following common fractions as a decimal fraction:*

   a. $\frac{7}{10}$ *f.* $\frac{35}{10000}$ *k.* $2\frac{8}{10}$

   b. $\frac{3}{100}$ *g.* $\frac{4}{10000}$ *l.* $3\frac{53}{100}$

   c. $\frac{35}{100}$ *h.* $\frac{156}{10000}$ *m.* $17\frac{126}{1000}$

   d. $\frac{48}{1000}$ *i.* $\frac{78}{100}$ *n.* $221\frac{46}{100}$

   e. $\frac{514}{1000}$ *j.* $\frac{1}{10000}$ *o.* $146\frac{753}{1000}$

3. *Write the following numbers as decimal fractions:*

   a. Six tenths ....;   nine tenths ....

   b. 15 hundredths ....; twenty-six hundredths ....

   c. nine and seventy-six hundredths ....; 15 and 6 hundredths ....

   d. Eight thousandths ....; one and 4 thousandths ....

   e. Five and 6 ten-thousandths ....; 4 hundred-thousandths ....

4. *Write each of the following numbers in words.*

   a. .8   *e.* 5.643   *h.* .14681

   b. .76   *f.* .4812   *i.* 10.64328

   c. 2.35   *g.* 7.3159   *j.* 123.96501

   d. .705

Rounding Off Decimal Fractions

Herbert went to the store to buy a note pad. He saw just the kind he wanted and noticed that the price was marked 3 for $.25.

"May I buy just one?" Herbert asked the clerk.

The clerk nodded. "You can buy one for $.09."

"But 9 times 3 is 27!" said Herbert, calculating rapidly.

"Well," laughed the clerk, "we can't sell you a pad for $.083333333, so we sell one for $.09."

Many times in our daily lives decimal fractions must be rounded off. As in the example above, decimal fractions may not be exact no matter how far they are carried out. Therefore, in a division that does not come out evenly, quotients are often carried out simply to the nearest tenth, hundredth or thousandth.

Notice that in business, prices are rounded to the next higher cent, instead of to the nearest cent. If the clerk had agreed with Herbert that $.083333333 could be rounded to $.08, the nearest cent, there would have been a small loss of money for the store.

Rule to Remember

In writing a number *correct* to a required number of decimal places, inspect *only* the number in the decimal place that is one place to the right of the decimal called for. If this next number is 5 or more, make the figure to the left of it 1 larger; if this next number is less than 5, leave the figure before it unchanged. Drop all decimals to the right of those required.

HOW TO DO THE EXAMPLE

When 4.16482 is rounded off:

to the *nearest ten-thousandth* it becomes **4.1648**

to the *nearest thousandth* it becomes **4.165**

to the *nearest hundredth* it becomes **4.16**

to the *nearest tenth* it becomes **4.2**

to the *nearest whole number* it becomes **4.**

EXERCISES

Rounding Off Decimals

1. *Round off each decimal to the nearest tenth:*
   a. .34
   b. .99
   c. .838
   d. 2.762
   e. 19.2127
   f. .76
   g. 1.46
   h. 3.61
   i. 32.325

2. *Round off each decimal to the nearest hundredth:*
   a. .632
   b. 6.545
   c. .82
   d. 10.064
   e. 15.119
   f. .477
   g. 2.499
   h. 8.199
   i. 5.395

3. *Round off each decimal to the nearest thousandth:*
   a. .7231
   b. .7650
   c. 9.7848
   d. .0536
   e. .6555
   f. .9246
   g. .8427
   h. .0025
   i. 3.5999

4. Round off each of the following to the nearest cent (nearest hundredth):
   a. $3.472
   b. $.062
   c. $2.664
   d. $31.125
   e. $4.577
   f. $.195
   g. $19.609
   h. $34.005
   i. $9.673
   j. $3.333
   k. $20.055
   l. $101.003

Comparing Decimal Fractions

An article in a leading magazine stated that the Latin American countries produce .2 of the world's lead, .97 of the world's nitrate, .19 of the world's oil and .186 of its tin.

Alice, who was reading the article, asked herself, "Do these countries produce a greater share of the world's lead, nitrate, oil or tin?"

To find the answer, she wrote each of the decimal fractions with the same number of places by adding one or two zeros to the end of some. This, she knew, would not change the value of the decimals, but would simply make them easier to compare.

.200 lead   .190 oil
.970 nitrate   .186 tin

Now she could see clearly that the Latin American countries' share in the world's production of nitrate was much greater than their share in the world's production of oil, lead, or tin. Of these three, their share was greatest in lead production, and smallest in the production of tin.

Principles to Remember

Before decimal fractions can be compared, the decimal fractions must have the same number of decimal places.

Zeros *annexed* (added) or dropped after the last figure to the right of the decimal point do not change the value of the decimal fraction. When this is done, the name of the decimal fraction is changed but not its value. For example:

.6 (six tenths) has the same value as .60 (sixty hundredths)

.07 (seven hundredths) has the same value as .070 (seventy thousandths)

HOW TO DO THE EXAMPLE

To compare decimal fractions, annex the number of zeros necessary to give each of the decimal fractions the same number of decimal places. Then compare the numbers.

(1) Which is larger .8 or .85?

.8 changed to hundredths is .80. Now we can see that .85 is larger.

(2) Which is larger .05 or .050?

.05 changed to thousandths is .050. We see now that neither is larger; .05 = .050.

EXERCISES

Comparing Decimal Fractions

1. *Change each of the following*
To hundredths:

a. .7	b. .8	c. .4	d. .9

To thousandths:

a. .2	c. .3	e. .04	g. .06
b. .70	d. .50	f. .11	h. .15

To tenths:

a. .600	c. .8000	e. .50	g. .100
b. .3000	d. .70	f. .90000	h. .600000

2. *In each of the following pairs of numbers, pick the larger number:*

a. .7 or .75	f. .38 or .383	k. .5 or .056
b. .3 or .28	g. .06 or .006	l. 8.3 or 8.31
c. .62 or .612	h. .5 or .555	m. .6 or .559
d. 4.6 or 4.06	i. .3 or .303	n. .2 or .026
e. .07 or .70	j. .1 or .011	o. 2.8 or .28

3. *Arrange each of the following groups of numbers according to size with the largest number first:*

a. .2, .002, .02, 2	d. 3.01, .301, .656, .066
b. 4.26, 4.255, 4.62, 4.608	e. 1.09, 10.9, .0019, 2.01
c. 6.04, .604, .008, 1.99	f. .6, .56, .056, .0612

GENERAL SKILL EXERCISE

How are you doing? Try the following test. If you get any wrong, turn to the pages shown after each question. Practice those problems until you have mastered them.

1. The number at the right of the decimal point stands for the .... of the decimal fraction (page 70).

2. If three digits are written after the decimal point, the denominator of the decimal fraction is .... (page 71).

3. When a fraction is to be written as a decimal fraction, there must be as many places to the right of the decimal point as there are .... in the denominator of the fraction (page 71)

4. The number 3.01 is called a .... decimal (page 72).

5. Moving a figure in a decimal fraction one place to the left causes the value of that figure to be multiplied by .... (page 72).

6. If the decimal fraction 3.4798 is to be expressed to the nearest hundredth, the number which determines how the decimal should be rounded is .... (page 74).

7. Are .7 and .70 different in value? .... (page 76).

8. The 6 in the decimal fraction 2.847653 is in the ....
place (page 71).

9. The decimal 18.649 is read eighteen and six hundred forty-nine
.... (page 72).

10. Before decimals can be compared, the decimals must have the
same number of .... (page 76).

My Score _____

Changing Decimals to Fractions

Since fractional parts of things may be written either as
common fractions or as decimal fractions, we should be able
to change a decimal fraction to a common fraction.

Essentials to Remember

A decimal fraction is a fraction whose denominator is
10, 100, 1000, or some higher power of ten.

To change a decimal fraction to a common fraction,
take out the decimal point and write the decimal number
as the numerator of the fraction. For the denominator
write the number as shown by the name of the last decimal
place. Reduce the common fraction to lowest terms.

HOW TO DO THE EXAMPLE

Problem 1. Write .85 as a common fraction.

Numerator
$$.85 = \frac{85}{100} = \frac{17}{20}$$
Hundredths

Problem 2. Write .002 as a common fraction.

Numerator
$$.002 = \frac{2}{1000} = \frac{1}{500}$$
Thousandths

[Continued on top of page 79]

Problem 3. Write 6.4 as a mixed number.

Numerator

$$6.4 = 6\tfrac{4}{10} = 6\tfrac{2}{5}$$

Tenths

Problem 4. Write $.12\tfrac{1}{2}$ as a common fraction.

Numerator

$$.12\tfrac{1}{2} = \frac{12\tfrac{1}{2}}{100} = 12\tfrac{1}{2} \div 100 =$$

Hundredths

$$\tfrac{25}{2} \div \tfrac{100}{1} = \tfrac{25}{2} \times \tfrac{1}{100} = \tfrac{1}{8}$$

A USEFUL TABLE TO REMEMBER

Decimal Fraction		Common Fraction	Decimal Fraction		Common Fraction
.25	=	$\tfrac{1}{4}$	$.87\tfrac{1}{2}$	=	$\tfrac{7}{8}$
.50	=	$\tfrac{1}{2}$	$.33\tfrac{1}{3}$	=	$\tfrac{1}{3}$
.75	=	$\tfrac{3}{4}$	$.66\tfrac{2}{3}$	=	$\tfrac{2}{3}$
$.12\tfrac{1}{2}$	=	$\tfrac{1}{8}$	$.16\tfrac{2}{3}$	=	$\tfrac{1}{6}$
$.37\tfrac{1}{2}$	=	$\tfrac{3}{8}$	$.83\tfrac{1}{3}$	=	$\tfrac{5}{6}$
$.62\tfrac{1}{2}$	=	$\tfrac{5}{8}$			

EXERCISES
Changing Decimals to Fractions

1. *Write each of the following numbers as common fractions in lowest terms:*

a.	.3	g.	.7	m.	.8	s.	.9
b.	.15	h.	.24	n.	.65	t.	.85
c.	.01	i.	.05	o.	.08	u.	.09
d.	.015	j.	.025	p.	.005	v.	.0075
e.	.375	k.	.625	q.	.875	w.	.750
f.	.0005	l.	.00125	r.	.0001	x.	.0025

2. *Write each of the following numbers as mixed numbers, with common fractions reduced to lowest terms:*

a.	1.5	f.	3.2	k.	5.8
b.	1.25	g.	2.75	l.	6.59
c.	2.125	h.	3.625	m.	7.725
d.	26.8	i.	66.5	n.	71.4
e.	725.50	j.	224.75	o.	905.625

Changing Common Fractions to Decimal Fractions

Since in a common fraction the line between the numerator and the denominator stands for *division*, a common fraction can easily be changed to a decimal fraction. The fraction $\frac{5}{8}$ may be read $5 \div 8$.

Rule to Remember

To change a common fraction to a decimal fraction, place a decimal point *after* the numerator, annex as many zeros as needed, and divide the numerator by the denominator.

HOW TO DO THE EXAMPLE

Problem: Change $\frac{5}{8}$ to a decimal fraction.

$$\frac{5}{8} = 5 \div 8 = \quad 8)\overline{\begin{array}{l} .62\frac{1}{2} \\ 5.00 \end{array}}$$

$$\begin{array}{r} 4\,8 \\ \hline 20 \\ 16 \\ \hline 4 \end{array}$$

By adding another zero, we can work the answer out to a complete decimal fraction.

$$\frac{5}{8} = 8)\overline{\begin{array}{l} .625 \\ 5.000 \end{array}}$$

$$\begin{array}{r} 4\,8 \\ \hline 20 \\ 16 \\ \hline 40 \\ 40 \\ \hline \end{array}$$

Review the table of common fractions and their corresponding decimals on page 79.

EXERCISES

Changing Common Fractions to Decimal Fractions

1. *Express each of the following common fractions as decimal fractions:*

   a. $\frac{6}{7}$ f. $\frac{3}{5}$ k. $\frac{1}{4}$

   b. $\frac{4}{9}$ g. $\frac{7}{11}$ l. $\frac{7}{25}$

   c. $\frac{7}{16}$ h. $\frac{8}{15}$ m. $\frac{5}{6}$

   d. $\frac{1}{200}$ i. $\frac{3}{10}$ n. $\frac{13}{50}$

   e. $\frac{19}{25}$ j. $\frac{9}{25}$ o. $\frac{1}{100}$

2. *Express each of the following common fractions as decimal fractions to the nearest tenth:*

   a. $\frac{3}{7}$ d. $\frac{2}{3}$ g. $\frac{4}{9}$

   b. $\frac{5}{6}$ e. $\frac{9}{12}$ h. $\frac{9}{11}$

   c. $\frac{5}{9}$ f. $\frac{19}{21}$ i. $\frac{25}{31}$

3. *Change each of the following common fractions to decimal fractions expressed to the nearest hundredth:*

   a. $\frac{3}{8}$ d. $\frac{8}{9}$ g. $\frac{17}{38}$

   b. $\frac{27}{42}$ e. $\frac{12}{19}$ h. $\frac{19}{24}$

   c. $\frac{9}{11}$ f. $\frac{9}{23}$ i. $\frac{5}{7}$

Arranging Common Fractions According to Size

Of all the immigrants coming into the United States in one year, $\frac{4}{25}$ were from Germany, $\frac{7}{152}$ from Poland, $\frac{1}{8}$ from Ireland and $\frac{4}{11}$ from Great Britain. From which of these countries did the United States receive the largest number of immigrants? From which country did the United States allow the fewest number to come?

We have already learned one way in which common fractions can be compared: we can find the lowest common denominator and compare the numerators. But, in this problem, the lowest common denominator would have to be very large, and it might take us a long time to find it.

Rule to Remember

Another way to compare common fractions is by changing the common fractions to decimal fractions. In this way we are still comparing fractions by finding a common denominator, this denominator being a power of 10.

HOW TO DO THE EXAMPLE

The numbers to be compared, from the problem on page 81, are these:

$$\frac{4}{25}, \quad \frac{7}{152}, \quad \frac{1}{8} \text{ and } \frac{4}{11}$$

Steps: Change each fraction to a decimal fraction, carried out to an equal number of decimal places.

$$\frac{4}{25} = \quad 25\overline{)4.000} \;\;\; \begin{array}{c}.160\end{array} = .160 \text{ from Germany}$$

$$\frac{7}{152} = 152\overline{)7.000} \;\;\; \begin{array}{c}.046\end{array} = .046 \text{ from Poland}$$

$$\frac{1}{8} = \quad 8\overline{)1.000} \;\;\; \begin{array}{c}.125\end{array} = .125 \text{ from Ireland}$$

$$\frac{4}{11} = \quad 11\overline{)4.000} \;\;\; \begin{array}{c}.364\end{array} = .364 \text{ from Great Britain}$$

By comparing the decimal fractions, we can see that $\frac{4}{11}$ is the largest of the common fractions, and that more Englishmen were allowed to enter the country than Germans, Irish or Poles. $\frac{4}{25}$, representing the German immigrants, is the next largest fraction, and $\frac{7}{152}$, representing the Polish immigrants, is the smallest.

EXERCISES

Arranging Common Fractions According to Size

Rewrite each of the following series according to size, with the largest first:

a. $\frac{1}{4}$ $\frac{1}{3}$ $\frac{2}{9}$ c. $\frac{1}{2}$ $\frac{3}{4}$ $\frac{5}{8}$ e. $\frac{1}{12}$ $\frac{1}{14}$ $\frac{1}{15}$

b. $\frac{3}{8}$ $\frac{3}{5}$ $\frac{1}{2}$ d. $\frac{3}{8}$ $\frac{4}{7}$ $\frac{3}{16}$ f. $\frac{6}{7}$ $\frac{6}{11}$ $\frac{6}{13}$

Adding Decimal Fractions

In the window of a jewelry store is a diamond brooch containing three large diamonds. A card alongside reads: "The center diamond is 12.08 carats. The diamond on the right weighs 9.23 carats and the one on the left 9.1 carats."

"How many carats do the three diamonds weigh?" wondered Jane, who was admiring the glittering display.

She arranged the addition problem in vertical form, making sure that all the decimal points, all the tenths and the hundredths were each in their separate columns. At the end of 9.1 she wrote a zero, so that the last column of numbers would be neat and clear. Then she added and she checked her addition in the same way that she added columns of whole numbers.

$$
\begin{array}{r}
12.08 \\
9.23 \\
9.10 \\
\hline
30.41 \text{ carats in the brooch}
\end{array}
$$

Rule to Remember

Decimal fractions are added in the same way that whole numbers are added. Since only like decimals can be added, that is, hundredths to hundredths, and tenths to tenths, the addends are arranged in a vertical column with the decimal points directly below one another, all the way down to the answer.

HOW TO DO THE EXAMPLE

Problem 1. Find the sum of the following numbers: 2.23, 4.8, 9 and .067.

1. Arrange numbers in columns
2. Annex zeros
3. Add

$$
\begin{array}{r}
2.230 \\
4.800 \\
9.000 \\
.067 \\
\hline
16.097 \text{ Answer}
\end{array}
$$

[Continued on top of page 84]

Problem 2. Add the following: 34.6, 13.82, 64.1 and .042

$$
\begin{array}{r}
34.600 \\
13.820 \\
64.100 \\
.042 \\
\hline
112.562 \quad \text{Answer}
\end{array}
$$

EXERCISES

Adding Decimal Fractions

1. *Add the following. Check your work.*

a. 4.36	*d.* .04	*g.* .5
5.47	.09	.4
		.1
b. $.69	*e.* 9	*h.* 7.125
1.60	.78	.81
4.89	7.5	19.455
	.02	2.8
c. .7321	*f.* $126.55	*i.* $1554.45
.9692	69.17	236.18
2.351	65.00	91.06
	118.29	1428.26

2. *Find the sum of the numbers in each of the following·*

   a. .4   .7
   b. .132   .246
   c. 1.09   2.06   3.04
   d. 96.212   18.4   26.66
   e. 21   2.1   .21   .021

   f. .09   .06
   g. .864   .948
   h. 5.12   6.21   7.96
   i. 27.896   35.221   6   23.64
   j. 36.4   60   29.86   .999

Subtracting Decimal Fractions

Decimal fractions are subtracted in the same way that whole numbers are subtracted.

Rule to Remember

The decimal fractions must be written so that the decimal point of the minuend, subtrahend and remainder are below each other. Zeros should be annexed so that both minuend and subtrahend are carried out to the same number of places. Check the answer the same way that you check the subtraction of whole numbers.

HOW TO DO THE EXAMPLE

Problem 1. Subtract 25.731 from 36.9

1.	Annex zeros	36.900
2.	Write numbers in proper positions	25.731
3.	Subtract	
		11.169 Answer

Problem 2. Mrs. Smith paid her grocery bill of $6.78 with a $10 bill. How much change did she receive?

1.	Write numbers in position	
2.	Annex zeros	$10.00
3.	Subtract	6.78
		$ 3.22 Answer

EXERCISES

Adding and Subtracting Decimal Fractions

1. *Subtract each of the following and check your work.*

a. .8	d. .9	g. .5	j. .19	m. .56
.3	.4	.1	.04	.42

b. .99	e. .07	h. .09	k. .654	n. .975
.54	.02	.01	.123	.555

c. .46	f. .55	i. 8.1	l. 7	o. 6.2
.021	.236	.05	.05	.504

p. 5.4	*r.* 6.1	*t.* 16.75	*v.* 8.432	*x.* 2.04
3.2	4.8	12.61	1.976	.63

q. 15.13	*s.* 8.556	*u.* 37.821	*w.* $126.42	*y.* $221
4.9641	6.419	15.964	19.01	18.63

2. *Subtract:*

a. 1.8 — .06	*f.* .46 — .09	*k.* 5.7 — 2.26
b. 17.6 — 2.8	*g.* 2.54 — .68	*l.* 7 — 2.6
c. 26.18 — .654	*h.* 200 — .26	*m.* 140 — .375
d. 646.52 — 220.7	*i.* 80.21 — 9.864	*n.* 109.35 — 51.4
e. 1.0041 — .006	*j.* 11.9861 — 1.031	*o.* 15.84 — 2.0693

3. On a trip a salesman covered the following distances: 212.6 miles, 127.8 miles, 319.4 miles and 400 miles. What was the total distance he covered?

4. Before starting out on a trip the speedometer of a car registered 8,624.8 miles. After completing the trip the speedometer read 9,142.9 miles. How many miles did the trip cover?

5. Henry has four pieces of wood which have the following lengths: 9.25 inches, 6.575 inches, 2.65 inches, and 7.372 inches. What is the total length of these pieces of wood?

6. Henry had $6.25 in his pocket. He paid James a debt of $2.56. How much money did he have left?

7. A neighborhood gasoline station took in the following amounts of money: Monday, $236.45; Tuesday, $190.09; Wednesday, $165.40; Thursday, $250.15; Friday, $298.95; and Saturday, $410.55. What was the total amount taken in during this week?

8. During one year the city of Mobile had 49.2 inches of rainfall. Galveston had 46.9 inches of rainfall. Which city had more rainfall? How much more?

9. Mr. Smith had $276.85 deposited in the bank. He made the following additional deposits: $62.48; $123.55; $86.50; $50; and $78.59. Find the total money he had in the bank after making his deposits.

10. A merchant sold material for $6146.95. The material cost him $5084.26. How much profit did he make?

11. During one working week, a truck delivered the following quantities of material: 2527.34 lbs., 1900.05 lbs., 2782.75 lbs., 2345.15 lbs., 1865.85 lbs. Find the total number of pounds delivered by the truck.

12. On January 1 Mr. Henry had $895.45 on deposit in the bank. During the month he deposited the following sums of money: $175.25, $642.50, $235.92, and $416.15. He also withdrew the following amounts: $85.16, $215.40, and $315.90. What was the balance at the end of the month?

GENERAL SKILL EXERCISE

How are you doing? Try the following test. If you get any wrong, turn to the pages shown after each question. Practice those problems until you have mastered them.

1. In changing a decimal fraction to a common fraction, the decimal number becomes the ......*7*............ of the fraction (page 78).

2. The decimal fraction .4 written as a common fraction is ....*2/5*............. (page 78).

3. To change a common fraction to a decimal fraction, the numerator of the common fraction is ......*divided*............... by the denominator (page 80).

4. ⅛ expressed as a decimal fraction is ....*.125*........... (page 80).

5. The values of common fractions can be compared after the common fractions have first been changed to *a decimal* (page 82).

6. Adding zeros after the decimals in a decimal fraction *will not* change the value of the decimal fraction (page 76).

7. Three dollars and sixty-seven cents expressed in decimal form is ......*3.67*............... (page 78).

8. Before decimals are added, they must be written so that the decimal points *on line* .... (page 83).

9. The amount of change obtained from $10 if the bill is $8.62 is ....*1.58*... (page 85).

10. How much less than 4.873 is 2.896? *2.018* .... (page 85).

My Score _____

Multiplying Decimals by Whole Numbers

In the world almanac, Arthur read that Halley's comet can be seen by people on the earth only once in every 76.02 years. Reading on, he learned that Halley's comet has returned 28 times since its first recorded appearance. To find out approximately how long ago Halley's comet was discovered, Arthur multiplied 76.02 by 28.

$$
\begin{array}{r}
76.02 \text{ years} \\
\times\ \ 28 \\
\hline
608\,16 \\
1520\,4\ \ \\
\hline
2128.56 = 2129 \text{ years, approximately}
\end{array}
$$

Rule to Remember

To multiply a decimal by a whole number, multiply as you would whole numbers. Then, begin at the right of the product and point off as many places as there are in the decimal fraction.

Zeros at the end of a decimal fraction may be dropped or added, without changing the value of the decimal fraction.

HOW TO DO THE EXAMPLE

Problem 1. Multiply 4.55 by 6

$$
\begin{array}{r}
4.55 \quad \text{(2 decimal places)} \\
\times\ 6\ \ \ \\
\hline
27.30 \quad \text{(2 decimal places)}
\end{array}
$$

$(27\frac{30}{100}) = (27\frac{3}{10}) = 27.3$ (dropping zero)

Problem 2. Multiply 3.671 by 12

$$
\begin{array}{r}
3.671 \quad \text{(3 decimal places)} \\
\times\ 12\ \ \ \\
\hline
7342\ \ \ \\
3671\ \ \ \ \\
\hline
44.052 \quad \text{(3 decimal places)}
\end{array}
$$

EXERCISE
Multiplying Decimals by Whole Numbers

Multiply each of the following:

a. .9	d. .8	g. 2.7	j. 5.6	m. 9.8
5	6	8	9	11
b. 6.73	e. .045	h. .006	k. .729	n. 46.231
8	5	7	9	54
c. 60.7	f. 29.5	i. 19.26	l. 23.034	o. 179.029
26	39	25	41	156

Multiplying a Decimal by a Decimal

Rule to Remember

In multiplying decimal fractions or mixed decimals, multiply as you do whole numbers. Then, starting at the right, mark off as many decimal places in the product as there are in the multiplier and multiplicand together.

HOW TO DO THE EXAMPLE

Problem 1. Multiply 3.62 by .7

3.62	(2 decimal places)
.7	(1 decimal place)
2.534	(3 decimal places)

Problem 2. Multiply 2.413 by .18

2.413	(3 decimal places)
.18	(2 decimal places)
19304	
2413	
.43434	(5 decimal places)

If the number of decimal places to be pointed off is greater than the number of figures in the product, place as many zeros to the *left* of the product as are needed to mark off the decimal point correctly.

[Continued on top of page 90]

Problem 3. Multiply $.14 by .6

$$
\begin{array}{ll}
\$.14 & \text{(2 places)} \\
\underline{\quad .6} & \text{(1 place)} \\
\$.084 & \text{(3 places—place zero in product)} \\
\end{array}
$$

or $.08

EXERCISES

Multiplying Decimals

1. *Multiply each of the following:*

a. 5.05	f. 1.4	k. 5.6	p. 9.8
1.5	2.1	4.2	2.2
7.5075	*2.94*	*23.52*	*21.56*
b. 1.67	g. 9.4	l. 7.81	q. 65.61
.02	.002	1.5	.1
.0534	*.0188*	*11.715*	*6.561*
c. 6.54	h. 8.56	m. .614	r. 25.69
.08	.73	.37	8.3
.5232	*6.2488*	*.22718*	*213.227*
d. 6.03	i. 2.275	n. .647	s. 6.195
1.06	.39	7.31	2.81
6.3918	*.88725*	*4.7957*	*17.40795*
e. 11.201	j. 9.043	o. 10.119	t. 41.639
.001	.05	.119	.936
.011201	*.45215*	*1.204161*	*38.97410*

2. *Multiply*

a. .36×.001	d. .175×.01	g. 6.7×.7
b. .79×.002	e. .7×.092	h. 1.6×.1
c. 3.8×.05	f. 19.04×.01	i. 13.15×.006

Finding a Part of a Number

Since a decimal fraction represents a part of a whole, we can find a fractional part of a number by using a decimal fraction.

Rule to Remember

To find a fractional part of a number, multiply the number by the decimal fraction.

HOW TO DO THE EXAMPLE

Problem: Mr. Smith owns 500 chickens, of which .04 are white. How many white chickens are there?

$$
\begin{array}{r}
500 \\
\times .04 \\
\hline
20.00
\end{array}
$$

Answer: 20 chickens are white.

EXERCISES

Finding Part of a Number

1. How much is .6 of $3.50?

2. There are 38 men in the Playfair Co. Of the 38, .5 stayed home because of illness. How many men didn't show up?

3. A farmer planted .75 of his 60-acre farm with wheat. How many acres of wheat did he have?

4. John earns $15 a week delivering papers after school. He saves .8 of his earnings. How much does he save each week?

Multiplying a Decimal or a Whole Number by 10, 100, 1000

Rules to Remember

To multiply a number by 10, 100, 1000 and so on, move the decimal point in the number being multiplied as many places to the right as there are zeros in the multiplier. If the multiplicand is a whole number, zeros must be annexed.

HOW TO DO THE EXAMPLE

Problem 1. Multiply 275.×10

1 zero

275.×10 = 2750. Decimal point moved one place to the right.

Problem 2. Multiply .275×100

2 zeros

.275×100 = 27.5 Decimal point moved *two* places to the right.

Problem 3. Multiply 275.×1000

3 zeros

275.×1000 = 275,000. Decimal point moved *three* places to the right

Problem 4. Multiply 27.5×10

1 zero

27.5×10 = 275. Decimal point moved *one* place to the right.

Note: The decimal point need not be expressed at all at the end of a whole number. It is written above after the whole numbers to clarify the rule explained.

EXERCISES

Multiplying a Decimal or a Whole Number by 10, 100 or 1000

1. *Multiply each of the following numbers by 10; then by 100; then by 1000.*

a.	$1.28	e.	.02	i.	.5	m.	7.6	q.	$2.125
b.	.8	f.	$15.98	j.	.008	n.	.014	r.	30
c.	$4.255	g.	181	k.	777	o.	3280	s.	10
d.	16.1029	h.	1258	l.	33.66	p.	256	t.	216.127

2. If a book costs $3.75, how much would 100 books cost?

3. James deposits $15 each week in the bank. How much will he have in 20 weeks?

4. Mr. Smith's phone bill is $15 per month. How much does the phone cost for the year?

5. There are 1,760 yards in a mile. How many yards are there in 1000 miles?

6. A man buys a 100-acre farm at $39.25 an acre. How much does he pay for the farm?

7. The average speed traveled by a jet plane is 726.82 miles per hour. How far does the plane travel in 10 hours?

8. High-test gasoline costs 41.9 cents per gallon. How much do 100 gallons cost?

9. A yard of cloth costs $4.75. What is the cost of a bolt of cloth containing 1000 yards?

Dividing Decimal Fractions and Mixed Decimals

The local community center bought 4 basketballs and paid $32.40 for them. How much did each basketball cost?

Rule to Remember

When a decimal is divided by a whole number, there are the same number of decimal places in the quotient as there are decimal places in the dividend.

[Continued on top of page 94]

HOW TO DO THE EXAMPLE

Method. In dividing a decimal by a whole number, write the decimal point in the quotient *directly above* the decimal point in the dividend. Then divide the dividend by the divisor as you would whole numbers.

Problem 1.

Divide $32.40 by 4

$$\frac{\$8.10}{4)\ \$32.40}\text{ per basketball}$$

Problem 2.

Divide .752 by 8

$$\begin{array}{r} .094 \\ 8)\overline{.752} \\ \underline{72} \\ 32 \end{array}$$

Problem 3.

Divide .84 by 12

$$\frac{.07}{12)\overline{.84}}$$

Problem 4.

Divide 1.86 by 6

$$\frac{.31}{6)\overline{1.86}}$$

EXERCISES

Dividing Decimals by Whole Numbers

Divide each of the following and check your work.

a. 3)$\overline{12.6}$ f. 8)$\overline{174.4}$ k. 4)$\overline{6.876}$
b. 2)$\overline{3.736}$ g. 8)$\overline{15.72}$ l. 9)$\overline{6.444}$
c. 21)$\overline{52.5}$ h. 18)$\overline{1533.6}$ m. 84)$\overline{1226.4}$
d. 77)$\overline{44.66}$ i. 16)$\overline{1315.6}$ n. 58)$\overline{83.52}$
e. 39)$\overline{1388.4}$ j. 22)$\overline{19.844}$ o. 28)$\overline{26.88}$

Avoiding Remainders in Division

Rule to Remember

Remainders can be avoided in some division problems by annexing zeros after the decimal point of the dividend and continuing to divide.

[Continued on top of page 95]

HOW TO DO THE EXAMPLE

Problem: Divide 867 by 2.

```
          433.5
     2) 867.0   zero annexed
        8
        ‒‒
         6
         6
        ‒‒
          7
          6
        ‒‒‒
         10
         10·
        ‒‒‒
```

EXERCISES
Avoiding Remainders in Division

Divide each of the following. Add enough zeros after the decimal point to make the division exact.

a. $6)\overline{39}$	f. $6)\overline{87}$	k. $4)\overline{42}$
b. $5)\overline{53}$	g. $2)\overline{17}$	l. $4)\overline{98}$
c. $12)\overline{270}$	h. $4)\overline{81}$	m. $4)\overline{863}$
d. $4)\overline{43}$	i. $25)\overline{79}$	n. $16)\overline{50}$
e. $16)\overline{100}$	j. $25)\overline{844}$	o. $8)\overline{94}$

Dividing by Decimal Fractions

Let us examine the following division examples involving whole numbers.

$$4)\overline{32} = 8 \qquad 40)\overline{320} = 8 \qquad 400)\overline{3200} = 8$$

What is true of the quotients? Notice that the quotients are the same but that the divisors and dividends have been multiplied by 10.

Division with decimals can be done in the same way as division with whole numbers. First, however, the divisor must be changed to a whole number. This is done by moving the decimal point to the right of all the numbers of the divisor;

that is, by multiplying the divisor by 10 or some power of 10. The dividend must also be multiplied by the same number that was used to multiply the divisor.

Principle to Remember

When both a divisor and its dividend are multiplied by 10, 100 or 1000, the value of the quotient does not change.

This principle is used in division by decimal fractions or decimal mixed numbers.

Method: When dividing by a decimal, follow these steps:

1. Move the decimal point of the divisor to the right of the last digit in the divisor and write a caret (∧) to indicate where the new decimal point will be.

2. Move the decimal point of the dividend to the right *the same number of places* as the decimal point was moved in the divisor, annexing zeros if necessary. Write a caret (∧) in place of the decimal point.

3. Place the decimal point in the quotient *directly above the caret* in the dividend. Divide in the same way as in the division of whole numbers.

HOW TO DO THE EXAMPLE

Problem 1. Divide 3.414 by .6

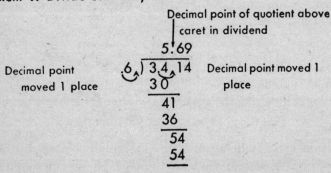

Decimal point of quotient above caret in dividend

Decimal point moved 1 place

Decimal point moved 1 place

[Continued on top of page 97]

***Problem* 2.** Divide 609.28 by .32

Decimal point of quotient above
caret in dividend

$$
\begin{array}{r}
1904\\
.32\,\overline{)\,609.28}\\
32\\
\overline{289}\\
288\\
\overline{128}\\
128
\end{array}
$$

Decimal point moved 2 places

Decimal point moved 2 places

***Problem* 3.** Divide 14.4 by .012

Decimal point in quotient
above caret in dividend

$$
\begin{array}{r}
1\,200.\\
.012\,\overline{)\,14.400}\\
12\\
\overline{24}\\
24
\end{array}
$$

Decimal point moved 3 places

Zeros annexed
Decimal point moved 3 places

Problem. 4. Divide 552 by 3.2

$$
\begin{array}{r}
17\,2.5\\
3.2\,\overline{)\,552.0\,0}\\
32\\
\overline{232}\\
224\\
\overline{80}\\
64\\
\overline{160}\\
160
\end{array}
$$

Estimating Quotients

In the lesson on division of whole numbers you learned how to estimate quotients. In working with decimals, estimating answers can help you to avoid many wrong answers.

By rounding off the divisor and the dividend, you can make a rough estimate. When the problem is solved the correct answer is sure to be close to the estimate.

HOW TO DO THE EXAMPLE

Problem: Divide 122.6 by 6.2

6.2 is about equal to 6 (using a close value that is easy to divide by)

122.6 is about equal to 120 (using a close value that can easily be divided by 6)

$120 \div 6 = 20$, *estimated quotient*

By actually dividing 122.6 by 6.2, we find that 19.8 is the correct quotient.

$$
\begin{array}{r}
19.77 \quad = 19.8 \text{ Answer} \\
6.2\overline{)122.6\,00} \\
62 \\
\overline{606} \\
558 \\
\overline{480} \\
434 \\
\overline{460} \\
434
\end{array}
$$

If you had obtained either 1.98 or 198. as a quotient, you would know it was not correct, since neither is close to your estimated answer, 20.

EXERCISES

Dividing by Decimals

1. *Estimate the quotients and then divide.*

   a. $.7\overline{)2.215}$ d. $.02\overline{)93.4}$ g. $.3\overline{).171}$

   b. $9.1\overline{)18.65}$ e. $.32\overline{)7.144}$ h. $.46\overline{)95.22}$

   c. $.09\overline{).8564}$ f. $.061\overline{)124.44}$ i. $.035\overline{)810.55}$

2. *Divide each of the following. Round off each answer to the nearest hundredth.*

   a. $.8\overline{)31.3}$ b. $.9\overline{)3.274}$ c. $.861\overline{)5.412}$

d. .13)$\overline{27.43}$ *g.* .37)$\overline{7.293}$ *j.* 7.64)$\overline{6.312}$

e. 24.2)$\overline{1079.77}$ *h.* .652)$\overline{189.32}$ *k.* .014)$\overline{1.1243}$

f. 19.11)$\overline{28.1}$ *i.* 21.12)$\overline{1.24}$ *l.* 14.12)$\overline{29.3}$

3. *Estimate the quotients and then find the correct answer.*

a. 13.9 ÷ 2.2   *d.* 72.7 ÷ 5.9   *g.* .1389 ÷ 6.9

b. 89.91 ÷ 2.1   *e.* .891 ÷ .029   *h.* .301 ÷ .051

c. 2.744 ÷ .51   *f.* 31.9 ÷ 8.1   *i.* 50.9 ÷ 9.8

4. *In each of the following division examples, the numbers in the quotients are correct but the decimal points have been left out. Place the decimal points in their correct places.*

$$\begin{array}{ccc} 274 & 233 & 91 \end{array}$$

a. .034)$\overline{9.316}$ *d.* .125)$\overline{29.125}$ *g.* .86)$\overline{78.26}$

$$\begin{array}{ccc} 1\ 38 & 2\ 149 & 128 \end{array}$$

b. 1.2)$\overline{16.56}$ *e.* .09)$\overline{19.341}$ *h.* 3.81)$\overline{4.8768}$

$$\begin{array}{ccc} 373 & 1\ 89 & 326 \end{array}$$

c. 2.36)$\overline{88.028}$ *f.* 24.6)$\overline{464.94}$ *i.* 4.11)$\overline{13.3986}$

Dividing by 10, 100 or 1000

For 10 days during his summer vacation, John took an automobile trip with his parents. They kept a record of their mileage from beginning to end, and found that they had traveled 2565 miles in all. John wondered what their average mileage was for each day.

He wrote out a problem of long division, dividing the total number of miles by 10. The answer was 256.5 miles per day.

When John's father saw the long division, he showed John how he might have done the problem in much less time. "Simply move the decimal point one place to the left," he said, "and you will get the same answer."

As we have seen, when a number is multiplied by 10, the decimal point is moved one place to the right; in a number multiplied by 100, the decimal point is moved two places to the right. Therefore, when we *divide* a number by 10 or any power of 10, we move the decimal point the same number of places as there are zeros in the divisor, but to the *left*.

Rule to Remember

To divide a number by 10 or any power of 10, move the decimal point in the dividend as many places to the left as there are zeros in the divisor. Add zeros when needed.

HOW TO DO THE EXAMPLE

$57 \div 10 = 5.7$ Move the decimal point *one* place to the left.

$136.4 \div 100 = 1.364$ Move the decimal point *two* places to the left.

$29 \div 1000 = .029$ Move the decimal point *three* places to the left.

PROBLEMS

1. *Divide each of the following numbers by 10, 100, and 1000.*

a. 9	h. 14	o. 26.1	v. 33.4
b. 126	i. 12.65	p. $19.53	w. 2362
c. $139.52	j. $1888	q. 26321	x. 38429
d. 4.27	k. .19	r. 412	y. 1000
e. .1	l. 1.11	s. 4.2	z. .003
f. .3131	m. 7.65	t. .2	
g. .04	n. 82.4	u. 600	

2. Mr. Smith owed $586 which he agreed to pay in 100 equal installments. How much is each payment?

3. Henry's father drives at an average speed of 45.5 miles per hour. How many hours does it take him to travel 300 miles? Find the answer to the nearest tenth of an hour.

4. A 9-foot piece of metal rod is to be divided into 100 equal parts. How long will each piece be?

5. A 20-trip railroad ticket to Hempstead costs $28.60. A single trip ticket costs $1.63. How much is saved on 20 trips if you purchase the 20-trip ticket?

6. The recipe for making a cake includes 3.5 cups of flour and .5 cup of butter. Mrs. Smith wishes to bake a cake which will be $\frac{1}{2}$ of the size given by the recipe. How much flour and how much butter must she use? How much must she use for $\frac{3}{4}$ of the recipe?

7. One cubic foot of fresh water weighs 62.5 lbs. How much will 600 cu. ft. weigh?

8. How many pieces of plywood each .25-inch thick are required to make a pile 1½ feet high?

9. Mrs. James paid $6.75 for a turkey which weighed 13.5 lb. What was the price per pound?

10. Frank has a second job at which he earns $1.85 an hour. Last week he worked 7½ hours. How much did he earn?

11. Mr. Smith bought 8000 writing pads for $400. How much did each pad cost him?

GENERAL SKILL EXERCISE

How are you doing? Try the following test. If you get any wrong, turn to the pages shown after each question. Practice those problems until you have mastered them.

1. When you multiply a decimal by a whole number, the product must have the same number of decimal places as the .... itself (page 88).

2. When two decimal fractions are multiplied, the product must have the same number of decimal places as there are in the .... and the .... (page 89).

3. Place the decimal point in the proper place: $27.85 \times .25 = 69625$ (page 89).

4. A sheet of cardboard is .03 inch thick. How high is a pile of 60 sheets? .... (page 88).

5. .01 of 1000 is .... (page 91).

6. $501 \times 100,000$ equals .... (page 92).

7. When you divide a number by 10,000, you move the decimal point .... places to the ....(pages 99, 100).

8. You can avoid a remainder in some division problems if you . ... zeros and continue to divide (page 94).

9. If you approximate an answer before beginning to do the problem, you are .... the answer (page 98).

10. If you multiply both the divisor and dividend of a problem by 1000, the value of the .... does not change (page 96).

My Score —————

Chapter Review

PRINCIPLES TO REMEMBER

1. A decimal fraction is a special type of fraction written without a denominator but in which the number of places at the right of the decimal point indicates whether the denominator is 10 or a higher power of 10.

2. If any figure of a number is moved one place to the left, the value of the figure is multiplied by 10.

3. To round off a decimal to a particular place, inspect the figure to the right of the required place: if it is 5 or over, change the last required digit to the next higher figure and drop all decimals to the right of the required figures; if it is less than 5, drop all decimals to the right of the required figure.

4. To compare decimal fractions, annex zeros so that the decimals have the same number of places.

5. A decimal fraction may be changed to a common fraction by: leaving out the decimal point, writing the decimal number as the numerator and the number shown by the name of the last decimal place as the denominator.

6. A common fraction may be changed to a decimal fraction by placing a decimal point after the numerator, adding zeros and then dividing the numerator by the denominator.

7. To determine which of a series of fractions has the greatest or least value, change the common fractions to decimal fractions with the same number of decimal places and compare the numbers.

8. Decimal fractions can be added by placing the decimal points under each other and keeping the decimal places in their proper positions. They are added as are whole numbers.

9. We subtract decimal fractions by adding zeros until there are as many places beyond the decimal point of the minuend as there are places in the subtrahend; by keeping the decimal places in their proper positions, and then subtracting as we do whole numbers.

10. Decimals are multiplied in the same way that whole numbers are multiplied. The product has as many decimal places as there are in the multiplier and multiplicand together.

11. A fractional part of a number is found by multiplying the number by the decimal fraction.

12. When a number is multiplied by 10, 100, 1000 and so on, the decimal point in the multiplicand is moved as many places to the right as there are zeros in the multiplier.

13. To avoid remainders in division, add zeros at the end of decimal fractions in the dividend and continue to divide.

14. Multiplying both a divisor *and* a dividend by 10 or any power of 10 does not change the value of the quotient.

15. When a number is divided by a decimal number, the decimal point is moved to the right the same number of places in both the divisor and the dividend. Division is then done in the same way as with whole numbers.

16. A number can be divided by 10 or a power of 10 by moving the decimal point to the left as many places as there are zeros in the divisor.

MASTERY TEST

A

1. The two parts making up a mixed decimal number are the .... number and the ....

2. To divide a number by 1000, move the decimal point .... places to the ....

3. The mixed decimal 1.754 expressed to the nearest hundredth is ....

4. The third place in a decimal fraction is called the .... place.

5. Six inches expressed as a decimal fraction of a foot is ....

6. To multiply a number by 100, move the decimal point .... places to the ....

7. You can change the name of a decimal fraction without changing its value by .... or dropping .... at the right of it.

8. Remainders may be avoided in division by .... zeros after the decimal point and continuing to ....

9. In rounding off a decimal fraction to the nearest hundredth, make the figure in the hundredth place 1 larger if the figure after it is .... or ....

10. If both the divisor and the .... are multiplied by 10, the value of the .... is not changed.

B

1. *Write each of the following decimals in words:*
   a. 3.475   b. .2461

2. *Write each of the following as decimal fractions:*
   a. $\frac{7}{10}$ b. $\frac{11}{15}$

3. *Write each of the following as common fractions or mixed numbers:*
a. .35   b. 1.45

4. *Change each of the following to decimal fractions correct to the nearest hundredth:*
a. $\frac{13}{21}$ b. $\frac{4}{7}$

5. Arrange the following numbers according to size, writing the largest number first: .07; .7; 7; .007

6. Find the sum of .375; 16; 22.25; .5; 1.125

7. $10 minus $3.79 equals?

8. Write in decimal form: seven and four thousandths.

9. Divide 77.095 by 8.5

10. If a boy's temperature rises from 98.6° to 101.2°, how many degrees does it rise?

11. What will be the cost of 50 feet of hose at $.12$\frac{1}{2}$ per foot?

12. John worked from 8:00 a.m. until 11:30 a.m. at the rate of $.60 per hour. How much did he receive for his work?

13. At 25 cents each, how many school lunches can be bought for $6?

14. Multiply 37.5 by .083

15. Find the product of 10,000 and .045.

16. Which one of the following numbers has the smallest value: .2; .22; .202; .022?

17. A year's subscription to a weekly magazine costs $9.75. If a single copy sells for 20 cents, how much will a person save by taking a year's subscription instead of buying a single copy each week?

18. The product of two numbers is 1.2. If one of the numbers is 8, what is the other number?

19. In four successive weeks a boy spent 18¢, $2.04, $1.53 and 28¢ in buying old stamps for his collection. What was the total cost per week for his hobby?

20. Mrs. Martin bought 2 dozen cans of peas and 4 loaves of bread. The cans of peas cost $3.36. The entire bill was $4.00. What was the cost of one loaf of bread?

4

PERCENTAGE

What Is Per Cent?

We have already learned two ways of writing fractional parts: common fractions and decimal fractions. Another method is by using per cents. Per cent tells the number of parts in every hundred. This number is followed by the per cent sign (%). The word per cent and the sign % actually refer to the denominator of a fraction expressed as hundredths. One *per cent* of a number means one-*hundredth* of a number; eight per cent of a number means eight-*hundredths,* and so on.

When working with per cent, we do not write the word but we use the sign. Thus, 20 per cent is written 20%, 1 per cent is written 1%, and so on. Therefore, when we see 20%, we know it means 20 parts of a hundred, $\frac{20}{100}$, or .20. 1% means 1 part of a hundred, $\frac{1}{100}$ or .01.

In working with problems involving percentage, we must be able to change per cents to decimals and decimals to per cents.

Changing Per Cents to Decimal Fractions

One day during a bad snowstorm 12% of the members of a social club missed the annual meeting. There were 150 members in the club.

To find the number of members absent, we must multiply 150 by 12%, but first we must change the per cent to a decimal fraction. Because 12% means 12 hundredths, we can also express it as .12. When we multiply 150 by .12, we find that 18 members were absent.

Essentials to Remember

To change a per cent to a decimal fraction, drop the per cent sign and move the decimal point two places to the left.

HOW TO DO THE EXAMPLE

Problem 1. Express 30% as a decimal fraction

$$30\% = .30$$

Same number of hundredths

Problem 2. Change $15\frac{1}{2}\%$ to a decimal fraction

$$15\frac{1}{2}\% = .15\frac{1}{2}$$

Problem 3. Write 5.1% as a decimal fraction

$$5.1\% = .051$$

EXERCISES

Changing Per Cents to Decimal Fractions

Change the following per cents to decimal fractions.

a. 20% =	g. 13% =	m. 5% =
b. 25% =	h. 6% =	n. 3% =
c. 50% =	i. 1.3% =	o. .5% =
d. $12\frac{1}{2}\%$ =	j. .3% =	p. 125% =
e. $33\frac{1}{3}\%$ =	k. $37\frac{1}{2}\%$ =	q. $87\frac{1}{2}\%$ =
f. $83\frac{1}{3}\%$ =	l. $16\frac{2}{3}\%$ =	r. $66\frac{2}{3}\%$ =

Changing Per Cents to Common Fractions

The Hobby Shop was planning to move and it was selling all its merchandise at reduced prices. Stephen went to see what bargains he could buy. He found one table of model airplane sets marked "$\frac{1}{3}$ off." A sign on another table said, "20% off."

To compare the amount of reduction so that he could tell which was the bigger bargain, Stephen changed 20% to a common fraction.

$$20\% = \tfrac{20}{100} = \tfrac{1}{5}$$

Then Stephen found the common denominator 15, and discovered that $\frac{1}{3}$ off was the greater reduction, since $\frac{1}{3}$ off $= \frac{5}{15}$ and $\frac{1}{5}$ off $= \frac{3}{15}$.

Essentials to Remember

To change a per cent to a common fraction, first write the per cent as a common fraction with a denominator of 100 and the given number as the numerator. Then, if possible, reduce the fraction to lowest terms.

► HOW TO DO THE EXAMPLE

Problem 1. Change 30% to a common fraction in lowest terms. $\qquad 30\% = \tfrac{30}{100} = \tfrac{3}{10}$

Problem 2. Change 25% to a common fraction

$$25\% = \tfrac{25}{100} = \tfrac{1}{4}$$

Problem 3. Change $33\frac{1}{3}\%$ to a common fraction.

$$33\tfrac{1}{3}\% = \frac{33\tfrac{1}{3}}{100} = 33\tfrac{1}{3} \div 100 =$$

$$\tfrac{100}{3} \div \tfrac{100}{1} = \tfrac{\cancel{100}}{3} \times \tfrac{1}{\cancel{100}} = \tfrac{1}{3}.$$

Meaning of 100%. If we change 100% to a common fraction, $100\% = \tfrac{100}{100} = 1$, we see that 100% stands for 1 whole thing or all of an object.

AN IMPORTANT TABLE OF PER CENT EQUIVALENTS

Per Cent	Fractional Equivalent	Per Cent	Fractional Equivalent
10% =	$\frac{1}{10}$	$12\frac{1}{2}\%$ =	$\frac{1}{8}$
20% =	$\frac{1}{5}$	25% =	$\frac{1}{4}$
30% =	$\frac{3}{10}$	$37\frac{1}{2}\%$ =	$\frac{3}{8}$
40% =	$\frac{2}{5}$	$62\frac{1}{2}\%$ =	$\frac{5}{8}$
50% =	$\frac{1}{2}$	75% =	$\frac{3}{4}$
60% =	$\frac{3}{5}$	$87\frac{1}{2}\%$ =	$\frac{7}{8}$
70% =	$\frac{7}{10}$	$16\frac{2}{3}\%$ =	$\frac{1}{6}$
80% =	$\frac{4}{5}$	$33\frac{1}{3}\%$ =	$\frac{1}{3}$
90% =	$\frac{9}{10}$	$66\frac{2}{3}\%$ =	$\frac{2}{3}$
100% =	1	$83\frac{1}{3}\%$ =	$\frac{5}{6}$

EXERCISES

Changing Per Cents to Common Fractions

1. *Change the following per cents to common fractions or mixed numbers in lowest terms.*

     a. 20%   c. 12%   e. 10%   g. 50%   i. 25%   k. 75%

     b. 40%   d. 125%   f. 1%   h. 15%   j. 5%   l. 6%

2. *Complete the following table:*

	Per Cent	Decimal Fraction	Common Fraction or Mixed Number
a.	5%	....	....
b.	....	....	$\frac{4}{5}$
c.	....	.15	....
d.	....	.06	....
e.	14%	....	....
f.	....	.62$\frac{1}{2}$	....
g.	....	....	$\frac{9}{10}$
h.	....	.025	....
i.	$\frac{1}{2}\%$	....	....
j.	....	....	$\frac{1}{8}$
k.	....	1.25	....
l.	....	....	$\frac{1}{100}$

Finding a Per Cent of a Number

John needed $60 to buy a new bicycle. His father promised to give him 25% of this amount, and said that John should save the rest. How much did his father give John? How much must John save?

Rule to Remember

To find a per cent of a number, change the per cent to either a decimal fraction or a common fraction. Multiply the number by the fraction.

HOW TO DO THE EXAMPLE

The problem requires a per cent of a number. In this case we must find 25% of $60.

1. Change 25% to a decimal fraction   25% = .25
2. Multiply .25 × $60.

$$\begin{array}{r} \$60 \\ \times .25 \\ \hline 300 \\ 120 \\ \hline \$15.00 \end{array}$$

Thus, John's father gave him $15. If we subtract $15 from $60, we find that John had to save $45.

In some per cent problems it may be easier to use a common fraction. For example, in the above problem, we could have changed 25% to $\frac{1}{4}$ and found $\frac{1}{4}$ of $60.

$\frac{1}{4} \times \$60 = \$15$ Amount John's father promised him.

EXERCISES

Finding a Per Cent of a Number

1. *Find the following percentages.*
   - a. 25% of $48
   - b. 13% of 50
   - c. 3% of 500 acres
   - d. 40% of 190 yards
   - e. 14% of 80 inches
   - f. 1% of $1000

g. 11% of $675

h. 15% of 420 apples

i. 99% of 1200 pupils

j. 65% of 50 yards

k. 18% of 50 feet

l. 100% of 75 apples

m. 93% of $750

n. 12% of $30

o. 16% of $530

p. 20% of 480 pupils

q. 75% of $400

r. 42% of $900

s. 72% of 250 bushels

t. 53% of $120

u. 48% of 700

v. 68% of 30 tons

w. 94% of 16 feet

x. 10% of $4000

y. 82% of $1750

z. 98% of 500 books

2. *In the following, find the percentages using common fractions:*

a. 20% of 30

b. 33⅓% of 180

c. 66⅔% of 1800

d. 37½% of 4880

e. 40% of 50

f. 87½% of 240

g. 62½% of 2400

h. 12½% of 560

i. 25% of 120

j. 50% of 1500

k. 83⅓% of 3600

l. 75% of 6400

PROBLEMS

1. In a newspaper quiz contest of 50 questions, John answered 86% of them correctly. How many questions did he get right?

2. John's father bought a new home for $12,000. He paid 40% immediately and the remainder was to be paid off in installments. How much did he pay immediately? How much was left to be paid off?

3. There are 2500 assemblers in an auto plant. Of these 26% go to work by car. How many workers use cars? How many workers do not?

4. In a shipment of potatoes a farmer estimates that 3% will spoil before they reach the market. In a shipment of 1800 bags of potatoes, how many bags will spoil?

5. In one season a baseball team played 140 games and lost 25% of them. How many games did they win?

6. In a department store sale an item was marked 20% off. If an article had an original price of $55, how much will you pay for it?

7. In a basketball tournament of 20 games, the Panthers won 25% of the games. How many games did they win?

8. In a mail carrier's test having 50 questions, Manuel had 40 questions right. In the next test having the same number of questions he had 10% more correct than he did in the first test. How many did he have right?

9. Henry bought a used car for $300. After using it for two weeks, he sold it at a loss of 20%. At what price did he sell the car?

10. Two men went into business and invested $12,000 together. Mr. Adams invested 35% of the total and Mr. Blake invested the remaining 65%. How much did each man invest?

GENERAL SKILL EXERCISE

How are you doing? Try the following test. If you get any wrong, turn to the pages shown after each question. Practice those problems until you have mastered them.

1. John had 79 answers correct out of 100 problems. The common fraction of the number he had correct out of all the problems is .... The per cent is .... (pages 105, 107).

2. Per cent means .... (page 105).

3. When you write $\frac{1}{2}$ as 50%, you have changed a .... to a .... (page 108).

4. Frank cut a pie into 6 parts and then ate 2 parts. The per cent of the pie Frank ate is .... (page 105).

5. 35% is .... hundredths (page 106).

6. 100% of $62\frac{1}{2}$ is .... (page 109).

7. $87\frac{1}{2}$% expressed as an equivalent common fraction is .... (page 108).

8. A man earns $40 and spends 75% of it. What per cent of his money does he save? .... (page 109).

9. If you have $20 and spend 60%, how much do you have left? .... (page 109).

10. The numerator of the fraction formed when 35% is changed to a common fraction and reduced to lowest terms is .... (page 107).

My Score _____

Finding What Per Cent One Number Is of Another Number

Out of 20 tries in a foul shooting contest, Walt sank 17 shots. What was his score expressed as a per cent? as a per cent?

In this example we must find what per cent 17 is of 20.

Helpful hint: The number connected with the word *is* (17), is the *numerator;* the number connected with the word *of* (20) is the *denominator.*

Essentials to Remember

To find what per cent one number is of another, first note what fraction the one number is of the other. Then change the fraction to a decimal by dividing the numerator by the denominator. Rewrite the decimal fraction as a per cent.

HOW TO DO THE EXAMPLE

Problem: 17 is what per cent (part) of 20?

$$\frac{17}{20}$$

Now change the common fraction $\frac{17}{20}$ to a decimal fraction.

```
      .85
20) 17.00              Check:                20
    16 0               85% of 20           ×.85
    ────                                    ───
    1 00   .85 = 85% answer                 100
    1 00   17 is 85% of 20.                 160
                                          ─────
                                          17.00
```

EXERCISES

Finding What Per Cent One Number Is of Another Number

1. *Find the following:*
   a. What per cent of $18 is $9?
   b. What per cent of a year is 8 months?
   c. What per cent of a foot is 2 inches?
   d. What per cent of an hour is 15 minutes?
   e. What per cent of a dollar is one cent?

2. *Give the answer to each of the following examples as* (1) *a common fraction* (2) *a decimal fraction* (3) *a per cent:*

	Common Fraction	Decimal Fraction	Per Cent
a. $6 is what part of $8?	....	....	....
b. $18 is what part of $25?	....	....	....
c. 20 minutes is what part of an hour?	....	....	....
d. 5 months is what part of a year?	....	....	....
e. 10 inches is what part of a yard?	....	....	....

PROBLEMS

1. In one season a baseball team played 200 games and won 180 of them. What per cent of the games did they win?

2. A man working as a radio inspector examined 25 radios. Of this number he passed 21. What per cent did he pass?

3. In a basketball game Henry took 18 shots at the basket. If he put the ball through the basket 5 times, what per cent of his shots were scoring shots?

4. In a plant employing 5,255 workers, 4,623 belong to a union. What per cent of the workers belong to the union?

5. In a shop of 42 workers, 5 were not given wage increases. What per cent of the workers were given increases?

6. A man earns $480 a month. What per cent of his salary does he save, if he saves $60 a month?

7. During one season a second-baseman fielded the ball 122 times and made 8 errors. What is his fielding per cent?

8. In a can of milk there are 30 quarts. If 2 quarts are butter fat, what is the per cent of butter fat?

9. During a baseball season the nine regular members of a team made this record. Find each player's batting average in per cent.

	Player	At Bat	Hits	Batting Per Cent
a.	Henry....	35	8	
b.	John.....	32	14	
c.	Murray...	37	13	
d.	Sam......	33	6	
e.	Joe......	35	12	
f.	Ray......	36	10	
g.	Hank.....	31	9	
h.	Charles...	33	7	
i.	Harvey...	30	11	

Rounding Off to the Nearest Per Cent

There are 36 employees in the ABC Co. Last Tuesday there were 34 employees present. What per cent of the employees was present?

$$
\begin{array}{r}
.944 \\
36\overline{)34.000} \\
32\ 4 \\
\hline
1\ 60 \\
1\ 44 \\
\hline
160
\end{array}
$$

Even though the division does not come out even in the hundredths place, we can still express the answer to the nearest whole per cent. Since the decimal fraction .944 is closer to .94 than to .95, rounded off to the nearest hundredth, therefore, .944 = 94%.

Rule to Remember

To change a common fraction to the nearest whole per cent divide the numerator by the denominator, carrying the division out to three decimal places. Then round off the quotient to the nearest hundredth, and express the hundredth as a per cent.

EXERCISES
Rounding Off to the Nearest Per Cent

1. *Find each of the following to the nearest per cent:*
  a. $48 is what per cent of $86?   d. $3.38 is what per cent of $52?
  b. What per cent of $16 is $5?   e. 15 is what per cent of 59?
  c. What per cent of 18 is 17?   f. 27 is what per cent of 35?

2. *What per cent of:*
  a. 10 is 6?   b. 50 is 12?   c. 12 is 4?   d. .16 is .08?

Rounding Off to the Nearest Cent

Mr. Russo wanted to buy a power lawn mower. He didn't know whether he would pay cash or pay in installments. The clerk said that he would save 2% of the selling price if he would pay cash. Actually, the clerk was offering Mr. Russo a 2% discount on the marked price of·$79.95. How much did Mr. Russo save by paying cash for the lawn mower?

Rule to Remember

In expressing an answer to the nearest cent, if the figure in the third decimal place is 5 or more, drop it and make the figure before it 1 larger; if the figure in the third decimal place is less than 5, simply drop this figure.

HOW TO DO THE EXAMPLE

Method:
1. Find 2% of $79.95.
2. Change the 2% to its decimal equivalent. 2% = .02

$$\begin{array}{r} \$79.95 \\ \times .02 \\ \hline \$1.5990 \end{array}$$

Since $1.5990 is closer to $1.60 than to $1.59, the answer to the nearest cent is $1.60.

Rounding Off to the Nearest Cent

1. *Find the following percentages and express them to the nearest cent.*

a.	2% of $16.48	*f.*	4% of $21.63
b.	3% of $26.81	*g.*	5% of $35.35
c.	8% of $45.45	*h.*	12% of $109.21
d.	18% of $134.15	*i.*	21% of $150.25
e.	35% of $169.25	*j.*	51% of $185.25

Finding a Number of Which a Per Cent is Given

In a local charity drive, volunteers sold 144 boxes of candy the first week of the drive. This was 16% of the total number they sold. How many boxes of candy did they sell during the entire drive?

In this type of example we are required to find a number when a certain per cent of that number is known.

HOW TO DO THE EXAMPLE

Method 1. Since 16% of the total number of boxes = 144

$$1\% \text{ of the total number} = 144 \div 16 = 9$$

Then 100% of the number sold =
$$9 \times 100 = 900$$

Therefore, the total number of boxes sold is 900.

Alternate Method:

Since 16% of ? = 144

Then $144 \div 16\% = 144 \div .16 = .16 \overline{)144.00}$ 900

In some problems the per cent may easily be changed to a common fraction. In this case another method may be used to solve the problem.

John spent $90 for tools. This was $66\frac{2}{3}\%$ of his earnings for one week. How much does he earn a week?

HOW TO DO THE EXAMPLE

Method. Change the per cent to an equivalent fraction and then divide the given number by the fraction.

$$\$90 \div \frac{2}{3} = \frac{\overset{45}{\cancel{90}}}{1} \times \frac{3}{2} = \$135 \text{ Answer}$$

Exercises and Problems

1. *Find a number of which:*
   - *a.* 5% is 6
   - *b.* 25% is 18
   - *c.* 33⅓ is 9
   - *d.* 87½ is 63
   - *e.* 54 is 200%
   - *f.* $40 is 10%

2. Eddie did 14 problems correctly. If this was 70% of the number of problems, how many did he have in all?

3. John works after school as a delivery boy. He saves 45% of his earnings. How much does he earn at his job if he saves $9.45 each week?

4. John delivered 63 packages, which is 70% of the total number he had to deliver. How many packages did John have to deliver?

5. On one delivery John rode a bus for 63 blocks, which was 90% of the total distance he had to go. How far did he have to travel?

6. Thirty-six boys, who make up 60% of Robert's Scout Troop, went on an overnight hike. How many boys are there in the troop?

7. Roberta is saving to buy a pair of ice skates. She has saved $4.50, which is 75% of the cost of the skates. How much do the skates cost?

8. Tommy bought a bike for $36 at a sale. This was 80% of the original price. What was the original price of the bike?

9. On a TV quiz program, 21 contestants made a score of more than 85%. These 21 contestants are 70% of the number of contestants. How many contestants are there on the program?

10. John's father bought a new home. The house costs him $1800 a year to run. This is 20% of his yearly income. What is his father's annual income?

Per Cents Over 100%

The population of Ourtown is 300% of what it was ten years ago. What does this statement mean?

This statement indicates that the new population is 3 times the size of the population in 1925, for $300\% = \frac{300}{100} = 3$. Thus, 300% of a number equals 3 times the number.

Similarly, 200% of a number equals 2 times the number; 400% of a number equals 4 times the number, and so on.

Suppose that the population of the town is 150% of what it was ten years ago. What does this mean? This tells us that the population is $1\frac{1}{2}$ or 1.5 times as large, since $150\% = \frac{150}{100}$ which equals $1\frac{1}{2}$ or 1.5.

Essentials to Remember

1. Any per cent larger than 100% is more than 1.

2. In finding more than 100% of a number, the result will be larger than the number.

HOW TO DO THE EXAMPLE

Problem: The Elmont Public Library had 2200 volumes of books last year. This year they have 108% as many. How many volumes do they now have?

To find 108% of 2200, change 108% to 1.08. Then multiply 2200 by 1.08.

$$108\% = \frac{108}{100} = 1.08$$

$$
\begin{array}{r}
2200 \\
\times 1.08 \\
\hline
176\,00 \\
2200\,0 \\
\hline
2376.00 \quad \text{Total number of volumes}
\end{array}
$$

EXERCISES
Percentages Over 100

1. *Complete each of the following:*
   a. 300% of a number equals .... times the number.
   b. 600% of a number equals .... times the number.
   c. 750% of a number equals .... times the number.
   d. 2700% of a number equals .... times the number.
   e. 3300% of a number equals .... times the number.

2. The Eron Manufacturing Company records show that they are doing 1400% as much business as they did when they started 20

years ago. When they began, they did $15,000 worth of business per year. How much are they doing now?

3. The enrollment at Epsilon College is 850% as much as when the college first opened. It began with 200 students. How many students does it have now?

Per Cent Increase or Decrease — Number Increase

In 1955, the population of a certain town was 98,250. Fifteen years later the population was 22% more than the original number. What is the new population?

HOW TO DO THE EXAMPLE

Method 1. Since the problem states that the new population was 22% more than it was 15 years later, it indicates that the population has increased by 22%. Therefore, we find 22% of the original number, and add this increase to the original number.

22% = .22

```
   98,250
   × .22
  196500
  196500
21,615.00  Increase in population
```

```
   98,250
 + 21,615  Increase of 22%
  119,865  New population
```

Method 2. Since the new population is 22% more than it was originally, it is now 100% + 22% or 122% as large as it was in 1955. Therefore, we multiply 98,250 by 1.22

$(122\% = \frac{122}{100} = 1.22)$.

```
     98,250
      1.22
    196 500
   1965 00
   9825 0
  119,865.00   New population
```

Remember: "More than" means there has been an increase.

Increases of Over 100%

Suppose the total industrial production of the United States *increased* 200% between 1950 and 1971. Would you say that production is twice as great?

Notice:
$$1950 = 100\%$$
$$+ \text{ Increase} = 200\%$$
$$1971 = 300\%$$

The total industrial production in 1971 was 3 times that in 1955.

Similarly, an *increase* of 100% in population means that the population is now 200% of its previous size: it has doubled. An *increase* of 300% in school enrollment would mean that 4 times as many students were enrolled.

Number Decrease

In Ourtown there are 1800 pupils who go to school by bus. Next year it is expected that there will be a 20% decrease in this number. How many pupils will travel to school by bus next year?

HOW TO DO THE EXAMPLE

Method 1. Since the example states that there will be a decrease, it means that there will be 20% fewer. Therefore, we find 20% or .20 of 1800 and subtract that amount from the 1800.

1800		1800	
×.20		−360	Decrease
360.00	Decrease	1440	pupils will travel by bus next year.

Method 2. Since there is a decrease of 20%, we subtract 20% from 100%. The new number will, therefore, be 80% or .80 of 1800.

1800
×.80
1440.00   pupils will travel by bus next year.

Finding the Per Cent of Increase

An item which cost $300 ten years ago now costs $400. What is the per cent of increase?

In this example we are trying to find what per cent of the *original price* the increase is.

To find the per cent of increase from the original amount,

1. Find the *amount* of increase by subtracting.
2. Compare the difference with the original number by forming a fraction, with the *difference* as the *numerator* and the *original* amount as the *denominator*.
3. Change this fraction to a per cent.

Rule to Remember

$$\text{Per Cent Increase} = \frac{\textit{Amount of Increase}}{\textit{Original Amount}}$$

HOW TO DO THE EXAMPLE

The solution has two steps:

1. Find the actual amount of increase in dollars and cents.

2. Find what per cent the increase is of the original number.

(1) $400   New amount
       −300   Old amount

       $100   Increase

(2) $100 = what per cent of the original price?

$\frac{\text{increase}}{\text{original}}$ $\frac{100}{300} = \frac{1}{3} = 33\frac{1}{3}\%$ increase

Finding the Per Cent of Decrease

At a special sale Jane's mother bought a dining room set for $500. The set had been selling for $600. What per cent of decrease was this?

In this problem we must find what per cent of the original number the decrease is.

Rule to Remember

$$\text{Per Cent of Decrease} = \frac{\text{Amount of Decrease}}{\text{Original Amount}}$$

HOW TO DO THE EXAMPLE

There are two steps in the solution of this problem:

1. Find the amount of decrease in dollars and cents.

2. Find what per cent the decrease is of the original price.

(1)
$600 Old amount
 500 New amount
$100 Decrease

(2) $100 = what per cent of the original price?

decrease
original $\frac{100}{600} = \frac{1}{6} = 16\frac{2}{3}\%$ decrease

---

EXERCISES

Finding Per Cent of Increase or Decrease

1. Two months ago oranges were selling for 45 cents a dozen. They are now selling for 60 cents a dozen. Find the per cent of increase in price.

2. James' salary was increased from $60 to $65 per week. What per cent of increase is this?

3. Mr. Adams raises rabbits. He has 350 rabbits and plans to sell 50 of them. What per cent of decrease will he have in the number of rabbits?

4. *Fill in the per cent of increase or decrease for each of the following:*

	Original Amount	New Amount	Per Cent Change	Increase or Decrease?
a.	$.80	$1.20	....	....
b.	.80	.60	....	....
c.	500	600	....	....
d.	75 feet	90 feet	....	....
e.	75 feet	60 feet	....	....
f.	$6	$5	....	....
g.	$1200	$1500	....	....
h.	$2600	$3000	....	....
i.	$9150	$9000	....	....
j.	$10,000	$11,000	....	....

5. In one year, the total number of television sets made in the United States was 210,000. Ten years later, the number of sets made was 8,000,000. What per cent of increase is this?

6. In one year, the total number of forest fires in the United States was 164,090. In the next year, the number rose to 188,277. To the nearest per cent, what is the per cent of increase?

7. Mr. Johnson has been adding a new fertilizer to the soil on his farm. If his crop increased from 220 bushels per acre to 275 bu. per acre, what was the per cent of increase in yield?

8. The price of a pair of shoes was reduced from $10.98 to $6.98. To the nearest per cent, what per cent of decrease is this?

GENERAL SKILL EXERCISE

How are you doing? Try the following test. If you get any wrong, turn to the pages shown after each question. Practice those problems until you have mastered them.

1. Of 100 bags of potatoes, 60 bags were sold. What per cent remained unsold? .... (page 112).

2. What per cent of a decade is 2 years? .... (page 112).

3. A batter's average is .367. To the nearest per cent, this is .... (page 114).

4. Express .543 to the nearest hundredth. .... (page 114).

5. Find 12% of $2.48 and express it to the nearest cent. .... (page 115).

6. If \$20 is 5% of a certain amount, what is that amount? .... (page 116).

7. What is 150% of \$200? .... (page 118).

8. Fifteen per cent more than 60 is .... (page 119).

9. 25% less than 80 is .... (page 120).

10. If a bicycle which originally sold for \$50 is now on sale for \$40, the per cent decrease is .... (page 121).

_____ *My Score*

Chapter Review

PRINCIPLES TO REMEMBER

1. A per cent, written with the % sign, represents parts of one hundred.

2. We can change a per cent to a decimal by dropping the per cent sign and moving the decimal point two places to the left.

3. We can change a per cent to a common fraction by writing a fraction with the given number as the numerator and 100 as the denominator.

4. One hundred per cent of a quantity is the entire quantity.

5. To find a per cent of a number, change the per cent to the equivalent decimal fraction or common fraction and multiply the number by the fraction.

6. To find the per cent one number is of a second number, form a fraction in which the first number is the numerator and the second number is the denominator. Divide the denominator into the numerator and change the decimal fraction to a per cent.

7. A common fraction is changed to the nearest whole per cent by dividing the numerator by the denominator, carrying the division to three decimal places, rounding off the quotient to the nearest hundredth and expressing the answer as a per cent.

8. To find a number when a per cent of it is known, change the per cent to an equivalent decimal fraction or common fraction and divide the given number by this fraction.

9. More than 100% of a number is a number larger than the original number.

10. To find an amount of increase, given a per cent of increase, take the per cent of the original number and add the product to the original number. To find an amount of decrease, take the per cent of the original number and subtract this amount from the original numbe

MASTERY TEST

1. *Complete each of the following:*
   a. 15% more than $40 is the same as ....% of $40 which equals $ ....
   b. 33⅓% more than $54 is the same as ....% of $54 which equals $ ....
   c. 100% more than $70 is the same as ....% of $70 which equals $ ....
   d. 30% less than $30 is the same as ....% of $30 which equals $ ....
   e. 45% less than $20 is the same as ....% of $20 which equals $ ....
   f. 66⅔% less than $180 is the same as ....% of $180 which equals $ ....

2. Because of a rainy day a baseball park had 40% less spectators than its usual crowd of 50,000. How many people were present?

3. There are 1150 people in East Village. An estimate shows that this number will probably decrease 10% by next year. How many people does the village expect to have next year?

4. *Find the following to the nearest cent.*
   a. 112% of $164
   b. 125% of $170
   c. 135% of $210
   d. 212% of $452
   e. 315% of $619
   f. 218% of $413.85
   g. 118% of $118
   h. 128% of $172
   i. 168% of $220
   j. 245% of $520
   k. 435% of $326.40
   l. 256% of $555.55

5. Last year Robert saved $56.25. Next year he plans to save 226% as much. How much does he expect to save?

6. The horsepower of a car was 90 last year. This year it is 55% greater. What is its new horsepower?

5

COMMON MEASUREMENTS

Look around you—at all the materials and objects that can be, and have been, measured. All materials which are bought and sold are measured; anything that is built or made is measured. Even the time is measured by the ticking of the clock. All things are measured to determine size, weight or duration.

Measurements are made by comparing the object being measured with a *standard unit of measure*: the inch, the hour, the minute, the yard and the mile.

Error in measurement always exists. Some measurements are made more accurately than others. The accuracy of your results depends on the measuring instrument you use and the care you take in making the measurement. The error in measurement should not be more than one-half of the smallest unit on your measuring instrument.

The Measurement of Length

The most common units for measuring length are the inch, the foot, the yard and the mile. Inches may be written ″; feet may be written ′. Thus, 6 feet is written 6′; 3 inches is written 3″.

Units of Linear Measure (Lengths of Lines)

12 inches (in.)	= 1 foot (ft.)
3 feet (ft.)	= 1 yard (yd.)
$16\frac{1}{2}$ feet	= $5\frac{1}{2}$ yards = 1 rod (rd.)
1760 yards	= 320 rods (rd.)
320 rods	= 1 mile (mi.)
1760 yards	= 1 mile
5280 feet	= 1 mile
1 nautical mile	= 1 knot = 1.15 land miles

Using a Ruler

The simplest and most commonly used instrument for making straight-line measurements is the *ruler*. Inches on a ruler may be subdivided into eighths, sixteenths, thirty-seconds or sixty-fourths of an inch. When used correctly and carefully, accurate measurements can be obtained with a ruler.

To determine the size of the smallest divisions on a ruler, count the small spaces between inch marks. If there are 16 spaces in an inch, the scale is marked in sixteenths; if there are 32 spaces, it is marked in thirty-seconds of an inch, and so on.

Rules to Remember

1. Use only rulers which have square, clean-cut ends. Worn or rounded ends result in inaccurate measurements. It is usually easiest to start measuring from any one of the inch marks on the ruler.

2. In measuring parts of square or rectangular objects, place the ruler parallel to the length being measured and not at an angle to it.

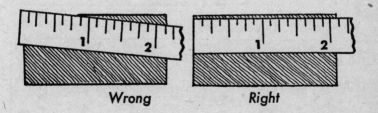

Wrong   **Right**

[Continued on top of page 128]

3. If the marked edge of the ruler does not come flat against the surface to be measured it is usually best to stand the ruler on edge so that the markings touch the surface. In the flat position the markings on the ruler may be too far from the object to allow accurate measurements.

4. To measure a line with a ruler, place the end of the ruler or the zero mark exactly on the line being measured. Make sure that the edge of the ruler is parallel with the line. Read the division mark on the ruler nearest where the line ends.

EXERCISES

Using a Ruler

1. *With a ruler measure each of the following lines to the nearest inch.*
a. ———————————   d. —————————————————
b. ——————————————   e. ————
c. ——————————————   f. ———————————

2. Measure each of the above lines to the nearest fourth of an inch.

3. Measure each of the above lines to the nearest eighth of an inch.

4. A ruler is placed against a metal plate as shown in the diagram. What is the length of the plate?

5. Draw a line $1\frac{1}{2}$ in. long. Mark it off in sixteenths of an inch.

6. What measurement is indicated by the arrow on the ruler pictured below?

7. Draw lines of the following lengths:
a. $2\frac{1}{16}$ in.   c. $4\frac{3}{4}$ in.   e. $2\frac{15}{16}$ in.   g. $\frac{5}{8}$ in.
b. $3\frac{3}{8}$ in.   d. $3\frac{3}{16}$ in.   f. $1\frac{9}{16}$ in.   h. $3\frac{5}{8}$ in.

8. Draw a line 2 inches long. Mark it off into eighths of an inch.

9. How many inches are there in 1 yard? in 5 yd?

10. How many feet are there in 1 mile? in ¼ mile? in ½ mile?

11. What fractional part of a yard is 9 inches?

12. A 29-inch length of ribbon contains how many more inches than a ¾-yard length of the same ribbon?

13. *a.* List three things measured in inches

    b. List three things measured in feet

    c. List three things measured in yards

14. How many yards are there in 2 rods?

Working With a Ruler

A ruler may be used to add and to subtract lengths.

How to Add With a Ruler

Problem: Find the total length of lines $\frac{1}{2}$ inch, $\frac{3}{8}$ inch and $1\frac{5}{16}$ inch long.

Draw a line $\frac{1}{2}$ inch long. At one end of the line draw a line $\frac{3}{8}$ inch long. Extend this line $1\frac{5}{16}$ inch. Measure the length of the entire line. The total length of the line is $2\frac{3}{16}$ inches.

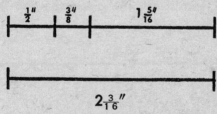

The length can be checked by the addition of fractions.

$$\frac{1}{2} = \frac{8}{16}$$
$$\frac{3}{8} = \frac{6}{16}$$
$$1\frac{5}{16} = 1\frac{5}{16}$$
$$1\frac{19}{16} = 2\frac{3}{16} \text{ inches}$$

EXERCISES

Working With a Ruler

*Find the total length of the lines in each of the following examples.
Check your answers by adding the fractions.*

a. $3\frac{5}{16}$ in., $4\frac{1}{2}$ in. and $2\frac{7}{8}$ in.

b. $1\frac{3}{4}$ in., $2\frac{1}{2}$ in., $\frac{5}{16}$ in. and $2\frac{7}{8}$ in.

c. $\frac{7}{16}$ in., $1\frac{1}{16}$ in., $3\frac{3}{4}$ in. and $\frac{1}{2}$ in.

d. $\frac{9}{16}$ in., $\frac{3}{4}$ in., $\frac{5}{8}$ in. and $2\frac{1}{8}$ in.

e. $1\frac{1}{4}$ in., $\frac{3}{4}$ in., $\frac{3}{16}$ in. and $\frac{1}{4}$ in.

f. $\frac{1}{2}$ in., $1\frac{3}{8}$ in., $\frac{7}{8}$ in. and $3\frac{3}{4}$ in.

g. 3 in., $1\frac{1}{4}$ in., $1\frac{3}{4}$ in. and $1\frac{1}{8}$ in.

Subtracting With a Ruler

John had a piece of wood which was $3\frac{5}{16}$ inches long. He used $1\frac{3}{8}$ inches of it. What was the length of the piece of wood that was left?

How to Subtract With a Ruler

Draw a line $3\frac{5}{16}$ inches long. Beginning at one end of the line, mark off $1\frac{3}{8}$ inches. Now measure the part of the original line that is left. The piece of wood that is left is $1\frac{15}{16}$ inches long.

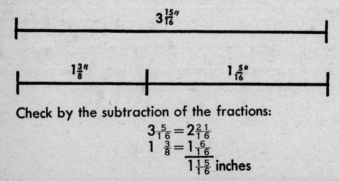

Check by the subtraction of the fractions:

$$3\frac{5}{16} = 2\frac{21}{16}$$
$$1\ \frac{3}{8} = 1\frac{6}{16}$$
$$\overline{\qquad 1\frac{15}{16} \text{ inches}}$$

EXERCISES

Subtracting With a Ruler

Using a ruler, find the lengths of the remaining portions of lines. Check your answers by subtracting fractions.

a. $3\frac{7}{8}$ in. cut off a line $5\frac{1}{2}$ in. long.

b. A piece of steel pipe $2\frac{11}{16}$ in. long cut from a 4 in. length.

c. A piece of ribbon $1\frac{3}{4}$ in. long cut from a $2\frac{1}{2}$ in. length.

d. $3\frac{9}{16}$ in. $-\frac{1}{4}$ in.   h. $2\frac{7}{16}$ in. $-\frac{3}{8}$ in.

e. $4\frac{1}{2}$ in. $-\frac{7}{16}$ in.   i. $3\frac{1}{4}$ in. $-\frac{11}{16}$ in.

f. $\frac{5}{6}$ ft. $-\frac{5}{8}$ ft.   j. $\frac{1}{2}$ ft. $-\frac{2}{8}$ ft.

g. $\frac{4}{8}$ in. $-\frac{1}{2}$ in.

Changing Measures of Length to Other Units

A *denominate* number is one in which the *name* of the unit of measure is given: 8 yards, 24 hours, 3 cups are all denominate numbers.

Frequently, measures of length are expressed in two or more units. Such numbers are called *compound denominate numbers*. For example, 3 yards 1 foot is a compound denominate number.

But suppose that a piece of material sells at $.69 per *yard*. Then we can not use yards and feet in computing the price. We must express the number in terms of *yards*, the unit specified. 3 yards 1 foot would be expressed as $3\frac{1}{3}$ yards.

To change measures of length, apply the following rules:

Rules for Changing to Larger Units

Rules to Remember

▶ Inches can be changed to feet by *dividing* the number of inches by 12.

Problem: Change 54 inches to feet.

$$54 \text{ in.} = 54 \div 12 = \frac{\overset{9}{\cancel{54}}}{1} \times \frac{1}{\underset{2}{\cancel{12}}} = \frac{9}{2} = 4\frac{1}{2} \text{ ft. or 4 ft. 6 in.}$$

▶ Inches can be changed to yards by *dividing* the number of inches by 36.

Problem: How many yards are there in 98 inches?

$$98 \text{ in.} = 98 \div 36 = \frac{98}{1} \times \frac{1}{36} = 2\frac{13}{18} \text{ yards.}$$

▶ Yards can be changed to rods by *dividing* the number of yards by $5\frac{1}{2}$.

Problem: Change 200 yards to rods.

$$200 \text{ yd.} = 200 \div 5\frac{1}{2} =$$

$$200 \div \frac{11}{2} = 200 \times \frac{2}{11} = 36\frac{4}{11} \text{ rods.}$$

General Rule to Remember

To change a measure of length to a larger unit of measure, divide the number of units given by the number of times the smaller unit is contained in each larger unit.

Rules for Changing to Smaller Units

Rules to Remember

▶ Miles can be changed to feet by *multiplying* the number of miles by 5280.

Problem: How many feet are there in 3 miles?

$$3 \text{ mi.} = 3 \times 5280 \text{ ft.} = 15,840 \text{ ft.}$$

▶ Yards can be changed to feet by *multiplying* the number of yards by 3.

Problem 1. How many feet are there in $6\frac{1}{3}$ yards?

$$6\tfrac{1}{3} \text{ yd.} = \tfrac{19}{3} \times 3 \text{ ft.} = 19 \text{ ft.}$$

Problem 2. Change 6 yards 1 foot to feet.

$$(6 \times 3 \text{ ft.}) + 1 \text{ ft.} = 19 \text{ ft.}$$

▶ Feet can be changed to inches by *multiplying* the number of feet by 12.

Problem 1. How many inches are there in $4\frac{1}{4}$ feet?

$$4\tfrac{1}{4} \text{ feet} = \tfrac{17}{4} \times \tfrac{12^{3}}{1} = 51 \text{ inches}$$

Problem 2. Change 4 feet 3 inches to inches.

$$(4 \times 12) + 3 = 48 \text{ in.} + 3 \text{ in.} = 51 \text{ inches}$$

▶ Yards can be changed to inches by *multiplying* the number of yards by 36.

Problem 1. Change $6\frac{1}{2}$ yards to inches.

$$6\tfrac{1}{2} \text{ yd.} = \tfrac{13}{2} \times \tfrac{36^{18}}{1} = 234 \text{ in.}$$

Problem 2. How many inches are there in 6 yd. $1\frac{1}{2}$ ft.?

$$(6 \times 36) + (1\tfrac{1}{2} \times 12) = 216 + 18 = 234 \text{ in.}$$

General Rule to Remember

To change a measure of length to a smaller unit
of measure, *multiply* the number of units by the number
of times the smaller unit is contained in the larger unit.

EXERCISES

Changing Measures of Length

1. *Change the following measures to feet and inches:*

    a.   68 in. = ... ft. .... in.

    b.   86 in. = ... ft. .... in.

    c.   94 in. = ... ft. .... in.

    d. 110 in. = ... ft. .... in.

    e. 210 in. = ... ft. .... in.

    f. 144 in. = ... ft. .... in.

    g.   59 in. = ... ft. .... in.

2. *How many inches are there in:*

    a. 9 ft. = ... in.   *e.* 6 yards 2 ft. = ... in.

    b. 3 ft. 4 in. = ... in.   *f.* 8 yards 1 ft. = ... in.

    c. 11 ft. 7 in. = ... in.   *g.* 12 yards 2 ft. = ... in.

    d. 5 yards = ... in.

3. *How many feet are there in:*

    a. 5 yards 1 ft. = ... ft.   *e.* 11 miles = ... ft.

    b. 12 yards 2 ft. = ... ft.   *f.* 21 miles 2 yards = ... ft.

    c. 38 yards 2 ft. = ... ft.   *g.* 26 miles 2 yards 2 ft. = ... ft.

    d. 4 miles = ... ft.

4. *Change to rods:*

    a. 5 miles = ... rods

    b. 8 miles = ... rods

    c. 12 miles = ... rods

    d. 10 miles 100 yards = ... rods

    e. 22 miles 200 yards = ... rods

    f. 3 miles 500 feet = ... rods

    g. 9 miles 60 yards = ... rods

GENERAL SKILL EXERCISE

How are you doing? Try the following test. If you get any wrong, turn to the pages shown after each question. Practice those problems until you have mastered them.

1. Measurements are made by comparing the size of an object with a .... (page 126).

2. The symbol (") stands for .... (page 126).

3. There are .... feet in a rod (page 126).

4. Using a ruler with .... ends may result in inaccurate measurements (page 127).

5. If we extend a known line a given distance and then measure the entire length, we are finding the length by .... with a ruler (page 129).

6. We can .... and .... lengths by using a ruler (page 129)

7. Measures expressed in two or more units are called.... (page 131).

8. If you divide the number of inches by 36, the answer is expressed in .... (page 132).

9. Rods can be changed to yards by the multiplication of the number of rods by .... (page 132).

10. There are .... feet in a mile (page 126).

My Score _____

Other Common Measures

How many times have we gotten on the scales? drunk a pint of milk? bought a pound of butter? waited for an hour?

On every one of these occasions we have used certain measures of weight, capacity or duration of time.

Sometimes, when we use these measures, we must change compound denominate numbers to single units. If we buy coal by the ton, it is more convenient to express the weight all in tons, rather than part in pounds. If we buy chickens by the pound, the weight, even the ounces, is expressed as parts of pounds. For this reason, we must know the quantities involved in each unit of measure.

UNITS OF WEIGHT

16 ounces (oz.)	**= 1 pound (lb.)**
100 pounds	**= 1 hundredweight (cwt.)**
2000 pounds	**= 1 ton (t.)**
2240 pounds	**= 1 long ton**

To change measures of weight, follow these rules:

Rules to Remember

▶ Pounds can be changed to ounces by *multiplying* the number of pounds by 16.

Problem 1. How many ounces are there in 2 pounds?

2 lb. $= 2 \times 16 = 32$ oz.

Problem 2. Change 3 lb. 2 oz. to ounces.

$(3 \times 16) + 2 = 48 + 2 = 50$ oz.

▶ Ounces can be changed to pounds by *dividing* the number of ounces by 16.

Problem 1. How many pounds in 48 oz.?

$\frac{48}{16} = 3$ lb.

Problem 2. Change 54 oz. to pounds.

$54 \div 16 = \frac{54}{16} = 3\frac{3}{8}$ lb.

▶ Pounds can be changed to tons by *dividing* the number of pounds by 2000.

Problem 1. Change 8000 pounds to tons

$\frac{8000}{2000} = 4$ tons.

Problem 2. Change 6500 pounds to tons and pounds.

6500 lb. $= \frac{6500}{2000} = 3$ tons 500 lb.

The four small boys weigh 3040 ounces. The man on the opposite scale weighs 190 pounds. Who weighs more? Sixteen ounces equal one pound. Therefore, the weight in pounds of the four small boys equals 3040 ÷ 16. The weight in ounces of the man equals 190 × 16.

EXERCISES

Changing Measures of Weight

1. *Change each of the following:*
   - *a.* 6 oz. = ... lb.
   - *b.* 59 oz. .... lb. .... oz.
   - *c.* 24 oz. = ... lb. ...... oz.
   - *d.* 64 oz. = ... lb.
   - *e.* 95 oz. = ... lb. .... oz.
   - *f.* 12 oz. = ... lb.

2. *How many ounces are there in each of the following:*
   - *a.* $1\frac{3}{4}$ lbs. = ... oz.
   - *b.* $\frac{5}{8}$ lb. = ... oz.
   - *c.* 3 lbs. 8 oz. = ... oz.
   - *d.* 15 lbs. 4 oz. = ... oz.
   - *e.* 18 lbs. 6 oz. = ... oz.
   - *f.* $6\frac{1}{8}$ lbs. = ... oz.

3. *Insert the proper number in each space.*
   - *a.* 2500 lb. = ... t. ...... lb.
   - *b.* 4800 lb. = ... t. ...... lb.
   - *c.* 8622 lb. = ... t. ...... lb.
   - *d.* 11,160 lb. = ... t. ...... lb.
   - *e.* 12,000 lb. = ... t. ...... lb.
   - *f.* 16,250 lb. = ... t. ...... lb.

UNITS OF LIQUID MEASURE

2 cups = 1 pint (pt.)
16 fluid ounces = 1 pint
2 pints (pts.) = 1 quart (qt.)
4 quarts (qts.) = 1 gallon (gal.)

The units of liquid measure are used to measure the volume of liquids. They do not measure weight.

To change liquid measures, apply the following rules:

Rules to Remember

▶Quarts can be changed to pints by *multiplying* the number of quarts by 2.

Problem 1. Change 9 quarts to pints.
    9 qt. = 9 × 2 = 18 pints

▶Gallons can be changed to quarts by *multiplying* the number of gallons by 4.

Problem 1. How many quarts are there in 4 gallons?
    4 gal. = 4 × 4 = 16 qt.

Problem 2. Change 3 gallons 2 quarts to quarts.
    3 gal. 2 qt. = (3 × 4) + 2 = 14 qt.

EXERCISES

Changing Liquid Measures

1. *How many quarts are there in each of the following?*
    a. 2 gal. 2 qt. = ... qt.   d. 26 gal. 2 qt. = ... qt.
    b. 2 gal. 1 qt. = ... qt.   e. 10 gal. 2 qt. 1 pt. = ... qt.
    c. 12 gal. 1 qt. = ... qt.   f. 1½ pt. = ... qt.

2. *How many pints are there in each of the following?*
    a. 2 gal. 1 qt. = ... pt.   d. 7 gal. 2 qt. 1 pt. = ... pt.
    b. 3 gal. 2 qt. = ... pt.   e. 10 gal. 1 qt. 1 pt. = ... pt.
    c. 4 gal. 1 qt. 1 pt. = ... pt.   f. 20½ gal. = ... pt.

UNITS OF DRY MEASURE

2 pints = 1 quart
8 quarts = 1 peck (pk.)
4 pecks = 1 bushel (bu.)

This man is holding one quart of orange juice and one quart of cereal. He is puzzled because he has forgotten that a liquid quart is about 14% smaller than a dry quart.

1. Which container holds the orange juice? Which contains the cereal?

2. How could he convert the dry quart into dry pints? How could he convert the liquid quart into liquid pints?

Dry measures are used to measure the volume of grain, fruits, vegetables and other dry quantities. The dry quarts and pints are different from the liquid quarts and pints. In fact, the liquid quart is about 14% smaller than the dry quart. The dry quart is 16% larger than the liquid quart.

To change dry measures, apply the following rules:

Rules to Remember

▶ Quarts can be changed to pints by *multiplying* the number of quarts by 2.

Problem: How many pints are there in 3 quarts?
$$3 \text{ qt.} = 3 \times 2 \text{ pints} = 6 \text{ pints.}$$

▶ Quarts can be changed to pecks by *dividing* the number of quarts by 8.

Problem: How many pecks are there in 40 quarts?
$$40 \text{ qt.} = 40 \div 8 = 5 \text{ pecks}$$

▶ Pecks can be changed to bushels by *dividing* the number of pecks by 4.

Problem: How many bushels are there in 12 pecks?
$$12 \text{ pecks} = \frac{12}{4} = 3 \text{ bu.}$$

EXERCISES
Changing Dry Measures

Complete each of the following:

a. 2 qt. 1 pt. = ... pints.
b. 16 qts. = ... pecks.
c. 2 bushels = ... pecks.
d. 6 pecks 1 quart = ... quarts.
e. 1 bushel 2 pecks = ... pecks.
f. 16 pecks = ... bushels.
g. 20 pints = ... pecks.
h. 25 pecks = ... bushels.
i. $1\frac{3}{4}$ pecks = ... quarts.
j. 1 peck 3 quarts = ... pints.

---

60 seconds (sec.) = 1 minute (min.)

60 minutes = 1 hour (hr.)

24 hours = 1 day (da.)

365 days
12 months } **= 1 year (yr.)**

To change units of time, apply the following rules:

Rule to Remember

To change minutes to seconds, *multiply* the number of minutes by 60.

HOW TO DO THE EXAMPLE

Problem 1. How many seconds are there in 2 minutes?
2 min. = 2 × 60 = 120 sec.

Problem 2. Change $3\frac{1}{2}$ minutes to seconds.
$3\frac{1}{2}$ min. $= \frac{7}{2} \times \frac{\overset{30}{\cancel{60}}}{1} = 210$ sec.

Rule to Remember

To change hours to minutes, *multiply* the number of hours by 60.

HOW TO DO THE EXAMPLE

Problem 1. How many minutes are there in 3 hours?
$$3 \text{ hr.} = 3 \times 60 = 180 \text{ min.}$$

Problem 2. Change 2 hours 15 minutes to minutes.
$$2 \text{ hr. } 15 \text{ min.} = (2 \times 60) + 15 = 135 \text{ min.}$$

Review the general rules for changing units of measure, pages 135-141. See also Reference Tables elsewhere in this book.

EXERCISES

Changing Units of Time Measure

Complete each of the following:

  a. 2 hr. 10 min. = ... min.
  b. 90 min. = ... hr.
  c. 75 min. = ... hr. .... min.
  d. 80 sec. = ... min.
  e. $\frac{1}{3}$ hr. = ... min.
  f. 3 yr. 6 mo. = ... mo.
  g. 6 wk. 2 da. = ... da.
  h. 30 min. = ... hr.
  i. 210 sec. = ... min.
  j. 2 da. 3 hr. = ... hr.

Working With Measures

Adding Measures

Henry had two pieces of wood. One piece was 5 ft. 9 in. long and the other was 4 ft. 7 in. in length. What was the total length of the two pieces?

Rule to Remember

To find the total of lengths, weights or duration, add the individual measures. In compound denominate numbers, place the numbers for the same units in the same columns; for example, feet in one column and inches in a separate column. If the total of the smaller units is equal to one or more of the larger units, increase the sum of the larger measure and express the remaining small units as part of a compound denominate number.

HOW TO DO THE EXAMPLE

Problem 1. Add 5 ft. 9 in. and 4 ft. 7 in.

$$\begin{array}{r} 5 \text{ ft. } 9 \text{ in.} \\ 4 \text{ ft. } 7 \text{ in.} \\ \hline 9 \text{ ft. } 16 \text{ in.} = 10 \text{ ft. } 4 \text{ in.} \end{array}$$

By adding the number of feet we get 9 ft. Then we add the number of inches and get 16 in. But 16 in. = 1 ft. 4 in. Therefore, 9 ft. 16 in. = 10 ft. 4 in.

Problem 2. Add 2 hr. 55 min. and 1 hr. 20 min.

$$\begin{array}{r} 2 \text{ hr. } 55 \text{ min.} \\ 1 \text{ hr. } 20 \text{ min.} \\ \hline 3 \text{ hr. } 75 \text{ min.} = 4 \text{ hr. } 15 \text{ min.} \end{array}$$

By adding the minutes we get 75 min. Then we add the hours and get 3. The total is 3 hr. 75 min. But 75 min. can be changed to 1 hr. 15 min. Therefore, 3 hr. 75 min. equals 4 hr. 15 min.

EXERCISES

Adding Measures

1. *Find the sum of the following:*

a. 6 ft. 3 in.	*b.* 5 ft. 1 in.	*c.* 12 ft. 9 in.
2 ft. 4 in.	7 in.	3 in.

d. 8 ft.
   1 ft. 6 in.

m. 11 ft. 5 in.
   2 ft. 9 in.

v. 21 ft. 8 in.
   9 ft. 6 in.

e. 4 hr. 18 min.
   6 hr. 15 min.

n. 3 hr. 40 min.
   2 hr. 15 min.

w. 2 hr. 53 min.
   7 min.

f. 7 hr. 28 min.
   3 hr. 37 min.

o. 1 hr. 45 min.
   2 hr. 25 min.

x.   8 hr. 48 min.
   10 hr. 45 min.

g. 4 hr. 35 min.
   6 hr. 48 min.
   3 hr. 26 min.

p. 7 ft. 7 in.
   9 ft. 8 in.
   10 ft. 9 in.

y. 10 ft. 1 in.
   8 ft. 8 in.
   4 ft. 3 in.

h. 3 lb. 7 oz.
   2 lb. 1 oz.

q. 7 lb. 5 oz.
   7 oz.

z. 6 lb. 4 oz.
   1 lb. 12 oz.

i. 9 lb. 6 oz.
   7 lb. 14 oz.
   4 lb. 8 oz.

r. 3 yd. 2 ft.
   8 yd. 1 ft.

aa. 12 yd. 2 ft. 9 in.
   10 yd. 1 ft. 3 in.

j. 4 gal. 1 qt.
   3 qt.

s. 6 gal. 3 qt.
   3 gal. 3 qt.

bb. 2 qt. 1 pt.
   3 qt. 1 pt.

k. 3 yr. 6 mo.
   4 yr. 3 mo.

t. 5 yr. 7 mo.
   2 yr. 5 mo.

cc. 8 yr. 8 mo.
   3 yr. 6 mo.

l. 4 wk. 3 da.
   5 wk. 4 da.

u. 8 wk. 5 da.
   3 wk. 2 da.

dd. 9 wk. 6 da.
   4 wk. 5 da.

ee. 1 da. 10 hr. 26 min.
   2 da. 2 hr. 34 min.

ff. 7 da. 17 hr. 52 min.
   5 da. 10 hr. 10 min.

gg. 1 yr. 305 da.
   2 yr. 90 da.

hh. 3 yr. 7 mon. 20 da.
   4 yr. 9 mon. 2 da.

Subtracting Measures

Mary's mother had a canister containing 8 lb. 4 oz. of sugar. She used 5 lb. 13 oz. in baking. How many pounds of sugar were left?

Essentials to Remember

To subtract compound denominate numbers, place the same units in the same column.

If the subtrahend is larger than the minuend in any column, change the minuend by taking 1 from the larger unit and changing it to its equivalent in the smaller units.

HOW TO DO THE EXAMPLE

To calculate the amount of sugar Mary's mother had remaining, we must subtract 5 lb. 13 oz. from 8 lb. 4 oz. First, we place the same units in a separate column. Since we cannot subtract 13 oz. from 4 oz. we must borrow 1 lb. or 16 oz. from 8 lb., leaving 7 lb. The borrowed 16 oz. is added to the 4 oz., making 20 oz.

Problem: From 8 lb. 4 oz. subtract 5 lb. 13 oz.

$$8 \text{ lb. } 4 \text{ oz.} = 7 \text{ lb. } 20 \text{ oz.}$$
$$5 \text{ lb. } 13 \text{ oz.} = \underline{5 \text{ lb. } 13 \text{ oz.}}$$
$$2 \text{ lb. } 7 \text{ oz.}$$

Therefore, **2 lb. 7 oz.** of sugar were left.

EXERCISE
Subtracting Measures

Subtract each of the following:

a. 7 lb. 8 oz.
  5 lb. 3 oz.

b. 2 hr. 40 min.
  1 hr. 50 min.

c. 6 yd. 9 in.
   11 in.

d. 18 yd. 2 ft. 9 in.
  14 yd. 1 ft. 5 in.

e. 23 gal. 2 qt. 1 pt.
  10 gal. 3 qt. 1 pt.

f. 9 lb. 5 oz.
   8 oz.

g. 10 yr. 6 mo.
  6 yr. 6 mo.

h. 8 yd. 1 ft.
  6 yd. 2 ft.

i. 12 lb. 6 oz.
  3 lb. 9 oz.

j. 3 wk. 2 da.
  1 wk. 4 da.

k. 10 hr.
  4 hr. 27 min.

l. 15 yd. 1 ft. 5 in.
  9 yd. 2 ft. 10 in.

m. 5 yr. 2 mo. 6 da.
  1 yr. 6 mo. 3 da.

Multiplying Measures

Mr. Jones plans to make a bookcase which has 6 shelves. Each shelf is to be 4 ft. 7 in. long. How long a piece of wood does he need from which he can cut the required length?

HOW TO DO THE EXAMPLE

Problem 1: Multiply 4 ft. 7 in. by 6.

$$\begin{array}{r} 4 \text{ ft. } 7 \text{ in.} \\ \times \quad 6 \\ \hline 24 \text{ ft. } 42 \text{ in.} = 27 \text{ ft. } 6 \text{ in.} \end{array}$$

Method : Multiply 7 in. by 6, which gives 42 in. Multiply 4 ft. by 6, which gives 24 ft. The result of the multiplication, therefore, is 24 ft. and 42 in. But 42 in. can be changed to 3 ft. 6 in. Thus, the answer is 27 ft. 6 in.

Problem 2. Multiply 4 ft. 6 in. by 5

Method : Another way of multiplying measures is: Change 4 ft. 6 in. to $4\frac{1}{2}$ ft. and then multiply by 5.

$$4\frac{1}{2} \times 5 = \frac{9}{2} \times 5 = \frac{45}{2} = 22\frac{1}{2} \text{ ft.} = 22 \text{ ft. } 6 \text{ in.}$$

EXERCISES

Multiplying Measures

Multiply each of the following:

a. 3 ft. 2 in.	*d.* 5 lb. 12 oz.	*g.* 2 hr. 17 min.	*j.* 5 pk. 2 qts.
3	4	5	9
b. 2 yd. 13 in.	*e.* 10 ft. 9 in.	*h.* 4 gal. 2 qt.	*k.* 2 hr. 10 min.
6	17	2	3
c. 4 t. 500 lb.	*f.* 15 min. 30 sec.	*i.* 6 yr. 6 mo.	*l.* 3 bu. 3 pk.
6	10	5	12

25 × 1000 lb   155 min   32 yr 6 mon   45 bu

Dividing Measures

Henry had a steel rod 6 ft. 3 in. long. He cut it into 5 equal parts. How long was each of the small pieces?

There are two ways of doing this example.

Rules to Remember

Change the compound denominate number completely to the smaller unit and divide.

Method 1

a. Change 6 ft. 3 in. to 75 inches.

b. Divide the 75 inches by 5.

c. Change the quotient back to compound denominate numbers.

HOW TO DO THE EXAMPLE

$$6 \text{ ft. } 3 \text{ in.} = (6 \times 12) + 3 = 75 \text{ in.}$$
$$\frac{75}{5} = 15 \text{ in.}$$
$$\frac{15}{12} = 1\frac{3}{12} = 1 \text{ ft. } 3 \text{ in.}$$

Divide the larger measure by the given divisor into as many units as it will be divided evenly. Change the remainder to the smaller unit, add it to the number of smaller units, and divide this number by the given divisor. Add the two quotients.

Method 2

a. Divide 6 ft. by 5. This gives 1 ft. with a remainder of 1 ft.

b. Change the 1 ft. remainder to 12 in. and add the 3 additional inches of the steel rod.

c. Divide the 15 in. by 5, getting 3 in.

d. Add the two quotients: 1 ft. + 3 in. = 1 ft. 3 in.

$\begin{array}{r} 1 \text{ ft.} \\ 5\overline{)6 \text{ ft.}} \\ \underline{5} \\ 1 \text{ ft. or } 12 \text{ in.} \end{array}$	$12 \text{ in.} + 3 \text{ in.} = 15 \text{ in.}$ $\begin{array}{r} 3 \text{ in.} \\ 5\overline{)15 \text{ in.}} \end{array}$ Answer: 1 ft. 3 in.

EXERCISES
Dividing Measures

Divide each of the following:

a. 4)8 lb. 4 oz.   e. 2)11 ft. 8 in.   i. 4)9 gal. 3 qt.

b. 3)8 ft.   f. 6)15 yr. 9 mo.   j. 8)16 hr. 40 min.

c. 4)7 bu. 3 peck   g. 4)9 wk. 2 da.   k. 5)40 min. 10 sec.

d. 10)15 yr. 9 mo.   h. 8)20 t. 1800 lb.   l. 4)16 mi. 300 ft.

GENERAL SKILL EXERCISE

How are you doing? Try the following test. If you get any wrong, turn to the pages shown after each question. Practice those problems until you have mastered them.

1. A unit that might be used to measure the weight of a slice of toast is the .... (page 136).

2. The abbreviation for hundredweight is .... (page 136).

3. There are .... pounds in $4\frac{1}{2}$ tons (page 136).

4. How many ounces are there in $\frac{3}{8}$ of a pound? .... (page 136).

5. If a glass can hold $\frac{1}{2}$ pint, how many glasses are needed to hold 2 quarts? .... (page 137).

6. If a bushel of apples weighs 50 pounds, how many bushels are there in 1 ton? .... (page 138).

7. A farmer delivers 8 gal. 1 qt. of milk every day. How much milk does he deliver in a 30-day month? .... (page 138).

8. A car leaves at 8:40 a.m. and arrives at its destination at 10:15 a.m. How long did the trip take? .... (page 144).

9. If fluid ounces are divided by 16, the answer is expressed in .... (page 137).

10. To change quarts to pecks, divide the number of quarts by .... (page 138).

————— *My Score*

Weights and Measures of Our Neighbors

In Canada and Mexico and in most of the countries in South America and Europe, the metric system, not the English system of weights and measures, is used.

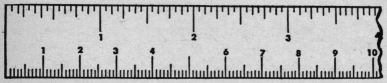

A ruler showing inches (top of ruler) and centimeters (bottom of ruler).

The metric system is a decimal system. Each unit is $\frac{1}{10}$ of the next larger unit. The *meter*, which is the basic unit of the system, is equal to 39.37 of our American inches. A *decimeter* is one tenth of a meter, and thus is equivalent to 3.937 inches. A *centimeter*, one hundredth of a meter, is equal to .3937 inch. A *millimeter*, one thousandth of a meter, is equal to .03937 in.

While the English system expresses distance in miles, the metric system expresses distance in kilometers. Each kilometer is 1,000 meters, and it equals approximately $\frac{5}{8}$ of our mile.

The metric system is used not only for linear measurements, but also for liquid weights and dry weights. The basic unit of dry weight is the *gram*. This equals only a small part of our ounce. The *kilogram*, which is 1000 grams, and is equal to approximately 2.2 of our pounds, is used more often. A *milligram*, which is .001 gram, is equal to .000035 ounce.

In liquid measurement, while we in the United States measure by quarts, the metric system uses the *liter*. A liter equals 1.057 quarts.

It is sometimes necessary to convert English units to the metric, or the metric units to English units.

Notice the prefix used for each of the units of measurement:

milli	= one-thousandth	(.001)	**deka**	= ten	(10)
centi	= one-hundredth	(.01)	**hecto**	= hundred	(100)
deci	= one-tenth	(.1)	**kilo**	= thousand	(1000)

When Don was visiting Canada, he got on a scale to weigh himself. The scale registered 54 kilograms. How many pounds did Don weigh?

HOW TO DO THE EXAMPLE

We know that 1 kilogram = 2.2 pounds. If one kilogram = 2.2 pounds, then to find the equivalent of 54 kilograms we must *multiply* 54 times 2.2 pounds.

Multiply:
$$\begin{array}{r} 54 \\ 2.2 \\ \hline 108 \\ 108 \\ \hline 118.8 \end{array}$$

Don weighed 118.8 pounds.

A strip of film is 8 mm. (millimeters) wide. How many meters wide is it? What part of an inch is it?

Essentials to Remember

Because a millimeter is $\frac{1}{1000}$ of a meter, to change millimeters to meters we must *divide* by one thousand— or move the decimal point three places to the left. To change meters to inches, *multiply* 39.37 inches by the number of meters.

HOW TO DO THE EXAMPLE

8 mm. $= \frac{8}{1000}$ meter or .008 meter.

We have learned that 1 meter = 39.37 inches. Then .008 meters must equal .008 × 39.37 inches.

$$\begin{array}{r} 39.37 \text{ in.} \\ \times .008 \\ \hline .31496 \end{array}$$

.31496 or approximately $\frac{3}{10}$ of an inch.

An exchange student from France measured a drawing and found it to be one inch long. His classmates asked him what one inch would equal in the metric system.

We know that one meter equals 39.37 inches. Then, to find the equivalent of one inch, we must *divide* 1 inch by 39.37.

$$1 \text{ in.} = \tfrac{1}{39.37} \text{ meter or } 39.37 \overline{) 1.00 \,000} \quad \begin{array}{c} .025 \text{ meter or 2.5} \\ \text{centimeters} \end{array}$$

Rule to Remember

To change one unit of measurement in the metric system to another unit of measurement in the metric system, we must simply move the decimal point. This is possible because each unit in the system is .1 of the next higher unit.

HOW TO DO THE EXAMPLE

Problem **1.** How many meters are there in 4.7 kilometers?

$$1 \text{ km.} = 1000 \text{ meters}$$
$$4.7 \text{ km.} = 4700\text{\textasciicircum} \text{ meters}$$

Problem **2.** How many meters tall is Ted if his height is 170 centimeters?

$$1 \text{ cm.} = .01 \text{ meters}$$
$$170 \text{ cm.} = 1.70 \text{ meters}$$

EXERCISES
Changing Units of Measurement

1. In 4 grams there are:
   a. .... milligrams   b. .... kilograms
2. How many quarts are in 6 liters of milk?
3. One mile equals:
   a. .... meters   b. .... kilometers
4. How many grams are there in:
   a. 4 milligrams 1 gram   b. 5 kilograms 4 milligrams
5. The thickness of a piece of cardboard was 1.5 millimeters. Expressed in inches, how thick was the cardboard?

6. When Roger was traveling with his family in London he saw a street sign which said, "Speed Limit, 80 km. (kilometers) per hour." How fast was Roger's father allowed to drive?

7. Roger's father stopped for gasoline. He bought 30 liters. How many gallons did he buy?

GENERAL SKILL EXERCISE

How are you doing? Try the following test. If you get any wrong, turn to the pages shown after each question. Practice those problems until you have mastered them.

1. The metric system is a .... system of weights and measures (page 148).

2. The relationship of one unit to the next larger unit in the metric system is .... (page 150).

3. The .... is the basic measure of linear measure in the metric system (page 148).

4. The .... is the basic unit of liquid measure in the metric system (page 148).

5. In the metric system, dry weights are measured by .... (page 148).

6. One .... or 1000 .... is equal to 2.2 pounds (page 148).

7. One .... equals nearly 40 inches (page 148).

8. Countries using the metric system would sell milk by .... rather than by quarts (page 148).

9. A chicken that weighs almost 4½ pounds would weigh approximately .... kilograms (page 149).

_____ *My Score*

Chapter Review

PRINCIPLES TO REMEMBER

1. Objects are measured to determine their size or weight. Duration is measured as length of time.

2. Length is expressed in inches, feet, yards and miles.

3. A ruler can be used to add or subtract lengths.

4. Numbers which are expressed in two units are called "com-

pound denominate numbers." An example of such a number is 2 yards 1 foot.

5. Weight is expressed in ounces, pounds or tons.

6. Liquid measure is expressed in fluid ounces, pints, quarts or gallons.

7. Dry measure is expressed in pints, quarts, pecks and bushels.

8. Time is expressed in seconds, minutes or hours.

9. Measures and compound denominate numbers can be added, subtracted, multiplied or divided.

10. In the metric system linear measurement is expressed in meters, dry weight in grams, liquid measure in liters.

11. To change one unit in the metric system to the next larger unit, move the decimal point one place to the left. To change one unit to the next smaller unit, move the decimal point one place to the right.

MASTERY TEST

1. Maria is 4 ft. 7 in. tall and her brother Manuel is 5 ft. 4 in. tall. How much taller is Manuel than Maria?

2. To change inches to feet would you *multiply* the number of inches by 12 or *divide* the number of inches by 12?

3. Henry produced 3 bu. 1 pk. of potatoes in his garden plot. Paul produced 1 bu. 3 pk. of potatoes in his garden plot. How much more did Henry produce than Paul?

4. If 12 pounds 8 ounces is divided equally among four people, how much does each receive?

5. If Joe sold 13 quart-containers and 11 pint-containers of ice cream from his truck in one day, how many gallons of ice cream did he sell?

6. What fractional part of a yard is 9 in?

7. Which is the greater distance, 5000 feet or one mile?

8. Fifty minutes is what fractional part of an hour?

9. John's father bought two turkeys. One weighed $12\frac{1}{2}$ lb. and the other $13\frac{3}{4}$ lb. How much did they weigh together?

10. If a dress factory uses $3\frac{1}{8}$ yards of cloth to make a dress, how many yards will it take to make 12 dresses?

11. A plane took off from an air base at 9:35 a.m. and returned at 1:33 p.m. Find the flying time in hours and minutes.

12. Mr. Jones feeds his horse 1 peck of oats each day. If he has 5 bushels of oats, how many days can he feed his horse with this supply?

13. If a plumber cuts two pieces of pipe, one $6\frac{3}{4}$ feet and the other $3\frac{1}{2}$ feet long, from a 12-foot length of pipe, how many feet of pipe are left?

14. How many quarts are there in 4 gallons? How many liters?

15. What fractional part of a year remains after June 30?

16. What fractional part of a yard is 12 inches?

17. A certain school has a one-quarter-mile track on its playground. How many times around the track would a boy have to run to complete a mile?

18. A girl was born on June 2, 1937. How old will she be on her next birthday?

19. Billy is making a knot exhibit. If he allows 20 inches of rope for each knot, how many feet of rope will he need to make 18 knots?

20. What fractional part of a year is a month?

21. What fractional part of a week is one hour?

22. Peter had 5 yards of lacing to cut into 20-in. pieces. How many pieces measuring exactly 20 in. each can be cut from the lacing?

23. One-half dozen eggs added to four eggs equals how many eggs?

24. From 3 feet 6 inches subtract 1 foot 10 inches.

25. How many slices, each $\frac{1}{4}$ in. thick, can be cut from an eighteen-inch piece of meat loaf? How many slices 1 cm. (centimeter) thick can be cut?

26. After four pieces each 1 ft. 5 in. long were cut from a board, a piece 4 in. long remained. What was the original length of the board?

27. Jane is 3 years and 3 months old. Her cousin is 4 times as old. How old is her cousin?

28. How far above the earth, to the nearest mile, is a plane flying at an altitude of 15,000 feet?

29. How many half-pint bottles can be filled with milk from a 10-gallon can of milk?

30. A friend expected at 5:30 p.m. was 1 hour and 40 minutes late. At what time did he arrive?

31. Paul is 5 ft. 4 in. tall and Sam is 62 in. tall. Which boy is taller?

32. Subtract 2 hours and 50 minutes from 5 hours and 12 minutes.

33. How many inches are there in 50 centimeters?

34. What is the shortest board a man must buy in order to cut three sections from it each 4 feet 8 inches long?

35. How many quart bottles can be filled from four 10-gallon cans of milk?

6 | SCALE DRAWING

Drawing to Scale

When an architect makes a plan or blueprint of a house, his drawing is much smaller than the actual house. The plan is reduced in size to fit the paper he is using. This process of reducing in size is called *drawing to scale*. The reduced drawing is known as a *scale drawing*.

In a scale drawing each line is a definite fractional part of the line it represents. A line in the scale drawing may be one-half of the line it represents, one-fourth of it, one-hundredth, one-thousandth, or any other definite part of it.

In a scale drawing the scale may be written:

$$\frac{1}{4}'' = 1'$$

This means that every $\frac{1}{4}$ inch length on the scale drawing represents a 1-foot length of the original object.

A scale drawing has the same shape as the original, but not the same size. Thus, we say that scale drawings are *similar* to the actual object.

Road maps, maps printed in textbooks and atlases, plans for parts of a machine are scale drawings. There is a definite relationship between two places on a map to the actual distances. For example, on a map the scale may be given as $\frac{1}{2}'' = 50$ miles. On another map the scale may be $1'' = 1000$ miles. This means that the actual distance between two points on a map $1\frac{1}{2}''$ apart, whose scale reading is $\frac{1}{2} = 50$ miles, is 150 miles.

Choosing Scales

In choosing a scale, we always pick one that is convenient to work with—not too large for the paper we are drawing on, nor too small to measure. It may be convenient to let $\frac{3}{4}$ inch equal 1 foot, $\frac{1}{2}$ inch equal 1 foot, or $\frac{1}{4}$ inch equal 1 foot. The scale depends upon the size of the original object and how much it must be reduced.

Once a scale is chosen, the same scale must be used in drawing all parts of the same object. Whenever a scale drawing is made, the scale being used must be stated. It is usually written at the bottom of the drawing.

Making a Scale Drawing

Mr. Martin wanted to make a scale drawing of his garage floor. The floor was a rectangle 20 feet long by 10 feet wide. He decided to use a scale in which $\frac{1}{2}$ inch = 5 feet.

First, he must divide the side into units of 5 feet each. $20 \div 5 = 4$ five-foot parts. Since in the scale $\frac{1}{2}$ in. = 5 ft., he would need $4 \times \frac{1}{2}$ inch or 2 in.

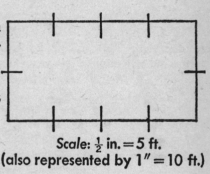

Similarly, to find the length of the line which would represent the 10-foot line:
$10 \div 5 = 2$ units of 5 feet each
$2 \times \frac{1}{2}$ inch = 1 in. to represent 10 feet.

Scale: $\frac{1}{2}$ in. = 5 ft.
(also represented by 1″ = 10 ft.)

EXERCISES

Making Scale Drawings

1. *The scale used in the following lines is $\frac{1}{4}$ in. = 1 ft. How many feet does each line represent?*

a. _____   c. _____
b. _____   d. _____
                 e. _____

2. *Using a scale of $\frac{1}{4}$ in. = 1 ft., give the length of the lines you would use to represent each of the following:*

a. 16 ft.   c. 14 ft.   e. $26\frac{1}{2}$ ft.   g. 48 ft.
b. 20 ft.   d. 23 ft.   f. 120 ft.   h. 10 ft.

3. *The scale used in making a scale drawing of a house is ¼ in. = 1 ft. What are the dimensions of the rooms represented by the following lines on the blueprint?*

a. 3 in. by 4 in.
b. $3\frac{1}{2}$ in. by 6 in.
c. $2\frac{3}{4}$ in. by $1\frac{1}{2}$ in.

d. $6\frac{1}{4}$ in. by $3\frac{1}{2}$ in.
e. $8\frac{1}{8}$ in. by $10\frac{3}{4}$ in.
f. $4\frac{1}{4}$ in. by $7\frac{1}{2}$ in.

4. *On a scale drawing where ⅛ in. = 50 miles, what distance does each of the following represent?*

a. $\frac{1}{4}$ in. .... mi.
b. $\frac{3}{8}$ in. .... mi.
c. $3\frac{1}{8}$ in. .... mi.

d. $2\frac{5}{8}$ in. .... mi.
e. $6\frac{1}{16}$ in. .... mi.
f. $5\frac{1}{8}$ in. .... mi.

5. a. Two cities are $3\frac{3}{4}$ in. apart on a map drawn to a scale of 1 in. = 40 mi. What is the distance in miles between the cities?

b. The scale of miles on a map is 1 in. = 50 miles. How long a line will have to be drawn on the map to show a distance of 1000 miles?

c. A house plan is drawn using the scale ¼ in. = 1 ft. In the plan the living room is 7 inches long; what is the actual length of the room?

Using Scale Drawings

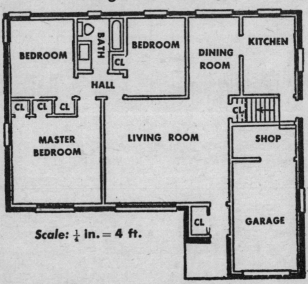

Scale: ¼ in. = 4 ft.

1. Read the floor plan shown on page 156.

   a. What are the dimensions of the master bedroom not including closets or entryway?
   b. How large is the living room?
   c. What are the dimensions of the garage?
   d. What is the measurement from side to side of the house?
   e. What is the measurement from front to back of the house?

Finding the Scale

What is the scale of a drawing if a line 2 inches long on the drawing represents 4 feet on the original object?

HOW TO DO THE EXAMPLE

A length of 4 feet is represented by 2 inches. To find out how many feet are represented by 1 inch, *divide* the actual measurement by the reduced measurement.

$$\frac{\text{actual 4 ft.}}{\text{reduced 2 in.}} = \frac{2 \text{ft.}}{1 \text{ in.}} \quad 1 \text{ inch} = 2 \text{ feet is the scale used.}$$

What is the scale of a drawing if a line $2\frac{1}{2}$ inches long on the drawing represents 25 feet on the original object?

HOW TO DO THE EXAMPLE

$2\frac{1}{2}$ inches $= 25$ feet. Therefore: $\dfrac{\text{actual 25 ft.}}{\text{scale } 2\frac{1}{2} \text{ in.}} =$

$$25 \div 2\frac{1}{2} = \frac{25}{1} \div \frac{5}{2} = \frac{25}{1} \times \frac{2}{5} = \frac{10 \text{ ft.}}{1 \text{ in.}}$$

OR $\dfrac{25 \text{ ft.}}{2\frac{1}{2} \text{ in.}} = \dfrac{25 \text{ ft.}}{2.5 \text{ in}} = 2.5\overline{)25.0}^{\,1\,0.} \quad 1 \text{ inch} = 10 \text{ ft. is the scale.}$

EXERCISES
Finding the Scale

1. *In each of the following (page 158) find the scale:*

Actual Length	Scale Drawing		Actual Length	Scale Drawing
a.	3 feet	9 inches	e.	15 miles	3 feet
b.	8 feet	4 inches	f.	24 feet	2.4 inches
c.	6 feet	3 inches	g.	$2\frac{1}{2}$ feet	10 inches
d.	12 miles	4 inches	h.	26 feet	$3\frac{1}{4}$ inches

2. A screwdriver 12 inches long is drawn to a scale of $\frac{1}{2}$. What will be the length of the line in the drawing which represents the length of the screwdriver?

3. A hammer $10\frac{1}{2}$ inches long is drawn to $\frac{1}{4}$ scale. What will be the length of the line in the drawing which represents the length of the hammer?

Scale as Ratio

Sam is six feet tall, while his friend Joe is only four feet tall. Sam is how many times as tall as Joe?

We can answer this question by forming a fraction, with Sam's height as the numerator:

$$\frac{\text{Sam's height} \quad 6 \text{ ft.}}{\text{Joe's height} \quad 4 \text{ ft.}} = \frac{3}{2} = \frac{1\frac{1}{2}}{1}; \text{ Sam is } 1\frac{1}{2} \text{ times as tall.}$$

Sometimes we leave the fraction in the form $\frac{3}{2}$, and say that the *ratio* of Sam's height to Joe's is 3 to 2.

Essentials to Remember

When two quantities of *like measure* are compared by dividing, the fraction formed is called a *ratio*. The ratio $\frac{1\frac{1}{2}}{1}$ is read "$1\frac{1}{2}$ to 1".

Ratios may also be written with a colon (:) in place of the fraction line. The ratio 3 to 2 may be written either $\frac{3}{2}$ or $3:2$.

To find the ratio of one number to a second, form a fraction with the *first number* as *numerator* and the *second* number as *denominator*.

What is the ratio of *size on a drawing* to *actual size*, if 1 inch on the drawing = 2 feet?

HOW TO DO THE EXAMPLE

Form a fraction, with the scale size as numerator:

$$\frac{\text{Size on drawing}}{\text{Actual size}} \quad \frac{1 \text{ inch}}{2 \text{ feet}} = \frac{1 \text{ inch}}{24 \text{ inches}} = \frac{1}{24}$$

The ratio is 1 in. to 24 in. or 1:24, or $\frac{1}{24}$.

Note that this ratio indicates a *reduction* of size, since the fraction is less than 1. The ratio 24:1 would indicate an *enlargement*, 24 times as large as the actual size.

Scale as Ratio and Proportion

Steve received a letter from Jim, who was traveling in Arkansas. In the letter Jim enclosed a snapshot of himself, standing in a cave next to a big limestone stalagmite. Steve wondered how tall this stalagmite was. He knew that the ratio of Jim's actual size to the stalagmite's actual size would equal the ratio of the boy's photographed size to the stalagmite's photographed size.

Steve knew also that Jim was 5'5", or 65" tall. He measured the photograph and found that here Jim was $1\frac{5}{8}$ inches tall. The height of the stalagmite in the photograph was $1\frac{1}{4}$ inches.

Steve wrote these measurements down to form a proportion. A *proportion* is a statement that two ratios are equal.

$$\frac{\text{Jim's ht. in photo } 1\frac{5}{8}''}{\text{Stalagmite's photo ht. } 1\frac{1}{4}''} = \frac{65'' \text{ Jim's actual ht.}}{? \text{ Stalagmite's actual ht.}}$$

If we could change the ratio $\frac{1\frac{5}{8}}{1\frac{1}{4}}$ to an equivalent fraction in which the numerator was 65, we could find the unknown height.

To find what number should be used to multiply both numerator and denominator, *divide* 65 by $1\frac{5}{8}$:

$$65 \div 1\tfrac{5}{8} = 65 \div \tfrac{13}{8} = \tfrac{65}{1} \times \tfrac{8}{13} = 40$$

Then change the known ratio to the equivalent fraction:

$$\frac{1\frac{5}{8}'' \times 40}{1\frac{1}{4}'' \times 40} = \frac{65''}{50''} \begin{array}{l}\text{Jim's actual height}\\\text{Stalagmite's height}\end{array}$$

Therefore, the actual height of the stalagmite is 50″, or 4′2″.

Essentials to Remember

A *proportion* is a statement that two ratios are equal. The proportion $\frac{2}{6} = \frac{1}{3}$ is read, "2 is to 6 as 1 is to 3."

If both ratios in a proportion are inverted, the proportion is still true:

If $\dfrac{1\frac{5}{8}}{1\frac{1}{4}} = \dfrac{65}{50}$ then it is also true that $\dfrac{1\frac{1}{4}}{1\frac{5}{8}} = \dfrac{50}{65}$

In a proportion, the *cross products* are equal. That is, in the proportion $\frac{1}{3} = \frac{2}{6}$, $1 \times 6 = 3 \times 2$. Therefore, when you have found the missing number in a proportion, you may check your answer by cross multiplying.

To find the missing number in a proportion, change the known fraction to an equivalent fraction by multiplying both the numerator and the denominator by the same number. The correct multiplier may be found by *dividing* the known term of the incomplete ratio by the *corresponding* term of the known ratio.

The scale drawing of a rectangle measured 6 inches wide and 8 inches long; find the actual dimensions of the rectangle if the scale shown is 2″ = 1′.

To find the actual dimensions, we must find a proportion.

HOW TO DO THE EXAMPLE

Problem 1. If 2 inches represents 1 foot, 6 inches represents —?—feet.

$$\frac{2}{1} = \frac{6}{?}$$

The problem is simply that of changing a fraction to higher or lower terms.

$$6 \div 2 = 3$$

Then $\frac{2 \times 3}{1 \times 3} = \frac{6}{3}$

Therefore, 6 inches represents 3 feet.   Answer.

Check: $\frac{2}{1} = \frac{6}{3}$

$$2 \times 3 = 1 \times 6$$

Problem 2. Knowing that the scale of the rectangle drawing is $2'' = 1'$, what length does $8''$ represent?

$$\frac{2}{1} = \frac{8}{?}$$

$$8 \div 2 = 4$$

$$\frac{2 \times 4}{1 \times 4} = \frac{8}{4}$$

Therefore, 8 inches represents 4 feet.   Answer.

Check: $\frac{2}{1} = \frac{8}{4}$

$$2 \times 4 = 1 \times 8$$

The dimensions of the original rectangle are $3'$ and $4'$

EXERCISES

Scale as Ratio and Proportion

1. *In each of the following express the scale as a ratio. State whether this is an enlargement or reduction in size of the original object.*

	Actual Length	Scale Drawing		Actual Length	Scale Drawing
a.	1 inch	42 inches	f.	26 inches	1 foot
b.	8 feet	1 foot	g.	$1\frac{1}{2}$ feet	$\frac{1}{2}$ inch
c.	1 foot	1 inch	h.	7.6 inches	76 inches
d.	1 mile	1 foot	i.	$2\frac{1}{2}$ feet	$7\frac{1}{2}$ inches
e.	5 feet	10 feet			

2. What scale would indicate that the scale drawing is the same size as the original object?

3. From this scale draw-
ing of a rectangle, find the
actual dimensions of the
rectangle.

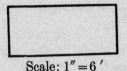

Scale: $1'' = 6'$

4. From this scale drawing
of a triangle, find the actual
dimensions of the triangle.

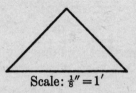

Scale: $\frac{1}{8}'' = 1'$

5. A rectangular picture 2 inches long and $1\frac{1}{8}$ inches wide is to be enlarged so that the width will be 8 inches. Find the length of the enlargement.

6. A rectangular picture 9 in. wide by $10\frac{1}{2}$ ins. long is to be reduced in size so that its width will be $4\frac{1}{2}$ inches. Find the length of the reduced picture.

7. The scale of drawing of a map is 1 inch = 80 miles. Find the distance between two cities $8\frac{1}{2}$ inches apart.

8. In a scale drawing, the scale is $\frac{1}{4}$ foot = 1 mile. What length on the scale drawing represents 22 miles?

9. In a scale drawing, the scale is 5 inches = 1 foot. What length on the scale drawing represents 20 feet on the object?

10. In a scale drawing, the scale is $\frac{5}{18}$ foot = 1 inch. What length on the scale drawing represents 4 inches on the object?

11. On a map the scale is $\frac{3}{8}$ inch = 1 mile. The distance between two cities on this map is $12\frac{1}{2}$ inches. What is the actual distance between the two cities?

12. In a scale drawing of a rectangle the length is 8 inches and the width is 5 inches. If the scale of drawing is 1 inch = $3\frac{1}{2}$ feet, find the dimensions of the original rectangle.

Finding Distances by Scale Drawings

A man started from point A and walked 3 miles north to B and then 4 miles east to C. Make a scale drawing to find the distance AC.

HOW TO DO THE EXAMPLE

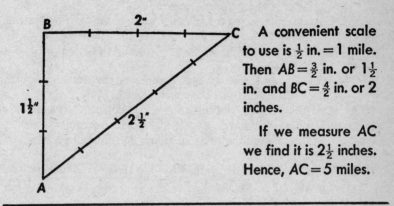

A convenient scale to use is $\frac{1}{2}$ in. = 1 mile. Then $AB = \frac{3}{2}$ in. or $1\frac{1}{2}$ in. and $BC = \frac{4}{2}$ in. or 2 inches.

If we measure AC we find it is $2\frac{1}{2}$ inches. Hence, $AC = 5$ miles.

EXERCISES

Finding Distances by Scale Drawings

1. A ladder 5 feet from a building leans against a wall at a point 20 feet from the ground. Make a scale drawing to find the length of the ladder.

2. A pole 25 feet high is secured with four guy wires fastened to it 12 feet from the ground. These wires are anchored in the ground 9 feet from the bottom of the pole. Make a scale drawing to find the length of each wire.

3. A man started from point A and walked east a distance of 10 miles to B. He then walked south a distance of 24 miles to C. Make a scale drawing to find the distance AC.

GENERAL SKILL EXERCISE

How are you doing? Try the following test. If you get any wrong, turn to the pages shown after each question. Practice those problems until you have mastered them.

1. A diagram of an object that has been reduced in size is called .... (page 154).

2. The comparison in size between the length of a line on the scale drawing and the actual length is known as the .... (page 154).

3. If the scale is $\frac{1}{4}$ in. = 2 ft.; then 1 in. .... ft. (page 154).

4. If the scale on a map is $1'' = 800$ miles, two cities $3\frac{1}{2}''$ apart are .... miles apart (page 154).

5. What is the scale ratio on a map if 1 inch on the map represents 2 feet on the object? .... (page 157).

6. If you draw an object in its complete size, the scale is .... (page 155).

7. The scale $\frac{1}{2}'' = 1'$ means that $\frac{1}{2}$ inch on the drawing equals .... of the object (page 157).

8. A drawing larger than the actual object is called ...... (page 159).

9. Once you have decided on a scale for a problem, you .... (may, may not) use another scale in doing a different part of the same problem (page 155).

10. If $\frac{1}{2}'' = 1'$ on a scale drawing, what are the original dimensions of a rectangle $1\frac{1}{2}''$ by $2''$ on the drawing? .... (page 160).

———— *My Score*

PRINCIPLES TO REMEMBER

1. A large object may be represented by a smaller drawing called a scale drawing.

2. The scale indicates the relation between the length of the lines on the scale drawing and the size of the object.

3. The same scale is used throughout a problem.

4. A scale may indicate an increase or reduction in size.

5. Scale drawings can be used to indicate distances between places on a map.

6. To find the scale of a drawing, divide the actual measurement of an object by its reduced measurement.

7. The comparison of two numbers by division is called a ratio.

8. A proportion is a statement that two ratios are equal.

9. A proportion is correct if the cross products are equal.

MASTERY TEST

1. *What is the scale of drawing if:*
   a. a book 10 inches long is represented by a $2\frac{1}{2}$ inch line?
   b. a postage stamp $\frac{3}{4}$ inch long is represented by a line 3 inches?
   c. a man who is $5'\ 8''$ is represented by a line 4 inches long?
   d. two cities 110 miles apart are separated on a map by a distance of 2 inches?

e. a flower pot 6 inches high is represented by a $\frac{1}{2}$ inch sketch?

2. *Using a convenient measure, draw to scale (state the scale you use for each):*

a. a telephone pole 35 feet high

b. a jet plane 38 feet long

c. a pair of scissors $7\frac{1}{2}$ inches long

d. a whale 13 yards 5 feet long

e. a nail $\frac{3}{8}$ inch long

f. the front of a house 40 feet long, which has a door in the center 80″ high × 36″ wide, a picture window at one side which measures 36″ high × 75″ wide, and two windows at the other side, each of which measures 30″ high by 24″ wide.

3. *Using the scale 1 inch = 5 feet, how many inches would you use to represent:*

a. a dog two feet high

b. a tennis court 36 feet wide by 78 feet long

c. a desk 28 inches high

4. Alice wants to have a photograph enlarged. It is now $3\frac{1}{2}$ inches long by $2\frac{1}{2}$ inches wide. She has asked for an enlargement which will be 6 inches long. What will be the width of the new photograph?

5. Donald's little sister has a doll house with miniature furniture. The miniature dining room table is 2 inches high. The actual dining room table is 30 inches high. If the diameter of a real plate is 10 inches, what will be the diameter of a miniature plate?

6. To go home from work, James walks straight down Main Street for $\frac{1}{2}$ mile, then he turns down Martin Road, which is perpendicular to Main, and walks $\frac{1}{4}$ mile. By making a scale drawing, find out how much distance James would save if he could follow a straight route from the factory to his home.

7. In an unabridged dictionary scale drawings often appear. Below each is a fraction or a whole number which indicates the size of the drawing in relation to its actual size. Measure the height of each of the following pictures and find the actual height.

$\frac{1}{4}$
$\frac{3}{8}$
$\frac{1}{35}$

7

ARITHMETIC IN BUSINESS

Commission

Mr. Chase works as a salesman in a television shop. Instead of getting a fixed salary, he receives 25% of the income from all the sales he makes.

The amount of money Mr. Chase earns is called his *commission*. The per cent he receives is called the *rate of commission*.

Suppose that during one week Mr. Chase sold $600 worth of merchandise. How much commission does he receive?

Rule to Remember

To find the commission, multiply the sales by the rate of commission.

Sales × Rate of Commission = Commission

HOW TO DO THE EXAMPLE

$$25\% = .25$$

Sales	$600
Rate of Commission	×.25
	3000
	1200
	$150.00 Commission

Let us assume that Mr. Chase was allowed to take his commission from the money the customer pays and return the remainder of the money to his employer. The money Mr. Chase would return is called the employer's *net proceeds*.

Rule to Remember

To find the net proceeds subtract the commission from the amount of sales.

Net proceeds = Sales — commission

HOW TO DO THE EXAMPLE

Sales	$600
Commission	−150
Net Proceeds	$450

A real estate salesman works on a $2\frac{1}{2}\%$ commission. If he sells a house for $12,500 how much commission does he earn?

Essential to Remember

To find $2\frac{1}{2}\%$ of $12,500, first change $2\frac{1}{2}\%$ to $.02\frac{1}{2}$ or .025 and then multiply the selling price by the rate of commission.

HOW TO DO THE EXAMPLE

$12,500
×.02½

6250
25000

$312.50 Commission

or

$12,500
×.025

62500
25000

$312.500 Commission

EXERCISES

Commission

1. *Complete the following:*

Sales	Rate of Commission	Commission
a. $50	$2\frac{1}{2}\%$	....

    b. $175   4½%   ....

    c. $508   6½%   ....

    d. $1200   7¼%   .   ...

2. A broker sold 600 bales of cotton at $15 a bale. His commission is 4% of the total sales. What was his commission?

3. At 18% commission, what amount of commission is earned by selling 32 dozen cards at $1.50 a dozen?

4. Mr. Adams works as an automobile salesman receiving 20% on each car he sells. One week he sold a car for $2350 and a station wagon for $3175. How much commission did he earn?

5. Jane sells Christmas cards. For each box of cards selling at 50 cents she gets 5% commission, and for each box of cards selling at $1 she gets 10% commission. If she sells 3 dozen 50-cent boxes and 2½ dozen $1 boxes how much commission does she earn?

6. A real estate salesman sold a piece of land for $22,500. If he received a 5% commission, how much does he earn from the sale? What were the net proceeds to the owner?

7. Mr. Adams works on a 3½% commission. If he sells $15,000 worth of merchandise, how much commission does he earn?

8. At 4½% commission, how much is earned by selling $19,000 of material?

9. A clerk in a store receives $60 a week and 2% commission on all he sells above $100. One week he sold goods amounting to $522. How much did he earn that week?

10. A farmer shipped to a commission merchant in New York 3,250 bushels of apples. Freight and trucking amounted to $430.50. If the apples were sold at an average of $1.15 a bushel and the commission merchant charged 4% for his services, how much money should he send back to the grower?

Finding the Rate of Commission

Of an $800 sale a salesman received $16 in commission. What rate of commission did he earn?

In this type of problem we are to find what per cent of the sales the commission is.

Essential to Remember

$$\text{Rate of Commission} = \frac{\text{Commission}}{\text{Sales}}$$

[Continued on top of page 169]

To find the rate of commission, make a fraction with the commission as the numerator and the sales as the denominator. Change the fraction to a per cent.

HOW TO DO THE EXAMPLE

$$\text{Rate of Commission} = \frac{\text{Commission } \$16}{\text{Sales } \$800} = \frac{1}{50} = .02 = 2\%$$

EXERCISES
Finding the Rate of Commission

1. *Complete the following:*

Sales	Commission	Rate of Commission
a. $50	$5	....
b. $48	$2.40	....
c. $80	$10	....
d. $152	$25	....
e. $750	$250	....

2. A salesman's commission for selling a car for $2250 is $67.50 What rate of commission is this?

Discount

A discount is an amount of money subtracted from the list or marked price of an object. For example, an auto mechanic bought a tool kit at a sale: the original price of the tool kit was $45 but it had been reduced 20% for the sale. How much did the mechanic pay for the tool kit?

Whenever any article is sold at less than its regular price, it is sold at a *discount*. The price at which the article was originally marked to be sold is called its *marked* or *list price*. The per cent given off the marked price is the *rate of discount*. The amount of money deducted from the marked price, or the amount, is called the *discount*. The price paid after the discount is taken off is the *net price* or *sales price*.

given off the marked price is the *rate of discount*. The amount of money deducted from the marked price, or the amount, is called the *discount*. The price paid after the discount is taken off is the *net price* or *sales price*.

Rule to Remember

Sales Price = Marked Price — Discount

HOW TO DO THE EXAMPLE

1. Find the discount.

$20\% = .20$ $45 Marked Price
            $\times .20$ Rate of Discount
         $9.00 Discount

2. Subtract the discount from the original price.

     $45.00 Marked Price
    —9.00 Discount
    $36.00 Net Price

EXERCISES

Discount

1. *Complete each of the following:*

	Marked Price	Rate of Discount	Discount	Net Price
a.	$19	30%	....	....
b.	$5.50	10%	....	....
c.	$18.75	20%	....	....
d.	$69.50	4%	....	....
e.	$22.98	50%	....	....
f.	$60	$12\frac{1}{2}\%$	....	....
g.	$31.20	$12\frac{1}{2}\%$	....	....
h.	$18	$37\frac{1}{2}\%$	....	....
i.	$31.50	$33\frac{1}{3}\%$	....	....
j.	$60.75	$66\frac{2}{3}\%$	....	....

2. At a sale a radio originally selling for $49.98 is being sold at a discount of 25%. What is the net price of the radio?

3. After using his bicycle for a year, Henry sold it at a discount of $33\frac{1}{3}$%. The bicycle originally cost him $69.99. How much did he receive for the bicycle?

4. Mr. Kane is a salesman in a department store that allows its employees a 15% discount on all merchandise bought in the store. If Mr. Kane buys a suit that is marked $49.95, how much does he pay for the suit?

5. A teacher is allowed a discount of 20% when he buys books. He bought books which were valued at $4.50, $3.00, $5.00 and $1.50. (*a*) How much did he save? (*b*) How much did he pay?

Rate of Discount

Mr. Jones paid $81 for a lawnmower that was marked $90. What rate of discount did he receive?

In this example we have to find what per cent of the marked price the discount is.

Rule to Remember

$$\text{Rate of Discount} = \frac{\text{Discount}}{\text{Marked Price}}$$

Find the discount by subtracting the net price from the original price. Then form a fraction with the discount as the numerator and the original price as the denominator. Change the fraction to a per cent.

HOW TO DO THE EXAMPLE

$90 Original price
−81 Net price
$ 9 Discount

$\dfrac{\text{Discount } \$}{\text{Marked Price } \$}$ $\frac{9}{90} = \frac{1}{10} = 10\%$ Rate of discount

EXERCISES

Finding Rate of Discount

1. *Complete each of the following:*

	Original Price	Net Price	Rate of Discount
a.	$50	$45	....
b.	$25	$19.75	....
c.	$.12	$.08	....
d.	$4	$3.50	....
e.	$16	$2	....
f.	$150	$120	....
g.	$112.50	$110.25	....

2. At a sale, Frank bought a sanding machine which was marked $37.50 reduced to $30. What rate of discount was this?

3. A man buys an electric motor for $54. He was given a discount of 40% from the list price. What was the list price?

4. What rate of discount is being offered on goods which are listed at $72.60 and sell for $60.50?

5. A man buys a watch at a sale. The price tag reads "Original Price $87.92, Sale Price $76.93." What per cent of discount is this?

Interest

Mr. Henry needed $2000 for his business. He went to the bank, which loaned him the money for one year. Mr. Henry agreed to repay the money plus interest at the rate of 7% per year.

When an individual or a business borrows money, he agrees to pay back at the end of a certain period of time the amount of money borrowed plus a per cent of the money in payment for the use of the money.

The amount of money that was borrowed is called the *principal*. The per cent is called the *rate of interest*. The amount paid for the use of the money is called the *interest*. The sum of the principal and the interest which is repaid is called the *amount*. The *time* in interest problems refers to the length of time for which the money is borrowed.

Let us assume that in the above problem Mr. Henry repays the money at the end of the year. How much interest does he pay? What is the amount he repays?

Rule to Remember

Rate × Principal = Annual Interest
Principal + Interest = Amount repaid

HOW TO DO THE EXAMPLE

1. Find the interest by multiplying the rate times the principal.

$$7\% = .07$$

$2000 Principal
× .07 Rate of Interest
————————
$140.00 Interest for 1 year

2. Find the sum of the interest and principal.

$2000 Principal
+ 140 Interest
————————
$2140 Amount repaid

In the above problem the money was borrowed for one year. In many cases, however, the time may be less or more than one year.

Time Less Than One Year

Mr. Adams borrowed $1400 from Mr. James for 6 months at 6%. How much interest does Mr. Adams pay? What amount does he repay?

Rule to Remember

Rate × Principal = Annual Interest
Annual Interest × Time in years = Interest

[Continued on top of page 174]

HOW TO DO THE EXAMPLE

1. Find the interest on the principal for 1 year.
$$6\% = .06$$
$\quad\$1400$ Principal
$\underline{\times .06}$ Rate of Interest
$\quad\$84.00$ Annual Interest

2. Since 6 months is $\frac{1}{2}$ year, take $\frac{1}{2}$ of the annual interest.
$$\frac{1}{2} \times \$84 = \$42 \text{ Interest for } \frac{1}{2} \text{ year}$$

3. Add the interest to the principal to find the amount.
$\quad\$1400$ Principal
$\underline{+\ 42}$ Interest
$\quad\$1442$ Amount repaid

Suppose that Mr. Adams had borrowed $600 for 4 months at $6\frac{1}{2}\%$ interest. How much interest would he have to pay?

HOW TO DO THE EXAMPLE

Step **1.** Find the interest on the principal at $6\frac{1}{2}\%$ for 1 year
$$6\frac{1}{2}\% = .06\frac{1}{2} \text{ or } .065.$$
$\quad\$600$ Principal
$\underline{\times .065}$ Rate of Interest
$\quad3\,000$
$\underline{36\,00}$
$\$39.000$ Interest for 1 year at $2\frac{1}{2}\%$ (Note: The last zero is omitted from the answer)

Step **2.** Since $\dfrac{4 \text{ months}}{12 \text{ months}}$ is $\frac{1}{3}$ of a year, take $\frac{1}{3}$ of the interest for 1 year.
$$\frac{1}{3} \times \$39 = \$13$$
Therefore, the interest at $6\frac{1}{2}\%$ for 4 months $= \$13$

Time More Than One Year

Suppose that Mr. Adams has borrowed $1400 for 2 years at 4% interest. How much interest does he pay?

HOW TO DO THE EXAMPLE

1. Find the interest for 1 year.

$$\begin{array}{r} \$1400 \\ .04 \\ \hline \$56.00 \end{array}$$

2. Multiply the interest for 1 year by the number of years given in the example. In our example we multiply $56 by 2.

$56 \times 2 = \$112$, the interest for 2 years.

Suppose that Mr. Adams has borrowed the money for $3\frac{1}{2}$ years. What will his interest be?

HOW TO DO THE EXAMPLE

1. Find the interest for 1 year. In the above example we found that the interest for 1 year is $56.

2. Multiply the interest by the time given in the example. In our example we multiply the 1 year interest by $3\frac{1}{2}$.

$56 \times 3\frac{1}{2} = \$196$, interest for $3\frac{1}{2}$ years.

Essentials to Remember

In computing interest, a year is counted as 360 days.

EXERCISES
Interest

1. *Find the interest on each of the following for 1 year.*

   a. $300 at 7%
   b. $900 at 5%
   c. $3156 at 8%
   d. $2542 at 6%

   e. $5379 at 4%
   f. $700 at 6%
   g. $425 at 4%

   h. $1735 at 5%
   i. $8525 at 6%
   j. $10,162 at 3%

2. *Find the interest on each of the following:*

	Principal	Rate	Time		Principal	Rate	Time
a.	$400	6%	3 years	e.	$125	4%	90 days
b.	$850	3%	2½ years	f.	$526	6%	60 days
c.	$700	6%	90 days	g.	$895	6%	30 days
d.	$3,500	4%	60 days	h.	$550	3%	90 days

3. *Complete each of the following:*

	Principal	Rate of Interest	Time	Interest	Amount
a.	$400	6%	4 mo.	....	....
b.	$620	5%	3 mo.	....	....
c.	$820	7%	6 mo.	....	....
d.	$1250	6%	8 mo.	....	....
e.	$440	8%	5 mo.	....	....
f.	$1500	4½%	2 yr.	....	....
g.	$4226	5½%	9 mo.	....	....
h.	$5238	6½%	6½ yr.	....	....

4. Mr. James borrowed $750 from a relative for 1 year at 4%. How much interest did he pay?

5. The Crane Company borrowed $13,500 at 6% for 2 years. How much interest did they pay?

6. Mr. Jones borrowed $1600 for one-quarter of a year at 6%. How much interest did he pay?

7. A man borrowed $450 to buy a car. If he paid 6% interest, how much interest did he have to pay back after 6 months?

Mortgages

Mr. Martinez had saved his money for a long time. Finally, he felt that he had enough money to buy a house for himself and his children. The house he wanted to buy cost $16,000. He knew that he could not afford to pay for the house in one lump sum payment. He knew that he would have to pay about $5,000 as a down payment and borrow the rest from a bank.

He went to a bank and the loan officer told him they would give him a *mortgage*. Under the terms of the mortgage, Mr. Martinez, as the *signer*, promises to pay the principal and the interest by a certain date. If the debt is not paid, the property is returned to the *holder*. The borrower pays the principal and the interest in regular installments.

principal and the interest by a certain date. If the debt is not paid, the property is returned to the *holder*. The borrower pays the principal and the interest in regular installments.

A mortgage is another way of borrowing money on interest. The *principal* is the amount borrowed, and the *per cent* is the rate of interest. The money paid to the holder of the mortgage sometimes includes yearly taxes and the cost of fire insurance. Let us work out a mortgage problem.

Mr. Barnes wanted to buy a house that cost $18,000. He paid $10,000 and gave the bank a mortgage on the remainder. By signing the mortgage, Mr. Barnes promised to pay interest at the rate of $6\frac{1}{2}\%$ on the unpaid balance. The date on which the mortgage expires (date of maturity), was 20 years from the time the mortgage was signed. If he paid a total of $3250 interest, what was the total amount that he paid after 20 years?

HOW TO DO THE EXAMPLE

Step 1. Find the principal.	Step 2. Find the amount.
$18,000 Cost	$8,000 Principal
− 10,000 Paid	+ 3,250 Interest
$ 8,000 Borrowed — Principal of mortgage	$11,250 Amount

If Mr. Barnes paid a total of $260 on the principal after the first year, how much interest did he pay the following year?

Step 1. Find the unpaid balance	Step 2.
	$7,740 Unpaid balance
	×.065 Rate of interest
$8,000 Principal	38700
− 260 Paid	46440
$7,740 Unpaid balance	$503.100 Interest paid in second year

EXERCISES

Mortgages

1. Mr. Adams bought a home for $9000. He paid $4500 and mortgaged the remainder. For how much was the house mortgaged?

2. On a mortgage of $8000, Mr. Grant paid $5238 interest over a period of 20 years. What was the total amount paid by the date of maturity?

3. Mr. Stevens was paying off a $6000 mortgage at the rate of 4% interest. After one year the unpaid balance was $5830. How much interest did he pay for the second year?

4. When he signed his mortgage, Mr. Hart agreed to pay $45 monthly for a period of 20 years. The monthly sum included principal and interest. What is the total amount Mr. Hart paid?

5. The bank showed Mr. Carr two plans by which he could pay off his mortgage in equal monthly installments. He could pay off the mortgage in 15 years by monthly installments (including principal and interest) of $47, or he could pay it off in 20 years by monthly installments of $39.50.

    a. How much would Mr. Carr pay each year if he chose the 15-year plan? How much would he pay in all if he chose this plan?

    b. How much would Mr. Carr pay each year if he chose the 20-year plan? How much would he pay in all?

    c. How much more would Mr. Carr pay in all under the more expensive plan? Why might he choose this plan in preference to the other?

    d. Interest was figured at 5%. If it were figured at 5.5%, would the monthly payments have been larger or smaller?

    e. If Mr. Carr had agreed on a plan which required payment in 10 years, would the monthly payments have been larger or smaller? Would the total amount repaid have been larger or smaller?

GENERAL SKILL EXERCISE

How are you doing? Try the following test. If you get any wrong, turn to the pages shown after each question. Practice those problems until you have mastered them.

1. The money earned by a salesman as a per cent of the selling price is called the .... (page 166).

2. The money left after a commission is subtracted is called the .... (page 167).

3. Complete: Sales minus .... equals net proceeds (page 167).

4. A commission of 20% of $150 equals $ .... (page 166).

5. If a boy earns $2 for selling an object for $10, his rate of commission is .... % (page 169).

6. Complete: Rate of Commission = $\dfrac{?}{\text{Sales}}$ (page 169).

7. When we buy an item at a certain per cent off the original price, we say that we have received a .... (page 169).

8. After the discount is subtracted from the marked price, the price you pay is called the .... (page 170).

9. Complete: Sales Price = ? − discount (page 170).

10. Complete: Rate of Discount = $\dfrac{?}{\text{marked price}}$ (page 171).

11. The sum of money paid for the use of money is called .... (page 172).

12. The money borrowed is called the ....(page 172).

13. The rate of interest is expressed as a .... (page 172).

14. The interest on $200 for 1 year at 6% is $ ...... (page 173).

15. The amount repaid on a loan of $200 for 1 year at 6% is .... (page 173).

16. A .... is a legal document by which the signer borrows money for property, agrees to pay the lender the principal plus interest within a given period of time, and gives the lender as security his written promise to turn over to the lender ownership of that property if the debt is not paid (page 176).

My Score ——————

Finding Interest by a Formula

In computing all of the previous interest examples you did the following: you multiplied the principal by the rate of interest and then multiplied the amount obtained by the time in years.

The rule you used in solving the interest problems is

Interest = Principal × Rate × Time

A short way of writing a rule is by means of a formula. A formula is made from a rule by using letters to represent the words or expressions that refer to numbers, and by using symbols to describe the arithmetic operations to be performed. Therefore, writing the above rule as a formula, it becomes

$$I = P \times R \times T \text{ or, it may be written } I = PRT$$

In this formula I stands for *interest*, P for *principal*, R for *rate* and T for *time in years*.

To find interest, using the formula, we replace the letters of the formula with the given numbers, and then perform the arithmetic operations.   Let's do the following problem:

A grocer borrowed $600 for 6 months at 6% interest. How much interest did he have to pay?

HOW TO DO THE EXAMPLE

1. Write the formula: $I = PRT$

2. In place of the P in the formula write $600; in place of the R write .06, and in place of T write $\frac{1}{2}$ since $\frac{6 \text{ months}}{12 \text{ months}} = \frac{1}{2}$ year.

$$I = PRT$$
$$I = 600 \times .06 \times \tfrac{1}{2}$$
$$I = 36 \times \tfrac{1}{2}$$
$$I = \$18$$

The interest is, therefore, $18

Find the interest and the amount to be repaid on $4000 at $7\frac{1}{2}\%$ for 3 years 4 months.

HOW TO DO THE EXAMPLE

$$I = PRT$$

$P = \$4000,$
$R = 7\frac{1}{2}\% = .075$

$I = 4000 \times .075 \times \frac{10}{3}$
$I = 300 \times \frac{10}{3} = \frac{3000}{3} = \$1000 \text{ Interest}$

Amount = Principal + Interest
$\$4000 + \$1000 = \$5000$

The owners of Gino's Pizzeria borrowed $2000 at 7% for 45 days. How much interest do they have to pay?

HOW TO DO THE EXAMPLE

1. Change the number of days to a fraction of the year. In interest problems, a month is usually counted as having 30 days and a year as having 360 days. Therefore, 45 days is $\frac{45}{360}$, which is $\frac{1}{8}$ of a year.

2. Now, place the numbers in the formula I = PRT:

$$P = 2000, R = .03, T = \tfrac{1}{8}$$

$$I = PRT$$

$$I = 2000 \times .03 \times \tfrac{1}{8}$$

$$I = 140 \times \tfrac{1}{8}$$

$$I = \$17.50$$

Gino's, therefore, has to pay $17.50 interest.

EXERCISES

Finding Interest by a Formula

1. *Find the interest on each of the principals for the time and rate of interest given:*

	Principal	Rate of Interest	Time	Interest
a.	$200	7%	$\frac{1}{2}$ year	....
b.	$500	7%	1 year	....
c.	$792	6%	$1\frac{1}{2}$ years	....
d.	$1250	5%	2 years	....
e.	$1625	3%	$2\frac{1}{2}$ years	....
f.	$1800	4%	3 years	....
g.	$2100	4%	$3\frac{1}{2}$ years	....

2. *Find the interest on each of the following:*

	Principal	Rate	Time		Principal	Rate	Time
a.	$400	6%	3 years	f.	$526	2%	60 days
b.	$850	3%	$2\frac{1}{2}$ years	g.	$895	3%	30 days
c.	$700	6%	$\frac{1}{2}$ year	h.	$550	3%	45 days
d.	$3,500	4%	90 days	i.	$1,450	4%	30 days
e.	$125	4%	90 days	j.	$490	3%	60 days

3. Mr. Adams borrowed $250 from a relative for 1 year at 4%. How much interest did he pay?

4. The Acme Company borrowed $3,500 at 6% for 2 years. How much interest did the company pay?

5. Thomas borrowed $250 from his brother for 4 years at 2%. How much interest did he pay? What was the total amount he paid back?

6. Mr. Ellery borrowed $600 at 7% for 90 days. How much interest did he pay?

7. Mr. Kane borrowed $1000 at 6% for one month. How much interest did he pay? What was the total amount he paid back?

8. Mr. Johnson borrowed $500 for 2 years at 7% interest. If he paid the interest in 4 equal payments, how much was each interest payment?

9. A man borrowed $460 for 2 years at 6½%. How much interest did he pay?

10. What is the interest on $600 for 8 months at 7%?

11. Mr. Henry needed money for a short period of time. He borrowed $1200 for 24 days at 4%. How much interest did he pay? How much money did he pay back?

Promissory Note

John Cole wanted to borrow $500 to fix up his house. He went to his friend, Allen King, who agreed to lend him the money. Even though they were friends, Mr. Cole insisted that, in order to protect his friend Allen, he would give him a promissory note and pay him 6% interest.

When the loan was made, the borrower or *maker* (John Cole) made a written promise to pay back the amount of the loan to the *payee* (Allen King) at a given time (90 days). This promise, on page 183, is called a *promissory note*. The amount of money to be paid back ($500) is called the *face* of the note. The date on which the money is to be repaid is called the *date of maturity*.

In this promissory note, the maker is Charles Lamar, the payee is Frank F. Farrell, the face is $1000, and the date of maturity is January 13, 1958.

Ed Allen borrowed $600 from a bank. The bank will give Mr. Allen at the time of the loan the face value of the note, $600, *minus* the interest from the date of the loan up to the day of maturity when the money is to be repaid. Thus, the interest is deducted in advance. This interest is the *bank discount*, and the amount of money the borrower receives after the discount is deducted is called the *proceeds*.

Find the proceeds of Mr. Allen's $600 loan, if the bank discounted his 60-day note at 6%.

HOW TO DO THE EXAMPLE

Step 1. Find the bank discount (which is also the interest.)

P = $600   I = PRT

R = 6% = .06 $I = 600 \times .06 \times \frac{60}{360}$

T = 60 days $I = 36 \times \frac{1}{6} = \$6$

Interest = $6 (bank discount)

Step 2. Subtract the bank discount from the face of the note.

$600   Face
−6   Discount
$594   Proceeds

EXERCISES

Promissory Notes

1. *Find the bank discount and the proceeds for each of the following
promissory notes.*

Face	Rate of Interest	Time
a. $400	6%	1 year
b. $800	5%	6 months
c. $1250	4%	90 days
d. $2200	3%	60 days
e. $3000	$7\frac{1}{2}$%	45 days

2. Mr. Adams borrows $350 for 60 days at 6%. How much is the
bank discount? How much does Mr. Adams receive? How much does
he pay back?

3. The Atomic Manufacturing Co. borrowed $6500 for 7 months
at 6% interest. How much is the bank discount? How much does the
company receive? How much do they pay back?

4. James Harper borrows $1800 for 120 days at $6\frac{1}{2}$% interest.
What is the face of the note? How much interest is paid? What is
the proceeds?

5. $400 is borrowed for $1\frac{1}{2}$ years at 7% interest. How much
interest is paid? What is the proceeds?

6. Mr. Jones needs $900 to buy new farm machinery. The bank
lends him the money at 6% for 180 days. How much does he get?

7. Mr. Clay wants to buy a shoe store. He needs $3000. The bank
lends him the money at 7% for 90 days. How much did the bank
give him?

8. Mrs. Frank wants to open a dress shop. She has $1000 and
needs an additional $700. Her bank agrees to lend her the money
for 120 days at 7% interest. How much money does the bank
give her?

Simple Interest

When a person opens a savings account at a bank, the bank
pays interest to the depositor at regular times on the amount
of money he has on deposit. The interest may be paid yearly—
annual interest; it may be paid every six months—*semi-
annual interest;* it may be paid every three months—*quarterly interest.*

Mr. Adams deposited $600 in a savings account on January 1, 1956. The bank pays 5% interest annually. How much interest is earned by the money in one year?

Rule to Remember

Interest paid on the principal only is simple interest.

HOW TO DO THE EXAMPLE

$$I = PRT$$

P = $600 Amount deposited   I = 600 × .05 × 1

R = 5% = .05 Interest rate   I = $30

T = 1 year

How much money did he have in the bank after he received the interest?

$600 Principal
+ 30 Interest
—————
$630 Amount

Compound Interest

Compound interest is the interest paid on the sum of the principal plus the interest it has already earned. This interest is said to be *compounded*. Most often it is compounded semi-annually. Sometimes it is compounded quarterly, or at another interval of time.

Mr. Charles deposited $480 in his compound interest account on January 1. The bank pays interest at the rate of 6% per year added to the account on June 30 and Dec. 31. If Mr. Charles made no withdrawals or deposits, how much interest did he receive on June 30? How much money did he have in his account after interest was paid on Dec. 31?

Rule to Remember

Compound interest is interest that is added to the principal at regular periods and the new amount draws interest for the next interest period.

HOW TO DO THE EXAMPLE

Step 1. Find the interest on the principal for 1 year.

$$6\% \text{ of } \$500 = .06 \times 500 = \$30.00$$

Step 2. Divide the interest by 2 or multiply by $\frac{1}{2}$ to obtain the interest for $\frac{1}{2}$ year.

$$\$30.00 \times \frac{1}{2} = \$15.00$$

Therefore, the interest on $500 for $\frac{1}{2}$ year at 6% is $15.00.

Step 3. Add the interest to the principal.

$$\begin{array}{ll} \$500.00 & \text{Principal} \\ +15.00 & \text{Interest} \\ \hline \$515.00 & \text{Amount on deposit, June 30.} \end{array}$$

Step 4. Find the interest on the new amount at 6% for $\frac{1}{2}$ year.

$$6\% \times \$515.00 = .06 \times \$515.00 = \$30.90$$
$$\$30.90 \times \frac{1}{2} = \$15.45$$

Step 5. Add the interest to the new amount.

$$\begin{array}{ll} \$515.00 & \text{On deposit, June 30} \\ +15.45 & \text{Interest} \\ \hline \$530.45 & \text{Amount on deposit, December 31.} \end{array}$$

Therefore, at the end of the year, Mr. Charles has $530.45 on deposit.

As you have seen, it takes quite some time to work out a compound interest problem. To avoid this, banks use a compound interest table that gives them the answer quickly.

The table below shows how much $1 will amount to at 3%, 4%, 4½%, 5%, and 6% interest, compounded by periods. Periods are usually figured as ½ year or one year. (All values are rounded to the nearest cent.)

VALUE OF $1 AT COMPOUND INTEREST

Periods	3%	4%	4½%	5%	6%
1	1.03	1.04	1.04	1.05	1.06
2	1.06	1.08	1.09	1.10	1.12
3	1.09	1.12	1.14	1.15	1.19
5	1.15	1.21	1.24	1.27	1.33
10	1.34	1.48	1.55	1.62	1.79
20	1.80	2.19	2.41	2.65	3.20

Mr. Smith deposited $1500 on July 1 in his local bank. The bank pays 6% semi-annually on the whole dollar amounts. What was Mr. Smith's balance on January 1, the following year? He made no deposits or withdrawals. Since his bank compounds interest semi-annually, there are 2 semi-annual periods in one year. Since the interest is 6% for 1 year, take ½ of 6% for each period, or 3%. In the table, opposite 2, under column 3%, is 1.06. Thus, $1 will amount to $1.06; $1500 will amount to

$1500 × 1.06 = $1590.00, Mr. Smith's amount on deposit at the end of the year.

EXERCISES

Compound Interest

1. On January 1 Jane had $284 in her bank account. The bank pays compound interest on June 30 and December 31 at the rate of 2% per year. If she makes no deposits or withdrawals, how much will she have on deposit at the end of the year?

2. If a bank pays interest at the rate of 5% per year, payable twice a year, how much interest is earned a year on a principal of $890?

3. *Complete each of the following:*

Principal	Rate of Interest	Interest Compounded	Amount at End of	Answer
a. $300	4%	Annually	1 year	....
b. $864	5%	June 30, Dec. 31	½ year	....

c.	$1250	3%	June 30, Dec. 31	1 year	....
d.	$2156	$4\frac{1}{2}$%	Annually	2 years	....
e.	$4588	5%	June 30, Dec. 31	1 year	....

4. From the compound interest table on page 187 find, to the nearest cent, what $50 would amount at compound interest for

a. 5 years at 4% compounded semiannually.

b. 5 years at $4\frac{1}{2}$% compounded annually.

c. 20 periods at $4\frac{1}{2}$% for each period.

d. 10 years at 4% compounded semiannually.

e. 40 periods at 3% for each period.

Profit and Loss

Jim Roberts, owned the Now Men's Shop. He bought an item for $2 and sold it for $3. He figured out his profit in this way: "I paid $2 for the item. This was my *cost*. Since my *selling price* was $1 more than it cost, I made a *gain* or *profit* of $1."

From this, it is easy to see that when the selling price is greater than the cost, a profit is made.

Rules to Remember

The selling price equals the sum of the cost of the article and the profit.

Selling Price = Cost + Profit

Sometimes the cost is greater than the selling price. When this is true, there is no profit and the difference between the cost and the selling price is the *loss*.

Loss = Cost − Selling Price

If a lawnmower costs a dealer $80 and he wishes to make 25% of the cost as profit, how much profit does he make? What is the selling price of the lawnmower?

HOW TO DO THE EXAMPLE

1. Take 25% of the cost to find the profit.

   Profit = 25% of $80

   $= \frac{1}{4}$ of $80 = $20 Profit

2. Add profit and cost to find the selling price.

   $80 Cost
   +20 Profit
   $100 Selling price

Therefore, the profit is $20 and the selling price is $100.

A shopkeeper paid $50 for a suit of clothes and sold it at a loss of 10%. What loss did he take? For what price did he sell the suit?

HOW TO DO THE EXAMPLE

1. Loss = 10% of $50   2. Cost $50
   $= \frac{1}{10} \times 50 Loss   −5
   = $5   Selling Price $45

Therefore, the loss is $5 and the selling price is $45.

Finding the Selling Price
When the Overhead Is Known

In order to stay in business, the owner must mark the price of his merchandise so that his margin or markup on each item is sufficient to pay his operating expenses and guarantee him a fair net profit. These operating expenses, sometimes called *overhead,* include rent for the store or building, salaries, light, taxes, freight charges, advertising and many other items.

The overhead must, therefore, be included in finding the selling price. To get the selling price when the overhead is given, we use this rule:

Selling Price = Cost + Overhead + Profit

Charles bought a used bicycle for $10.50. He bought a new tire for $3.50 and he spent $.50 for a can of paint. He planned to make $2.50 profit. What should be the selling price of the bicycle?

HOW TO DO THE EXAMPLE

$10.50	Cost
4.00	Overhead
2.50	Profit
$17.00	Selling Price

Finding Profit

Mr. Johnson bought a defective television set for $48.00. He spent $32.50 on parts for repairing the set, and he sold it for $100. How much profit did he make?

Rule to Remember

Selling Price − (Cost + Overhead) = Profit

HOW TO DO THE EXAMPLE

1.
$48.00	Cost
+32.50	Overhead
$80.50	Cost + overhead

2.
$100.00	Selling Price
−80.50	Cost + overhead
$ 19.50	Profit

Rule for Finding Overhead

Overhead = Selling Price − (Cost + Profit)

EXERCISES

Finding Selling Price When Overhead Is Known

1. *Complete the following table:*

	Cost	Overhead	Profit	Selling Price
a.	$120	10% of cost	$15	?
b.	$300	$40	20% of cost	?
c.	$500	$60	?	$700
d.	$1200	?	25% of cost	$1700
e.	$2400	15% of cost	10% of cost	?

2. A merchant buys rugs at $110. Freight charges are $6. At what price must he sell these rugs in order to make a profit of $33\frac{1}{3}\%$ of their total cost?

3. A suit that costs $30 was sold for $38. The merchant estimates the overhead at 30% of the cost. Was the suit sold at a profit or loss? How much was the profit or loss?

4. A man bought a car for $200. He bought new tires which cost him 30% of the cost. If he wants to make a profit of $50, what must the selling price of the car be?

5. A couch, which cost the dealer $280, was damaged in the dealer's shop. In order to sell it, he had to mark it at 40% off his cost price. What was the selling price of the couch?

6. A grocer bought merchandise for $150 which he sold at a profit of 100%. How much did he receive for the merchandise?

Expressing Profit or Loss as a Per Cent of Cost

Very often businessmen would like to find what per cent of the cost the profit or the loss is. Let us see how it is done.

Mr. Jones bought a desk for $20 and sold it for $25. Find the profit and the per cent of profit based on the cost.

Rule to Remember

$$\text{Rate of Profit} = \frac{\text{Profit}}{\text{Cost}} = \dots\dots\%$$

HOW TO DO THE EXAMPLE

$$\begin{array}{rl} \$25 & \text{Selling Price} \\ -20 & \text{Cost} \\ \hline \$\ 5 & \text{Profit} \end{array}$$

Comparing the profit with the cost, we say that the

Rate of Profit $= \frac{\$\ 5\ \text{Profit}}{\$20\ \text{Cost}} = \frac{1}{4} = 25\%$

Therefore, the profit is 25% of the cost.

EXERCISES
Expressing Profit or Loss as a Per Cent of Cost

1. *Complete the following table:*

	Cost	Rate	Loss	Profit	Selling Price
a.	$150	?		?	$175
b.	$300	?	?		$250
c.	$535	?	$15		?
d.	$17.50	?		$2.50	?
e.	$324	?	$45		?
f.	$1680	?	?		$1500

2. A man bought a car for $175. He spent $50 for repairs. If he sold the car for $250, what per cent of the total cost did he gain?

3. Henry bought 15 dozen eggs for $4.50 and sold them at $.42 per dozen. He spent $.55 for carfare while selling them and $.25 for

boxes and paper. (*a*) What was his profit? (*b*) What was the per cent of profit on the cost?

4. A sofa which cost $200 was sold for $175. What was the per cent of loss?

Assets and Liabilities

In order to earn money for a local fund drive, five women decided to bake and sell cookies. They borrowed $50.00 to begin their business. A friend gave them 10 cookie tins, worth $1.98 each, and from the $50.00 the women spent $18.00 for flour, milk, sugar and other ingredients.

The women made 50 dozen cookies, and the first day they began to sell them at 10 cookies for 50¢. They sold 180 cookies and received $9.00.

At the end of the first day, the women wanted to find the *net worth* of their business; that is, they wanted to know exactly how much their business was worth. First they listed their *liabilities*. A liability is a debt, or money owed. Their only debt was the $50.00 they borrowed.

Next they listed their *assets*. An asset is anything owned, including money and supplies. The women listed these assets and added them:

```
$19.80 ten cookie tins @ $1.98
 12.00 ingredients (2/3rds of the original ingredients
          were left)
 32.00 cash (remainder of $50.00)
  9.00 cash (from sale of cookies)
  6.40 cost of cookies not sold
$79.20 total assets
```

Net worth = assets − liabilities. Therefore, the women subtracted:

```
$ 79.20 assets
−50.00 liabilities
$ 29.20 net worth
```

EXERCISES
Assets and Liabilities

1. *For each of the following, compute the total assets and the total liabilities, find the net worth of the business, and state whether or not the business is solvent.*

a. assets	liabilities	b. assets	liabilities	c. assets	liabilities
$1258.00	$625.30	$49.00	$82.40	$524.92	$724.00
297.97	850.10	42.87	100.00	620.00	68.98
322.00	50.00	2.98	9.98	1903.23	94.20
83.39		90.90		602.88	
107.02					

2. John and Jane began a business selling second-hand books at school. They borrowed $35 from John's parents to help them begin their business, and they bought 20 used text books for a total of $29.50, a metal stand for the books for $3.75, 2 erasers at 5¢ each and a roll of scotch tape for 25¢. They received a bill from the school for $5 for a license to sell books on school grounds.

At the end of one week John and Jane had received $7.20 for four books, which had cost them $4.35.

What were their assets at the end of the first week? What were their liabilities? Was their business solvent?

3. Jim was business manager of the school newspaper. For one issue, Jim recorded that 367 copies of the paper were sold at 10¢ each, and $42.90 was received from advertisements. As business manager, Jim received a bill from the printer for $78.00. If the newspaper had on hand $89.20, what was its net worth?

4. Mrs. Rogers had a cake booth at the county fair. She borrowed $40 to begin the business. She paid $15 for a license to sell, $10.80 for ingredients for the 12 cakes, $3.98 for a chair behind the counter, and $3.20 for paper plates, forks and napkins.

Mrs. Rogers cut each cake into 8 pieces and sold each piece for $.20.

On the first day she sold $2\frac{3}{4}$ cakes. On the second day there was a severe wind and rain storm, the stand was overthrown, all the remaining cakes were ruined and the paper plates, forks and napkins were spoiled.

What were Mrs. Roger's assets? What are her liabilities? Was the business solvent?

Investing in a Business

Richard and five of his friends decided to go into business together. They wanted to make and sell wooden tables and bookcases. When they had figured the expenses of wood, hammers, nails, shellac and other items, they decided that they would need $1000 with which to begin.

To raise the money, the men decided to form a corporation and sell 2000 *shares of stock* at $.50 each. Each person who bought a share became a *shareholder* or *stockholder*, which made him a part owner in the business. The price of each share, $.50, was the *par value* of the stock, and the $1000 which the men had after all the shares were sold was the *capital*.

The business was named the Woodshop Company. It held its first stockholders' meeting, and the stockholders elected the six men *directors* of the corporation. As directors, they would manage the corporation, declare dividends, and decide how dividends would be distributed.

Dividends are profits of the corporation divided among the stockholders. The stockholders who own *preferred* stock receive a given amount, usually a certain per cent of par value, each time dividends are given. The dividends paid to the holders of *common* stock vary with the profits that the corporation makes. Thus, owners of preferred stock are always paid their dividends first. The remainder of the profits, whether more or less per share than the amount paid to the preferred stock owners, is divided among the holders of common stock.

The annual *yield* of a stock is the annual income (from dividends) divided by the cost. Thus, if Mr. Jade bought 200 shares of common stock of the Woodshop Company at $.50 each and received dividends of $7.75 in June and $4.25 in January, he would figure his yield in this way:

$$\begin{array}{r} \$\ 7.75 \\ +\ 4.25 \\ \hline \$12.00 \end{array}$$

$$\text{Yield} = \frac{12.00 \text{ Annual income}}{\$100 \text{ Cost}} \times 100, \text{ or } 12\% \text{ Yield}$$

The directors of the Woodshop Company decided to issue dividends semiannually. After the company had been in existence for six months, the treasurer submitted the following

report, and from this report the directors computed the
dividends to be paid.

Treasurer's Report on the Woodshop Company

Receipts:		Capital: $1000	
20 tables @ $30	$ 600		
14 tables @ $50	700	Expenses:	
25 bookcases @ $40	1000	Wages—330 hrs.	
18 bookcases @ $60	1080	@ $3.00	$990
	$3380	Materials	$537

EXERCISES

Investing in a Business

Using the table above, answer these questions.

1. Find the profit of the Woodshop Company.

2. If the company paid dividends of 6% of par value to holders
of preferred stock, and if each share of stock cost $.50, how much did
a holder of 150 shares of preferred stock receive when dividends
were paid?

3. If 800 of the shares were preferred stock and the company
paid a dividend of 6% semiannually, how much did the company
pay to holders of preferred stock at the end of six months?

4. The company decided to keep $500 as capital to cover future
expenses. Find the amount that would be divided among the common
stockholders after dividends on preferred stock had been paid.

5. 1200 shares of the stock were common stock. How much
in dividends would a man receive who owned 35 shares of
common stock?

6. Mr. Pitt bought 35 shares of common stock. If his dividend
after the next six months was the same as his dividend after the first
six months what would be Mr. Pitt's annual yield? Express as
per cent.

7. Mr. Brewer owned 20 shares of preferred stock. What was his
per cent annual yield?

Buying Stocks

Large corporations issue many hundreds, and often many
thousands, of shares of stocks. Thousands of shares are bought

and sold every day. The buying and selling transactions take place at a *stock exchange*. The two largest exchanges are the New York Stock Exchange and the American Stock Exchange. The person who handles the orders for buying and selling is called a *broker*, and the fee or commission that he charges for this service is *brokerage*.

There are two kinds of stock: *common* and *preferred*. Those who own common stock receive a dividend (payment) that varies as the profits of the company vary. Those who own preferred stock expect to receive a fixed dividend each year, regardless of the amount of profit that the company makes. When the company issues dividends, those who own preferred stock are paid first. The remaining profits are then divided among the holders of common stock.

A government agency, the Securities and Exchange Commission (SEC), supervises the sale and purchase of stocks to prevent the sale of worthless stock.

Every day in many daily newspapers the selling price or *market value* of the stocks of large corporations are published. The following table indicates the market value of certain stocks on January 31.

	Open	High	Low	Close	Net Change
American Motors	$5\frac{5}{8}$	$5\frac{7}{8}$	$5\frac{5}{8}$	$5\frac{7}{8}$	$+\frac{1}{4}$
American Telephone and Telegraph	$177\frac{3}{8}$	$177\frac{3}{8}$	$176\frac{1}{2}$	$176\frac{3}{4}$	$-\frac{5}{8}$
Chrysler	66	$67\frac{1}{4}$	$65\frac{1}{2}$	$65\frac{1}{2}$	$-\frac{1}{2}$
Coca Cola	$105\frac{1}{2}$	$105\frac{1}{2}$	$104\frac{1}{2}$	$104\frac{1}{2}$	-1
Eversharp	$15\frac{5}{8}$	$15\frac{3}{4}$	$15\frac{5}{8}$	$15\frac{5}{8}$	$-\frac{1}{8}$
Food Fair	$39\frac{1}{8}$	$39\frac{1}{8}$	39	39	$-\frac{1}{8}$

After American Motors, we see in the first column $5\frac{5}{8}$. This means that on January 31 the opening price of one share of American Motors was $\$5\frac{5}{8}$. The highest market value (see next column) of American Motors stock that day was $\$5\frac{7}{8}$. The lowest value was $\$5\frac{5}{8}$. At the closing of the transactions of the day, the stock sold at $\$5\frac{7}{8}$. The last column is headed, "Net Change." This figure compares the closing price on the day reported with the closing price on the day before. American

Motors' change was $+\frac{1}{4}$. Therefore, the market value rose $\$\frac{1}{4}$ since the last sale on the day before. If the closing price on January 31 was $\$5\frac{7}{8}$, then the closing price on January 30 must have been $\$5\frac{7}{8}-\frac{1}{4}$, or $\$5\frac{5}{8}$.

EXERCISES

Buying Stocks

Use the stock quotation table on page 197 to answer the following questions.

1. What was the highest price that one share of American Telephone and Telegraph reached on January 31?

2. What was the closing price of Eversharp on January 30?

3. In which of the companies listed was there the largest change between the closing price of January 30 and the closing price of January 31?

4. *a.* Mr. Miller bought 100 shares of Coca Cola at the lowest market value on January 31. How much did he pay for the stock?

   b. In addition to the cost of the stock, Mr. Miller paid $.35 per share for a brokerage fee. How much did he pay in all?

5. How much did Mrs. Wilson pay for 50 shares of American Motors if she bought them at the closing price on January 30?

6. Mr. Frank bought 100 shares of Food Fair at the lowest market value on January 31. Mr. Stevens bought 100 shares of Food Fair at the closing price on January 30. Who paid more? How much more?

7. Mr. Lipe bought 100 shares of Eversharp at its lowest price on January 31.

   a. What is the lowest price at which he could have bought the stock?

   b. If he paid a brokerage fee of $.15 per share, how much did the stocks cost him?

8. Which of the companies listed had the greatest change in market value on January 31?

Bonds

Sometimes the federal government, a city, town, village, a large business or a corporation wants to borrow money rather than share its business by selling stocks. Then the organization will issue bonds.

A *bond* is a kind of promissory note by which a business or organization promises to repay to the *bondholder* a certain sum of money at a given time and at a given rate of interest. The length of this time is usually from 10 to 30 years. The principal, called the *face value* or *par value*, is usually $1000 or more, with the exception of the United States Savings Bonds.

The United States Savings Bond is an investment in the government of the United States. If a man invests $18.75, for example, in 1967, he will receive $25 in 1977. The difference between $25 and $18.75 ($6.25) is interest. The value of the bond in 1977 is the *maturity value*.

These are the United States Savings Bonds of Series E:

$18.75 bond matures to $28.10 in ten years.

$37.50 bond matures to $56.25 in ten years.

$75.00 bond matures to $112.50 in ten years.

$375.00 bond matures to $562.50 in ten years.

$750.00 bond matures to $1111.25 in ten years.

Sometimes the bondholder needs the money he has invested before the date of maturity. Then he may *redeem* the bond, receive the money he invested and still receive some interest on it.

Mr. Jansen bought a $50 U.S. Savings Bond issued at $37.50. In ten years it matured. How much interest did he receive? What average annual per cent interest on his money did he receive?

HOW TO DO THE EXAMPLE

$56.25 maturity value
$- 37.50$ issue price
$\overline{\$18.75}$ interest

$$\frac{\text{interest received}}{\text{money invested}} \quad \frac{18.75}{37.50} = \frac{5}{1} = 50\% \text{ total interest}$$

$50\% \div 10 \text{ years} = 5\%$ annual rate of simple interest

Buying and Selling Bonds

Many corporations issue bonds for a similar reason and in a similar way. These bonds, however, do not have a fixed price at which they are issued. The *quoted price*, or the price at which the bond may be bought or sold, varies with the prosperity of the business. The quotation is in terms of a face value of $1000.

Thus, if a $1000 bond is quoted at 96, the selling price of the bond is 96% of the face value, or $960. If the bond is quoted at 106, the selling price is 106% of $1000, or $1060.

Bonds usually pay interest semiannually. There are coupons attached to the bond for this purpose, each of which bears a date on which a payment of interest is due. When that date arrives, the bondholder tears off the coupon and presents it to the company for payment.

Written on the coupon also is the value of the coupon. The value of coupons for one year is the interest for that year; the rate of interest paid on the bond is called the *coupon rate*.

Therefore, if a $1000 bond has a coupon rate of 4% and pays interest semiannually, each coupon will be worth 2% of $1000, or $20.

The *rate of return*, or the *current yield* of the bond is the per-cent of the total cost that the bond earns in interest each year.

Mr. Darrow bought a $1000 bond quoted at 93 and paying 4% interest, payable semiannually. He paid $5 for a brokerage fee. What was the quoted price of the bond, the value of each coupon, and the rate of return?

Rule to Remember

$$\text{Rate of return} = \frac{\text{Annual income}}{\text{Total cost}} = \text{........}\%$$

HOW TO DO THE EXAMPLE

1. What was the quoted price of the bond?
   93% of $1000 = $930 quoted price

[Continued on top of page 201]

2. Find the value of each coupon.

The annual coupon rate is 4%.
4% ÷ 2 = 2% of face value paid semiannually
2% of $1000 = $20 value of each coupon

3. What is the rate of return?

$930 price of bond
+ 5 brokerage fee
‾‾‾‾‾‾
$935 total cost

4% of $1000 = $40 annual income

$$\frac{\$40}{\$935} = .0428 = 4.28\% \text{ rate of return}$$

EXERCISES

Buying and Selling Bonds

Where necessary, refer to table of U.S. Savings Bonds on page 199

1. Sally saved her money to buy a $25 United States Savings Bond
   a. If she saved $5 each week, how soon could she buy the bond?
   b. When the bond matured, how much did Sally receive?
   c. What amount of the maturity value was interest?
   d. What is the average annual rate of interest that Sally received?

2. Ronald bought a $50 U.S. Savings Bond. After six years he redeemed the bond, and received $42.00.
   a. How much more than Ronald paid did he receive?
   b. What total rate of return did he receive for the money he invested?
   c. What was the average annual rate of interest?

3. What is the maturity value of a U.S. Savings Bond issued at $375? at $750?

4. On January 31, 1971, the American Tobacco Company issued $1000 bonds at 3%, quoted at 96½, and maturing in 1976. Mr. Rourke bought one bond and paid a brokerage fee of $5.
   a. In how many years would the bond mature?
   b. What was the market value of the bond?
   c. Interest was given semiannually. What was the value of each coupon?

d. What was the rate of return?

e. What amount did Mr. Rourke receive in interest by the date of maturity?

5. Disregarding brokerage, find the cost of:

   a. two $1000 bonds quoted at 103½

   b. five $1000 bonds quoted at 89¼

   c. three $1000 bonds quoted at 111⅛

   d. two $1000 bonds quoted at 98½

   e. five $1000 bonds quoted at 100

Taxation

It costs money to run a government, and to provide services for the people. Some of the services are national and are paid for through *federal taxes*. Others are paid for through *state taxes*, and others through *local taxes*.

Federal Taxes

Our federal government receives its money from two general sources: *internal revenue*, or taxes on items within the country, and *customs revenues* or *duties*, which are taxes on items brought here from other countries. In one year our federal government collected more than 75 billion dollars from internal revenue alone, five-eighths of which was from taxes on income.

Federal income tax is placed on the incomes of individual persons and of corporations. Any citizen who receives more than a certain income in one year must file a record of his income with the government. The total amount of income received during that year is his *gross income*. The amount of income on which he pays tax depends upon his *exemptions*, which will vary with the number of persons he supports, physical disabilities, age and several other conditions. The tax rate on taxable income depends chiefly on the amount of that income.

Income Tax

Mr. Lynd, who is married and has a child, last year had an income of $8520. He was allowed by law $600 for each exemption, including himself, and he spent $982 on charity, business entertainment expenses and other deductible items. What was Mr. Lynd's income tax if the rate on his income was $800 plus 22% of taxable income over $4000?

Rule to Remember

Taxable income = gross income — deductions

HOW TO DO THE EXAMPLE

Step 1 a. Find the amount deductible for exemptions

```
  $600 For each exemption
×    3 Exemptions
$1800 Amount of exemptions
```

b. Add the deductions to the amount of exemptions

```
  $1800
  + 982
  $2782 Total deductions
```

c. Subtract deductions from gross income

```
  $8520 Gross income
—  2782 Deductions
  $5738 Taxable income
```

Step 2 a. Since Mr. Lynd pays $800 plus 22% of income over $4000, we must find the amount of taxable income over $4000.

```
  $5738 Taxable income
—  4000
  $1738 Taxable income over $4000
```

b. Take 22% of taxable income over $4000

```
  $1738
  ×  .22
  34 76
  347 6
  $382.36  =  22% of taxable income
                   over $4000
```

c. Find the total tax payable.

```
  $382.36
   800.00
  $1182.36 Income tax payable
```

Other Federal Taxes

In a jewelry store Mrs. Johns bought a necklace that was marked $3.98 plus 10% federal tax. How much did Mrs. Johns pay for the necklace?

$3.98 × .10 = $.398 = $.40 federal tax

$3.98
+.40
_____
$4.38 Total price of necklace

EXERCISES

Taxes

1. Mr. Roberts is not married and has no dependents. He makes $8850 each year. His total deductions one year amounted to $929. The tax rate on his taxable income was $1240 plus 22% of any excess taxable income over $7000. Find the amount of Mr. Roberts' income tax.

2. Mr. Anderson works in the same plant as Mr. Roberts, and he also makes $8850 each year. He is married but has no children. In addition to the $600 allowed for each exemption, he deducted $890. On his taxable income he paid $700 plus 22% on the excess over $6000. How much did Mr. Anderson pay to the federal government for income tax?

3. In the problems above, Mr. Anderson's exemption put him in a lower income bracket than Mr. Roberts' bracket. How much more income tax was paid by Mr. Roberts than by Mr. Anderson?

4. Mrs. Hart received a telephone bill for $8.38. This amount included a 10% federal tax. How much did she pay for federal tax?

5. Mr. Gerard bought a cigarette lighter marked $4.50 plus 10% federal tax. How much did he pay for the lighter?

City and Town Taxes

Each year towns and cities have to raise large amounts of money to maintain public services and to pay the salaries of public employees and officials. The estimate of the amount of money that will be required to run the city is known as the city *budget*. A large part of the required money is raised by levying a tax on real property or real estate, which includes land and buildings. Certain town officials, called *assessors*, examine and fix the value of all the property to be taxed. This value placed on real property is called the *assessed valuation*. For example, suppose the budget of a town is $37,500 and the assessed valuation of all the property in the town is $1,000,000.

The tax rate is determined by dividing $37,500 by $1,000,000 which gives .0375. This means that every property owner must pay a tax of .0375, or 3.75% of the assessed valuation of his property. This rate may also be expressed in other ways:

In cents per dollar — $3\frac{3}{4}$ cents per dollar of assessed valuation.

In dollars per $100 — $3.75 per $100 of assessed valuation.

In dollars per $1000 — $37.50 per $1000 of assessed valuation.

The village of East Valley had to raise $62,500 to run its local government. The assessed value of its real estate was $5,000,000. What is the tax rate per $100?

Rule to Remember

$$\text{Tax Rate} = \frac{\text{Amount to be raised}}{\text{Assessed valuation}} = \dots\dots\%$$

Multiplying $100 by this per cent will give the tax rate per $100

HOW TO DO THE EXAMPLE

$$\text{Rate} = \frac{\text{Amount to be raised}}{\text{Assessed valuation}}$$

$$= \frac{62,500}{5,000,000} = \frac{1}{80} = .0125 = 1\frac{1}{4}\%, \text{ tax rate}$$

$$\$100 \times .0125 = \$1.25 \text{ per } \$100, \text{ tax rate.}$$

David Rose lives in East Valley and owns a house assessed at $4000. What amount does Mr. Rose have to pay in taxes?

Rule to Remember

Taxes = Assessment (expressed in hundreds) × Tax Rate (per $100).

HOW TO DO THE EXAMPLE

$$\frac{4000}{100} = 40 \text{ hundreds}$$

$$40 \times \$1.25 = \$50 \text{ Taxes}$$

EXERCISES

Real Estate Taxes

1. *Find the tax rate on each of the following:*

	Money to be raised	*Assessed value*
a.	$50,000	$1,000,000
b.	$1,500	$95,000
c.	$30,000	$1,500,000
d.	$25,500	$950,000
e.	$35,000	$1,750,000
f.	$275	$45,000
g.	$5,325	$125,000
h.	$360,000,000	$15,000,000,000

2. A man owns a house which is assessed at $15,000. How much does he pay in taxes if the tax rate is 2% of the assessed value?

3. A man owns a lot whose assessed value is $1,200. What is the amount of his tax if he pays $2.50 on $100?

4. The tax rate is $.035 on $1. What is the tax per $1000? per $100?

5. A man owns three pieces of property which are valued at $25,500; $13,500; $60,000. Find the amount of taxes he must pay if the rate is $2.25 on $100.

6. The school budget in a district of which the assessed valuation was $4,500,000 was $90,000. (a) What was the school tax per thousand? (b) If a man's property was assessed at $4,550 how much tax did he pay?

7. The cost of a house is $10,000. The assessed valuation is ¾ of the cost. What is the amount of taxes paid if the tax rate is $2.80 per hundred?

8. A man's property is assessed at $6,500. His tax is $195. (a) What is his tax rate on $100? (b) The estimated expenses of the village for which this tax was raised amount to $7,600. What is the assessed valuation of all the property in the village?

9. A village needs to raise $20,250 on an assessed valuation of $750,000. (a) Find the tax rate per thousand. (b) If Mr. Fox owns two pieces of property assessed at $12,500 and $17,300 find his total tax.

10. A rural school district with an assessed valuation of $940,500 needed to raise $11,286 for its school system. (a) What would be the tax rate per $1,000? (b) The owner of a house in this district valued it at $7,500. The house was assessed at 75% of this value. For how much was it assessed? (c) What was the amount of the school tax on this house?

Insurance

Fire Insurance

Losses resulting from fires in the United States have reached almost one billion dollars a year. Since no one knows when or where a fire will break out, people who rent apartments, own their own home or business purchase a fire insurance policy to protect them against loss or damage resulting from a fire. The insurance purchased involves a contract called a *policy*.

The person taking out the policy is the *insured*, or *policy holder*. The amount for which the property is insured is called the *coverage* or *face of the policy*. The amount of money the policy holder pays for the policy is called the *annual premium*. This annual premium is based on the amount of insurance carried and the *rate* that is being charged for each $100 of insurance. Insurance may also be paid for every three months, or quarterly.

Let us see how the annual premium is figured.

Mr. Johnson insured his house for $9000 at the rate of $.68 per $100. What is his annual premium for this policy?

Rule to Remember

To find the annual premium, multiply the rate per $100 by the number of $100's contained in the face of the policy

$$\text{Annual premium} = \frac{\text{Face of policy}}{\$100} \times \text{Rate per } \$100$$

HOW TO DO THE EXAMPLE

Step 1. Find the number of $100's in the face of the policy.

$$\frac{\$9000}{\$100} = 90$$

Step 2. Multiply 90 by the rate per $100

$$90 \times \$.68 = \$61.20 \text{ Annual premium}$$

EXERCISES

Fire Insurance

1. A man insured his house for $12,000 against fire for 1 year. If the rate is $.48 per $100, find the premium for the year.

2. Mr. Roberts insured his house against fire for $10,500 for 1 year. If the annual rate is $.42 per $100, find the premium for the year.

Complete each of the following:

	Face	Rate per $100	Annual Premium
a.	$4,500	$.25	?
b.	6,200	.32	?
c.	7,000	.38	?
d.	9,500	.41	?
e.	12,500	.46	?
f.	15,800	.49	?
g.	25,000	.62	?
h.	46,000	.75	?
i.	115,000	.90	?

Life Insurance

The main reason a person buys life insurance is to leave his family with money in the event he dies. A person buys only as much insurance as he can pay for. When he buys insurance, he makes an agreement with the company which is clearly stated in his policy. He agrees to make a certain number of payments, called the *premiums*, over a certain period of time. The insurance company, in return for receiving premiums, agrees to pay a specified amount of money at the time of the insured's death or any other agreed upon time. The sum paid by the company is called the *benefit* and the person to whom the benefit is paid is the *beneficiary*.

The four main types of life insurance policies are: *ordinary whole-life policy*, *term policy*, *limited-payment life policy*, and *endowment policy*:

1. Ordinary (Straight) Life Policy

In an *ordinary life policy*, the insured person pays a fixed premium every year of his life. The benefit is paid to the beneficiary at the time of the insured person's death. This policy may be turned in to the company before the insured's death, and the company will pay the insured the *cash surrender value* which is based on the amount of money that has accumulated in his account.

2. Limited Life Payment Policy

The *limited payment life* policy is similar to the ordinary life policy except that the premiums are paid only for a fixed period of time—ten to thirty years. At the end of the premium-paying period the policy is said to be *paid up*. No further premiums are paid and the policyholder is insured for the rest of his life.

3. Endowment Policy

An *endowment policy* requires the payment of premiums for a specified number of years—usually twenty to thirty. If the insured is alive at the end of this time, the face value of the policy will be paid to him. If he dies during this time, the beneficiary receives the full amount of the policy.

4. Term Insurance

In *term insurance*, a person is insured only for a definite and limited number of years, such as five or ten years. The insurance company will pay the benefit only if the insured person dies during this time. When the policy expires, the person must take out a new policy if he wishes to continue his insurance. Premiums on term insurance are very low since the company is liable for only a few years, and there is no cash surrender value if the policy is canceled.

The table below shows three types of policies and the annual premiums from age 20 to age 40.

ORDINARY STRAIGHT LIFE			20-PAYMENT LIFE			20-YEAR ENDOWMENT		
Age	Annually	Semi-Annually	Age	Annually	Semi-Annually	Age	Annually	Semi-Annually
20	17.17	8.76	20	27.06	13.80	20	46.02	23.47
21	17.59	8.97	21	27.57	14.06	21	46.11	23.52
22	18.03	9.19	22	28.08	14.32	22	46.19	23.56
23	18.49	9.43	23	28.61	14.59	23	46.29	23.61
24	18.96	9.67	24	29.15	14.87	24	46.39	23.66
25	19.46	9.92	25	29.71	15.15	25	46.51	23.72
26	19.99	10.19	26	30.30	15.45	26	46.63	23.78
27	20.53	10.47	27	30.89	15.75	27	46.77	23.85
28	21.10	10.76	28	31.49	16.06	28	46.92	23.93
29	21.69	11.06	29	32.12	16.38	29	47.09	24.02
30	22.32	11.38	30	32.76	16.71	30	47.26	24.10
31	22.96	11.71	31	33.43	17.05	31	47.46	24.20
32	23.65	12.06	32	34.12	17.40	32	47.67	24.31
33	24.36	12.42	33	34.83	17.76	33	47.89	24.42
34	25.11	12.81	34	35.56	18.14	34	48.15	24.56
35	25.89	13.20	35	36.31	18.52	35	48.42	24.69
36	26.72	13.63	36	37.09	18.92	36	48.72	24.85
37	27.59	14.07	37	37.89	19.32	37	49.05	25.02
38	28.49	14.53	38	38.73	19.75	38	49.40	25.19
39	29.45	15.02	39	39.61	20.20	39	49.79	25.39
40	30.44	15.52	40	40.51	20.66	40	50.21	25.61

Premiums are based on $1000 of insurance.

EXERCISES

Life Insurance

In the following exercises, refer to the table above.

1. Mr. Smith bought an ordinary life policy for $5000 at the age of 25. What annual premium did he pay? If he paid the premiums semiannually how much did he pay?

2. What is the annual cost of an ordinary life policy for $6000 when taken out at the age of 20 years? What is the annual premium of the policy if bought at age 30 years? What is the semiannual premium if bought at age 40?

3. A 35-year-old man is trying to decide what type of a life insurance policy to purchase. At his age, how much less per year will an

ordinary life policy for $8000 cost him than an $8000 20-payment life policy?

4. A 40-year old man buys a $1000 20-payment life policy. What is the annual premium? If he dies when he is 51 years old, how much will he have paid in premiums?

5. Mr. Johnson bought a $10,000 20-year endowment policy when he was 30 years old. After paying 5 annual premiums, he died. How much more was paid to the beneficiary than Mr. Johnson paid in?

6. Mr. Jones, age 30, took out a 20-year endowment policy for $5000. After paying for 10 years he died. How much would he or his beneficiary have received:

    a. if he had taken an ordinary-life policy?

    b. if he had taken a 20-payment life policy?

Automobile Insurance

In most states in our country, a car owner must have certain forms of insurance before license plates will be issued to him. Car insurance protects the owner against financial loss to himself in case of fire, theft, bodily injury to others and damage to property. The main types of insurance are:

1. *Policies which protect the owner:*
   a. *Comprehensive insurance* will protect the owner against damage caused by malicious mischief.
   b. *Fire insurance* protects the owner from losses suffered when the car is destroyed or damaged by fire.
   c. *Theft insurance* protects the owner when his car is stolen.
   d. *Collision insurance* protects the owner whose car is damaged by collision with another car. Companies limit the cost of repairs to $50 or $100 deductible; that is, they will pay all costs above those sums.
2. *Policies with which you protect others:*
   a. *Bodily injury insurance* protects the owner up to the sum of the policy in case of bodily injury caused by his car.
   b. *Property damage liability insurance* covers the owner or person driving the car against claims for damage done to property by the use of the owner's car.

Suppose your father carries comprehensive insurance on his car, which is insured for $3000. He pays an annual rate of $1.50 per $100. How much is his annual premium?

$$\$3000 \div \$100 = \$30 \times \$1.50 = \$45.00$$

For liability coverage your father carries $10,000 to $20,000 or more insurance. This means that the insurance company will pay $10,000 to each person injured, and up to $20,000 on any accident caused by your father's car. For property damage coverage he pays $30 for $5000.

GENERAL SKILL EXERCISE

How are you doing? Try the following test. If you get any wrong, turn to the pages shown after each question. Practice those problems until you have mastered them.

1. An expression in which a rule is represented by letters and signs is known as a(an) .... (page 178).

2. Complete: I = P × ____ × T (page 178).

3. P above stands for the .... (page 178).

4. In solving interest problems we must know that 60 days represents what fractional part of a year? .... (page 180).

5. The interest on $200 at 6% for 180 days is .... (page 180).

6. The signed paper which is a promise to repay a loan is called a .... (page 182).

7. The day when borrowed money is to be repaid is called the .... (page 182).

8. Interest paid once on deposited money is a type of interest called .... (page 185).

9. Interest paid on principal and interest is known as .... (page 185).

10. Complete: Loss = Cost − .... (page 188).

11. Complete: Selling Price = Cost + Overhead + ... (page 190).

12. Complete: Rate of Profit = $\dfrac{?}{Cost}$ expressed as a per cent (page 191).

13. Complete: Tax Rate $= \dfrac{\text{Amount to be Raised}}{?}$ expressed **as a** per cent (page 205).

14. The amount of money a policy holder pays an insurance company each year is called the .... (page 207).

15. The type of policy which is paid for every year of the policy-holder's life is a (an) .... (page 209).

16. A person who owns stock is a .... (page 195).

17. The .... rate is the rate of interest paid on a bond (page 200).

18. The .... of a bond equals the annual income

19. The taxable income = ... income − deductions (page 203).

20. Insurance which protects a car owner against claims for bodily injury caused by this car is called .... insurance (page 211).

21. The .... price of a bond is the price at which it may be bought or sold (page 199).

22. The .... rate is the rate of interest paid on a bond (page 200).

23. The .... of a bond equals the annual income from the bond divided by the total cost (page 199).

24. Taxable income = ... income − deductions (page 203).

25. Insurance which protects a car owner against claims for bodily injury caused by this car is called .... insurance (page 211).

_____ *My Score*

MASTERY TEST

1. The difference between the total cost and the selling price is the ....

2. A deduction made from a debt, a bill or a price is called a ....

3. The sum to be paid after a discount has been taken off is called ....

4. Money paid for the use of money is called ....

5. The amount left on deposit in a bank is the ....

6. Selling price = ... + ... + ...

7. A written promise to repay borrowed money is called a ....

8. Interest paid in advance on a promissory note is called the ....

9. Protection against loss of money due to fire is called ....

10. Money earned on bank deposits is called ....

11. For a sale, the price of a shirt was dropped from $4 to $3.50. What was the per cent of decrease in the price?

12. A merchant sold hardware for $75, making a profit of $15. What was the per cent of profit on the selling price?

13. The cost of soup to a grocer was 9 cents per can and he sold it for 16 cents per can. If he allowed 25% of the selling price for expenses, what was his profit on each can of soup?

14. A girl sold $24.60 worth of seeds at a $33\frac{1}{3}\%$ commission. How much did she earn?

15. Find the interest on $500 for 3 months at an annual interest rate of 4%.

16. An agent sold 200 boxes of apples at $4 a box and charged a commission of 5%. What was his commission?

17. A canoe marked $150 was sold for $120. What was the rate of discount?

18. For a sale, the price of a suit was reduced from $40 to $35. What was the per cent decrease in the price?

19. If a discount of 20% is given on an article marked $17.50 what is the selling price?

20. A class earned $60 commission from the sale of magazine subscriptions. This amount was a 25% commission on all sales. How many dollars' worth of magazine subscriptions did they sell?

21. What is the simple interest on $460 for 2 years at $2\frac{1}{2}$?

22. If the annual rate for comprehensive insurance is $1.23 per $100, what is the annual cost for $2300? $1950? $2950? $1760?

23. A clerk worked in a store 8 hours a day at the rate of $2 per hour. In addition to his regular pay, he received 2% commission each day on the amount of his sales above $75. During 4 consecutive days, his sales were as follows: first day, $95, second day $178.50, third day $70, fourth day $128.

    a. How much did he receive as regular pay for the 4 days?

    b. How much extra did he earn in commission?

    c. What was his total pay for the 4 days?

24. A savings bank pays 5% interest on its deposits and adds the interest to the depositor's account on June 1 and December 1 of each year. On June 1, 1956, Mr. Adams deposited $300. If he made no withdrawals, how much did Adams have on deposit on December 1, 1957?

25. For a recent school year a school district purchased 24,000 gallons of oil at $.32 per gallon, less a discount of 12½%.
   a. What was the actual cost of the oil per gallon?
   b. During the year it was necessary to burn 22,800 gallons of the oil. How much did the oil cost that was used to heat the building?
   c. What per cent of the oil was used?

26. A salesman worked on a weekly salary of $80 with an added commission of 5% on all sales over $500. If his sales for one week amounted to $1750, what was his total salary for the week?

27. A savings bank pays interest semiannually on its deposits at the rate of 4½% annually. Interest is credited to the depositor's account on January 1 and July 1. On July 1, 1968, H. O. Lathrop deposited $400. He withdrew $75 on July 1, 1969. How much did Lathrop have on deposit on January 1, 1970?

28. Mr. Ames borrowed $2650 for 45 days at 4%. How much is the bank discount? How much does Mr. Ames receive? How much does he pay back?

29. Mr. Tarant bought a home that cost $14,000. He paid $7000 and mortgaged the rest at 4% interest for 20 years.
   a. Find the principal of the mortgage.
   b. What is the average monthly payment on the principal that Mr. Tarant must make?
   c. Mr. Tarant had paid $615 of the principal by the end of the second year. If the interest was taken annually, how much interest did Mr. Tarant pay for the third year?

30. Martha and Lynn decided to make a vegetable garden in their back yard and to sell the vegetables they grew. To begin their business they borrowed $15 from their parents. They bought seeds for $3.50, fertilizer for $1.80, a watering can for $.98, a hoe for $2.98, and a shovel for $3.20. At the end of the season they sold their products and received $7.59 for tomatoes, $6.22 for asparagus, $1.80 for carrots and $1.05 for radishes. What were their liabilities? What were their assets? Was the business solvent? Explain.

8

USING
ARITHMETIC
IN THE HOME

Every household should be run like a business. Then the income, the money earned by the members of the family, can be wisely planned and managed, and not spent without first figuring out if it can be afforded. Every household needs money for food, clothing, rent, doctor bills, education, recreation, taxes, gifts, carfare, and other items. And money will have to be saved in order to meet emergencies that may suddenly come up. A division of probable expenditures, based upon income, is called a *budget*.

In order to set up a budget for any given period of time, a person must

1. Know the approximate income for that period.
2. List necessary living expenses.
3. Plan to have money for insurance, savings and education.
4. Limit the amount to be spent on each item according to income.

The following budget has been suggested for a family of four with an income of $5600 per year.

Food . . . . 18%   Health 3%
Clothing . . . . 10%   Education and recreation 10%
Housing . . . . 15%   Taxes 8%
Expense of   Gifts and contributions 6%
operating house   12%   Savings and insurance 12%
Transportation 6%

Every family should work out its own budget, for the per cents will vary according to income, number of persons in the family and individual needs.

You, too, will find that you can plan your spending and saving more wisely if you budget your allowance or income.

EXERCISES

Budgets

1. Mrs. Smith, with an income of $5900, spends 18% for food. How much does she spend in one year for food? How much does she spend in one month?

2. If Mr. Jones' income is $8800 and he spends $1320 for clothing, what per cent of his budget does he allow for clothing?

3. Alice's mother saves $45 a month from her husband's salary. If this is 12% of his monthly earnings, how much does he earn a month?

4. The Jones' family income was $5600. Of this $1400 was spent for food, $2100 for clothing, $700 for shelter, and $350 for life insurance. The family saved the remainder.
   a. What per cent of the income is each item?
   b. How much of his income was saved?
   c. What per cent of the income was the saving?

5. The Martin family earned $10,000 in one year. Out of these earnings, $3500 was spent for food, $2100 for clothing, $1200 for rent, $350 for life insurance, $180 for gifts and $500 for a vacation. The Martin family put the remainder in a bank.
   a. Total the expenditures and find the net savings.
   b. What per cent of the family's income was saved?
   c. What per cent of the family's income was each of the items?

Keeping Accounts

After a budget has been set up, a record should be kept of all the money received and paid out. Such a record is called a *cash account*. A cash account makes it possible to know how closely the budget has been followed. In addition to its being a record of all money spent, it is a good indication as to whether or not certain items have been estimated correctly in the budget.

Making the Cash Account

A record is kept of the money received, the *receipts*, and of the money spent, the *expenditures*. The cash account is balanced, usually at the end of each month. The sum of all money received should equal the sum of all money spent, plus money left over, which is called *cash on hand*.

Let us study the cash account record kept by Mrs. Allen for the month of April.

RECEIPTS					EXPENDITURES			
April	1	Cash on hand	$76	40	April	1	Savings	$30	00
	2	Salary	450	80			Rent	80	00
	15	Dividends	20	00			Food	160	40
						7	Clothing	62	46
							Gas	4	35
							Electricity	5	70
							Telephone	6	55
						10	Automobile	21	00
						14	Plumbing Repairs	18	50
						15	Taxes	66	80
						20	Gifts	15	00
							Insurance	60	00
							Total	530	76
		Total	547	20			Balance	16	44
May	1	Cash on Hand	16	44					

Note: Cash on hand = Total Receipts − Total Expenditures.

EXERCISES
Keeping Accounts

1. In the following examples, rule paper as on page 218 and make a cash account record. Find the totals and the balance at the end of each month.

    a. September 1. Receipts: cash on hand, $24.65; salary, $359.70. Expenditures: Rent, $62.50; food, $124.60; clothing, $26.50; electricity, $3.40; gas, $2.80; car expense, $18.26; telephone, $4.75; savings, $40.

    b. February 1. Receipts: cash on hand, $18.23; salary $416.28; dividends, $12.25.
    Expenditures: Rent, $70; clothing, $18.25; food, $148; electricity, $4.85; gas, $3.15; car expense, $26; telephone, $5.50; savings, $35.

    c. June 1. Receipts: cash on hand, $22.50; salary, $390.60. Expenditures: Rent, $75; clothing, $33.89; food, $132.46; electricity, $3.69; gas, $2.98; car expense, $12.80; telephone, $5.10; savings, $38.00.

2. John expects to work after school for 4 weeks earning $20 a week. Make a cash account for his monthly receipts and expenditures.
    Receipts: $80
    Expenditures: Bus fares, $2.00; lunches at school, $5.40; entertainment, $3.75 a week; clothing, $10; school expenses, $6.10. Would he have enough money left over to buy an $18.75 bond?

Thrifty Purchasing

A thrifty housewife always tries to save money by buying at sales or in large quantities or during certain seasons when particular foods are abundant. Her careful planning, thoughtful selection and quantity-buying often help balance her budget or increase her cash on hand.

EXERCISES
Thrifty Purchasing

1. Jane's mother bought two 100-pound bags of potatoes in the fall at $2.50 a bag. In the winter the price of potatoes was 6 cents per pound. How much did she save by buying the bags of potatoes in the fall?

2. At a supermarket sale a certain brand of orange juice which ordinarily sells for 20 cents a can is being sold for $2.05 for a case of 12 cans. How much is saved by buying a case?

3. One store is selling canned peas at 3 cans for $1. Another sells the same peas at 30 cents per can. How much is saved on 2 dozen cans if bought at the lower price?

4. Mrs. Caine usually buys soap powder which sells at 36 cents for 1½ pounds. At a sale, she bought 25 pounds for $4.49. What did she save per pound?

5. A certain brand of tomato juice sells at 30 cents for a 46-ounce can and at 12 cents for a 12-ounce can. How much is saved by buying the larger can?

6. Mr. Roberts drives his car over a toll bridge every day on his way to and from work. The toll is either 15¢ for each fare, or $5.00 for a book of fifty tickets. On fifty trips, how much will Mr. Roberts save by buying the book of tickets?

7. Cream comes in three sizes: a quarter-pint for 16¢, a half-pint for 28¢ and a pint for 49¢. Mrs. Willard uses a quarter of a pint a day. She finds that the cream becomes sour if she keeps it in her refrigerator for more than 3 days. What size would be most thrifty for her to purchase? Why?

8. Mr. and Mrs. Walker use 2 ounces of toothpaste each week. They can buy a 2-ounce tube of toothpaste for 47¢, or a 4-ounce tube for 88¢. How much can they save in four weeks by buying the larger size?

Sales Checks

Most places of business give *sales slips* to customers when they make purchases. Since each sales slip indicates what items were bought and how much they cost, the sales slip provides a complete record of all purchases.

When the customer pays his bill, the clerk gives him another kind of slip—a *receipt*.

The receipt is a written statement indicating that a bill has been paid. Usually, the bill is marked "Paid," and is signed by the individual receiving the payment.

I. J. Frank, Inc.
Food Super Market

Phone: HEmpstead 3-1786

Front and Main St.
Hempstead, N. Y.

Oct. 10, 1955__

Sold to: <u>Mrs. John Harris</u>

<u>No. 173 Oak Drive</u>

3 loaves of bread @ 22¢		66
3 cans of corn @ 18¢		54
2 packages Jello		25
5 lb. potatoes @ 6¢		30
10 lb. sugar		90
7 lb. rib roast @ 98¢	6	86
1 lb. bacon		79
Total	10	30

EXERCISES

1. Make out a bill from your butcher to your mother for: 3 lb. rib roast at 90¢ per lb.; 9 lb. chicken at 53¢ per lb.; 4 lb. calves' liver at $1.50 per lb.; 2 lb. frankfurters at 45¢ per lb.; 2½ lb. chopped meat at 39¢ per lb.; 2 lb. lamb chops at 89¢ per lb.

2. Make out a form, show the extensions and total for the following items. Your mother paid cash. Show the receipted bill.

3½ yd. silk @ 79¢ per yd.   4 spools thread @ 9¢ per spool
2 doz. buttons @ 34¢ per doz.   2¼ yd. trimming @ 80¢ per yd.
2 yd. binding at 14¢ per yd.   1 pkg. needles at 28¢ per pkg.

3. Make out bills for these items. Supply all information such as dealer's name, dates of purchases, etc. Make the extensions. The bill was paid in 5 days after purchase. Receipt the bill.

36 math books @ $1.25   38 notebooks @ 36¢
28 history books @ 90¢   4 doz. pencils @ 40¢ per doz.
34 English books @ 95¢   2¼ doz. memo pads at 28¢ per doz.

Writing and Endorsing Checks

Mrs. Rogers bought several items from Kelmer's Department Store in New York City, and she put the items on her charge account. At the end of the month she received a bill for $21.68.

Mrs. Rogers wanted to send the money rather than pay it in person, so she made out a *check*. On the check she wrote the date, the number of the check, the store to which the money was owed, the amount and her signature. Before she tore out the check, she wrote on the stub at the left of it (which would remain in the checkbook) the date, amount of the check, to whom it was paid and the balance of money remaining in her checking account. (See check below.)

When Kelmer's Department Store received the check, a person in charge *endorsed* it and deposited it to the store's account.

To endorse a check means to sign it on the back to show that you received the money. When a check is made out to an individual, then that particular person must endorse the check on the back on the top of the left hand side in exactly the same way that the check is made out to him. (If it is made out to Mrs. Edward R. Rogers, it must be endorsed *Mrs. Edward R. Rogers*. If it is made out to Edna Rogers, it must be so endorsed.)

After she has endorsed the check, she may either cash it (receive money for it) or deposit it to her account in the bank.

How the check shown on the bottom of page 222 would be endorsed by Kelmer's Dept. Store.

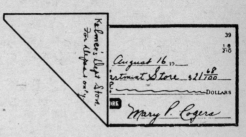

Mrs. Rogers paid the department store with a *personal check*. Once, when she went on a trip to Canada, she used another kind of check: a *traveler's check*.

Traveler's checks are issued by private companies for travelers who do not want to carry large sums of money with them. Wherever persons travel the checks can be spent like cash. They are issued in denominations of $10, $20, $50 and $100. The charge for the checks is $1 per $100.

Traveler's checks may be bought at banks or at express companies. Like personal checks, they must be endorsed. But unlike the personal check, each one is signed by the traveler at the time he buys it. When the traveler wants to cash a check, he signs his name in the presence of the payee in the lower

A TRAVELER'S CHECK

left-hand corner, inserting the date and name of the payee. The payee then compares the two signatures to see that they are alike.

Every traveler's check has a number. If a check is lost or stolen before being endorsed, the owner reports the serial number, and the value of the check is returned to him.

EXERCISES

Checks

1. Why is it better to pay a bill by check rather than by cash?

2. In how many ways is the amount of a personal check written? Why?

3. If a check has erasures on it, why may the bank refuse to pay cash for the check?

4. Suppose that you have $44.30 in your checking account. You have received a bill from Bower's Book Store for $6.96. Draw the proper lines on your paper to represent the check and the stub. Fill in both, making the check payable to the book store. Assume that this is the first check in a new checkbook.

5. The Block family took a trip to New Orleans. Before they left, Mr. Block bought $800 worth of traveler's checks. How much did he pay for the checks?

6. When Mr. Arnold purchased his traveler's checks, he copied the number of each one. Explain why.

7. A hotel manager accepted a traveler's check from a guest at the hotel. Why did he ask the guest to sign the check in his presence?

8. Mr. Lynn paid $606 for traverer's checks. What was the value of the checks?

Installment Buying
("Buying on Time")

Many people buy their cars, refrigerators, washing machines, television sets and other big items like these on installment plans. This means that they do not pay the complete price at once but, instead, they pay only a *down payment* at the time of the purchase. They plan to pay weekly or monthly payments until the total is paid. Meanwhile, they take the article home for use.

Often the people who buy on installment do not realize that they are paying more than marked price. Today, as a result of new law, anyone who buys on the installment must be told what per cent he is paying and how much more he is paying than he would if he were to pay cash. If he purchases an item on the installment plan, a *service charge* or *carrying charge* is added to the marked price. In effect, the person who buys by installment is paying interest for borrowing money.

A used car that is priced at $800 for cash can be purchased on the installment plan for $150 down and $30 each month for 24 months. Find the carrying charge (the difference between the cash price and the installment price.)

HOW TO DO THE EXAMPLE

1.

Down Payment	$150
Installment payments $30×24	+720
Total installment price	$870

2.

Installment Price	$870
Cash Price	−800
	$70

The carrying charge, therefore, is $70

Mr. Smith buys a $200 television set on an 18-month payment plan. He makes a down payment of $50 and will pay a 6% carrying charge on the unpaid balance. How much is each monthly installment?

HOW TO DO THE EXAMPLE

1. Purchase price $200
   Down payment   − 50
   Unpaid balance $150

2. Carrying charge 6% × $150 = $9

3. $150 + $9 = $159 to be repaid

4. The balance is to be repaid in 18 payments. Therefore, we must divide the total by 18.

   $159 ÷ 18 = $8.84 for each monthly installment

EXERCISES
Installment Buying

1. The cash price for a television set is $225. On the installment plan, the set is sold for $80 down plus $15 a month for one year. What is the carrying charge?

2. A company sells deep freezers for $240. On the installment plan, the carrying charge equals $5\frac{1}{2}$% of the selling price. What will a deep freezer cost if it is bought on the installment plan?

3. Janet wants to buy a radio. She likes a radio that sells for $28. On the installment plan, the radio will cost her 25% down plus $3 a week for 7 weeks. If she buys the radio on the installment plan:
   a. how much must she pay down?
   b. what will be the carrying charge?

4. Jim wants a bicycle that will cost $58 on the installment plan. He must pay $18 down and 20% of the balance each month until the bicycle is paid for.
   a. How much money must he pay each month?
   b. How soon will the bicycle be paid for?
   c. If the bicycle sells for $54.20 in cash, what is the per cent carrying charge? (Find to the nearest whole per cent.)

5. Mr. Hart sells electric dishwashers priced at $180. He requires that customers buying on the installment plan pay a carrying charge

of 5% on the unpaid balance, a down payment of ¼ of the price, and 7 equal monthly payments on the balance.

  a. How much down payment is required?

  b. What is the carrying charge on an electric dishwasher bought on the installment plan? What is the selling price?

Electricity in the Home

The electric bill is based upon the amount of electricity used. This amount of electric current is expressed in *watt-hours*. An electric bulb marked 100 watts would use 100 watt-hours of electricity if it were allowed to burn one hour. In ten hours, therefore, a 100-watt bulb would use 10×100 watts or 1000 watt-hours of electricity. 1000 watt-hours equal 1 *kilowatt-hour*, abbreviated K.W.H. or kw.hr.

A 60-watt bulb is kept burning for 100 hours. How many kilowatt-hours of electricity have been consumed?

Rule to Remember

To change watt-hours to kilowatt-hours, divide the number of watt-hours by 1000 by moving the decimal three places to the left.

HOW TO DO THE EXAMPLE

$60 \times 100 = 6000$ watt-hours

$\frac{6000}{1000} = 6$ kilowatt-hours

or 6000 watt-hours $= 6.000$ K.W.H.

EXERCISES

Kilowatt Hours

1. A 75-watt bulb is burned for 20 hours. How many watt-hours of electricity are used? How many kilowatt-hours (kw.hr.)?

2. How many kw.hr. are used by a 60-watt lamp in 10 hours? in 18 hours?

3. Change each of the following watt-hours to kw.hr.

a. 675	*d.* 4,692	*g.* 30,128	*j.* 5,384
b. 2100	*e.* 329	*h.* 7,923	*k.* 926
c. 3520	*f.* 42,986	*i.* 1,115	*l.* 62,134

Reading an Electric Meter

The electric meter measures the amount of electricity used in a building or an apartment. It consists of four dials, whose readings together give the amount of electricity used, expressed in kilowatt-hours.

To read a meter, start with the left dial and read all the dials together as you would read a four figure number. The left dial is read in thousands. This indicates that as the pointer moves from one number to the next, 1000 kw.hr. of electricity have been used. The second dial indicates the number of 100 kw.hr. of electricity; the third, ten, and the fourth, one.

The hands on an electric meter move around the face of the meter in this pattern: first and third move in a counter clockwise direction; the second and fourth move in a clockwise direction.

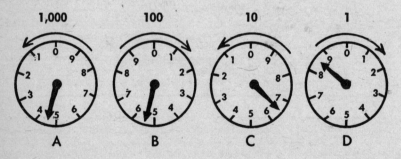

1,000   100   10   1

A   B   C   D

Principles to Remember

Always read the dial number which each hand has *passed;* that is, if the hand is between two numbers, read the *smaller* of the two numbers.

If a hand points between 9 and 0, read 9, since the hand has passed 9.

HOW TO DO THE EXAMPLE

On dial A, the hand is between 4 and 5 so we read the dial as 4.

On dial B, the hand is between 5 and 6 so we read the dial as 5.

On dial C, the hand is between 6 and 7 so we read the dial as 6.

On dial D, the hand is between 8 and 9 so we read the dial as 8.

Therefore, the meter indicates that 4568 kilowatt-hours of electricity have been used.

Paying for Electricity

To compute the electric bills for its customers, the electric company reads the meter each month. The difference between the monthly readings represents the amount of electricity in kilowatt-hours used for the month. This is multiplied by the cost per kilowatt-hour.

The dials for the Jones Co. electric meter shows the following readings on July 31 and on August 30. At the rate of 4 cents a kilowatt-hour, find the electricity cost for August.

July
31

August 30

Rule to Remember

Cost of electricity = Kilowatt-hours used × Cost per Kilowatt-hour.

HOW TO DO THE EXAMPLE

August 30 reading   6532 kw.hr.
July 31 reading   − 4318 kw.hr.
                   2214 kw.hr. of electricity used
                × .04 kw.hr.
                  $88.56 cost of electricity

Electrical Appliance Ratings

Most electrical appliances are rated. That is, a mark on the appliance states the amount of electricity it uses. Here are some appliances and their ratings (the number of watts each uses per hour):

Electric clock . . . . 2 watts   Electric iron . . . . 1000 watts
Toaster . . . . 1250 watts   Table model radio . . . . 30 watts
Vacuum cleaner . . 200 watts   Waffle iron . . . . 660 watts

Referring to this list when necessary, answer the following questions.

EXERCISES

Paying for Electricity

1. How many kw.hr. of electricity does an electric clock use in a 30-day month? At the rate of 4 cents a kw.hr., what is the cost of the electricity needed to run this clock per month?

2. Mr. Smith leaves a 25-watt light burning on the average of 10 hours each night in his store as a safety measure. At the rate of 5 cents a kw.hr., what is the cost of keeping the bulb lit for a 30-day month?

3. Roberta's mother uses the vacuum cleaner for 30 minutes a day for 5 days and for 2 hours on the sixth day. How much does it cost her to use the vacuum cleaner for 5 weeks if electricity in her town costs her $5\frac{1}{2}$ cents a kw.hr.?

4. Mrs. Harris listens to the radio while she irons. She irons twice a week for 3 hours each time. At 5 cents a kw.hr., what is the cost of the electricity used while she does her ironing during a 4-week period?

5. Mrs. Barnes does her ironing on Mondays for $3\frac{1}{2}$ hours and she uses her vacuum cleaner on Tuesdays for 2 hours. If electricity costs 5 cents a kw.hr., how much will she spend in 4 weeks for electricity used for house work?

6. Read the following meters:

a.

b.

c.

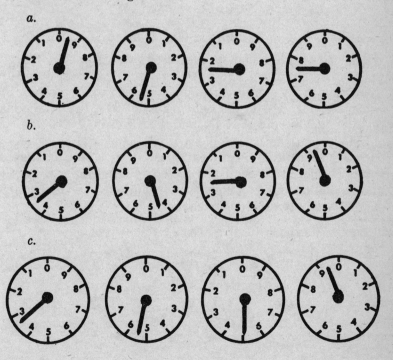

7. Convert the readings on the meters (p. 231) to watt-hours.

8. Figured at a cost of 6 cents per kw.hr., find the cost of electricity for the following meter readings.

March 31

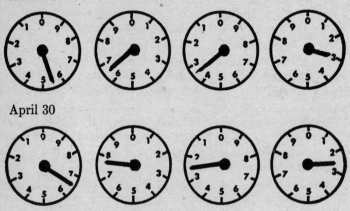

April 30

Reading a Gas Meter

The gas used in a home is measured by a gas meter. The gas meter measures in cubic feet the amount of gas used. There are three dials in a gas meter; reading are taken to the nearest 100 cubic feet. The dial on the right reads in 100's, the middle dial reads in 1,000's, and the left-hand dial reads in 10,000's.

Thus, when the hand on the right hand dial has made a complete revolution, ten times 100 cu. ft. or 1000 cubic feet of gas have passed through the meter. When the hand on the middle dial has made a complete revolution, 10,000 cubic feet of gas have passed through the meter.

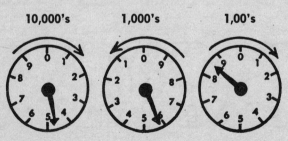

10,000's   1,000's   1,00's

How to Read a Gas Meter

To read the gas meter shown on the bottom of page 232, start at the left dial and read as you would read a five-place number. When the hand is between two numbers, always read the lower. The dials read:

$$40,000$$
$$5,000$$
$$\underline{800}$$

Adding these numbers, we find that the meter reads 45,800 cu. ft.

EXERCISES

Reading a Gas Meter

1. *Read the following gas meters:*

   a.

   b.

2. *Draw gas meters to show the following meter readings:*

a. 12,800 cubic feet	*f.* 38,700 cubic feet
b. 17,500 cubic feet	*g.* 45,900 cubic feet
c. 25,600 cubic feet	*h.* 60,000 cubic feet
d. 2,600 cubic feet	*i.* 59,200 cubic feet
e. 19,200 cubic feet	*j.* 30,300 cubic feet

Reading a Railroad Timetable

Suppose that you are going on a railroad trip. One of the first things you must do in planning your trip is to refer to a timetable printed by the railroad company you are going to use. The timetable will tell you the time certain trains leave and arrive at various places and the distance between cities serviced by that railroad.

Below is the timetable published by a railroad for its run between Cincinnati and Cleveland.

Cincinnati to Dayton, Columbus and Cleveland

Miles	Table No. 22	444 Daily	426 Daily	312 Daily	424 Daily	16 Daily	442 Daily	302 Daily
		AM	AM	AM	PM	PM	PM	PM
0 0	Lv Cincinnati......(E.T.) (Union Terminal)...	CAPITAL CITY SPECIAL	8 45	9 00	3 30	4 15	11 00	11 30
4.7	Lv Winton Place........		8 56	9 11	3 41	4 26	11 11	11 41
31 5	Lv Middletown..........		9 32	9 47	4 14	4 56	11 47	12 17
42.3	Lv Miamisburg..........							
52.3	Lv Dayton.............		10 05	10 20	4 42	5 22	12 25	12 50
63.6	Lv Fairborn...........							
77.4	Ar Springfield.........		10 45	11 00	5 20	5 56	1 10	1 35
77.4	Lv Springfield.........		10 45		5 20	5 56	1 10	
96.9	Lv London.............		11 07					
122.4	Ar Columbus...........		11 38		6 07	6 43	1 57	
122.4	Lv Columbus...........	8 00	11 50		6 20	6 50	2 38	
146.5	Lv Delaware...........	8 36	12 29					
163.1	Lv Cardington........	f 8 53						
167.7	Lv Edison (Mt. Gilead)..		f12 52	CLEVELAND SPECIAL	THE QUEEN CITY	THE CINCINNATI MERCURY		
180 6	Lv Galion.............	9 20	1 18		7 20	ƒ7 50	3 50	
184.8	Lv Crestline..........	9 32	1 33		7 30		4 12	
193.3	Lv Shelby.............	9 44	1 50					
205.5	Lv Greenwich..........							
213.0	Lv New London.........	10 08	ƒ2 14					
224 0	Lv Wellington.........	10 22	2 30		♦8 11	OHIO STATE LIMITED Does not enter Cleveland Union Terminal	NIGHT SPECIAL	MICHIGAN SPECIAL
235 1	Lv Grafton...........	f10 35						
253 8	Lv Linndale...........	10 55	3 05		8 45		5 22	
260.0	Ar Cleveland (Union Terminal)....	11 10	3 25		9 00		5 40	

EXERCISES

Reading a Timetable

Referring to the timetable on page 234, answer the following questions:

1. How long does it take on the Ohio State Limited to go from Winton Place to Galion?

2. How many miles is it from Middletown to Wellington?

3. At what times does the Night Special leave Dayton? arrive at Cleveland?

4. Which is the fastest train from Cincinnati to Middletown?

5. How far is it from Columbus to Cleveland? How long does it take the Cleveland Special to go from Columbus to Cleveland?

6. Which train stops at Edison? At Grafton?

7. What is the average rate of speed of the Cincinnati Mercury traveling from Cincinnati to Cleveland?

8. You are expected in Columbus, Ohio, at 6:20 p.m.

   a. Which train will you take from Dayton?

In the Kitchen

Cindy decided to make some biscuits. She found a recipe which would make 20 biscuits that called for:

1 cup milk
1 teaspoon salt
3¾ tablespoons shortening
2 teaspoons baking powder
2 cups flour

When Cindy looked into the refrigerator, she found that she had only ¾ cup milk.

a. If she uses this amount of milk, how much must she use of every other ingredient?

b. How many biscuits will the new recipe make?

GENERAL SKILL EXERCISE

How are you doing? Try the following test. If you get any wrong, turn to the pages shown after each question. Practice those problems until you have mastered them.

1. Planning to spend income wisely for household expenses and other necessities is called .... (page 216).

2. One fact you must know before making a budget is the number of .... in the family (page 217).

3. The item that constitutes the major portion of a budget is .... (page 217).

4. A record which shows the amount of money received and the amount paid out is called a (an) .... (page 218).

5. Money spent is called .... (page 218).

6. The difference between the money spent and the money received is known as the .... (page 218).

7. A housewife can usually save money by buying in .... rather than buying individual items (page 219).

8. The written statement which indicates that a bill has been paid is called a (an) .... (page 220).

9. By .... a check, a person acknowledges the receipt of the money (page 222).

10. The price of electricity is usually so many cents per.................... (page 227).

_____ *My Score*

Chapter Review

PRINCIPLES TO REMEMBER

1. Each family should budget its money so that it can spend and save the proper amounts, according to its particular income and needs for expenditure.

2. A cash account should be kept to indicate the money received, the money spent and the cash on hand.

3. Quantity buying is a means of saving money.

4. A purchaser receives a sales slip as a record of purchases, and a receipt as a record of money paid.

5. A record of a check made out is kept on the check stub in the checkbook. By endorsing a check, one acknowledges receipt of the money.

6. Installment buying requires a down payment of part of the total price. The balance is paid in weekly or monthly payments. The total charge on the installment plan equals the marked price plus the carrying or service charge.

7. The price of electricity is determined by finding the number of kilowatt-hours and multiplying this by the cost per kilowatt-hour.

8. The amount of gas or electricity used is determined by reading meters.

MASTERY TEST

1. Each week Alice spends approximately $2.50 for food, $.40 for school supplies, $1.00 for recreation and $1.50 for miscellaneous items. She gets an allowance of $4.00 and she earns $2.00 a week baby sitting. She saves the remainder. Work out a budget for Alice.

2. Mr. Alban has an income of $5200. He allows 12% of this money for clothing for him and his family. How much does he spend on clothing?

3. Sandy keeps a cash account record for each month. For the month of January she recorded in the receipt column: cash on hand, $6.20; allowance, $16. In the expenditures column she recorded: lunches, $8.30; movies, $1; books, $2.98: gifts, $.80; personal items, $1.25. What was Sandy's cash on hand at the end of January?

4. The laundry and dry cleaning store had a sign in the window which said, "Cash and Carry—15% discount." That is, the customer who brings and calls for his own laundry pays 15% less than the customer who uses the delivery service. Mrs. Rand had her clothes laundered on the cash and carry system. At the end of the month she got a bill for $12.75. How much would she have paid if she had used the delivery service?

5. The price of frozen orange juice is $.63 for 3 cans. One can alone

costs $.24. How much is saved on three dozen cans of orange juice by buying 3 cans each time?

6. At the end of February Mrs. Carney had $173.92 in her checking account. During the month of March she wrote a check for $22.98 for a dress, $7.50 for a tablecloth and napkins, $9.96 for shirts for her husband and $10 to pay for television repairs. What was her balance at the end of March?

7. Jack saw an English bicycle marked $89.98. He decided to buy it on an installment plan for $15 down payment 'and $5 weekly for 18 weeks. How much did Jack pay for the bicycle? What per cent increase is the installment plan price over the original price?

8. Mr. Kenny used 12,650 watt-hours of electricity during the month of October. If his electricity cost 4¢ per kw.hr., what was his bill for the month?

9. Mrs. Sacks has a 900-watt electric iron. She uses the iron four hours each week. If electricity cost 5¢ per kw.hr., what was her bill for the month of February?

10. The first day of January Mr. Stark's gas meter registered 1 on the left hand dial, 2 on the middle dial and 2 on the right hand dial. The first day of February the dials showed, from left to right, 1, 4 and 3.

  a. How many cubic feet of gas were consumed during the month of January?
  b. If gas costs $.20 per 100 cubic feet, how much will Mr. Stark pay for his gas for the month?

11. Draw electric meters to show these readings:

  a. 3820 kw. hr.   d. 6904 kw. hr.
  b. 460 kw. hr.   e. 3865 kw. hr.
  c. 3333 kw. hr.   f. 1008 kw. hr.

12. Draw gas meters to show these readings:

  a. 16,400 cubic feet   d. 6,200 cubic feet
  b. 8,000 cubic feet   e. 43,800 cubic feet
  c. 39,900 cubic feet   f. 97,400 cubic feet

13. Mr. Bowers bought $750 worth of traveler's checks. How much did he pay for the checks?

14. Mrs. Pinto bought an electric dishwasher on an installment plan for a total of $190. The carrying charge was 6% of the selling price. What was the selling price to the nearest dollar?

9

GRAPHS

By use of the graph we can present number relationships in an interesting, pictorial manner. The lines, pictures or bars on a graph show comparisons so that they can actually be seen.

There are four basic types of graphs or charts:

1. the pictograph
2. the bar graph
3. the line graph
4. the circle graph

A good graph clearly shows particular facts and the comparison between them. It is neatly drawn, its scales have been labeled, and it has been given a suitable title.

The Pictograph

A graph in which pictures of objects are used to represent numbers is called a *pictograph*. Each object or symbol represents a definite quantity.

MOTOR VEHICLES IN THE UNITED STATES

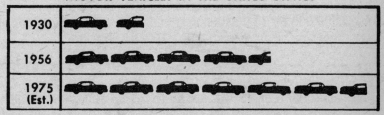

(Each symbol = 15,000,000 vehicles)

1. How many motor vehicles were in use in this country in 1956?

First, we count the number of symbols next to the year 1956. There are $4\frac{1}{2}$. Since each symbol represents 15,000,000 vehicles, the number of motor vehicles in use in 1956 was $4\frac{1}{2}\times15$ million, or 67,500,000.

2. How many motor vehicles will be in use in 1975?

$6\frac{2}{3}$ symbols $\times$ 15,000,000 = 100,000,000

3. How many more vehicles were in use in 1956 than in 1930?

We know there were 67,500,000 vehicles in use in 1956. For 1930 we find there are $1\frac{2}{3}\times15,000,000$, or 25,000,000 vehicles. By subtracting 25,000,000 from 67,500,000 we find that there were 42,500,000 more vehicles in 1956 than in 1930.

4. Find the per cent of increase in the number of vehicles in use in 1956 over the number in use in 1930.

Find the number increase:

$$\begin{array}{r} 67,500,000 \\ -25,000,000 \\ \hline 42,500,000 \end{array}$$

Form a fraction with the number increase as the numerator and the number before the increase as the denominator:

$$\frac{\text{increase}}{\text{original number}} \quad \frac{42,500,000}{25,000,000} = \frac{170}{100} = 170\% \text{ increase}$$

5. If it is estimated that 85,000,000 motor vehicles will be in use in 1965, how many symbols should be used to picture this on the graph?

Since each symbol represents 15,000,000 vehicles, we divide 85,000,000 by 15,000,000 and find the answer: $5\frac{2}{3}$ symbols.

EXERCISES

The Pictograph

1. Improvements in medicine have greatly increased the average life expectancy in America. In 1900 an American could expect to live for 47.3 years. In 1920 his life expectancy was 54.1 years. In 1930 life expectancy had increased to 59.7 years, by 1950 he could expect

to reach 68 and in 1970 he could expect to live to 74 years.
Make a pictograph representing these facts. You may want to
let a rectangular calendar page or some other figure represent a
certain number of years.

2. The chart below represents growth in high school enrollment
in the United States from 1880 to the present time.

a. What does the pic-
tograph show you
about growth in
high school enroll-
ment between 1880
and 1900?

b. What was the per-
cent of persons who
did not attend high
school in 1920?

c. What percent of per-
sons aged 14-17 in-
clusive were going
to high school in
1940? What per-
cent attend now?

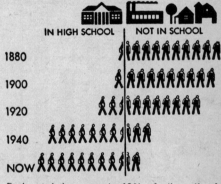

GROWTH IN HIGH SCHOOL ENROLLMENT

IN HIGH SCHOOL | NOT IN SCHOOL

1880

1900

1920

1940

NOW

Each symbol represents 10% of all youth of
high school age (14-17 inclusive)

d. Express in percentage points how many more persons are
going to high school now than in 1900 and in 1920.

The Bar Graph

A graph in which bars are used to represent numerical facts
is called a *bar graph*. Bar graphs represent quantities visually
by comparing bars of varying lengths but of uniform widths.
They are usually used to show size or amount of different items,
or size or amount of the same item at different times. If the bars
are drawn straight up and down, that is, at right angles with
the horizontal base line of the graph, a *vertical bar graph* is
formed. If the bars are drawn horizontally, or across the page,
the graph is called a *horizontal bar graph*.

The numbers on one margin of the graph indicate the *scale*
used; the labels on the other margin are a *key* to the items
graphed. The scale on every bar graph should begin with a
zero value.

Reading a Vertical Bar Graph

William Graves works as a salesman on commission. He kept a record of his sales for five weeks. Using the information shown on the graph, answer the following questions:

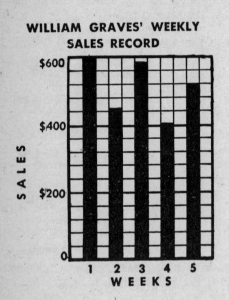

WILLIAM GRAVES' WEEKLY SALES RECORD

1. What were Graves' sales during the third week?

First, we locate the bar representing the third week's sales. Since each of the lines represents $40, the bar indicates sales of $580.

2. In which week did he make the smallest total sales?

Looking at the graph we find the shortest bar is the bar for week 4. The amount of sales this week was $400.

3. In which two weekly periods were his sales nearest the same amount?

We look for two bars that are almost equal in length. These are the bars representing the sales for the first and third weeks. The sales for the first week were $600. For the third week they were $580.

4. By what amount did his sales for the second week differ from his sales for the fourth week?

The sales for the second week were $450 and the sales for the fourth week were $400. By subtracting we find that the second week's sales were $50 greater.

5. What were his average sales for the five-week period?

Sales

Week 1—$600
Week 2— 450
Week 3— 580
Week 4— 400
Week 5— 520
$2550

$$\frac{2550}{5} = \$510 \text{ average sales}$$

6. If he received 15% commission on all sales, what total commission did he earn for the entire five-week period?

Since the total sales were $2550 we take 15% of this amount. His total commission was $382.50.

Reading a Horizontal Bar Graph

The following horizontal bar graph shows the distance in miles from New York City to various other cities.

Using the graph we can determine that the approximate distance from New York City to:
a. Albany is 145 miles
b. Montreal, Canada, is 384 miles
c. Scranton, Penn. is 126 miles

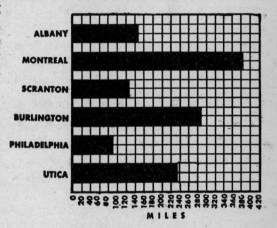

**DISTANCE FROM NEW YORK CITY
TO OTHER CITIES**

d. Burlington, Vermont, is 287 miles
e. Philadelphia, Penna., is 90 miles
f. Utica, New York, is 235 miles

Making a Bar Graph

The following suggestions will help you to make a bar graph. Choose a subject for a bar graph. It might be your personal record of test marks; it might be the number of workers absent from their job each day for a week. Read the suggestions below as you make the graph.

How to Make a Bar Graph

1. Use graph paper—a special type of paper with ruled lines that form many small squares.

2. Decide what type of bar graph you will make—vertical or horizontal.

3. Choose a suitable scale, letting each space represent a certain number. Choose a scale so that the longest bar will fit on the paper.

4. Mark off the scale numbers on the graph paper, directly opposite the lines, starting with zero. On a vertical bar graph, write the scale at the left of the graph, beginning at the bottom with zero. On a horizontal bar graph, write the scale at the bottom, with zero at the left.

5. Make all the bars the same width and the proper length.

6. Give the graph a title.

7. Make the graph neat and attractive.

EXERCISES

The Bar Graph

1. On a TV quiz program, of 20 questions given, four panelists gave the following number of correct answers: Helen, 18; John, 16; Irving, 15; Anna, 11. Make a horizontal bar graph to represent this information.

2. On a certain day in September at 2 p.m. the following temperatures were recorded in the following cities: New York, 76°; Washington, 84°; Chicago, 68°; Miami, 90°; Galveston, 94°; San Francisco, 77°. Make a vertical bar graph to represent this information.

3. Using an almanac, find the length of 5 rivers in the United States. Make a horizontal bar graph of this information.

4. Look up the height of 5 of the tallest peaks in the world. Represent your information with a vertical bar graph. From the graph

determine how many times the height of the shortest peak the highest is.

5. Represent the information from the picture below in a bar graph.

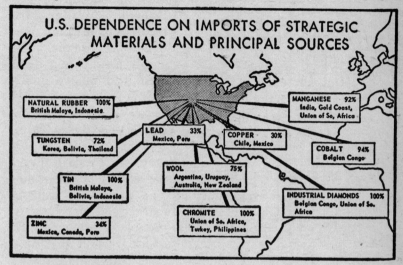

Line Graphs

A graph in which a line is used to represent number facts is called a *line graph*. This type of graph shows changes such as an increase or decrease in a quantity by the rising or falling of the line. The line on a line graph actually connects a number of points.

Stated simply, a line graph shows how things change together. For example, in the line graph, when there is a change in the hour there is also a change in the temperature.

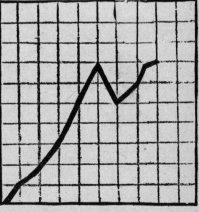

Reading a Line Graph

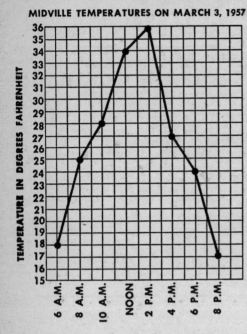

MIDVILLE TEMPERATURES ON MARCH 3, 1957

This line graph represents the official Weather Bureau temperature readings on a winter day.

Let us examine the graph closely and then read it. First we notice that a line graph has two scales—a vertical scale and a horizontal scale. The vertical scale on this graph is marked off in degrees of temperature. The horizontal scale is marked off in hours of the day. Reading the scales we find that at 6 a.m. (horizontal scale) the temperature (vertical scale) was 18°; at 6 p.m. the temperature had risen to 24°.

How to Make a Line Graph

1. Use graph paper.
2. Choose two scales—a vertical scale and a horizontal scale. Be certain that the scale you pick allows the largest number to be placed on the graph. Do not choose a scale that will make the graph too long or too wide.
3. Label the scales.
4. Place a dot on the graph to represent the information given. Each dot represents two related facts—one is interpreted by the vertical scale, the other by the horizontal scale.
5. Connect the points by drawing a straight line between them.
6. Give the graph a title.

Anton kept a record of his arithmetic marks for a week. His marks were: Monday, 70%; Tuesday, 80%; Wednesday, 85%; Thursday, 85%; Friday, 95%. Make a line graph to represent these facts.

Let us choose for our vertical scale, one box = 5%. Then we can plot the points. We locate

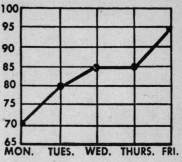

ANTON'S ARITHMETIC MARKS

Monday on the vertical scale and 70% on the horizontal scale. We place the dot where the two lines meet. In the same way we plot all other points, and we connect them with straight lines.

Essential to Remember

Be sure that the *interval* represented between scale divisions is the *same* along the full length of the scale, even when there is no data to be plotted for some scale divisions, and data is to be plotted *between* other scale divisions.

EXERCISES

Making a Line Graph

1. At a certain place a river is 90 feet wide. At intervals of 10 feet all the way across the depth of the river is measured in feet and found to be as follows: 18, 22, 26, 20, 19, 12, 8, 6.

  a. Make a graph representing the bottom of the river as determined by these measurements. Let the horizontal scale represent feet wide and the vertical scale, feet deep.
  b. How far from the right shore is the deepest part of the river?
  c. How far from the left shore is the deepest part of the river?

2. An employer pays his help $20 a day. Make a graph which will make it possible for the employer to find how much he owes his employees for working any number of days from 1 to 23, in any month.

   a. From this graph find how much he owes a man for working
      8 days; 6½ days; 8¼ days.

   b. From this graph find how many days a man must work to
      earn $60; $130; $410; $500.

   c. As the number of days a man works increases, his wages
      ....

3. A man kept a record of his income month by month, for two
years, as follows:

	1st Year	2nd Year		1st Year	2nd Year
Jan.	$496	$517	July	$415	$437
Feb.	$503	$546	Aug.	$432	$458
Mar.	$484	$497	Sept.	$485	$495
April	$460	$440	Oct.	$503	$512
May	$450	$425	Nov.	$489	$537
June	$427	$446	Dec.	$512	$551

   a. By means of a double line graph compare his income for the
      two years.

   b. In which year did he earn more during a greater number of
      months?

4. The population of the United States from 1850 to 1956 is listed
below (rounded off to the nearest million). Make a line graph to show
the growth during this period of time. 1850, 23 million; 1860, 30
million; 1870, 39 million; 1880, 50 million; 1890, 63 million; 1900,
76 million; 1910, 92 million; 1920, 106 million; 1930, 123 million;
1940, 132 million; 1950, 151 million; 1956, 168 million.

5. The following graph shows the noon temperature at a certain
weather station on seven consecutive days in June.

   a. On what day was the noon temperature the highest?

   b. For what two consecutive days was the change in noon tem-
      perature the least?

   c. For what two consecutive days was the change in noon tem-
      perature the greatest?

   d. What was the average noon temperature for the week?

   e. How many degrees warmer was it at noon on June 9 than at
      noon on June 12?

NOON TEMPERATURES AT MIDVILLE, PA.
SECOND WEEK OF JUNE, 1957

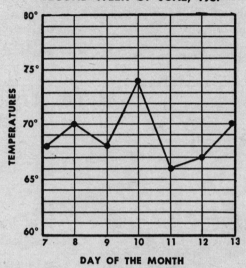

DAY OF THE MONTH

Apportionment Graphs

An apportionment or distribution graph shows how a particular whole is divided or apportioned. It may represent a day; it may represent a dollar; it may represent a budget. There are two types of apportionment graphs: the circle graph and the divided-bar graph. Whether in circle or in bar form, the graph represents 100% of the whole it expresses.

The Circle Graph

A chart which consists of a circle broken down into subdivisions is called a *circle graph* or a *pie graph*. A circle graph is used to show how all the parts are related to the whole. The entire circle, which equals 360°, represents the entire thing. Often, circle graphs are used to represent such things as the expenses of the government, causes of deaths, a budget, or daily apportionment of time.

Below are two circle graphs. One represents where each dollar of the government comes from. The other represents how each of the government's dollars is spent.

You may change the ¢-signs to %-signs in these graphs, for 59¢, for example, equals $\frac{59}{100}$ or 59% of a dollar.

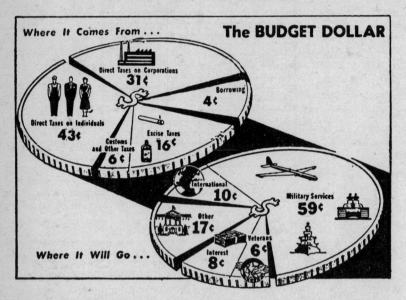

The circles above have been divided into *sectors;* each sector has *part of the circumference* (circle) for one edge and *two radii* for its other two edges.

The size of a sector depends upon the size of the angle between the two radii. The number of degrees which should be in each central angle is found by determining the fractional part of the whole that each sector is to represent, and multiplying each fraction by 360°.

Mrs. Brown counted the women in her club and made a circle graph of the colors of hair. She found that 12 women had black hair, 12 had brown hair, 6 were blonde and 6 had red hair.

Since there were 36 women in the club, Mrs. Brown divided the circle as follows.

HAIR COLORING OF PUPILS IN JOHN'S CLASS

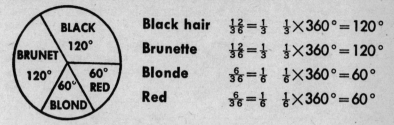

Black hair $\quad \frac{12}{36} = \frac{1}{3} \quad \frac{1}{3} \times 360° = 120°$

Brunette $\quad \frac{12}{36} = \frac{1}{3} \quad \frac{1}{3} \times 360° = 120°$

Blonde $\quad \frac{6}{36} = \frac{1}{6} \quad \frac{1}{6} \times 360° = 60°$

Red $\quad \frac{6}{36} = \frac{1}{6} \quad \frac{1}{6} \times 360° = 60°$

How to Make a Circle Graph

1. Draw a circle large enough for you to represent all the facts clearly.

2. Find the number of facts to be graphed and express them as fractions or per cents, using the circle as 100% or 360.° Arrange the facts in a table.

3. Use a protractor to mark off sectors of the circle which will contain the required number of degrees. Label the sectors.

4. Give the graph a title.

EXERCISES

Circle Graph

1. Each week John receives an allowance of $6.00. He spends it as follows: carfare, $1.70; snacks, $.80; movies, $1.25; other expenses, $1.25; savings, $1.00. Show these facts in a circle graph.

2. In a certain high school the student body is divided into the following groups: seniors, 18%; juniors, 20%; sophomores, 25%; freshmen, 37%. Make a circle graph of these facts.

3. In Henry's shop there are 36 men. Six are rated superior; 10 are rated above average, 12 are rated average and 8 below average. Show this on a circle graph.

4. Study the following series of circle graphs, which show the per cents of United States farm output which are exported.

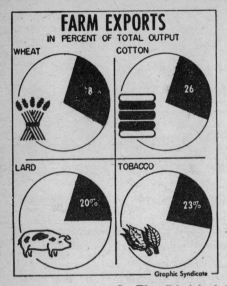

a. By how many percentage points did the per cent of wheat exported exceed the per cent of lard exported?

b. Figuring the total output of each of these products as 100% what per cent of tobacco was used in the United States?

c. What is the ratio of the cotton used domestically to the cotton exported?

2. The Divided-Bar Graph

A second kind of apportionment graph is the divided-bar graph. A single bar is divided into portions, each of which represents a part of the whole.

Suppose that Mrs. Brown (see p. 251) wanted to make a divided-bar graph rather than a circle graph to represent the types of hair in her club. She would find what part each number is of the whole, select a convenient length, draw a bar, and divide the bar into the proper proportions.

She has already determined that the bar will be divided into $\frac{1}{3}$, $\frac{1}{3}$, $\frac{1}{6}$ and $\frac{1}{6}$. Therefore, if she chooses $2\frac{1}{4}$ inches as the length of her bar, the parts will be:

$$\frac{1}{3} \times 2\frac{1}{4} = \frac{1}{3} \times \frac{9}{4} = \frac{3}{4} \text{ inch—black hair}$$
$$\frac{1}{3} \times 2\frac{1}{4} = \frac{1}{3} \times \frac{9}{4} = \frac{3}{4} \text{ inch—brunette}$$
$$\frac{1}{6} \times 2\frac{1}{4} = \frac{1}{6} \times \frac{9}{4} = \frac{3}{8} \text{ inch—blonde}$$
$$\frac{1}{6} \times 2\frac{1}{4} = \frac{1}{6} \times \frac{9}{4} = \frac{3}{8} \text{ inch—red hair}$$

BLACK   BRUNETTE   RED BLOND

HAIR COLORS OF MEMBERS OF MRS. BROWN'S CLUB

EXERCISES

Divided-Bar Graph

1. Study the divided-bar graph that Mrs. Brown made.
   a. Measure the length of the portion of the graph that represents black hair.
   b. Using the length of the first portion and referring to the
   numbers on p. 251, determine mathematically the length of
   every other division.
   c. Suppose she had made the length of the first division 1″.
   Knowing what portion this is of the whole, find mathematically what the total length would be.
   d. Why did Mrs. Brown choose a $2\frac{1}{4}″$ total length instead of
   choosing a bar one inch longer?

2. Make a divided-bar graph showing approximately how you
spend each school day. Use these divisions: time spent eating, sleep-
ing, in class, for recreation, doing homework, miscellaneous.

Graphing a Formula

We have learned that a formula is a method of expressing a
relationship. By substituting values for letters in the formula,
the value of any unknown can be determined.

Suppose that a boy walks at the rate of 2 miles per hour.
We can write a formula which can be used to find the distance
the boy travels in any period of time. With D representing
distance in miles and t representing *time, or number of hours
traveled*, the formula is:

$$D = 2t$$

By substituting values in the formula, we can find the value
for D that corresponds with each value of t. Below we have
arranged the values of t and the corresponding values of D
in a table.

t	0	1	2	3	4	5	6	7
D	0	2	4	6	8	10	12	14

Using these values we can draw the graph for the formula.
First, we draw a horizontal line for the horizontal scale. On this

scale we indicate the time (t) or the number of hours the boy walked. Next we draw the vertical scale, on which we represent the distance covered. We use each pair of values in the table above to locate a point on the graph.

Starting with the first pair, we plot t as 0 and D as 0. Then we plot the values $t=1$, $D=2$, and so on. When we have connected all the plotted points, we see that they all lie on the same straight line. This straight line, with relationship to the horizontal and vertical scales, represents the formula $D=2t$.

EXERCISES

Graphing a Formula

1. Mr. Mathew mortgaged his house for $12,500 and agreed to pay 5% interest. Substituting the value for PR in the formula I = PRT, make a table showing interest for times ranging from one to ten years. Plot the points on a line graph.

    a. From the graph, find how much interest Mr. Mathew will have paid at the end of 10 years.

    b. After how many years will Mr. Mathew have paid $2500?

2. Mr. Reynolds pays his employees $2.50 an hour. (The salary of the worker is equal to $2.50 times the number of hours he works.) Write a formula for the salary of the worker. Arrange a table extending from one to twelve hours. From the information on this table, make a line graph.

    a. How much does one employee make in 8 hours?

    b. How much more does he make in 8 hours than in 2 hours?

    c. How much can four employees make if they work together for one hour?

GENERAL SKILL EXERCISE

How are you doing? Try the following test. If you get any wrong, turn to the pages shown after each question. Practice those problems until you have mastered them.

1. In a ...., a definite quantity is represented by a picture (page 239).

2. In a bar graph, the lines are of .... widths but of .... lengths (page 241).

3. A complete whole is represented in a(an) .... graph. Two types of this graph are the .... graph and the .... graph (page 249).

4. When we graph a formula we first form a table of values by .... (page 254).

5. The bars on a .... bar graph are drawn across the page (page 241).

6. To show the changes in one particular quantity or item we would use a .... graph (page 245).

7. John would show approximately how he spends his weekly allowance on a .... graph (page 249).

8. Another name for a circle graph is a ....graph (page 249).

9. One portion of a circle graph is called a ....(page 250).

10. Every line graph or bar graph has a horizontal and a vertical .... (page 246).

My Score ————————

Chapter Review

PRINCIPLES TO REVIEW

1. A graph presents numerical relationships in a visual form.

2. In a pictograph, each picture or symbol represents a definite quantity.

3. The lengths of bars in a bar graph represent numerical facts. The bars are of varying lengths but of the same width.

4. The bars of a vertical bar graph are drawn straight up and down; those of a horizontal bar graph are drawn across the page.

5. The line graph shows the changes in a quantity by the rising or the falling of a line. The position of the line with relation to the horizontal and the vertical scales represents number facts. The line connects a number of points.

6. An apportionment or distribution graph shows the relationship of all the parts of a particular whole. The whole graph represents 100%.

7. The circle or pie graph, and the divided-bar graph, are types of the apportionment graph. Each division of the circle graph is called a sector.

MASTERY TEST

1. *Study the following graph and answer the questions below.*

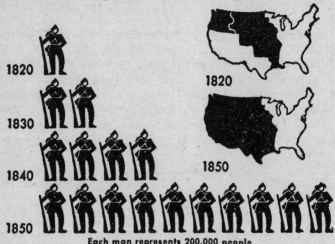

1820

1830

1840

1850

Each man represents 200,000 people

1820

1850

THE AMERICAN WEST—1820 to 1850

  a. What does the graph tell you about the trend in population in the West from 1820 to 1850?

  b. For every 100 people that lived in the West in 1830, how many hundreds lived in the West in 1840?

  c. How many people had settled in the West by 1850?

  d. The great California gold rush was in 1849. Does the graph indicate anything about its effects?

  e. How does the per cent increase from 1820 to 1830 compare with the per cent increase from 1830 to 1840?

  2. **Make a vertical bar graph to represent the heights of the following well-known structures: Empire State Building, 1250 feet; Eiffel Tower, 1000 feet; Washington Monument, 550 feet; Great Pyramid of Egypt, 450 feet; Leaning Tower of Pisa, 180 feet.**

  3. **The population in a certain high school was distributed as follows: seniors, 450; juniors, 630; sophomores, 1050; freshmen, 1480. Make a horizontal bar graph to represent this information.**

4. On a certain day in a city the temperature readings were as follows:

6 a.m.	− 6°	noon	+ 15°
7 a.m.	− 3°	1 p.m.	+ 16°
8 a.m.	− 1°	2 p.m.	+ 17°
9 a.m.	+ 2°	3 p.m.	+ 14°
10 a.m.	+ 8°	4 p.m.	+ 8°
11 a.m.	+ 14°	5 p.m.	+ 3°

　　a. Make a line graph of this information.

　　b. From the graph determine the approximate time when the temperature was 0°.

　　c. From the graph determine the approximate temperature at 3:30 p.m.

5. The rainfall in inches in a city during a certain year was as follows: January, 3.8 inches; February, 3.6 inches; March, 2.4 inches; April, 0.8 inches; May, 0.6 inches; June, 0.2 inches; July, 0.0 inches; August, 0.3 inches; September, 0.5 inches; October, 0.9 inches; November, 1.8 inches; December, 2.7 inches.

　　a. Make a line graph of this data.

　　b. In what month was the rainfall greatest?

　　c. In what month the least?

6. A doctor's income for one year was as follows: January, $2425; February, $2190; March, $1980; April, $1995; May, $2380; June, $1925; July, $1670; August, $1830; September, $1945; October, $2075; November, $2580; December, $2610.

　　a. Make a line graph to picture the trend of the doctor's income during the year.

　　b. At what time of the year is his income greatest?

　　c. How can you explain this?

　　d. What might have caused the income to be so small during the month of July?

7. One day Arthur spent his day as follows: sleep, 9 hours; school, 6 hours; meals, 1 hour; homework, 3 hours; travel, 1 hour; play, 2 hours; miscellaneous, 2 hours. Make a circle graph showing this information.

8. Mr. Atkinson cultivates a farm of 120 acres on Long Island. He planted his crops in the following manner: corn, 40 acres; tomatoes, 30 acres; celery, 15 acres; lettuce, 20 acres; beets, 5 acres; string beans, 5 acres; cauliflower, 5 acres. Make a circle graph to picture this data.

9. *From the graph, answer the questions below.*

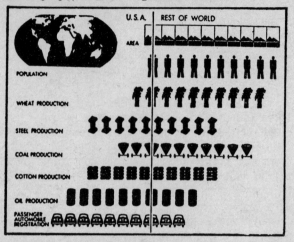

 a. What per cent does each picture or figure represent?

 b. For every person who lives in the United States, how many people live in the rest of the world?

 c. What is the ratio of the cotton production in the United States to the cotton production in the rest of the world?

 d. The area of the United States is approximately 3 million square miles. What is the approximate area of the world?

 e. What per cent of the world's wheat does the United States produce?

 f. Make a circle graph showing the population of the United States and the population of the rest of the world.

 g. Make a circle graph, allotting one portion for the United States and one portion for the rest of the world, showing automobile registration.

 h. Compare the two graphs which you have just made. What do they indicate about the standard of living of each person in the United States compared with the standard of living of the average person in another part of the world?

10

ALGEBRA

Algebra is used in many walks of life, from that of the philosopher to that of the manual laborer. The skilled worker may use algebra to determine the location of the center or the size of holes he must drill. Doctors, engineers, and scientists use algebra in their research. In 1905, Albert Einstein discovered an algebraic formula which led to the discovery of atomic energy: $E = mc^2$. His formula meant that *energy* equals *mass* times the square of the *speed of light*.

By the use of algebra we can reduce complex problems to simple formulas. We can find the answers to problems about the universe, and to problems of sewing, building, cooking, measuring, buying and selling as well.

Symbols of Operation

From arithmetic you are familiar with the symbols $+$, $-$, $\times$, $\div$ and $=$. Each of these signs indicates a particular arithmetic operation, and all of these arithmetic operations are essential in algebra. In algebra one additional symbol is used: a dot to indicate multiplication.

Algebraic Numbers

The Arabic numerals that we use in our everyday work, such as 1, 2 and 3, are used to represent *arithmetic numbers*. In algebra, however, we use letters as well as numerals to represent those

What is *X*? What is *Y*? What is the unknown? Letters in algebra problems represent unknown values. We can identify those values by finding their relationship to the numbers around them. If $10y \div 2 = 5$, then *y* must equal 1. If $10x \div 2 = 25$, then *x* must equal 5.

1. What is the value of *y* if $5 + y = 33$?

values. These letters are called *literal numbers*. Expressions containing letters are called *literal expressions*. Thus, the literal expression indicating the sum of *a* and *b* is written $a + b$. The literal expression indicating the difference between *a* and *b* is written $a - b$ or $b - a$.

An *equation* is a statement that one expression is equal to a second expression.

$5a = 20$ is an equation; $a + b = c$ is an equation.

Symbols to Remember

$+$ indicates add, sum of, increased by.

$-$ means subtract, difference of, diminished by.

$\times$
$\cdot$ } indicate multiply, times, the product of.

$\div$ means divide, find the quotient.

$=$ means equals.

Expressing Products

The product of the two numbers, *a* and *b*, may be written as $a \times b$. Then the product of *x* and *y* would be $x \times y$. To avoid confusion between the letter *x* and the multiplication sign $\times$, we use a dot placed above the line and between the two letters to indicate multiplication.

Thus, the product of x and y may be written $x \cdot y$ (not $x.y$). Notice the difference between 2.3 and 2·3). But when one or both of the numbers are literal numbers, the dot is omitted. The product of x and y is simply written xy. Similarly, a times b is ab; $3x$ means 3 times x. But the product of 49 and 62 cannot be written 4962; it is written (49) (62) or 49·62 or 49×62.

Let us use the symbols of operation to represent the following as algebraic expressions.

HOW TO DO THE EXAMPLE

Problem 1. The sum of r and s.

Using the symbol $+$ to indicate addition, we find the answer:

$$r+s, \text{ or } s+r$$

Problem 2. The product of 2 and m.

Because the symbol for multiplication is omitted when a literal number is used, the answer is $2m$.

Problem 3. The difference when 5 is subtracted from t.

Using the symbol $-$ to indicate subtraction or difference, we find the answer: $t-5$

Problem 4. 3 less than twice x.

Twice the number x is $2x$; the symbol for "less than" is $-$. Thus, the answer is: $2x-3$.

Problem 5. b divided by 7.

Division can be represented by a fraction. Therefore, the answer is: $\dfrac{b}{7}$

Problem 6. The sum of a and b diminished by 3 times c.

Answer: $a+b-3c$

Represent as an algebraic equation: A is 8 less than B.

Rule to Remember

= means "is equal to". The expression "less than" is represented by a minus sign.

HOW TO DO THE EXAMPLE

The expression "8 less than B" would be expressed algebraically as $B-8$.

The statement "A is 8 less than B" would be written

$$A = B - 8$$

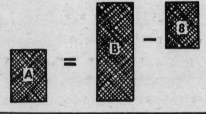

If H represents Henry's money and R represents Ralph's money, write an equation expressing the fact that Henry's money exceeds twice Ralph's money by $24.

Rule to Remember

Exceeds means *is more than.*

HOW TO DO THE EXAMPLE

Twice Ralph's money is $2R$.

An amount which "exceeds twice Ralph's money by $24" would be written $2R + \$24$.

The equation $H = 2R + \$24$ tells us that Henry's money (H) is $24 more than twice Ralph's money (R).

If b pencils cost c cents, how much will m pencils cost?

HOW TO DO THE PROBLEM

If b pencils cost c cents, then one pencil will cost $\dfrac{c}{b}$ cents.

Therefore, m pencils cost m times as much as one pencil;

that is, $m \cdot \dfrac{c}{b}$ or $\dfrac{m}{1} \cdot \dfrac{c}{b}$ or $\dfrac{mc}{b}$ cents.

EXERCISES

Symbols of Operation

1. *Write in algebraic language the answer to each of the following:*

   a. 9 plus 14
   b. 8 plus 6
   c. n plus 5
   d. 15 plus b
   e. 8 more than 6
   f. l more than w
   g. 3 more than n
   h. 5 increased by 9
   i. b increased by a
   j. r increased by 13
   k. 8 less than 15
   l. C less than d
   m. 7 less than l
   n. 15 decreased by 11
   o. r decreased by b
   p. 9 decreased by s
   q. 8 times 5
   r. l times w
   s. 5 times n
   t. the product of 7 and 8
   u. the product of a and b
   v. the product of 7 and a
   w. 18 divided by 7
   x. d divided by r
   y. n divided by 5
   z. 10 divided by x

2. *If n represents a certain number, write:*

   a. four more than the number
   b. twice the number
   c. five less than the number
   d. one-half of the number
   e. two-thirds of the number
   f. the number increased by seven
   g. the number increased by a
   h. the product of b and the number
   i. two more than twice the number
   j. seven less than three times the number
   k. three times the number increased by a
   l. B less than a times the number

3. *If r and s represent two numbers, write:*
   a. the first number plus the second number
   b. three times the first number increased by six
   c. five less than twice the second number
   d. the product of the two numbers
   e. three times the first number increased by two times the second number
   f. six times the second number diminished by four times the first number

4. *Represent the number of:*

   a. inches in f feet
   b. inches in y yards
   c. feet in y yards
   d. cents in d dollars
   e. cents in q quarters
   f. cents in h half-dollars
   g. nickels in d dollars

   h. nickels in q quarters
   i. pints in g gallons
   j. ounces in p pounds
   k. quarts in p pecks
   l. feet in i inches
   m. dollars in c cents
   n. quarts in p pints

5. An apple costs 5 cents. Represent the cost of n apples.
6. An orange costs 4 cents. Represent the cost of n dozen oranges.
7. A dozen lemons cost n cents. Represent the cost of a lemon.
8. Six apples cost b cents. Represent the cost of 2 dozen apples.
9. If 5 apples cost 15 cents, represent the cost of n apples.
10. If 4 pens cost c cents, represent the cost of 9 pens.
11. If n is a whole number, what is the next larger whole number?
12. If n is a whole number, what is the next smaller whole number?
13. If William weighs w pounds, represent his weight after he gains 5 pounds.
14. If Helen weighed h pounds and gained 3 pounds, how much does she weigh?
15. If Mary weighed m pounds and lost 7 pounds, how much does she weigh?
16. If Howard weighs h pounds and intends to lose 6 pounds, how much will he weigh?
17. If an express train travels e miles an hour, represent the rate of a local train which travels 5 miles an hour less than the express train.
18. A boy went to the store with a \$5 bill. If he spent d dollars, how much did he have left?
19. A boy is b years old now. How old will he be 5 years from now?
20. A girl is g years old now. How old will she be a years from now?
21. A man is x years old now. How old was he 5 years ago?

22. A woman is w years old now. How old was she a years ago?

23. A boy bought 10 articles, each of which cost c cents. How much change should he get from a dollar bill?

24. A girl bought r articles at c cents each. How much change should she receive from a $5 bill?

25. The width of a rectangle is w inches. How long is it if the length is 7 inches more than its width?

26. State in words the meaning of the following algebraic expressions:

a. $x+5$	e. $8-a$	h. $y+b$	k. pr
b. $x-7$	f. $2x+7$	i. $5-c$	l. $\dfrac{d}{r}$
c. $3x$	g. $\dfrac{x}{3}$	j. rt	
d. $15+y$			

Evaluation of Algebraic Expressions

The process of finding the value of an algebraic expression is called *evaluating* an expression.

Rule to Remember

The arithmetic value of an algebraic expression may be found by substituting arithmetic values for the literal numbers and then following these rules for the order of operations: *First*, find each indicated *product* or *quotient;* *then*, perform all indicated addition or subtraction.

HOW TO DO THE EXAMPLE

Evaluate: $5x-3y+6z$ when $x=10$, $y=2$, and $z=5$

Substitute the given values in the given equation:

$$5x-3y+6z = 5(10)-3(2)+6(5)$$
$$= 50-6+30$$
$$= 74$$

Make an evaluation table for the formula $l = 5w$.

HOW TO DO THE EXAMPLE

Suppose that $w = 1$; then $l = 5\cdot1$ or 5.

Suppose that $w = 2$; then $l = 5\cdot2$ or 10.

Suppose that $w = 3$; then $l = 5\cdot3$ or 15.

List these values in an evaluation table:

$w =$	1	2	3	
$l =$	5	10	15	

EXERCISES
Evaluating Algebraic Expressions

1. If $l = 3w$, complete the following table:

w	1	2	3	4	5	6	7
l	3	6					

2. If $p = 4s$, complete the following table:

s	1	2	3	4	5
p	4	8			

3. If $y = x + 7$, make a table showing the values of y when $x = 1,2,3,$ 4, 5, 9, 10 and 12.

4. If $y = x - 4$, make a table showing the values of y when $x = 4,$ 5, 6, 10, 12 and 14.

5. If $y = 2x + 1$, make a table showing the values of y when $x = 1, 2, 3, 5, 7, 20, 22$ and 25.

6. If $y = 3x - 2$, make a table showing the values of y when $x = 1, 2, 3, 4$ and 5.

7. The formula for the perimeter of a triangle whose sides are a, b and c is $p = a + b + c$. Find the perimeter of a triangle whose sides are:

a. 15, 12 and 24	*c.* 16, 12 and 20	*e.* 13, 14 and 15
b. 3, 4 and 5	*d.* 6, 4 and 9	*f.* 5, 12 and 13

8. The formula for the perimeter, p, of an isosceles triangle two of whose sides are each equal to a, and whose base is equal to b, is $p = 2a + b$. Find the perimeter of each of the following isosceles triangles:

a. $a = 10$ and $b = 4$	*d.* $a = 9.1$ and $b = 3.8$
b. $a = 9$ and $b = 5$	*e.* $a = 8\frac{3}{4}$ and $b = 5\frac{1}{4}$
c. $a = 11.5$ and $b = 8$	*f.* $a = 5$ and $b = 2$

9. The formula for the perimeter of an equilateral triangle each of whose sides is s is $p = 3s$. Find the perimeter of the equilateral triangle whose sides are:

a. 5   *b.* 2   *c.* 5.5   *d.* $3\frac{1}{3}$ *e.* 9   *f.* 6

10. The formula for the perimeter of a square is $p = 4s$. Find the perimeter of a square whose sides are:

a. 4   *b.* 7   *c.* 3.5   *d.* 6.3   *e.* $4\frac{1}{2}$ *f.* 8

11. The formula for the circumference of a circle is $C = \pi D$. Find the circumferences of the circles whose diameters are: (Use $\pi = \frac{22}{7}$)

a. 7   *b.* 14   *c.* 21   *d.* 5   *e.* 8   *f.* 4.3

12. The formula for the area of a square is $A = s^2$. Find A when s equals:

a. 5   *b.* 10   *c.* 12   *d.* 15   *e.* 3.4   *f.* 9.9

Factors

If two or more numbers (arithmetic or literal) are multiplied, the result of the multiplication is called a *product*. Each number that has been multiplied to arrive at that product is called a *factor* of the product. For example, since $2 \cdot 7 = 14$, then 2 and 7 are factors of their product, 14. Similarly, the number 210 can be written as $2 \cdot 3 \cdot 5 \cdot 7$. Two, three, five and seven are called the prime factors of 210. A prime factor is a factor that is not divisible by anything other than itself or unity. Two is a factor of 210; so is $2 \cdot 3$ or 6, $2 \cdot 3 \cdot 5$, or 30 and so on. Consider the number $6ab$, which can be written as $2 \cdot 3 \cdot a \cdot b$. Then $6ab$ has the following factors: 2, $3ab$, a, b, 6, $6a$, and so on.

Coefficients

Any factor of a product may be called the *coefficient* of the product of the remaining factors. For example, in the expression $7xyz$, 7 is the coefficient of the remaining factors xyz, or $7x$ is the coefficient of the remaining factors yz, etc.

A coefficient which is an arithmetic number is called a *numerical coefficient*. Thus, 8 is the numerical coefficient in the expression $8xy$. If a letter is written without a number before it, the coefficient is understood to be 1. For example, x means $1x$, and ab means $1ab$.

Combining Terms

An algebraic expression consists of one or more terms. If an algebraic expression consists of more than one term, as for example, $3a + 2b + e$, the terms are separated by plus ($+$) or minus ($-$) signs.

A *term* or a *monomial* consists of numbers connected only by signs of multiplication or division. For example, $2xy$, and $\frac{ab}{5c}$ are terms or monomials. Thus, the algebraic expression $3x - 2ab + 4$ has 3 terms: $3x$, $2ab$, and 4.

Consider the following questions:
1. What is the sum of 8 eggs and 2 eggs?
2. What is the sum of 8 eggs and 2 chairs?

The first question is a reasonable question and one which can be answered. The second is not reasonable and cannot be answered. The purpose of adding or subtracting numbers or objects is to find out how many of the *same kind* we have.

The sum of $3ab$ and $7ab$ is $10ab$, because 3 ab's and 7 more like them would yield $10ab$'s. However, $2a$ and $3b$ cannot be added because these are unlike terms.

Like terms have the same literal factors. Thus, $3a$ and $5a$ are like terms, and xy and $4xy$ are like terms. *Unlike terms* do not have the same literal factors. $3d$, $7x$, $2y$ and $5xy$ are all unlike terms.

Adding and Subtracting Like Terms

An algebraic expression containing two or more like terms can be simplified by combining like terms. Since unlike terms cannot be added or subtracted we merely indicate their addition or subtraction by signs. For example, $3x + 6a - 2b$.

Rule to Remember

To combine like terms, add or subtract their numerical coefficients as indicated by the sign of operation, and write the result as the coefficient of the common literal factor.

HOW TO DO THE EXAMPLE

Problem 1. Find the sum of 6x and 3x.

Since these are like terms, we add only the numerical coefficients. $6x+3x=9x$

Problem 2. Subtract 7xy from 12xy

Since these are like terms, we subtract their numerical coefficients. $12xy-7xy=5xy$

Problem 3. Find the sum of 7x and 3xy

Since these are unlike terms, we merely indicate their sum by the addition sign. $7x+3xy=7x+3xy$

Problem 4. Combine $6a+7b+2a+3b$

When numbers are added, the answer will always be the same, regardless of the order in which we add the numbers.

$$6a+7b+2a+3b=6a+2a+7b+3b=8a+10b$$

(In such simple problems it is not necessary to rewrite the expression before adding.)

Problem 5. Combine $1.2x+13y+.6x-7y$
$$1.2x+13y+.6x-7y=1.8x+6y$$

Problem 6. Add the following:

$$\begin{array}{ll}
(a) \quad \begin{array}{r} 4x \\ x \\ \hline 5x \end{array} & \qquad (b) \quad \begin{array}{r} 4a+3b \\ 8a+9b \\ \hline 12a+12b \end{array}
\end{array}$$

EXERCISES

Adding and Subtracting Terms

1. *Add:*

   a. 12 feet
      7 feet
       feet

   d. $10f$
      $3f$
      f

   g. $11f+6i$
      $3f$
      f i

   b. 5 inches
      4 inches
       inches

   e. $6i$
      $3i$
      i

   h. $5i$
      $2i$
      i

   c. 12 yards
      6 yards
       yards

   f. $12y$
      $4y$
      y

   i. $12y+f$
      $6y+f$
      y f

2. *Add:*

   a. $5x$
      $7x$

   d. $5\frac{2}{3}d$
      $6\frac{2}{3}d$

   g. $5.6d$
      $.9d$

   j. s
      $12s$

   b. $20r$
      r

   e. $8y$
      $6y$

   h. $8\frac{1}{2}x$
      $9\frac{2}{3}x$

   k. $4\frac{1}{2}a$
      $5\frac{1}{2}a$

   c. $1.8x$
      $2.5x$

   f. $19x$
      x

   i. $12x$
      $9x$

   l. $5\frac{5}{6}y$
      $\frac{2}{3}y$

3. *Simplify:*

   a. $9x+4x$
   b. $8t-5t$
   c. $12s+3\frac{1}{2}s$
   d. $9a-8a$
   e. $1.6t-.8t$

   f. $\frac{10}{3}b-\frac{5}{3}b$
   g. $\frac{7}{8}a-\frac{1}{2}a$
   h. $4.3d-1.7d$
   i. $\frac{5}{7}a+\frac{2}{7}a$

   j. $1.5x-.5x$
   k. $6y+\frac{2}{3}y$
   l. $9x-\frac{2}{3}x$

4. *In the following examples subtract:*

   a. $9x$
      $5x$

   c. $16a$
      $9a$

   e. $9.8t$
      $.6t$

   g. $16\frac{1}{8}r$
      $11\frac{3}{8}r$

   b. $14a$
      $9a$

   d. $22b$
      b

   f. $4.2d$
      $1.8d$

   h. $2\frac{3}{10}c$
      $\frac{9}{10}c$

5. *Simplify:*

a. $6x+9x+x$

b. $12x+3x$

c. $8.3a+9.7a$

d. $10n+.8n+3x$

e. $8\frac{1}{2}b+4\frac{2}{3}b$

f. $8t+9t+s+4t$

g. $16y+2y+8y$

h. $4.6c+.8c+1.2c+1.2d$

i. $2\frac{1}{5}d+5\frac{2}{5}d+6\frac{4}{5}d$

j. $.6a+2w+2\frac{1}{2}w+5\frac{1}{3}w$

Algebraic Equations

An equation is a mathematical statement that two quantities are equal. The sign of equality, or equals sign, $=$, is used to indicate that one expression or quantity is equal to another expression or quantity. The expressions on either side of the equals sign are called *members of the equation*.

These are equations:

$$x=6, \quad x+2=8, \quad x-9=5.$$

In the equation $x+2=8$, $x+2$ is called the left member of the equation and 8 the right member.

In an equation, the letter whose value must be found is called the *unknown number* or the *unknown*. The equation $x+2=8$ means that 2 added to an unknown number equals 8.

Writing Algebraic Equations

Problem 1. If 10 is added to a number, the result is equal to 48. Write this statement as an algebraic equation.

Method: Pick any letter and let it stand for the number that you must find.

Let $x =$ the unknown number

$x+10$ means 10 added to x.

Since "is equal to" is represented by an equals sign ($=$), the equation is

$x+10=48$

Problem 2. John's weight exceeds twice Sam's weight by 5 pounds. Express this statement as an algebraic equation.

[Continued on top of page 273]

Method: Let J = John's weight
$\qquad\quad$ S = Sam's weight
Twice Sam's weight is represented by 2S.
"Exceeds" means is more than and is represented by $+$.
John's weight is equal to 5 more than twice Sam's weight.
Therefore, the equation is $J = 2S + 5$.

> **Problem 3.** Eight times a number diminished by 4 is 20.
> Write this statement as an algebraic equation.
>
> Method: Let y = the unknown number
>
> $\qquad$ Eight times the number is represented by 8y.
> "Diminished by" is represented by $-$. The
> equation is:
>
> $$8y - 4 = 20$$

EXERCISES

Writing Algebraic Equations

Write the equations for solving the following problems. (Do not solve.)

1. The cost of 3 pens is $15. What is the cost of one pen?
2. The cost of 5 apples is 60 cents. What is the cost of an apple?
3. A man travels 250 miles in 5 hours. How far does he travel in one hour?
4. Five times a certain number is 4.5. How large is the number?
5. One-third of a number is 12. Find the number.
6. Eight times Henry's savings is $96. How much has he saved?
7. In 12 days a man earned $308. How much did he earn each day?
8. Two-fifths of a number is 8. Find the number.
9. A basketball player scored one-third of the team's final score. If he scored 13 points, how many points did the team score?

10. A number increased by 5 equals 25. Find the number.

11. A number decreased by 15 is equal to 23. Find the number.

12. Two numbers add to 25. If the larger is four times the smaller, find the two numbers.

13. One number is seven times another number. If their difference is 42, find the numbers.

14. A number increased by $\frac{1}{3}$ of itself is equal to 40. Find the number.

15. A pound of steak costs 99 cents. How many pounds can I buy for $4.95?

16. A shirt and a tie cost $4.50. If the shirt costs twice as much as the tie, find the cost of the tie.

17. Three times a certain number decreased by 5 is equal to 25. Find the number.

18. One-half a certain number increased by 9 is equal to 15. Find the number.

19. Twice a number increased by 7 is equal to 21. Find the number.

20. A boy saves 3 times as much as his sister. Together they save $48. How much does each save?

21. John has $20 and buys a shirt. If he has $17.50 left, how much does the shirt cost?

22. A certain sum of money invested at 6% yields $36 in one year. How much money was invested?

23. After John worked 50 hours he finished $\frac{1}{3}$ of the job. How many hours were required to do the complete job?

GENERAL SKILL EXERCISE

How are you doing? Try the following test. If you get any wrong, turn to the pages shown after each question. Practice those problems until you have mastered them.

1. To indicate the expression "increased by", you use the symbol .... (page 260).

2. The symbol (=) means .... (page 260).

3. Letters used to represent numbers are known as ...... (page 259).

4. The product of 53 and 74 is written algebraically as .... (page 261).

5. "Exceeds" is written in algebra as .... (page 262).

6. Three less than twice a number is written as .... (page 262).

7. When you evaluate an expression you find the ....
of the expression (page 265).

8. A product is the result of .... (page 267).

9. In the expression 6*ab*, 6 is called the .... of
ab (page 268).

10. Only .... (like, unlike) terms can be added (page 269).

My Score _____

Solving an Equation

The two members of an equation are said to balance each
other, just as the opposite sides of a balanced seesaw do. To
solve an equation means to find the value of the literal number,
or unknown, which will make the statement of the equality
true.

Rule to Remember

Every equation represents a balance of two members.
In order to maintain this balance, every operation performed on one side of the equation must also be performed
on the other side.

The Equation as a Balance

Suppose we had a seesaw and we placed a weight of 30
pounds on one end of the seesaw. At the other end we place a
40-pound weight. How much more weight will we have to
place at the end holding 30 pounds so that the seesaw will be
in balance?

If we let x be equal to the weight needed, then the equation
we must solve is $30 + x = 40$. The answer we get is 10 pounds.
If a weight of 10 pounds is placed at the end with the 30-
pound weight, then the weights on both ends will be the same
—40 pounds. The seesaw is balanced.

If an additional weight of 6 pounds is now placed at one
end of the seesaw, then a weight of 6 pounds must be placed

at the other end so that the weights at both ends will be the same and the seesaw will remain balanced.

Now you can see if the balance is to be kept, whatever is done at one end of the seesaw must also be done at the other. In other words, the same number must be added to both sides of the equation to keep the balance.

Rules for Solving Equations

Rule of Division

Both members of an equation may be divided by the same number; the resulting quotients will form a new equation.

Illustrative example:

$$100 = 100$$
$$5 = 5$$

$$\frac{100}{5} = \frac{100}{5}$$ Dividing both sides of the first equation by the number 5.

Rule of Multiplication

Both members of an equation may be multiplied by the same number.

Illustrative example:

$$8 = 8$$
$$3 = 3$$

$$8 \times 3 = 8 \times 3$$ Multiply both sides of the equation by the number 3.

$$24 = 24$$

Rule of Addition

The same number may be added to both sides or members of an equation.

Illustrative example:

$$4 = 4$$
$$+3 = +3$$

$4+3 = 4+3$ Add the number 3 to both sides of the equation.

$$7 = 7$$

Rule of Subtraction

The same number may be subtracted from both sides of an equation.

Illustrative example:

$$8 = 8$$
$$-2 = -2$$

$8-2 = 8-2$ The same number, 2, is subtracted from both sides of the equation.

$$6 = 6$$

Solving Equations by the Rule of Division

If we *subtract* a certain amount from a number and then *add* the same amount, the result is the same as the original number. Subtracting and adding the same amount are opposite or *inverse* operations. Similarly, if we *multiply* a number by a certain amount and then *divide* the result by the same amount, we find the original number. Multiplying and dividing by the same number are *inverse* operations.

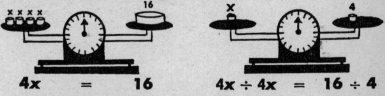

| $4x$ | $=$ | 16 | | $4x \div 4x$ | $=$ | $16 \div 4$ |

Both sides of the equation must be divided by the same number to keep the balance.

Rule to Remember

To solve equations, we use inverse operations. That is, we undo what has been done. Therefore, we must first determine what has been done to the unknown so that we can do the opposite operation to obtain the unknown by itself.

HOW TO DO THE EXAMPLE

Problem: Solve and check the equation $3x = 12$

Method. We would like an equation in which x alone will equal some quantity. Upon examining the equation we see that the unknown, x, has been multiplied by 3. The opposite operation of multiplication by 3 is division by 3.

Since in an equation the value of the left member is the same as the value of the right member, what is done to the left side must also be done to the right side in order to keep the equality of both sides.

Therefore, if we divide the left side by 3, we must also divide the right side by 3. Hence,

$$3x = 12$$
$$\frac{3x}{3} = \frac{12}{3} \quad \text{Dividing both sides by 3}$$
$$x = 4 \quad \text{Answer}$$

Checking. In order to be sure we did not make a mistake, we must substitute the value 4 for x in the original equation. If the left side is then equal to the right side, we know that the answer is correct.

Check $3x = 12$
$$3(4) = 12$$
$$12 = 12$$

The answer, 4, is called the *root* of the equation $3x = 12$.

Solve and check the equation: $.2x = 16$

HOW TO DO THE EXAMPLE

x has been multiplied by .2. The inverse operation is division by .2. Therefore:

$.2x = 16$

$\dfrac{.2x}{.2} = \dfrac{16}{.2}$ Dividing both sides by .2

$x = 80$

$$\begin{array}{r} 80. \\ .2\overline{)\,16.0} \end{array}$$

Check:

$.2x = 16$

$(.2)(80) = 16$

$16.0 = 16$

Solve and check the equation: $18 = \frac{2}{5}m$

HOW TO DO THE EXAMPLE

m is multiplied by $\frac{2}{5}$. The inverse operation is division by $\frac{2}{5}$. Therefore:

$18 = \frac{2}{5} m$

$\dfrac{18}{\frac{2}{5}} = \dfrac{\frac{2}{5} m}{\frac{2}{5}}$ Dividing both sides by $\frac{2}{5}$.

$18 \div \frac{2}{5} = m$

$\frac{\cancel{18}^{9}}{1} \times \frac{5}{\cancel{2}} = m$

$45 = m$

Check

$18 = \frac{2}{5} m$

$18 = \frac{2}{5}(45)$

$18 = 18$

Solve and check the equation: $\frac{3}{2}y = \frac{9}{8}$

HOW TO DO THE EXAMPLE

y is multiplied by $\frac{3}{2}$. The inverse operation is division by $\frac{3}{2}$. Hence:

$\frac{3}{2}y = \frac{9}{8}$

$\dfrac{\frac{3}{2}y}{\frac{3}{2}} = \dfrac{\frac{9}{8}}{\frac{3}{2}}$ Dividing both sides by $\frac{3}{2}$

$y = \frac{9}{8} \div \frac{3}{2}$

$y = \frac{9}{8} \cdot \frac{2}{3}$

$y = \frac{3}{4}$

Check:

$\frac{3}{2}y = \frac{9}{8}$

$\frac{3}{2} \cdot \frac{3}{4} = \frac{9}{8}$

$\frac{9}{8} = \frac{9}{8}$

EXERCISES

Solving Equations by the Rule of Division

Solve the following equations. Check each result.

1. $2x = 14$	7. $28 = 7d$	13. $5 = 2\frac{1}{2}x$
2. $3x = 21$	8. $39 = 13e$	14. $1.2v = 3.6$
3. $9x = 81$	9. $3t = 10$	15. $4.5d = 9$
4. $5x = 30$	10. $4t = 18$	16. $.05n = 2$
5. $14x = 42$	11. $7\frac{1}{2}c = 15$	17. $1.3s = 2.6$
6. $15 = 3c$	12. $9\frac{1}{2}y = 19$	18. $23 = \frac{3}{4}y$

Solving Equations by the Rule of Multiplication

Solve and check the equation: $\dfrac{x}{4} = 3$

HOW TO DO THE EXAMPLE

In the equation, x has been divided by 4. The inverse of division by 4 is multiplication by 4. But if the left side of the equation is multiplied by 4, then the right side must be multiplied by 4 to maintain the balance.

$$\frac{x}{4} = 3$$
$$4\left(\frac{x}{4}\right) = 4(3) \quad \text{Multiplying both sides by 4}$$
$$x = 12$$

Check
$$\frac{x}{4} = 3$$
$$\frac{12}{4} = 3$$
$$3 = 3$$

Another way of solving the problem is by writing $\frac{x}{4}$ as $\frac{1}{4}x$ and dividing both sides by $\frac{1}{4}$. (See page 279).

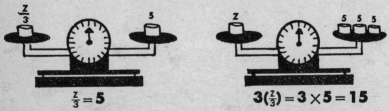

$$\frac{z}{3} = 5 \qquad\qquad 3\left(\frac{z}{3}\right) = 3 \times 5 = 15$$

Both members of an equation must be multiplied by the same number to keep the balance.

Solve and check the equation: $\frac{1}{3}x = \frac{3}{8}$

HOW TO DO THE EXAMPLE

$\frac{1}{3}x$ is the same as $\frac{x}{3}$. Therefore:

	Check
$\frac{x}{3} = \frac{3}{8}$	$\frac{1}{3}x = \frac{3}{8}$
$3\left(\frac{x}{3}\right) = \left(\frac{3}{8}\right)3$ Multiplying both sides by 3	$\frac{1}{3} \cdot \frac{9}{8} = \frac{3}{8}$
$x = \frac{9}{8}$ or $1\frac{1}{8}$	$\frac{3}{8} = \frac{3}{8}$

EXERCISES

Solving Equations by the Rule of Multiplication

Solve each of the following equations and check your results.

1. $\frac{x}{3} = 7$
2. $\frac{1}{4}y = 5$
3. $\frac{c}{7} = 2$
4. $\frac{d}{8} = 3$

5. $\frac{x}{3} = 4$
6. $\frac{c}{8} = 15$
7. $\frac{x}{5} = 12$
8. $\frac{t}{7} = 42$

9. $\frac{t}{5} = 7$
10. $\frac{d}{8} = 9$
11. $\frac{1}{4}b = 86$
12. $\frac{r}{34} = 4$

Solving Equations by the Rule of Subtraction

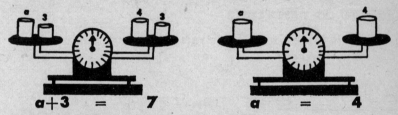

$a + 3 \quad = \quad 7$ $\qquad a \quad = \quad 4$

The same number must be subtracted from both members to keep the balance in an equation.

Solve and check the equation: $x + 4 = 10$

HOW TO DO THE EXAMPLE

We notice that 4 has been added to x. If x is to stand alone, then the 4 must be taken away or subtracted from the left member. If 4 is subtracted from the left side of the equation, it must also be subtracted from the right side to maintain the balance.

[Continued on top of page 282]

$$x + 4 = 10$$
$$\underline{-4 = -4} \text{ Subtracting 4 from both sides}$$
$$x = 6$$

Check
$$x + 4 = 10$$
$$6 + 4 = 10$$
$$10 = 10$$

Solve and check the equation: $y + 2.5 = 6.9$

HOW TO DO THE EXAMPLE

2.5 has been added to y. The inverse operation is subtraction of 2.5. Therefore:

$$y + 2.5 = 6.9$$
$$\underline{-2.5 = -2.5} \text{ Subtracting 2.5 from}$$
$$y = 4.4 \quad \text{both sides}$$

Check
$$y + 2.5 = 6.9$$
$$4.4 + 2.5 = 6.9$$
$$6.9 = 6.9$$

Solve and check the equation: $2\frac{1}{4} + z = 5$

HOW TO DO THE EXAMPLE

$2\frac{1}{4}$ is added to z. The inverse operation is subtraction of $2\frac{1}{4}$. Therefore:

$$2\frac{1}{4} + z = 4\frac{4}{4}$$
$$\underline{-2\frac{1}{4} \quad -2\frac{1}{4}} \text{ Subtracting } 2\frac{1}{4} \text{ from both}$$
$$z = 2\frac{3}{4} \quad \text{sides}$$

Check
$$2\frac{1}{4} + z = 5$$
$$2\frac{1}{4} + 2\frac{3}{4} = 5$$
$$5 = 5$$

EXERCISES

Solving Equations by the Rule of Subtraction

Solve each of the following equations and check the answer.

1. $a + 7 = 9$
2. $b + 2 = 8$
3. $x + 9 = 12$
4. $x + 6 = 11$

5. $a + 7 = 7$
6. $9 = r + 6$
7. $5.8 = c + 4.9$
8. $a + 6\frac{3}{8} = 9\frac{1}{2}$

9. $5y + 58 = 70$
10. $S + \frac{5}{8} = 26$
11. $4x + 9 = 21$
12. $z + 9.1 = 16.8$

13. $d+15=15\frac{3}{4}$ 15. $b+1.4=8.6$ 17. $R+6.5=8$

14. $S+4\frac{1}{2}=9$ 16. $w+4.5=5.86$ 18. $19\frac{2}{5}=x+18\frac{4}{5}$

Solving Equations by the Rule of Addition

 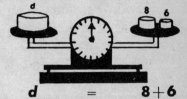

$$d-6 \quad = \quad 8 \qquad\qquad d \quad = \quad 8+6$$

The same number must be added to both members to keep the balance in an equation.

Solve and check the equation: $x-6=13$

HOW TO DO THE EXAMPLE

We notice that 6 has been subtracted from x. To obtain x alone, we must perform the inverse operation of *subtraction*, that is, adding the 6. But if 6 is added to the left side of the equation, it must also be added to the right side. Therefore:

$$x-6= 13$$
$$\underline{+6=+6} \text{ Adding 6 to both sides}$$
$$x \quad = 19$$

Check
$$x-6=13$$
$$19-6=13$$
$$13=13$$

Solve and check the equation: $y-3.2=1.6$

HOW TO DO THE EXAMPLE

3.2 is subtracted from y. The inverse operation is the addition of 3.2 to both sides. Therefore:

$$y-3.2=1.6$$
$$\underline{+3.2=+3.2} \text{ Adding 3.2 to both}$$
$$y \quad = \quad 4.8 \quad \text{sides}$$

Check
$$y-3.2=1.6$$
$$4.8-3.2=1.6$$
$$1.6=1.6$$

Solve and check the equation: $3 = y - 5$

HOW TO DO THE EXAMPLE

5 is subtracted from y. The inverse operation is addition of 5. Therefore:

		Check
$3 = y - 5$		$3 = y - 5$
$\underline{+5 = \ +5}$ Adding 5 to both sides		$3 = 8 - 5$
$8 = y$		$3 = 3$

EXERCISES
Solving Equations by the Rule of Addition

Solve and check the following equations:

1. $r - 3 = 12$
2. $s - 6 = 19$
3. $t - 12 = 9$
4. $x - 5 = 1$
5. $y - 10 = 10$
6. $c - 5\frac{1}{2} = 10$
7. $d - 6\frac{1}{4} = 12$

8. $a - 4\frac{1}{2} = 8\frac{1}{2}$
9. $x - 3\frac{2}{3} = 9$
10. $x - 5\frac{1}{5} = 5\frac{3}{5}$
11. $x - 5\frac{1}{4} = 8\frac{1}{2}$
12. $x - 1.2 = 4.8$
13. $y - 1.4 = 9.3$
14. $c - 1.25 = 4.6$

15. $l - .4 = 1.68$
16. $39 = x - 16$
17. $p - .6 = .8$
18. $d - \frac{3}{5} = 1$
19. $25 = g - 16\frac{1}{4}$
20. $z - 20 = 89$

Solving Equations by the Combination of Rules

Often, more than one rule must be used in solving an equation. In the following examples we shall learn how to use more than one rule to find the value of an unknown in an equation.

Solve the following equation for x and check: $\frac{2x}{3} = 8$.

Rule to Remember

When more than one inverse operation must be performed to solve an equation, *arithmetic terms* of the member which contains the unknown are eliminated *first*, using the rules of addition or subtraction. Then numerical coefficients of the unknown can be eliminated, using the rules of division or multiplication. [Continued on top of page 285]

HOW TO DO THE EXAMPLE

Since in the equation, $\frac{2x}{3} = 8$, the unknown was divided by 3, we must multiply both sides of the equation by 3. Then, since the unknown was multiplied by 2, we divide the result by 2.

Method 1.

$$\frac{2x}{3} = 8$$
$$3 \cdot \frac{2x}{3} = 8 \cdot 3 \quad \text{Multiply by 3}$$
$$2x = 24$$
$$\frac{2x}{2} = \frac{24}{2} \quad \text{Divide by 2}$$
$$x = 12$$

Check
$$\frac{2x}{3} = 8$$
$$\frac{2(12)}{3} = 8$$
$$8 = 8$$

We can combine these two operations into one operation by multiplying $\frac{2}{3}$, the coefficient of x, by $\frac{3}{2}$, the reciprocal of $\frac{2}{3}$. An inverted fraction is the *reciprocal* of the original fraction.

Method 2.

$$\frac{2x}{3} = 8$$
$$\frac{3}{2} \cdot \frac{2x}{3} = 8 \cdot \frac{3}{2} \quad \text{Multiply both sides by } \frac{3}{2}.$$
$$x = 12$$

Solve and check the following equation: $2x + 5 = 13$

HOW TO DO THE EXAMPLE

In the equation 5 is added to 2x. The inverse operation is the subtraction of 5. If 5 is subtracted from both sides, the 2x will remain alone on the left side. Then, since the unknown has been multiplied by 2, we divide both sides by 2.

$$2x + 5 = 13$$
$$\underline{-5 = -5} \quad \text{Subtracting 5 from both sides}$$
$$2x = 8$$
$$\frac{2x}{2} = \frac{8}{2} \quad \text{Dividing both sides by 2}$$
$$x = 4$$

Check
$$2x + 5 = 13$$
$$2(4) + 5 = 13$$
$$8 + 5 = 13$$
$$13 = 13$$

Solve and check the equation: $\frac{y}{3} - 5 = 7$

HOW TO DO THE EXAMPLE

	Check
$\frac{y}{3} - 5 =\;\; 7$	$\frac{y}{3} - 5 = 7$
$\underline{+5 = +5}$	$\frac{36}{3} - 5 = 7$
$\frac{y}{3}\;\;\; =\; 12$	$12 - 5 = 7$
$3 \cdot \frac{y}{3} = 12 \cdot 3$	$7 = 7$
$y = 36$	

Solve and check the equation: $x + 2x = 21$

Rule to Remember

Whenever like terms appear in one member of an equation that has to be solved, the like terms are combined before any other operation is done.

HOW TO DO THE EXAMPLE

$x + 2x = 21$

$3x = 21$ The like terms x and 2x
have been combined

$\frac{3x}{3} = \frac{21}{3}$

$x = 7$

Check

$x + 2x = 21$

$7 + 2(7) = 21$

$7 + 14 = 21$

$21 = 21$

Solve and check the equation: $8 + 3x = 7x$

HOW TO DO THE EXAMPLE

The unknown, x, appears on both sides of the equation. We must have x on only one side. We notice that 3x is added to 8. If 3x is subtracted from both sides of the

[Continued on top of page 287]

equation, 8 will be on the left side and the x's on the right side. We can then divide both sides by the number of x's.

$$8+3x = 7x$$

$$\underline{-3x = -3x}$$ Subtracting 3x
$$8 \quad = \quad 4x$$ from both sides

$$\frac{8}{4} \quad = \quad \frac{4x}{4}$$ Dividing both sides by 4

$$2 = \quad x$$

Check

$$8+3x = 7x$$
$$8+3(2) = 7(2)$$
$$8+6 \quad = 14$$
$$14 = 14$$

Solve and check the equation: $8x-4 = 3x+21$

HOW TO DO THE EXAMPLE

3x has been added to 21. If 3x is subtracted from both sides, the literal term will appear only on the left. 4 has been subtracted from 8x. If 4 is added to both sides, the numerical term will appear only on the right side. Hence:

$$8x-4 = 3x+21$$

$$\underline{-3x = -3x}$$ Subtracting 3x from both sides

$$5x-4 = 21$$

$$\underline{+4 = +4}$$ Adding 4 to both sides

$$5x = 25$$

$$\frac{5x}{5} = \frac{25}{5}$$ Dividing both sides by 5

$$x = 5$$

Check

$$8x \; -4 = 3x+21$$
$$8(5)-4 = 3(5)+21$$
$$40 \; -4 = 15+21$$
$$36 = 36$$

EXERCISES

Solving Algebraic Equations

Solve and check the following equations:

1. $3x + 2x = 25$
2. $9x + 3x = 36$
3. $6x - 4x = 18$
4. $5s - 4s = 10$
5. $5r + 7r = 48$
6. $9c - 48 = 24$
7. $22a + 11a = 66$
8. $15c - 8c = 21$
9. $1\frac{1}{2}d + 4\frac{1}{2}d = 24$
10. $5\frac{3}{7}e - 2\frac{3}{7}e = 30$
11. $\frac{1}{2}x - \frac{1}{3}x = 6$
12. $\frac{2}{3}a + \frac{5}{3}a = 7$
13. $1.8d + 3.2d = 40$
14. $2A - 3 = 9$
15. $3A - 15 = 3$
16. $4A - 3 = 25$
17. $6A - 3 = 9$
18. $15 = 2N - 7$
19. $5B - 6 = 14$
20. $3T - 2 = 15$
21. $2T - 5 = 6$

22. $2R - 4\frac{1}{2} = 5\frac{1}{2}$
23. $3v - 6\frac{2}{3} = 8\frac{1}{3}$
24. $3x - \frac{1}{2} = 1$
25. $3x - \frac{1}{5} = 10$
26. $2w - 1.2 = 4.8$
27. $3t + 2.4 = 4.2$
28. $5t - 1.5 = 3.7$
29. $2s + 1.25 = 4.5$
30. $3b - 4.3 = 8.06$
31. $5d + 6.5 = 12.8$
32. $3.6a - 2.4a = 24$
33. $\frac{1}{2}e + \frac{1}{4}e = 6$
34. $\frac{2}{3}f - \frac{1}{5}f = 20$
35. $\frac{1}{5}r + \frac{1}{4}r = 10$
36. $\frac{1}{3}x - \frac{1}{8}x = 6$
37. $3A + 5 = 14$
38. $2B + 9 = 21$
39. $5C + 8 = 28$
40. $6n + 3 = 21$
41. $15 = 3n + 3$
42. $24 = 2n + 8$

43. $2c + 4.5 = 12.5$
44. $3y + 7 = 7$
45. $9t + 5 = 23$
46. $2t + 3 = 14$
47. $2t + 3\frac{1}{2} = 9\frac{1}{2}$
48. $3c + 14 = 25$
49. $3x + 4\frac{1}{2} = 6$
50. $4r + 7 = 28$
51. $15 = 3t + 15$
52. $\frac{1}{4}t - \frac{1}{6}t = 4$
53. $9s - .2 = 17.8$
54. $5x + 3x - 2 = 14$
55. $6x - 3x - 5 = 7$
56. $5x + 5 + 4 = 19$
57. $7x - 1 - 2 = 11$
58. $3x + 2 + 5x = 18$
59. $3x + 5 - 3 = 16$
60. $x + 2x + 2 = 17$
61. $6C - 7 - 4C = 17$
62. $40 = 7d + 2d - 5$
63. $50 = 5y - 3y + 8$

GENERAL SKILL EXERCISE

How are you doing? Try the following test. If you get any wrong, turn to the pages shown after each question. Practice those problems until you have mastered them.

1. Whatever is done to one side of an equation must be .... (page 276).

2. Both members of an equation must be .... (page 276).

3. Algebraic equations can be solved by using .... operations (page 277).

4. In solving an equation, you must always obtain the unknown .... (alone, combined) on one side of the equation (page 278).

5. Finding the value of the unknown of an equation is called .... the equation (page 275).

6. The operation opposite to division is .... (page 280).

7. The fraction $\frac{2}{5}$ is the .... of the fraction $\frac{5}{2}$. (page 285).

8. When more than one inverse operation is performed, the rules of addition and subtraction may be used .... (before, after) the rules of division or multiplication (page 284).

9. Like terms are always .... before any other operation is performed (page 286).

10. When an equation is solved, the unknown is on .... , whereas the numbers are on the .... (page 287).

My Score _____

The Formula

The selling price of an article is equal to the sum of the cost of the article and the gain on the cost. If we let $S.P.$ stand for the selling price, C for the cost and G for the gain, then a rule for finding the selling price can be written as the equation:
$S.P. = C + G$

If the driver knows the distance he must go and the rate of speed he can travel, he can find the time it will take him to arrive at his destination by using a formula.

1. Write a formula for the time it will take the driver to reach his destination.

The *distance* that a car will travel is equal to the product of the average *rate* and the *time* required for the trip. If we let d stand for the distance, r for the average rate, and t for the time, then a rule for finding the distance any car will travel in a given time can be written as the equation: $d = rt$

In both examples, above, the *rules* were translated into equations which contain symbols. Such equations are called *formulas*.

A formula is easier to remember than a long statement of the rule, and it saves time and space.

Rule to Remember

A formula is an equation which contains algebraic symbols and expresses a rule or a principle.

HOW TO DO THE PROBLEMS

Problem **1.** Write a formula for the number of inches *i* in *f* feet.

Method. There are 12 inches in 1 foot. In *f* feet there are *f* times as many inches. Therefore, the formula is

$$i = 12f$$

This can be read, "the *number* of inches is 12 times the *number* of feet."

Problem **2.** If *h* hats cost *d* dollars, write a formula for the cost *C* in dollars of one hat.

Method. If *h* hats cost *d* dollars, then one hat will cost *d* dollars divided by *h*. Therefore, the formula is

$$C = \frac{d}{h}$$

Problem **3.** Write as a formula: The average *A* of 3 numbers is equal to their sum divided by 3.

Method. Let the numbers be represented as *x, y* and *z*, respectively. Then

$$A = \frac{x + y + z}{3}$$

Problem **4.** Write as a formula the rule: The number of points (*P*) that a basketball team will score in a game is equal to the sum of the number of fouls (*F*) and twice the number of goals (*G*).

$$P = F + 2G$$

Writing the Rule a Formula Expresses

Often we have to write the rule which is being expressed briefly as a formula.

How to Write the Rule of a Formula

Problem 1. State the rule for the formula $r = \dfrac{d}{t}$ if $r =$ the average rate, $d =$ the distance, and $t =$ the time.

Rule. The average rate is equal to the quotient of the distance divided by the time. Or, the average rate is equal to the distance divided by the time.

Problem 2. The total value V in cents of a number of stamps is given by the formula $V = 2a + 3b$. If $a =$ the number of two-cent stamps, and $b =$ the number of three-cent stamps, write a statement of the formula.

Statement. The total value in cents of a number of 2 and 3-cent stamps can be found by multiplying 2¢ by the number of two-cent stamps, multiplying 3¢ by the number of three-cent stamps, and adding these two products.

Problem 3. State the rule for the formula $C = 20a$ if $a =$ the number of pounds of apples and $C =$ the cost in cents.

Answer: The cost in cents of apples is equal to the product of 20 multiplied by the number of pounds.

This formula may be used when the price of apples is 20¢ per pound.

EXERCISES

The Formula

1. If an automobile travels 50 miles an hour, write the formula for the distance, d, that it will cover in t hours.

2. An apple costs 8 cents. Write the formula for the cost, c, of n apples.

3. Mr. Samuel earns $28 every day he works. Write the formula for his salary, S, if he works d days.

4. Candy sells for $1.69 a pound. Write the formula for the cost, c, of p pounds.

5. John is 4 times as old as Henry. Represent in symbols.

6. Mary is 5 years older than Helen. Represent this in literal numbers.

7. A man earns 6 per cent interest on his investment. Write the formula for the interest i he should get if he invests p dollars.

8. A man saves $5 a week. Write as a formula the amount he saves, s, in w weeks.

9. Write as a formula, "The area of a rectangle is equal to the base multiplied by the altitude."

10. Write as a formula, "The area of a triangle is equal to one-half the product of the base and the altitude."

11. Write as a formula, "The circumference of a circle is the product of π and the diameter."

12. Write the formula for the average of three numbers x, y and z.

13. Write as a formula, "The sum of three angles, A, B and C, of a triangle is 180°."

14. The length of a rectangular room is l inches and its width is w inches. Write a formula for the perimeter, the total distance around all four sides of the room.

15. Write a formula for the number of days in a weeks and b days.

Evaluation of Formulas

If the value of every letter but one in a formula is known, the value of the unknown letter can be found. This is known as *evaluating* a formula for the unknown. To evaluate a formula we substitute numerical values for literal numbers, and solve the problem.

How to Evaluate Formulas

Problem 1. If $R = \dfrac{D}{T}$ find the value of R when $D = 60$ and $T = 10$.

Method. $R = \dfrac{D}{T}$

$R = \frac{60}{10}$ Substituting values in the formula

$R = 6$

[Continued on top of page 293]

Problem 2. Using the formula $d=rt$, find the value of d when $r=30$ and $t=4$.

Method. $d=rt$

$d=(30)(4)$

$d=120$

Problem 3. The area of a rectangle is 120 sq. ft. Find the length if the width is 5 feet. Use the formula $A=LW$.

Method. $A=LW$

$120= L (5)$

$\dfrac{120}{5}= \dfrac{L}{5} (5)$ Dividing both sides by 5

24 feet $=L$ Length is 24 feet.

Problem 4. The volume of a rectangular solid is 200 cubic feet. The length is 20 feet and the width is 5 feet. Using the formula $V=lwh$, find the height.

Method. $V=lwh$

$200=(20)(5) h$

$200=100 h$

$\frac{200}{100}=\frac{100}{100} h$

2 ft. $=h$ Height is 2 feet.

EXERCISES

Evaluation of Formulas

1. The formula for the perimeter of a triangle whose sides are a, b and c is $p=a+b+c$. Find the perimeter of a triangle whose sides are:

a. 15, 12 and 24

b. 3, 4 and 5

c. 16, 12 and 20

d. $6x$, $4x$ and $9x$

e. $3x$, $4x$ and $5x$

f. $5x$, $12x$ and $13x$

2. The formula for the perimeter, p, of an isosceles triangle two of whose sides are each equal to a, and whose base is equal to b, is $p=2a+b$. Find the perimeter of each of the following isosceles triangles:

   a. $a=10$ and $b=4$ *d.* $a=9.1$ and $b=3.8$
   b. $a=9$ and $b=5$ *e.* $a=8\frac{3}{4}$ and $b=5\frac{1}{4}$
   c. $a=11.5$ and $b=8$ *f.* $a=5x$ and $b=2x$

3. The formula for the perimeter of an equilateral triangle is $p=3s$. Find the perimeter of the equilateral triangles whose sides are:

   a. 5   *c.* 5.5   *e.* $9x$
   b. 2   *d.* $3\frac{1}{3}$ *f.* $6x$

4. The formula for the perimeter of a square is $p=4s$. Find the perimeter of each of the following squares whose sides are:

   a. 4   *c.* 3.5   *e.* $4\frac{1}{2}$
   b. 7   *d.* 6.3   *f.* $8x$

5. The formula for the circumference of a circle is $C=\pi D$. Find the circumferences of the circles whose diameters are: (Use $\pi = \frac{22}{7}$)

   a. 14   *c.* 21   *e.* 8
   b. 7   *d.* 5   *f.* 4.3

Exponents

Exponents provide a mathematical shorthand. An *exponent* is a number that indicates the number of times a number is to be multiplied by itself. The number to be multiplied by itself is called the *base*.

The exponent is written as a small number to the right of and above the base. For example, in the expression x^2, the 2 is the exponent and the x is the base. In the expression y^5, y is the base and 5 is the exponent. In the expression $2a^3$, 3 is the exponent and a is the base. If the base has no written exponent then the exponent 1 is understood.

a^1 means a, x^2 means $x \cdot x$, y^5 means $y \cdot y \cdot y \cdot y \cdot y$, $2a^3$ means $2 \cdot a \cdot a \cdot a$

x^2 is read as *x to the second power, x square* or *x squared; x^3* is read as *x to the third power,* or *x cubed.*

Evaluating Expressions Having Exponents

Problem 1. If $y = 4$, what is the value of y^4?

Solution: $y^4 = 4^4$

              $4^4 = 4 \times 4 \times 4 \times 4 = 256$

              $y^4 = 256$

[Continued on top of page 295]

Problem 2. If $y = 4$, what is the value of $2y^2$?

Solution:
$$y^2 = 4^2$$
$$4^2 = 4 \times 4 = 16$$
$$2y^2 = 2 \cdot 4^2 = 2 \cdot 16 = 32$$
$$2y^2 = 32$$

Problem 3. If $y = 4$, what is the value of $\left(\dfrac{3}{y}\right)^3$?

Solution:
$$\left(\frac{3}{y}\right)^3 = \left(\frac{3}{4}\right)^3$$
$$\left(\frac{3}{4}\right)^3 = \frac{3}{4} \times \frac{3}{4} \times \frac{3}{4} = \frac{27}{64}$$
$$\left(\frac{3}{y}\right)^3 = \frac{27}{64}$$

EXERCISES
Evaluating Formulas

1. The formula for the area of a square is $A = s^2$. Find A when s equals:

a. 3	d. 5	g. $\frac{1}{2}$	j. $\frac{3}{4}$	m. .8	p. 4.6
b. 6	e. 12	h. $\frac{1}{3}$	k. $\frac{2}{8}$	n. .7	q. 7.8
c. 8	f. 15	i. $\frac{1}{7}$	l. $\frac{7}{13}$	o. .25	r. 1.25

2. The formula for the total surface area of a cube is $S = 6e^2$. Find the total surface area of each cube if the edge, e, is:

a. 2	c. $\frac{1}{2}$	e. .9	g. 1.3
b. 4	d. $\frac{3}{5}$	f. .75	h. 4.2

3. If $x = 2$ and $y = 3$ find the value of each of the following algebraic expressions:

a. $3x + 6y$	c. $x^2 - y$	e. $y^2 - 3x$
b. $5x - 3y$	d. $x^2 + y^2$	f. $x^2 + 3x - y^2 + 2y$

Finding Formulas from Tables

In finding formulas, we are usually given the values of the related numbers to determine how each one relates to or depends upon the other. The related numbers are called *variables*, for their values vary. When we understand how the numbers vary, we can express in a formula the relationship between the variables.

How to Find Formulas from Tables

Problem 1. Write a formula which will express the relationship between N, the number of hats, and C, the cost of each hat as shown in the following table:

N	1	2	3	4	5	6	7
C	5	10	15	20	25	30	35

Method: Notice that the value of C is always 5 times the value of N. The formula that expresses this relationship is $C = 5N$.

Problem 2. Write a formula which expresses the relationship between the numbers in the following table. Fill in the missing values.

Gallons of gas	1	2	3	4	5	6	?
Cost	$.30	$.60	$.90	$1.20	?	$1.80	$2.10

Method: Since one gallon of gas costs $.30, the total cost of any number of gallons may be obtained by multiplying the number of *gallons* by $.30. This gives the formula $C = \$.30N$. Using this formula, we see that the first missing value may be obtained by multiplying $.30 by 5. The first missing value, therefore, is $1.50. The second missing value is 7, since $2.10 \div \$.30 = 7$.

Problem 3. Write a formula which expresses the relationship between the numbers in the following table.

Time in City A	1	2	3	4	5	6
Time in City B	3	4	5	6	7	8

Method: By studying the table we see that the time in City B is always 2 hours later than the time in City A. This gives the formula $B = A + 2$, which may also be expressed as

$$B - A = 2 \quad \text{or} \quad A = B - 2.$$

EXERCISES

Finding Formulas from Tables

1. The following table shows the cost of fountain pens at $2 each.

n	1	2	3	4	5	6
c	2	4	6	8	10	12

   a. As n changes from 1 to 6, c changes from .... to ....

   b. To find each value of c, multiply the corresponding value of n by ....

   c. The formula for this table is ....

2. The following table shows the cost of books at $3 each.

n	1	2	3	4	5	6
c	3	6	9	12	15	18

   a. As n changes from 2 to 5, c changes from .... to ....

   b. Each value of c is .... times the corresponding value of n.

   c. This table represents the formula ....

3. A father is 23 years older than his son. The table shows their **ages** from the time the father is 30.

s	7	8	9	10	11	12	13	14
f	30	31	32	33	34	35	36	37

   a. As the father's age changes from 32 to 37, the son's age changes from .... to ....

   b. To compute the father's age, ... must be .... to the son's age.

   c. Write a formula for this table.

   d. What will the father's age be when the son is 25?

   e. How old will the son be when the father is 50?

4. The following is a table for the distance that a train will **cover** when it travels 50 miles an hour.

t	1	2	3	4	5	6	7	8
d	50	100	150	200	250	300	350	400

   a. As *t* changes from 2 to 6, *d* changes from ....
        to ....

   b. To find *d* multiply each corresponding value of *t* by ....

   c. Write the formula for this table.

  5. Study each of the following tables and write a formula to represent the facts.

(*a*)

n	3	4	5	6	7	8
c	15	20	25	30	35	40

(*d*)

x	4	5	6	7	8
y	1	2	3	4	5

(*b*)

t	2	3	4	5	6	7
d	40	60	80	100	120	140

(*e*)

x	2	3	4	5	6
y	5	7	9	11	13

(*c*)

x	0	1	2	3	4
y	2	3	4	5	6

(*f*)

x	6	8	10	12	14
y	3	4	5	6	7

  6. Make a table for each of the following expressions. Let *x* equal each of the expressions and use the numbers 4 to 10 for *n*.

   a. $n+6$ *e.* $3n$ *h.* $4n+2$

   b. $n-3$ *f.* $2n+1$ *i.* $2n-1$

   c. $n+5$ *g.* $3n+5$ *j.* $4n-3$

   d. $n-1$

  7. If $l=3w$, complete the following table:

w	1	2	3	4	5	6	7
l	3	6					

  8. If $p=4s$, complete the following table:

s	1	2	3	4	5
p	4	8			

  9. If $y=x+7$, make a table showing the values of *y* when $x=$ 1, 2, 3, 4, 5, 9, 10 and 12.

  10. If $y=x-4$, make a table showing the values of *y* when $x=$ 4, 5, 6, 10, 12 and 14.

  11. If $y=2x+1$, make a table showing the values of *y* when $x=$ 1, 2, 3, 5, 7, 20, 22 and 25.

  12. If $y=3x-2$, make a table showing the values of *y* when $x=$ 1, 2, 3, 4 and 5.

Signed Numbers

Signed numbers are arithmetic or literal numbers which are preceded by a + (plus) or a − (minus) sign. A number preceded by a plus sign is called a *positive* number. Thus +8, +$\frac{1}{2}$ and +*ab* are positive numbers. A number preceded by a minus sign is called a *negative* number. Thus, −6, −$\frac{3}{7}$ and −*bc* are negative numbers. These positive and negative numbers are signed numbers.

The number itself indicates a *quantity* or *magnitude;* the sign indicates the *direction* in which the amount is measured. For this reason, signed numbers are also called *directed numbers.*

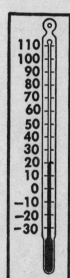

The + and − signs of signed numbers indicate opposite directions or meanings. The + sign indicates the direction of a gain, an income or a distance upward. The − sign indicates the direction of a loss, an expense or a distance downward. For example, +25° means 25 degrees above zero; −10° indicates 10 degrees below zero.

At the end of a year one business reported the result of the year's operation as +$20,000. In another business the year's result was −$8,000. The first business had a $20,000 profit; the second business had an $8,000 loss.

Signed numbers can be compared with the numbers on a Centigrade thermometer (at left). After locating zero on the thermometer, we always find the positive numbers above zero and the negative numbers below zero.

The *absolute value* of a number is its numerical value or the number of units it contains regardless of its sign. For example, +7, and −7 have the same absolute value, 7, since there are 7 units in either number.

If a number is written without a sign in front of it, it is understood to be a positive number. For example, 8 means the same as if it were written +8.

EXERCISES

Signed Numbers

1. If 5° above 0 is represented by 5°, 5° below zero is **represented** by ....

2. Represent each of the following temperatures using **signed** numbers:

    a. 10 degrees above zero   *d.* 15 degrees below **zero**
    b. 7 degrees above zero   *e.* 2 degrees above **zero**
    c. 12 degrees below zero   *f.* 8 degrees below **zero**

3. The temperatures reported for a city on a certain day **were** as follows:

Hour P.M.	1	2	3	4	5	6	7	8	9	10	11	12
Temp.	0	+2	+3	+1	−2	−5	−7	−11	−9	−9	−8	−1

    a. What was the temperature at 6 p.m.? at 1 p.m.?
    b. What was the highest temperature?
    c. What was the lowest temperature?

4. If north of the equator is considered a positive direction **and** south of the equator is considered a negative direction, express **each** of the following as a positive or negative number.

    a. 50 miles north   *c.* 100 miles north
    b. 30 miles south   *d.* 350 miles south

5. If a positive number is used to express the height above a cer-tain fixed level, then a .... number is used **to** express a depth below the fixed level.

6. Express the following as signed numbers:

    a. a balloon is 350 feet above sea level
    b. an airplane is 1500 feet above sea level
    c. a submarine descended 85 feet below **sea level**
    d. a boat sank in 123 fathoms of water
    e. a mountain is 9000 feet high
    f. a monument is 565 feet high
    g. the depth of a river is 36 feet

h. an elevator is 615 feet above the main floor

i. an elevator is 32 feet below the main floor

7. If deposits in a bank are represented by positive numbers, then withdrawals are represented by .... numbers.

8. Represent the following through the use of signed numbers:

    a. a deposit of $500   *c.* a withdrawal of $50

    b. a withdrawal of $125   *d.* a deposit of $67

9. If a profit is represented by a positive number, then a loss is represented by a .... number.

10. Explain the meaning of a business transaction resulting in:

    a. +$9   *c.* −$50

    b. −$18   *d.* +$70

Addition of Signed Numbers with Like Signs

Adding refers to the combining of two or more numbers into a single number which represents the sum of the numbers. The numbers that are being added may either be positive or negative. The sum of the numbers may also be either positive or negative.

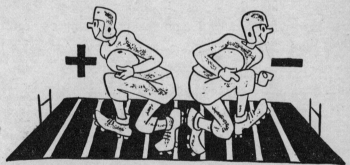

Joe was a member of the Blue Team. He carried the football to +8. But on the next play the opposing team moved the ball −3. To find the location of the ball now, Joe added +8 and −3 and he found that the ball was at +5.

1. On the third play the opponents had a victory of −7. Where was the ball?

2. On the fourth play, the Blue Team scored +16. Where was the ball now?

Positive Numbers

If a man has $5, represented by $+5$, in one pocket and $10, represented by $+10$, in another pocket, he has a total of $+15$, or $15. The addition can be written either vertically or horizontally.

$$\begin{array}{r} +\ 5 \\ +10 \\ \hline +15 \end{array} \quad \text{or} \quad (+5)+(+10)=+15$$

If two positive numbers are added the result is a positive number.

Negative Numbers

If a man owes one person $200, represented by -200, and another person $50, represented by -50, then he owes a total of -250, or $250. The addition can be written vertically or horizontally.

$$\begin{array}{r} -200 \\ -\ 50 \\ \hline -250 \end{array} \quad \text{or} \quad (-200)+(-50)=-250$$

Thus, if we add two negative numbers the result is a negative number.

Rule to Remember

When adding signed numbers having like signs, add their absolute values and place the common sign before their sum.

Addition of Signed Numbers with Unlike Signs

Mr. Smith has $40, represented by $+40$. He owes Mr. Henry $10. This debt is represented as -10. The result of combining or "adding" the two leaves Mr. Smith with $30. This is the same as saying that adding $+40$ and -10 gives $+30$ or $30 as the result.

If Mr. Smith had $10, represented as $+10$, and owed $40, represented as -40, then he would still owe Mr. Henry $30.

Therefore, the result of adding or combining $+10$ and -40 is -30.

The above two examples indicate that if a man *has more* than he owes, then he will end up *having the difference* between what he has and what he owes. If he *owes more* than he has, the result is that he *owes the difference* between what he owes and what he has.

Rule to Remember

When adding two signed numbers having *unlike* signs, *subtract* the smaller absolute value from the larger and place in front of the difference the sign of the *larger* absolute value.

HOW TO DO THE PROBLEMS

Problem 1. Perform the following additions:

Solution.
$$\begin{array}{c} +2 \\ +5 \\ \hline 7 \end{array} \quad \begin{array}{c} -6 \\ -4 \\ \hline -10 \end{array} \quad \begin{array}{c} +8 \\ -6 \\ \hline 2 \end{array} \quad \begin{array}{c} -4 \\ +12 \\ \hline 8 \end{array} \quad \begin{array}{c} +3 \\ -3 \\ \hline 0 \end{array}$$

Remember: If no sign is written in front of a number, it is understood to be a positive number. Zero is neither positive nor negative.

Problem 2. Find the sum of -2 and -3

Solution. The question is "How much is -2 and -3?" Writing this as a vertical addition, it becomes

$$\begin{array}{c} -2 \\ -3 \\ \hline -5 \end{array}$$ The answer is, therefore, -5.

Problem 3. Find the sum in each of the following:

a. $-7, +11$ c. $+3, -17$
b. $+6, +12$ d. $-1.2, -3.5$

[Continued on top of page 304]

Solution

    a. $-7 + 11 = +4$ *c.* $+3 - 17 = -14$

    b. $+6 + 12 = +18$ *d.* $-1.2 - 3.5 = -4.7$

Problem 4. Combine: $-2x + 4y - 3x - 6y$

Solution. First we combine like terms, following the rules for adding signed numbers:

    $-2x$ and $-3x = -5x$

    $4y$ and $-6y = -2y.$

Now we connect the terms with signs of operation. Therefore,

    $-2x + 4y - 3x - 6y = -5x - 2y$

EXERCISES

Addition of Signed Numbers

1. *Add:*

a. $+10$ $\ +3$	*e.* -10 $\ -3$	*i.* $+10$ $\ +3$	*m.* -10 $\ -3$
b. $+21$ $\ +7$	*f.* -41 -17	*j.* -21 $\ -7$	*n.* -17 -14
c. $+6$ $+9$	*g.* -5 -1	*k.* $+5$ $+5$	*o.* -6 -6
d. $+10$ $\ \ 0$	*h.* $\ \ 0$ -11	*l.* $+12$ $+22$	*p.* -9 -11

2. *Add:*

    a. $(+2)+(+8)$ *c.* $(-6)+(+6)$ *e.* $(+15)+(-20)$

    b. $(-12)+(+6)$ *d.* $(-9)+(-4)$ *f.* $(-9)+(+9)$

3. *Add:*

a. $+8$ -14	*b.* $+26$ -14	*c.* -29 -15	*d.* -14 $+12$

e. $+8.8$
  -3.5

k. -9.6
  $- .5$

q. -10.85
  $+12.72$

w. -6.72
  $+4.58$

f. $-7\frac{1}{2}$
  $+6\frac{1}{2}$

l. $-7\frac{1}{4}$
  $+5\frac{3}{4}$

r. $-5\frac{4}{5}$
  $+3\frac{2}{5}$

x. $-12\frac{1}{7}$
  $- 5\frac{1}{7}$

g. $- 8$
  $+10$
  $- 5$

m. -12
  $- 6$
  $+20$

s. $+8\frac{1}{2}$
  $-6\frac{3}{4}$
  $+2\frac{1}{4}$

y. -4.5
  $+5.7$
  -3.8

h. $+12n$
  $+14n$

n. $- 6x$
  $-12x$

t. $+ 9T$
  $+12T$

z. $-15R$
  $+22R$

i. $-6H$
  $+8H$

o. $- 5a$
  $-10a$

u. 0
  $+12a$

aa. $-14b$
  0

j. $+8\frac{3}{5}t$
  $-5\frac{2}{5}t$

p. $-4\frac{1}{3}r$
  $-5\frac{1}{3}r$

v. $-6.7a$
  $+5.8a$

bb. $-5\frac{3}{4}b$
  $+2\frac{1}{3}b$

4. *Solve each of the following as an addition example:*

  1. An elevator goes 30 feet up and then 40 feet down.
    a. In what direction is the elevator from the starting point?
    b. How far is it from the starting point?

  2. A man travels 5 miles east and than 10 miles west.
    a. In what direction is he from the starting point?
    b. How far is he from the starting point?

  3. At 10 p.m. the thermometer reads 1° below zero. During the next hour the temperature dropped 4°. What is the temperature at 11 p.m.?

  4. A man had $500 in the bank and withdrew $350. How much did he have left?

  5. A man traveled 100 miles north and then 150 miles south.
    a. In what direction is he from the starting point?
    b. How far is he from the starting point?

Subtraction of Signed Numbers

Jane has savings of $18.90. Tom has no savings, and he has a debt of $3. What is the difference between Jane's money and Tom's money? In other words, how many dollars more must Tom have to equal the amount Jane has?

We represent Jane's savings as $+18.90$ and Tom's debt of $3 as -3. To find the difference we must subtract -3 from $+18.90$. Subtracting a negative value is equivalent to adding its inverse positive value. That is, we must change the sign of the subtrahend and add.

$$
\begin{array}{rcl}
+18.90 & = & +18.90 \\
\text{Subtract} - \underline{3.00} & & \text{Add} + \underline{3.00} \\
& & +21.90
\end{array}
$$

Thus, the difference between the money Jane has and what Tom owes is $21.90. Tom must get $21.90 to have savings equal to Jane's.

One December day in Wisconsin the temperature reached 18°. The lowest temperature in that place on that particular date was $-26°$. How many degrees must the mercury drop from its position at 18° to equal the lowest temperature on that date? We must find the difference between the final temperature, -26 and the beginning temperature, $+18$. Subtracting a positive value is equivalent to adding its inverse negative value: change the sign of the subtrahend and add.

$$
\begin{array}{rcl}
-26 & = & -26 \\
- \underline{+18} & & + \underline{-18} \\
& & -44
\end{array}
$$

The temperature must decrease by 44°. That is, the mercury dropped 44°.

Rule to Remember

To subtract signed numbers, change the sign of the subtrahend and add.

[Continued on top of page 307]

HOW TO DO THE PROBLEMS

Problem 1. Subtract the following:

a.
$$\begin{array}{r} +16 \\ -\ 8 \end{array} = \ \begin{array}{r} +16 \\ +\ +\ 8 \\ \hline +24 \end{array}$$

c.
$$\begin{array}{r} +76 \\ +19 \end{array} = \ \begin{array}{r} +76 \\ +-19 \\ \hline +57 \end{array}$$

b.
$$\begin{array}{r} -28 \\ -22 \end{array} = \ \begin{array}{r} -28 \\ +\ +22 \\ \hline -\ 6 \end{array}$$

d.
$$\begin{array}{r} -82 \\ +60 \end{array} = \ \begin{array}{r} -82 \\ +-60 \\ \hline -142 \end{array}$$

Problem 2. Find the difference:

a. $(+4x)-(-2x)=(+4x)+(+2x)=+6x$

b. $(-5b)-(-4b)=(-5b)+(+4b)=-b$

c. $(-2x)-(+6b)=(-2x)+(-6b)=-2x-6b$

d. $(-8t)-(-13d)=(-8t)+(+13d)=-8t+13d$

e. $(5a)-(+3c)=(5a)+(-3c)=5a-3c$

EXERCISES

Subtraction of Signed Numbers

Subtract the second number from the first:

1. 3, −3
2. −9, +4
3. +63, +33
4. 3z, −5z
5. −6, −82
6. 45a, +a
7. −d, +8d
8. +52, +21
9. −3x, +2x
10. −5a, −4a
11. 98s, −43s
12. 4, +56
13. +8a, −2a
14. −98w, −17w
15. +16, +16
16. +32d, +3d
17. −.9, +.34
18. +23d, +9d
19. 3s, −5s
20. 78, +8d

State each of the following as a subtraction example, and solve.

1. A fish was beneath the water at a distance represented by −20f. The top of a fishing rod was above the water at a distance represented by +2.5f. What is the distance from the fish to the top of the fishing rod?

2. 0 represented the beginning score of each person playing a certain game. +20 was the highest possible score, and −20 was the lowest possible score.

a. Bob received +17. How many points was he from the highest possible score? How many points was he from the lowest possible?

b. Alice received −8. How many points was she from the highest possible score? How many points from the lowest possible?

Multiplication of Signed Numbers

Multiplication is a short way of finding the sum of equal quantities.

If Jim earns $15 a day, represented by +15, in five days he will have earned $75, since

$$5(+15) = +75$$

If Jim's living expenses average $13 a day, represented by −13, in five days he will have spent $65, since the sum of five −13's is −65.

$$5(-13) = -65$$

In algebra, multiplication can also help find the total when a number of equal quantities are subtracted.

If $1 of Jim's daily income is deducted, or subtracted, for income tax, the effect this has on his salary is to lower it $5 each week. Subtracting five $1 payments would be written −5(+1).

To subtract, change the sign of the subtrahends, and proceed as in addition:

$$-5(+1) = +5(-1)$$

Since the sum of five −1's is −5,

$$-5(+1) = +5(-1) = -5$$

If Steve decides to give up smoking so that he can subtract this $2 monthly expense from his budget, he will be $24 ahead at the end of a year. Subtracting twelve $2 expenses would be written

$$-12(-2)$$

Following the rule for subtraction, we find that

$$-12(-2) = +12(+2) = +24.$$

Notice the signs of the answers to the multiplications done on page 308.

$+15$	-13	$+1$	-2
$+\ 5$	$+\ 5$	-5	-12
$+75$	-65	-5	$+24$

Rules to Remember

1. When two numbers having *like* signs are multiplied, the product is *positive*.

2. When two numbers having *unlike* signs are multiplied, the product is *negative*.

3. When three numbers are to be multiplied, find the product of two numbers, and multiply this product by the third number.

HOW TO DO THE EXAMPLE

1. $(+3) (+6) = +18$
2. $(-3) (-6) = +18$
3. $(+3) (-6) = -18$
4. $(-3) (+6) = -18$
5. $(-3a) (-6b) = +18ab$
6. $(+3a) (-6b) = -18ab$
7. $(+3) (-2a) (+3b) = -18ab$
8. $(+3a) (+6a) = +18a^2$

EXERCISES
Multiplication of Signed Numbers

Multiply:

1. $(-4) (-5)$
2. $(+60) (-2)$
3. $(4a) (5b)$
4. $(-3) (-2) (-8)$
5. $(+5) (-6a)$
6. $(22) (-24)$
7. $(50a) (2)$
8. $(+8c) (-8c)$
9. $(+52) (-3) (+a)$
10. $(-20) (2) (-4)$
11. $(a) (-b)$
12. $(-4) (-44)$
13. $(+54) (-6)$
14. $(4a) (-2)$
15. $(+34) (-6)$
16. $(45) (-4) (2a)$
17. $(90) (5) (f)$
18. $(+8) (-78)$
19. $(-42x) (+5)$
20. $(+48) (+ab)$

Division of Signed Numbers

Multiplication examples can be checked by division. If we check a multiplication exercise whose product is known to be correct by dividing the product by one of the multipliers, the quotient must be equal to the other multiplier.

Multiply $+15$ Check $\dfrac{+75}{+5} = +15$
            $+\ 5$
            $\overline{+75}$

Multiply -13 Check $\dfrac{-65}{-13} = +\ 5$
            $+\ 5$
            $\overline{-65}$

Multiply $+1$ Check $\dfrac{-5}{+1} = -5$
            -5
            $\overline{-5}$

Multiply -2 Check $\dfrac{+24}{-12} = -2$
            -12
            $\overline{+24}$

Rules to Remember

1. When numbers having *like* signs are divided, the quotient is positive.

2. When numbers having *unlike* signs are divided, the quotient is *negative*.

HOW TO DO THE PROBLEMS

1. $\dfrac{+10}{+5} = +2$ 5. $\dfrac{+10a}{+5a} = +2$

2. $\dfrac{-10}{-5} = +2$ 6. $\dfrac{-10a}{+5} = -2a$

3. $\dfrac{+10}{-5} = -2$ 7. $\dfrac{+10ab}{-5a} = -2b$

4. $\dfrac{-10}{+5} = -2$ 8. $-10 \div -5 = +2$

EXERCISES

Division of Signed Numbers

Divide:

1. $+50 \div +25$

2. $\dfrac{-8}{+2}$

3. $+6a \div +a$

4. $\dfrac{-22bc}{-11c}$

5. $\dfrac{-54ab}{+9a}$

6. $\dfrac{+82b^2}{-4b}$

7. $\dfrac{+7z}{+7}$

8. $\dfrac{-72}{+.3}$

9. $\dfrac{+20t}{+5}$

10. $\dfrac{-64abc}{-2bc}$

11. $\dfrac{-25c^4}{+5c^2}$

12. $\dfrac{+84d}{+12d}$

13. $\dfrac{-80g^2}{-4g^2}$

14. $\dfrac{-22a}{-22}$

15. $\dfrac{+95}{-5}$

16. $\dfrac{-244d^2c}{+4dc}$

17. $\dfrac{+36d}{+12}$

18. $\dfrac{-240z}{-6}$

19. $\dfrac{+82pr}{+4r}$

20. $-355t \div 5t$

How to Solve Algebraic Problems

1. Read the word statement of the problem slowly and carefully two or three times.

2. If it will be helpful, draw a picture or diagram and label the given facts on it.

3. Notice what facts are given and determine what must be found.

4. Represent the quantity to be found by a letter.

5. Using this letter, express all the given facts in algebraic symbols.

6. Write the equation to express the relationship stated in the problem.

7. Solve the equation.

8. Does the value of the literal number answer the question asked?

9. Check the answer by substituting its value in the written problem, using arithmetic to see whether the answer is correct.

John spends $\frac{2}{3}$ of his earnings each week. If last week he spent $12, how much did he earn?

How to Solve the Problem

Let $x =$ dollars John earned, then $\frac{2}{3}x =$ dollars spent

$\frac{2}{3}x = \$12$

$\frac{3}{2}(\frac{2}{3}x) = (12)\frac{3}{2}$ Multiplying both sides by $\frac{3}{2}$

$x \ = \$18$ John earned

Check: If John spends $\frac{2}{3}$ of his earnings, and his earnings were $18, he would have spent $\frac{2}{3} \times \$18$ or $12, which checks with his expenses as given in the problem.

PROBLEMS

Solve each of the following problems using algebraic equations.

1. One number is twice another number. The sum of the two numbers is 36. Find the number.

2. I have a number in mind. If I double this number the result is 48. Find the number.

3. Four times Albert's savings is $100. How much has he saved?

4. A man travels 90 miles in 3 hours. How far does he travel in one hour?

5. A train travels 40 miles an hour. Find how many hours it takes to cover 240 miles.

6. How much money must be invested at 3% to yield an annual income of $180?

7. The area of a rectangle is 48 square inches. If the length of the rectangle is 8 inches, find the width.

8. In a baseball game John scored $\frac{1}{8}$ of the number of runs his team scored. If John scored 3 runs, how many runs did his team score?

9. Mary spent $\frac{2}{5}$ of her savings. If she spent $8, how much had she saved?

10. The length of a rectangle is 11 feet. This represents $\frac{1}{4}$ of the perimeter. Find the perimeter.

11. There are 24 boys in a class. If $\frac{2}{3}$ of the number of pupils are boys, find the number of pupils in the class.

12. John and Henry caught 60 fish. If John caught twice as many as Henry, how many did each catch?

13. Mary is 4 times as old as Jane. The sum of their ages is 25 years. Find the age of each.

14. Two boys earned $24 while working on a farm. If Samuel worked three times as long as Harry, how much should each receive?

15. A man left $6000 for his son and daughter. He left twice as much to his son as he left to his daughter. How much did each receive?

16. Find each side of a square whose perimeter is 64 inches.

17. Find each side of an equilateral triangle whose perimeter is 27 inches.

18. The length of a rectangle is twice its width. Find the length and width if the perimeter is 120 feet.

19. One number is 7 times another and their sum is 88. Find the numbers.

20. A number increased by one-half that number is 21. Find the number.

21. Separate 36 into two parts so that one part is 5 times the other part.

22. What number increased by $\frac{2}{5}$ of itself is equal to 56?

23. Separate $5\frac{1}{7}$ into two parts so that one part is 8 times as large as the other.

24. The width of a rectangle is one-half of its length. Find the two dimensions if the perimeter is 90 feet.

25. A man bought a tie, a shirt and a hat. He paid twice as much for the shirt as for the tie, and five times as much for the hat as for the tie. If he spent $8 for all three items, how much did each item cost him?

26. After spending $10 in a store, a man had $15 left. How much money did he have originally?

27. How old is John if he was 12 years of age eight years ago?

28. What number increased by 9 is equal to 27?

29. After decreasing my rate of speed by 10 miles an hour, my car was traveling 25 miles an hour. What was the original rate of speed of the car?

30. A boy is 3 years older than his sister. If the boy is 21, how old is the sister?

GENERAL SKILL EXERCISE

How are you doing? Try the following test. If you get any wrong, turn to the pages shown after each question. Practice those problems until you have mastered them.

1. An equation containing algebraic symbols and expressing a rule is called a (an) .... (page 272).

2. The formula for the number of inches in m yards is .... (page 290).

3. If a bats cost s dollars, one bat costs .... dollars (page 263).

4. The formula $t = \dfrac{d}{r}$ means .... (page 289).

5. Find the value of I in the formula $I = PRT$ if $P = 6$, $R = .50$ and $T = 3$ .... (page 290).

6. Find the length, using the formula $P = 2l + 2w$, if $P = 400$ and $w = 60$ .... (page 293).

7. In the expression a^3, the 3 is called the .... and the a is called the .... (page 294).

8. Using $A = s^2$, what is the value of A if $s = 6$? .... (page 294).

9. Numbers which have either a $(+)$ or $(-)$ sign in front of them are called .... numbers (page 299).

10. The numerical value of a number regardless of its sign is called its .... (page 299).

11. To subtract signed numbers, change the sign of the subtrahend and .... (page 306).

12. The product of $+5$ and -6 is .... (page 306).

——————— *My Score*

PRINCIPLES TO REMEMBER

1. In algebra, letters are used to represent numbers. These letters are called *literal numbers*.

2. The symbol $(+)$ means *the sum of, add* or *more than;* the symbol $(-)$ means *subtract, less,* or *the difference between.* The symbol $\div$ means *divided by.* The symbol $=$ means *is equal to* or *equals.*

3. Evaluating an expression means substituting values for letters to obtain the value of the given expression.

4. A product is the result of multiplication. Any one of the numbers that has been multiplied is a factor of the product.

5. Only like terms may be added or subtracted.

6. An equation indicates that two quantities are equal. In an equation the letter whose value must be determined is called the *unknown*.

7. Since an equation represents a balance, anything done to one side of an equation must be done to the other side.

8. In solving an equation, inverse operations are performed. The inverse operation of addition is subtraction; the inverse operation of multiplication is division.

9. When more than one inverse operation is used to solve an equation, the rules of addition or subtraction may be used before the rules of multiplication or division.

10. An equation which contains algebraic symbols and expresses a rule or principle is called a *formula*.

11. The value of any letter in a formula is found by substituting the given values for the other letters, and solving the equation for the unknown.

12. An exponent is a number that indicates how many times the base is to be multiplied by itself.

13. Signed numbers are numbers, arithmetic or literal, which have a $(+)$ or $(-)$ sign in front of them.

14. The absolute value of a number is its numerical value regardless of its sign.

15. When you add signed numbers having like signs, you find their absolute values and write the common sign before their sum.

16. When you add signed numbers having unlike signs, you subtract the smaller absolute value from the larger and give the excess the sign of the larger absolute value.

17. When you subtract signed numbers, you change the sign of the subtrahend and proceed as in adding signed numbers.

18. When numbers having like signs are multiplied, the product is positive; when numbers having unlike signs are multiplied, the product is negative.

19. When two numbers having like signs are divided, the quotient is positive; when two numbers having unlike signs are divided, the quotient is negative.

MASTERY TEST

1. *Evaluate each of the following when $x=5$, $y=2$ and $z=10$.*
   a. $x+y+z$
   b. $20x-z$
   c. y^3
   d. z^2+y
   e. $3x+6z$
   f. $52+x^2-z$
   g. $\dfrac{5z}{x}$
   h. $y+3z^3$
   i. $\dfrac{z^2}{x^2}$
   j. $2x+\dfrac{6x}{y}$

2. *Add:*
   a. $6xy$, $7xy$
   b. $+5$, -18
   c. $2a$, $2c$
   d. $-16, -8, -52$
   e. $44x$, $-3x$
   f. $2x$, $5a$, $6x$, $-2a$
   g. $+5$, $-9a$
   h. x, $5x$, $6xw$
   i. $-16a$, $+5a$
   j. $4x$, $-4x$

3. *Perform the following:*
   a. $6x-x$
   b. $18a-(-9a)$
   c. $2y-\frac{1}{2}y$
   d. $(-19)-(+5)$
   e. $4r^2-3r^2$
   f. $(-18t)-(-5t)$
   g. $14d-3d$
   h. $(+22a)-(+20a)$
   i. $5ad-ad$
   j. $\frac{1}{2}r-\frac{1}{4}r$

4. *Multiply:*
   a. $ab \cdot a$
   b. $6x \cdot 6$
   c. $5x \cdot 4y$
   d. $3b \cdot 3a \cdot 2s$
   e. $16x\,(-4)$
   f. $-56\,(+4)$
   g. $-7a\,(-7a)$
   h. $16\,(-5d)$
   i. $\frac{1}{2}x\,(7x)$
   j. $-8x\,(-x)\,3x$

5. *Divide:*
   a. $\dfrac{6a}{a}$
   b. $\dfrac{x^4}{x^2}$
   c. $\dfrac{-10}{-5}$
   d. $\dfrac{60a}{-3}$
   e. $\dfrac{+20ab}{+4a}$
   f. $b \div a$
   g. $6g \div g$
   h. $25ab \div -5b$
   i. $a^4 \div x^2$
   j. $-120c^2 \div -6c^2$

6. *Solve the following equations:*
   a. $16x=4$
   b. $5y+25=4y$
   c. $\frac{3}{4}x=36$
   d. $\dfrac{a}{7}=28$
   e. $\dfrac{15r}{5}=27$
   f. $2p-9=1+p$
   g. $3x-2x=40$
   h. $\frac{1}{2}m=22$
   i. $\dfrac{4t}{2}=70$

j. $6m = \frac{2}{3}$

k. $6x - x = 23 - 4x$

l. $3t - 18 = 24$

m. $\frac{y}{3} = 14$

n. $5x - 3 = 16x - 8$

o. $7r = \frac{4}{5}$

p. $20x - 2 = 62$

q. $y = -y + 9$

r. $\frac{z}{8} = 24$

s. $16f - \frac{1}{4}f = 261$

t. $\frac{d}{12} = \frac{144}{24}$

7. *Write the formulas for the following tables of values and find the missing values:*

a.

x	1	2	3	4	?
y	2	4	6	?	10

d.

x	1	2	3	4	?
y	1	4	9	?	25

b.

x	5	6	7	8	?
y	4	5	6	?	9

e.

x	1	2	3	4	?
y	1	3	5	?	9

c.

x	2	3	4	5	?
y	5	6	7	?	12

f.

x	1	2	3	4	?
y	3	12	27	?	75

8. *Write the formula for each of the following:*

   a. The cost, C, in cents of sending a telegram of n words, n being greater than 10, if the cost of sending the first ten words is 24 cents and each additional word costs 2 cents.

   b. The cost, C, in cents of sending a telegram of n words, n being greater than 10, if the cost of sending the first ten words is 31 cents and each additional word costs 3 cents.

   c. The charge, C, in cents for a telephone conversation between two towns lasting n minutes, n being greater than three, if the charge for the first three minutes is 38 cents, and each additional minute costs 10 cents.

   d. The charge, C, in cents for borrowing a book from a lending library for n days, n being greater than seven, if the charge for the first week is 25¢ and each additional day costs 3¢.

9. *Solve the following:*

   a. A man is 4 years younger than his wife. If the man is 49, how old is the wife?

   b. I had $12 in the bank. I worked for 13 hours and put my earnings in the bank. I then had $51. How much did I earn each hour?

   c. I multiply a number by 7 and then add 3. My result is 45. What was the number?

d. I multiply a number by 4 and then subtract 9. My result is 31. What was the original number?

e. One-half a number, decreased by 4, is equal to 28. What was the number?

f. Mary withdrew half of her money from the bank and went shopping. After spending $5, she had $10 left. How much money did she have originally in the bank?

g. After adding 5 gallons of gasoline to the number of gallons he had in his tank a man had a full gas tank, or 16 gallons of gasoline. How many gallons did he have originally?

h. A man had a certain number of quarts of oil in his car and needed more. After adding as many more quarts as he had originally and then driving his car until he had used one quart of oil, he had 5 quarts left. How many quarts did he have originally?

i. If I added $10 to twice the amount I have, I would then have $100. How much money do I have?

j. Two boys worked a total of 25 hours. If John worked 5 hours longer than Henry, how many hours did each work?

10. Two angles are complementary if their sum is 90°.
    Two angles are supplementary if their sum is 180°.

    a. If an angle is 4 times as large as its complement, find the angle.

    b. If an angle is one-half the size of its complement, find the angle.

    c. An angle is 3 times as large as its supplement. Find the angle and its supplement.

    d. An angle is one-fifth of its supplement. Find the angle and its supplement.

11. The sum of the angles of a triangle equals 180°.

    a. If one angle of a triangle is equal to twice the second angle, and the third angle is equal to the sum of the other two, find each angle of the triangle.

    b. Find each angle in a triangle if its angles are all equal to each other.

12. The perimeter of a square can be found by the formula:
$$p = 4s$$
The area of a square can be found by the formula:
$$A = s^2$$
If the perimeter of a square is 40 inches, find the area of the square.

GEOMETRY

Engineers, architects, artists and people of many other professions use lines and figures in their daily work. The study of lines and the closed figures made by lines is called *geometry*.

Points and Lines

Points

A point has no length, width or thickness. It merely indicates position. To represent a point in geometry, we mark a dot and label it with a capital letter. For example $\overset{.}{A}$ or ·A would be called "point A."

Lines

A line has no width or thickness. It has length and direction. An infinite number of straight lines can be drawn through one point.

Since a line extends indefinitely in either direction, we must work with *line segments*, or portions of lines. The segment is represented by two capital letters, one placed at each end. A_____B is the line segment *AB* or *BA*. It can also be represented by a small letter. Hence, ____*a*____ is line segment *a*.

A line joins two points. Only one straight line can be drawn between two points. There are three kinds of lines: straight, curved and broken.

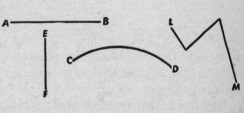

AB and *EF* are straight lines; *CD* is a curved line. *LM* is a broken line. Notice that the lines are labeled by capital letters placed at the end of the line.

Lines that extend from left to right as the horizon does, are called *horizontal lines*. Examples of horizontal lines are lines on writing paper and all level lines which we find in man-made structures.

Lines that go straight up and down with respect to the earth are called *vertical lines*. Examples of vertical lines are telephone poles, trees, and plumb lines.

Any straight line which is neither a horizontal nor a vertical line is a *slanting* or *oblique line*.

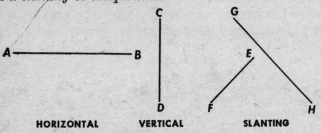

HORIZONTAL   VERTICAL   SLANTING

Examples of slanting lines are the limbs of most trees or the banister of a stairway.

Lines that have the same direction and are always the same distance apart are called *parallel lines*. They may be vertical, horizontal or oblique.

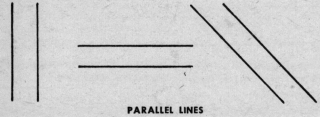

PARALLEL LINES

No matter how far they extend, parallel lines will never meet. The opposite edges of a street, the opposite edges of a ruler, and railroad tracks are examples of parallel lines.

Straight lines that cross each other are called *intersecting lines*. The verticals and horizontals of graph paper intersect. The lines of roads intersect at corners. Intersecting straight lines meet at only one point.

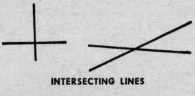

INTERSECTING LINES

Constructing Equal Lines

A line may be drawn on a paper. We can construct another line exactly equal in length using only a compasses and a straightedge.

The instrument used for drawing circles or arcs is a *compasses.* It consists of two pointed legs joined at the top by a pivot. One of the pointed legs is usually a pencil or a piece of lead.

A *straightedge* is a tool used to construct a straight line, but not for measuring it. It looks like a ruler, but it contains no units of measurement.

How to Construct Equal Lines

Problem: Construct a line equal to line *a.*

a
_____

Method

Step 1: Draw line *ST* longer than given line *a.*

S———————————————*T*

Step 2: Place the sharp point of your compasses on one end of line *a*, and put the pencil point of the compasses on the other end. Tighten your compasses so that it will keep this span.

Step 3: Keeping the same span on the compasses put the sharp end on point *S* of line *ST*. Draw a short arc cutting line *ST* at *U.* The line segment *SU* will be equal to the line segment *a.*

S———————————|——*T*
|U

Bisecting a Line

To *bisect* a line means to divide that line into two equal parts. We can bisect a line with compasses and a straightedge.

How to Bisect a Line

Problem: Bisect line segment *AB*

Method:

Step 1: Open your compasses to a span greater than one-half the line *AB*.

Step 2: Place the point of your compasses at *A* and draw an arc above and below *AB*.

Step 3: Keep the same span. Place the point of your compasses at *B* and draw an arc above *AB* and below *AB*, crossing the first arcs at points *D* and E.

Step 4. Join points *D* and *E* with a straight line crossing line *AB* at *X*.

Line *DE* is the *bisector* of line *AB*. Point *X* is the middle of line *AB*, and line *AX* is equal to line *XB*.

EXERCISES

Lines

1. How many straight lines can be drawn through a point?

2. Draw any two straight lines that are not parallel. In how many points do they meet, no matter how far you extend them?

3. Select any two points. Draw a straight line between them with a ruler. Can you draw a different straight line between them? How many different straight lines can be drawn between any two points?

4. Draw three lines to illustrate each of the following:
   a. horizontal lines   b. vertical lines   c. parallel lines

5. Draw and label:
   a. two horizontal lines   d. two parallel lines
   b. two vertical lines   e. two curved lines
   c. two intersecting lines

6. *Draw:*
   a. A line equal to the first horizontal line you drew in 5a above.
   b. Bisect this line.

Angles — Measuring Angles

An angle is formed when two straight lines meet at a point. The lines are called the *sides* of the angle. The point at which the sides meet is called the *vertex* of the angle. The angle is read as angle *BAC* or *CAB*.

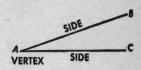

The size of an angle depends upon the amount one side has turned away from the other. The length of the sides of an angle does not determine its size.

The unit of measure used in measuring an angle is the *degree*. A degree is a unit that equals $\frac{1}{90}$ of a right angle and $\frac{1}{360}$ of a circle. A right angle, therefore, contains

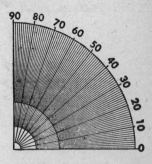

90 degrees (90°), and a circle contains 360 degrees (360°). The size of an angle is the number of degrees through which one side of the angle has turned away from the other side.

Kinds of Angles

1. Right Angle. If one side of an angle turns a quarter of a complete circle away from the other side, the angle that is formed is a right angle. It contains 90°. A right angle is represented by this sign: ⌐

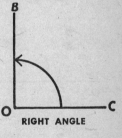

RIGHT ANGLE

a. Complementary angles. When two angles put together form a right angle, and thus their sum is 90°, the angles are *complementary*. For example, angle *ABC* is the complement of angle *CBD* since their sum (60°+30°) equals 90°.

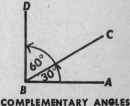

COMPLEMENTARY ANGLES

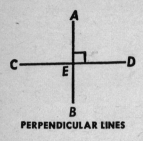

PERPENDICULAR LINES

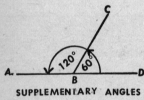

STRAIGHT ANGLE

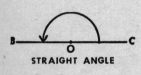

SUPPLEMENTARY ANGLES

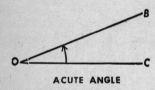

ACUTE ANGLE

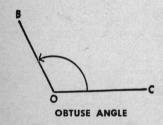

OBTUSE ANGLE

b. Perpendicular lines. When two lines intersect at right angles, the lines are *perpendicular*. Each angle formed by a perpendicular line contains 90°.

2. Straight Angle. If one side of an angle turns half of a complete circle away from the other side, the angle that is formed is a *straight angle*. The sides of a straight angle lie in the same straight line.

Notice that a straight angle is twice the size of a right angle since in a straight angle the side has made half a complete turn, or two quarter turns. The number of degrees in a straight angle is 180°.

3. Supplementary Angles. When the sum of two angles is 180°, the angles are said to be *supplementary*. For example, angle *ABC* is the supplement of angle *CBD* since their sum (120°+60°) is 180°.

4. Acute Angle. If one side of an angle turns less than a quarter of a circle away from the other side, the angle formed is an *acute angle*. An acute angle, therefore, is smaller than a right angle, or less than 90°.

5. Obtuse Angle. If one side of an angle turns more than a quarter circle but less than half a half circle away from the other side, the angle formed is an *obtuse angle*. Therefore, an obtuse angle is greater than a right angle but smaller than a straight angle. It contains more than 90° but less than 180°.

6. *Reflex Angle.* If one side of an angle turns more than half a circle (180°) but less than a complete circle (360°) away from the other side, the angle formed is a *reflex angle.* Therefore, a reflex angle is greater than a straight angle.

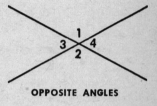

REFLEX ANGLE

7. *Opposite or Vertical Angles.* When two lines cross each other four angles are formed.

Angles 1 and 2, formed by the intersecting lines, are called *opposite* or *vertical angles.* What other angles are opposite angles? Since opposite angles have been formed by the same amount of turning, they are equal. Notice also that ⊀1 is the supplement of ⊀3. ⊀2 is the supplement of ⊀3. Because supplements of the same angle must be equal, ⊀1 must equal ⊀2.

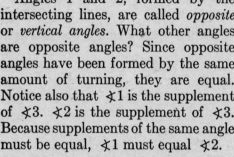

OPPOSITE ANGLES

8. *Size of Angles.* The size of an angle does not depend on the length of its sides.

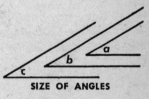

SIZE OF ANGLES

From the diagram we can see that the size of any angle depends only on the amount of turning of one side of the angle away from the other.

EXERCISES

Angles

1. How many degrees are there in a right angle?

2. When one side of an angle has turned through half of a circle, it has turned through ....°.

3. A straight angle contains ....°.

4. An acute angle contains less than ....°.

5. An obtuse angle contains more than ....° but less than ....°.

6. An angle that contains more than 180° but less than 360° is called a (an) ....

7. How many degrees are there in a complete rotation, or a circle?

8. In each of the figures in this question name the angle by the use of three letters and tell what type of angle it is.

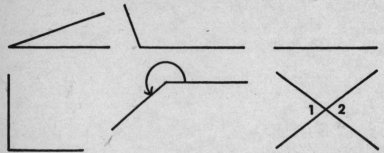

9. Draw an acute angle; an obtuse angle; a right angle; a straight angle; a reflex angle.

10. Name the type of angle that is formed by the hands of a clock at each of the following hours:

    a. 6:00   *c.* 7:15   *e.* 4:30
    b. 2:20   *d.* 9:00   *f.* 12:45

11. Name by means of three letters all the angles there are in the figure at the right. Name the vertex and sides of each angle. Tell what type of angle each one is. Do not include reflex angles.

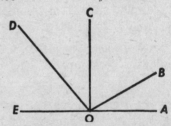

12. How many degrees are in the angle formed by the hands of a clock at:

    a. 3 o'clock   *c.* 6 o'clock
    b. 2 o'clock   *d.* 9 o'clock

13. Find the complement of each of the following angles:

    a. 40°   *d.* 67°   *g.* 88°   *j.* 68$\frac{2}{3}$°
    b. 70°   *e.* 32°   *h.* 23°   *k.* 42.4°
    c. 45°   *f.* 15°   *i.* 60°   *l.* 58.25°

14. An angle contains the same number of degrees as its complement. Find the number of degrees in the angle.

15. An angle is eight times as large as its complement. Find the angle and its complement.

16. An angle is one-third of its complement. Find the angle and its complement.

17. If the sum of two angles is 180°, they are ....

18. Write an algebraic statement which says that angle A and angle B are supplementary.

19. Find the supplement of each of the following angles:

a. 20°	*d.* 90°	*g.* 123°	*j.* $136\frac{1}{3}$°
b. 140°	*e.* 15°	*h.* 156°	*k.* 47.8°
c. 59°	*f.* 78°	*i.* $19\frac{2}{5}$°	*l.* 139.25°

20. An angle contains the same number of degrees as its supplement. Find the number of degrees in the angle.

21. An angle is three times its supplement. Find the angle and its supplement.

22. An angle is one-half of its supplement. Find the angle and its supplement.

Measuring and Constructing Angles with a Protractor

Angles of any given size may be drawn, or the size of an angle may be measured, by using an instrument called a *protractor*.

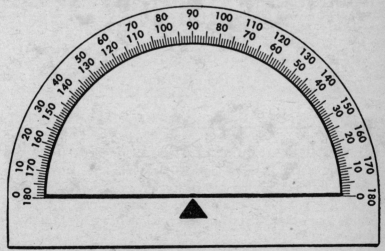

A protractor is used to measure angles. The inside numbers show degrees in angles beginning at 0° and going counterclockwise. The outside numbers mark degrees in angles from 0° going clockwise.

Notice that the upper part of the protractor is half a circle; it contains 180°. The half circle is divided into 180 parts. The center of the semicircle or protractor is at point ▲. Notice that there are two sets of numbers on the curved edge so arranged that one set of numbers begins at the right side of the protractor and the other set begins at the left side. This arrangement permits us to measure angles that open at the left or the right sides.

Finding Number of Degrees in an Angle

Problem: Find the number of degrees in angle EFG.

Method: Place the center of the protractor at point F so that point ▲ of the protractor is on point F and the zero division line at S on the protractor lies on side FG of the angle. Now read the scale where line FE crosses the protractor. Reading from the zero at the right we find that angle EFG contains 29°.

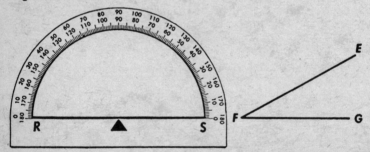

If you were to use the outside scale which starts at zero on the left side of the protractor, the reading would be 151°. Since a 151° angle would be obtuse, and ∢EFG is acute, you would not have the correct measurement for the angle.

Drawing Angles with a Protractor

Problem: Draw an angle of 50°.

Method:

1. Draw a line to represent one side of the desired angle. Label this line *EF*.

2. If *E* is to be the vertex of the angle, place the protractor with center *A* on point *E* and the zero division line at *R* on line *EF*.

3. Now, reading from the zero at the left, find the 50° mark on the protractor and place a point opposite it. Call this point *D*.

4. Remove the protractor and draw a line from *E* to the point *D*. Angle *DEF* contains 50°.

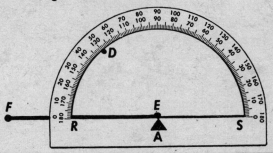

EXERCISES

Measuring and Constructing Angles

1. Using a protractor, find the number of degrees in each of the following angles:

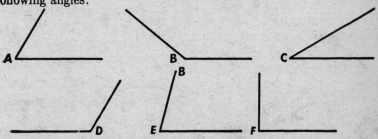

2. Draw angles equal to angles (*c*) and (*d*) from question 1. Use a protractor.

3. With a protractor draw the following angles:

　a. 10°　　*c.* 40°　　*e.* 110°　　*g.* 65°　　*i.* 60°　　*k.* 123°　　*m.* 90°
　b. 20°　　*d.* 80°　　*f.* 135°　　*h.* 30°　　*j.* 45°　　*l.* 75°　　*n.* 162°

Constructing Equal Angles with Compasses

Suppose that angle *DEF*, page 329, was already drawn and you wanted to copy it so as to get another 50° angle without having to use the protractor; that is, you wanted to construct an angle equal to ∢*DEF*. This is what you could do.

How to Construct Equal Angles

Step 1: Draw base line *GH.*

Step 2: Now turning to angle *DEF*, place the sharp point of your compasses on E and draw an arc cutting *DE* at *K* and *EF* at *L.*

Step 3: Using *G* as the center on line *GH*, draw an arc of the same radius and approximately the same length, cutting *GH* at *M.*

Step 4: On angle *DEF*, place one point of your compasses at *L* and the other point of your compasses at *K*, so that the span of the compasses will equal the distance between points *K* and *L.*

Step 5: Keeping this radius, place your compasses on point *M* and draw an arc cutting the arc you have drawn in point *O.*

Step 6: Join points *G* and *O* with a line.

Angle *OGH* equals angle *DEF*. Thus, if the original angle is 50°, then the angle you have drawn will be 50° also.

Constructing Parallel Lines

Parallel lines, you have learned, are lines that are always the same distance apart. When you know how to contruct equal angles, you can also construct parallel lines.

A line that cuts two or more other lines is called a *transversal*. In the construction below you must use a transversal.

In the diagram below (step 2), *k* and *c* are corresponding angles. Angles *n* and *f* are corresponding, too. Can you name two other pairs of corresponding angles? If corresponding angles formed by a transversal are equal, the two lines it cuts will be parallel. This is the principle we will use for the construction.

How to Construct Parallel Lines

Problem: To construct a line parallel to line AB.

Method 1: Using a compasses

Step 1: Draw a slanting line (transversal) cutting AB and forming angles c, d, e and f.

Step 2: Choose a point above AB on the slanting line and construct an angle equal to angle d. YZ is parallel to AB.

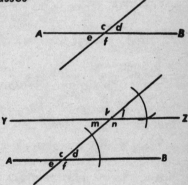

Method 2: With a protractor

Step 1: Follow directions of Step 1 above.

Step 2: Place the base of your protractor on the slanting line, using the point of intersection as the center. Now measure angle d.

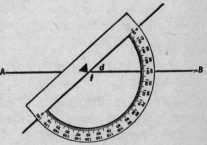

[Continued on top of page 332]

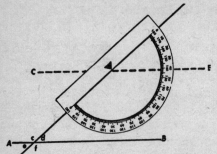

Step 3: Slide your protractor on the slanting line to a point above *AB* and construct an angle equal to *d*.

The side, *CE*, of the angle you have drawn is a line parallel to line *AB*.

Constructing Right Angles and Perpendicular Lines

Perpendicular lines are lines that meet so as to form right angles. You can construct one line perpendicular to another by using a compasses and straightedge or by marking off an angle of 90° with your protractor.

Right Angles and Perpendicular Lines

Problem: 1: Using compasses and a straightedge, construct a line perpendicular to line *CD*.

Step 1: Set your compasses so that it has a radius larger than half of line *CD*.

Step 2: Place the sharp point of your compasses on *C* and draw a long arc cutting *CD*.

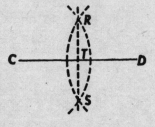

Step 3: Place the point of your compasses on *D* and draw a long arc intersecting the arc you have just drawn at *R* and *S*.

Step 4: Draw a line through points *R* and *S* intersecting line *CD* at *T*.

RS is perpendicular to *CD*. *RS* also *bisects*, or *divides CD* into two equal parts. That is, *CT* equals *TD*. Thus, we call *RS* the *perpendicular bisector* of *CD*.

[Continued on top of page 333]

Measure *CT* and *TD* with your compasses. Are they equal?

If *RS* is perpendicular to *CD*, how many degrees does ∢*RTC* contain? What kind of angle is it?

Problem 2: From point *L*, construct a perpendicular to line *MN*.

Step 1: Place the sharp point of your compasses on *L*. Draw an arc intersecting *MN* at two points, *D* and *E*.

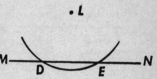

Step 2: Place your compasses point on *D*. Draw a short arc directly below *L*.

Step 3: Keeping the same radius, place your compasses point on *E*. Draw an arc intersecting the arc you have just drawn at *H*.

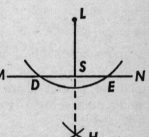

Step 4: Join points *L* and *H* with a straight line. (Note: The perpendicular line need not extend to *H* unless required. It may stop at the line *MN*.)

LH (or *LS*) is perpendicular to *MN*. Therefore, ∢*LSM* and ∢*LSN* are right angles.

Problem 3: From point *R* on line *ST*, construct a perpendicular to *ST*.

Step 1: Place your compasses point on *R*. Draw an arc intersecting *SR* at *A* and an arc of the same radius intersecting *RT* at *B*.

[Continued on top of page 334]

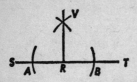

Step 2: Lengthen the span of the compasses. With A and B as centers, and with equal radii draw intersecting arcs above line ST. Label the point of intersection V.

Step 3: Join points V and R with a straight line. VR is perpendicular to ST at R.

Bisecting an Angle

You have learned how to bisect a straight line, page 321. Now you will learn how to bisect an angle; that is, to divide the angle into two equal parts.

How to Bisect an Angle

Problem: Bisect ⟨ DEF.

Step 1: Place your compasses point on E and draw an arc cutting both sides of the angle, at K and P.

Step 2: Using K and P respectively as centers and with equal radii, draw short arcs that intersect at A.

Step 3: Join points A and E.
AE is a bisector. ⟨ DEA equals ⟨ AEF.

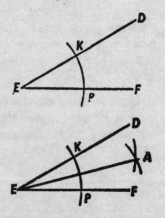

EXERCISES
Measuring and Constructing Angles

1. With your protractor, find the number of degrees in angles *a* and *b*.

2. Using compasses and a straightedge
   a. copy angles *a* and *b*.
   b. bisect each.

3. With compasses and straightedge
   a. construct a right angle;
   b. construct an angle of 135° (Hint: right angle + ½ right angle)

4. Draw line *ST* and, with compasses and straightedge, construct line *OP* parallel to it. Use a perpendicular transversal.

5. Determine whether lines *AB* and *CD* are parallel by measuring with your protractor angles *e*, *f*, *g* and *h*.

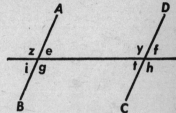

6. If the lines above are parallel and angle *z* above measures 127°, how many degrees are contained in angle *y*? in angle *t*? in angle *h*?

7. Using a straightedge draw three triangles (3-sided plane figures) of different sizes and shapes. With your protractor measure the angles of each of the triangles. Find the sum of the angles of each triangle. Write a general rule of the sum of the angles of a triangle.

GENERAL SKILL EXERCISE

How are you doing? Try the following test. If you get any wrong, turn to the pages shown after each question. Practice those problems until you have mastered them.

1. A portion of a line is called a .... (page 319).

2. The number of lines that can be drawn between any two points is .... (page 319).

3. A line may be curved, broken or .... (page 319).

4. The upright corner of a room is an example of a .... line (page 320).

5. Lines that are always the same distance apart no matter how far extended are called .... lines (page 320).

6. The size of any angle is determined by the .... (page 323).

7. A straight angle contains ....° (page 323).

8. Two angles whose sum is 180° are .... (page 324).

9. Opposite angles are always .... (page 325).

10. The unit used in measuring angles is the .... (page 323).

11. To .... a line or an angle means to divide that line or angle into two equal parts (page 321).

12. The sides of an angle meet at the .... (page 323).

13. A (An) .... angle is more than 90° but less than 180° (page 324).

14. A (An) .... is an instrument divided into 180° (page 321).

15. A line which meets another line at a 90° angle is ....
to that line (page 324).

_____ *My Score*

Plane Figures

Figures that lie on a flat surface are called *plane figures*. They have only two dimensions — length and width. Closed plane figures with straight lines are called *polygons*, from the Greek meaning "many angles." A *regular polygon* is a polygon with equal sides and equal angles.

Kinds of Polygons

Triangles. A triangle is a plane figure bounded by three straight lines and containing three angles. The sum of the angles of every triangle is 180°.

1. Naming Triangles

A triangle is identified by naming its vertices in any order. Thus, the first triangle below may be called △ABC, △BAC, △BCA, △CAB, △CBA or △ACB. The symbol △ means triangle.

2. Types of Triangles According to Length of Sides

A *scalene* triangle is a triangle of which no two sides are equal. $\triangle ABC$ is a scalene triangle.

An *isosceles* triangle is a triangle which has two equal sides. The equal sides are called the *legs*, as DE and EF in the

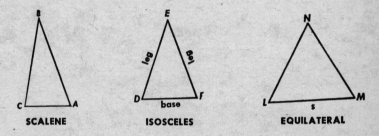

SCALENE   ISOSCELES   EQUILATERAL

triangle *DEF*. The third side is called the base, as *DF* in the triangle *DEF*. The angles *D* and *F* at the base are called *base angles*. Angle *E*, formed by the two equal sides, is called the *vertex angle*.

An *equilateral triangle* is a triangle with three equal sides. $\triangle LMN$ is an equilateral triangle.

3. Types of Triangles According to Angles

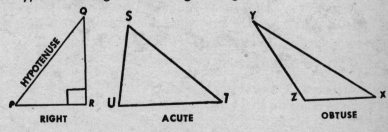

RIGHT   ACUTE   OBTUSE

A *right triangle* is a triangle which contains one right angle. No more than one angle of a triangle can be a right angle. Why? In a right triangle the side opposite the right angle is called the hypotenuse. Thus, $\triangle PQR$ (page 337), is a right triangle.

An *acute triangle* is a triangle which has three acute angles. Thus, $\triangle UST$ is an acute triangle.

An *obtuse triangle* is a triangle which contains one obtuse angle. $\triangle XYZ$ is an obtuse triangle.

A triangle whose angles are equal, and therefore contain 60° each, is an *equiangular* or *equilateral triangle*.

A triangle whose base angles are equal to each other but not equal to the third angle is an *isosceles triangle*.

EXERCISES

Plane Figures

Match column II with column I. There is one *definition for each term.*

I	II
( ) *a.* scalene triangle	1. All three sides are equal.
( ) *b.* right triangle	2. The sum of its angles is 180°.
( ) *c.* acute triangle	3. No two sides are equal.
( ) *d.* isosceles triangle	4. Two sides only are equal.
( ) *e.* obtuse triangle	5. All three angles are less
( ) *f.* equilateral triangle	than 90° each.
( ) *g.* triangle	6. It contains an angle of 90°.
	7. One angle is more than 90°.

How to Construct a Triangle When the Lengths of the Three Sides Are Known

Triangles may have many different dimensions. By using a ruler, compasses and a protractor, you can easily construct a triangle when sufficient information is given.

HOW TO DO THE EXAMPLE

Problem: Construct a triangle *PBD* with a base of 2 inches, one side of $1\frac{1}{4}$ inches and one side of 1 inch.

[Continued on top of page 339]

Equipment: ruler and compasses

Solution: Step 1: With the ruler draw base line *BD* two inches long.

Step 2: Give your compasses a radius of $1\frac{1}{4}$ inches. With the point at *D*, draw a short arc above the base line.

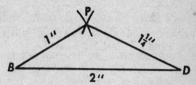

Step 3: Give your compasses a radius of 1 inch. With the point at *B*, draw a short arc intersecting at *P* the arc you have just drawn.

Step 4: Draw *PD* and *PB*.

  △*BPD* is the required triangle.

How to Construct a Triangle When One Angle and the Lengths of the Sides of That Angle Are Known

HOW TO DO THE EXAMPLE

Problem: Construct triangle *GER*, one angle of which is 35°. The sides of that angle are $\frac{3}{4}$ inch and 1 inch in length.

Equipment: ruler, compasses and protractor

Solution:

Step 1: With the ruler, draw base line *ER* one inch long.

Step: 2 Using your protractor and making *E* the vertex, draw an angle of 35°.

Step 3: Give the compasses a radius of $\frac{3}{4}$ inch. Place the compasses point at *E* and mark off leg *GE*.

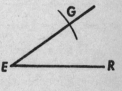

Step 4: Draw line GR.

  △*GER* is the required triangle.

Construct a Triangle When the Sizes of Two Angles and the Length of the Side Between Them Are Known

HOW TO DO THE EXAMPLE

Problem: Construct triangle *BEF* if the base *EF* is 2 inches, ∡*BEF* is 100° and ∡*BFE* is 30°.

Equipment: ruler, compasses and protractor

Solution:

Step 1: With the ruler, draw the base line *EF* 2 inches long.

Step 2: With the protractor, construct an angle of 100° (∡*BEF*) at vertex *E*.

Step 3: Construct an angle of 30° (∡*BFE*) at vertex *F*.

Step 4: Extend the two legs until they intersect at *B*.

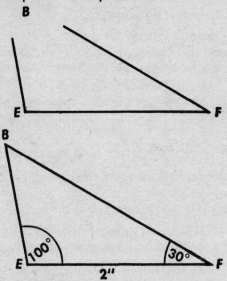

△*BEF* is the required triangle.

EXERCISES
Triangles

1. Draw an acute triangle; an obtuse triangle; a right triangle.
2. Using compasses and a straightedge, construct an isosceles triangle; an equilateral triangle.
3. How many right angles can there be in a triangle?
4. How many obtuse angles can a triangle contain?
5. How many acute angles *must* every triangle contain?
6. What is the sum of the three angles of a triangle?
7. Write the algebraic formula for the sum of the three angles *A*, *B* and *C* of a triangle.
8. Find the third angle of a triangle if the first two are:
      a. 30° and 60°   *b.* 90° and 45°   *c.* 18.2° and 86.5°

    d. 40° and 80°   *f.* 72° and 46°   *h.* 37.4° and 121.5°
    e. 120° and 10°   *g.* 128° and 21°   *i.* $37\frac{1}{2}$° and $57\frac{1}{3}$°

  9. Find the base angles of an isosceles triangle if the vertex angle is:

    a. 30°   *c.* 62°   *e.* 90°   *g.* 36.8°   *i.* 124.68°
    b. 50°   *d.* 130°   *f.* 57°   *h.* $47\frac{1}{2}$°

  10. Find the vertex angle of an isosceles triangle if the base angles are each:

    a. 60°   *c.* 55°   *e.* 51°   *g.* $32\frac{1}{2}$°   *i.* 18.3°
    b. 40°   *d.* 45°   *f.* 80°   *h.* $43\frac{3}{4}$°

  11. Construct an equilateral triangle by constructing angles with a protractor. (Do not measure sides to construct the figure.)

  12. Construct a triangle the sides of which measure 3″, 2″ and $2\frac{1}{4}$″. Use a ruler and compasses. What kind of triangle is this?

  13. The vertex angle of a triangle is 25°. One leg of that angle measures 1″. The other leg measures $1\frac{3}{4}$″. Using a protractor, compasses and ruler, construct the triangle.

Quadrilaterals

  A quadrilateral is a plane figure bounded by four straight lines. There are several kinds of quadrilaterals.

  1. *Parallelogram.* A parallelogram is any quadrilateral in which two pairs of opposite sides are parallel.

  2. *Rectangle.* A rectangle is a parallelogram whose angles are all right angles.

  3. *Square.* A square is a rectangle in which all the sides are equal in length.

  4. *Trapezoid.* A trapezoid is a quadrilateral in which only one pair of opposite sides are parallel.

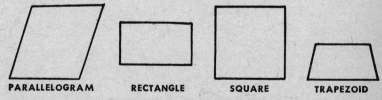

PARALLELOGRAM   RECTANGLE   SQUARE   TRAPEZOID

  The rectangle and the square both have four right angles. You have learned how to draw a 90° angle with a protractor and construct the angle with compasses. Using this knowledge, you can construct rectangles and squares.

How to Construct a Square

Problem 1: Construct any square, PQRS.

Step 1: Draw base line QR. At Q and R construct perpendiculars.

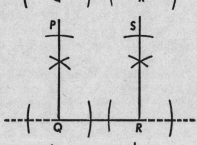

Step 2: Give your compasses a radius equal to the distance between points Q and R. Using this radius, mark off PQ and RS on the perpendicular sides.

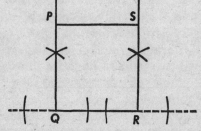

Step 3: Join points P and S.

PQRS is the required square.

Problem 2: Construct rectangle MNOP having a base of 2 inches and sides of $1\frac{1}{4}$ inches.

Step 1: With a ruler, draw base line NO 2 inches long. At N and at O construct perpendiculars d and e.

Step 2: Using a ruler, mark off point M on segment d $1\frac{1}{4}$ inches from N. Mark off point P on segment e $1\frac{1}{4}$ inches from O.

Step 3: Join points M and P.
MNOP is the required rectangle.

To construct a parallelogram, you must construct two sets of parallel lines (see p. 332). To construct a trapezoid, you must construct one set of parallel lines.

Other Plane Figures

1. *Pentagon.* A pentagon is a polygon which has five sides.
2. *Hexagon.* A hexagon is a polygon which has six sides.
3. *Octagon.* An octagon is a polygon which has eight sides.
4. *Decagon.* A decagon is a polygon which has ten sides.

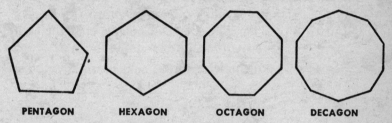

PENTAGON   HEXAGON   OCTAGON   DECAGON

Since a *regular* polygon has equal sides and equal angles, all the vertices are equidistant from the center.

A *circle* is a curved line all points of which are equidistant from the center. Therefore, if we inscribe a regular polygon inside of a circle, every vertex of the polygon will rest on the line of the circle.

Constructing Stars and Regular Polygons

To construct a regular polygon of more than four sides draw a circle and divide it into equal arcs.

How to Construct a Regular Hexagon

Problem: Construct a regular hexagon.

Method: Every circle has 360°. Every hexagon has 6 sides. Therefore, we must divide the circle into parts of 360° ÷ 6, or 60°.

Step 1: With compasses, draw a circle.

[Continued on top of page 344]

Step 2: Using the center O as the vertex, with a protractor mark off a central angle of 60°.

Step 3: Set your compasses so that the radius is equal to the distance between A and B.

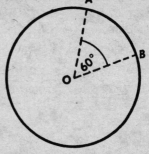

Step 4: Putting your compasses point on B, draw a short arc through the circle and label the point of intersection C. Then put the compasses point on C and draw an arc through point D. Continue until you have reached F. (You may erase the first angle that you drew.)

Step 5: Join each point with the next consecutive point.

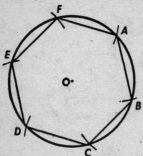

ABCDEF is a regular hexagon

A star is similar to a regular polygon. In fact, the construction of a five-pointed star follows the basic principles of construction of a regular pentagon, and constructing a six-pointed star is similar to constructing a regular hexagon.

How to Construct a 5-Pointed Star

Problem: Construct a five-pointed star.

Method:

Step 1: Draw a circle.

[Continued on top of page 345]

Step **2**: Find the number of degrees which must be contained in each of the parts of the circle. 360° in the circle ÷ 5 parts = 72° in each part.

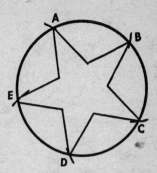

Step **3**: Draw an angle of 72° within the circle, using a protractor and keeping the center of the circle as the vertex. When you have found points A and B where the sides of the angle meet the line of the circle, erase the angle you have drawn.

Step **4**: Set your compasses so that it has a span equal to the distance between A and B. Using this span, mark off the five equal parts of the circle.

Step **5**: Draw AD, DB, BE, EC and CA. Erase the lines in the middle of the star.

Notice that if you had drawn lines AB, BC, CD, DE and EA, you would have constructed a regular pentagon instead of a five-pointed star.

EXERCISES

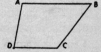

Plane Figures

1. How many angles does a parallelogram have?
2. Three of the following sentences are correct. Tell which, and explain why.
   - *a.* All rectangles are parallelograms.
   - *b.* All parallelograms are rectangles.
   - *c.* All squares are rectangles.
   - *d.* All rectangles are squares.
   - *e.* All quadrilaterals are parallelograms.
   - *f.* All parallelograms are quadrilaterals.

3. If *AB* is parallel to *CD* in the figure at the right, what kind of figure is *ABCD*?

4. Using a compasses and a straightedge, construct:

a. a rectangle   d. a parallelogram

b. a square   e. an 8-pointed star

c. a trapezoid

(Hint for e: For the central angle, construct and bisect a right angle. When 8 arcs are marked off, connect every other point so as to form two squares. If the 8 points are named consecutively A, B, C, D, E, F, G, and H, try drawing lines AD, DG, GB, BE, EH, HC, CF, and FA.)

5. In this room are many geometrical figures. Find:

a. 2 circles

b. 3 rectangles

c. 2 pentagons

d. a parallelogram

e. a trapezoid

f. 3 triangles

g. a sector

h. parallel lines

i. an acute angle

j. an octagon

k. a pyramid

l. a cylinder

m. a rectangular prism

Perimeter

The *perimeter* of a plane figure is the distance around it. The perimeters of each of the figures we have been studying would equal the sum of the lengths of its sides.

Perimeter of a Rectangle

Mr. Jones had a rectangular garden plot. Its length was 14 feet and its width was 10 feet. How many feet of wire were needed to fence in the plot?

To find the perimeter we must add all the sides. Since the length of one side equals the length of the other side, and the width of one side equals the width of the other side, we must find the sum of twice the length plus twice the width. The perimeter, we find, is 48 feet. We simply add:

$$10+10+14+14=48$$

The perimeter of a rectangle can be expressed by a formula.

If we let w stand for the width of the rectangle, l for the length and P for the perimeter, we find that the perimeter of the rectangle is:

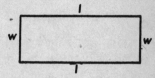

$$P=l+l+w+w$$

We can combine the lengths and the widths and express the formula in a shorter form.

Rule to Remember

The perimeter of a rectangle equals two times the length plus two times the width.

$$P=2l+2w \text{ or } P=2 (l+w).$$

Perimeter of a Square

Since a square is a rectangle having four equal sides, we can represent each of the sides by the letter s. The perimeter of the square is expressed by the formula:

$$P=s+s+s+s, \text{ which is written as:}$$

$$P=4s$$

Rule to Remember

The perimeter of a square equals the length of one side multiplied by 4.

$$P=4s$$

Perimeter of a Triangle

Let a, b, and c represent the three sides of a triangle.

Adding the lengths of the sides, we find the perimeter.

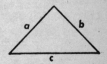

Rule to Remember

The perimeter of a triangle equals the sum of the three sides.

$$P = a + b + c$$

Perimeter of an Isosceles Triangle

Since an isosceles triangle is a triangle in which two sides are equal, the sides may be represented as a, a and b. The perimeter of the triangle is expressed by the formula:

$$P = a + a + b$$

which is written

$$P = 2a + b$$

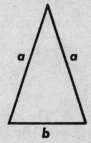

Rule to Remember

The perimeter of an isosceles triangle equals the length of the base plus two times the length of a leg.

$$P = 2a + b$$

Perimeter of an Equilateral Triangle

Since an equilateral triangle is a triangle having three equal sides, each of the sides is represented by the letter s. The perimeter of the triangle is expressed by the formula

$$P = s + s + s, \text{ which is written as}$$
$$P = 3s$$

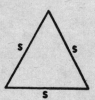

Rule to Remember

The perimeter of an equilateral triangle equals 3 times the length of one side.

$$P = 3s$$

EXERCISES

Perimeter

1. Write the formula for the perimeter of a rectangle whose length is l and whose width is w.

2. Find the perimeter of the rectangles whose dimensions are:
   - a. 5 inches by 8 inches
   - b. 6 feet by 4 inches
   - c. $4\frac{1}{2}$ yards by $3\frac{1}{4}$ yards
   - d. $8\frac{1}{3}$ feet by $6\frac{1}{2}$ feet
   - e. 4.5 inches by 6.7 inches
   - f. 7.25 feet by 9.15 feet
   - g. 4 yards by 12 yards
   - h. 3 yards 1 foot by 2 yards 1 foot

3. The perimeter of a rectangle is 48 inches. If its length is 18 inches, find its width.

4. Write the formula you would use to find the perimeter of a triangle whose sides were represented by a, b and c.

5. The legs of the right angle of a right triangle are 4 inches and 6 inches. Construct this triangle, measure with a ruler the length of the hypotenuse, and find the perimeter.

6. How much ceiling molding is needed for a room 19 feet 6 inches long and 17 feet 3 inches wide?

7. What is the perimeter of a square, one side of which is:
   - a. 22 feet
   - b. 6 yards
   - c. $\frac{1}{2}$ inch
   - d. 1 foot 6 inches
   - e. $5\frac{1}{2}$ inches
   - f. 19 miles

8. The base of an equilateral triangle is 16 yards. What is the perimeter of the triangle?

9. An isosceles triangle has a perimeter of 36 inches and a base of 8 inches. How long is each of the two legs?

10. The sides of a triangle measure t, t and t. Write the formula for the perimeter of this triangle. What kind of triangle is it? How large is the vertex angle?

Perimeter of a Right Triangle

If we know the lengths of the three sides of a right triangle, we will, of course, add $a+b+c$ to find the perimeter. But, suppose we know the length of only two sides of a right triangle. We can still find the perimeter by finding the length of the third side.

The side of a right triangle opposite the right angle is called the *hypotenuse*. The hypotenuse is always the longest side of the triangle.

If we know the length of two sides of a right triangle, we can find the length of the third by following a formula discovered by a Greek mathematician. It is called the *Rule of Pythagoras*. This is the rule:

Rule to Remember

The square of the hypotenuse is equal to the sum of the squares on the other two sides. If the hypotenuse is c, and the two legs are a and b, then

$$c^2 = a^2 + b^2$$

Suppose that, in this diagram, the hypotenuse is 5″, one leg is 3″ and the other leg is 4″, and suppose that each square represents one square inch.

Following the Rule of Pythagoras, we would find that

$$5^2 = 3^2 + 4^2$$

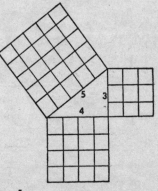

Since squaring a number means to multiply that number by itself, the equation is equivalent to

$$25 = 9 + 16$$
$$\text{or} \quad 25 = 25$$

If you count the squares in the diagram, you will find that there are 25 squares on the hypotenuse and 25 squares on the two legs combined.

But, of course, we ordinarily use the Rule of Pythagoras when one of the sides of a right triangle is unknown. Then we work with an equation like this: $c^2 = 3^2 + 4^2$.

When we combine the terms on the right side of this equation, we find the value of c^2, which is 25, and we must then find the square root of that number.

Squares and Square Roots

To square a number, you have learned, you must multiply that number by itself. The square root of a number is just the opposite. When you find the square root of a number, you are finding what number multiplied by itself gives you the number you began with. The sign for the square root is $\sqrt{\ }$. Thus, the square root of 25 is represented by $\sqrt{25}$.

25 is a perfect square. That is, a whole number (5) multiplied by itself will give you 25. Most numbers are not perfect squares. In that case, to get the square root of a number we may either find it by taking an arithmetic square root or by using a table.

How to Find the Square Root of a Number

Problem: Find the square root of 2894.44.

Method: Step 1: Place the number under a square root sign. Place the decimal point for your answer directly above the one in the given example. Mark off the digits of $\sqrt{28'94'.44'}$ the given number from the decimal point in either direction into periods of two digits each. Every period except the extreme left one must contain two digits. If the last period does not have two digits, add a zero.

Step 2: Find a number that has a square as close to the first period as possible, but does not exceed it. In this example, it is 5. So, place 5 above the first period. Square 5 and place the result under the first period. Now subtract and get a remainder of 3.

$$\begin{array}{r} 5 \cdot \\ \sqrt{28'94'.44'} \\ 25 \\ \hline 3 \end{array}$$

[Continued on top of page 352]

Step 3: Bring down the next period, 94. Multiply the 5 in the answer by 20, giving a trial divisor of 100. Place this to the left of 394, separating it as indicated. Dividing the trial divisor into 394 gives 3. Place this 3 above the second period. Now add 3 to the trial divisor, making 103, and then multiply the new divisor by the 3 and place the result under 394. Subtracting this gives a remainder of 85.

$$
\begin{array}{r}
5\ 3 \\
\sqrt{28'94'.44'} \\
25 \\
\hline
{}^{100}\ \ 394 \\
{}^{+3}\ \ 309 \\
{}^{103}\ \ \overline{85}
\end{array}
$$

Step 4: Bring down the last period of 2 digits. Get the new trial divisor by taking the answer so far times 20. Place this to the left of 8544 as shown. Dividing, the trial divisor goes into 8544 eight times. Place 8 above the last period in your answer; add it to the trial divisor; and then multiply the new divisor by 8.

$$
\begin{array}{r}
5\ 3\ .\ 8 \\
\sqrt{28'94'.44} \\
25 \\
\hline
{}^{100}\ 394 \\
{}^{+\ 3}\ 309 \\
\hline
{}^{103} \\
{}^{1060}\ 85\ 44 \\
{}^{+\ 8}\ 85\ 44 \\
\hline
{}^{1068}
\end{array}
$$

Place this product under the 8544, subtract, and the remainder is zero. The required square root then is 53.8.

HOW TO TELL IF YOUR ANSWER IS RIGHT:

To check your square root, multiply it by itself:

$$
\begin{array}{r}
53.8 \\
\times 53.8 \\
\hline
4304 \\
1614 \\
2690 \\
\hline
2894.44 \quad \text{Ans.}
\end{array}
$$

The answer, 2894.44, is the number you started with, so you have proved that your square root of 53.8 is correct.

EXERCISES
Squares and Square Roots

1. Find to the nearest tenth the square root of each of the following. Show your work.

a. 61   *c.* 64   *e.* 23   *g.* 92   *i.* 19   *k.* 28   *m.* 32   *o.* 115
b. 12   *d.* 118   *f.* 5   *h.* 26   *j.* 40   *l.* 10   *n.* 130

2. Find the square of each of the following to the nearest tenth. *Do not* use the table of Squares and Square Roots.

a. 23   *c.* 14   *e.* 511   *g.* 35   *i.* 7   *k.* 27   *m.* 128   *o.* 8
b. 83   *d.* 102   *f.* 33   *h.* 2   *j.* 96   *l.* 18   *n.* 64

Finding Square Roots from a Table

Finding square roots by arithmetic as shown takes much time. Therefore, square roots have been compiled in tables. In the table on page 354 you will find the square root and the square of every whole number from 1 to 150.

Look at this table to find the square root of 15. Here you find the square root is 3.87. If you multiply the square root by itself you will find that 3.87^2 equals 14.9769.

Since 3.87 has three significant figures, 3.87^2 should be rounded off to three significant figures: $14.9769 = 15.0$, which is the correct square.

How to Find Square Root from a Table

Problem 1: Find the square root of 85.

Method: Look down the column "No." (page 354) until you reach 85. Now, on the same line, but under the column "Square Root," you will find the square root, 9.22.

To Check: $9.22^2 = 9.22 \times 9.22 = 85.0084 = 85.0$

Problem 2: Find the square root of 961.

Method: Look down the "Square" column until you find 961. To the left of it, under "No.", you will find 31. Thus, the square root of 961 equals 31.

To Check: $31 \times 31 = 961$

Problem 3: Find the square root of 340.

Method: On checking the table under "Square" you do not find the number 340. However, 340 is between 324 and 361 in the table. We see that under column "No.", that 340 is between 18 and 19. Since 340 is less than half way from 324 to 361, we try the figure 18.4.

In the table at the right we see that 340 is nearer to 338.56 than it is to either 331.24 or 346.89. Therefore, the square root of 340 equals 18.3 to the nearest tenth.

$$18.2^2 = 331.24$$
$$18.3^2 = 334.89$$
$$18.4^2 = 338.56$$

Tables of Squares and Square Roots of Numbers

No.	Square	Square Root	No.	Square	Square Root	No.	Square	Square Root
1	1	1.00	51	2,601	7.14	101	10,201	10.05
2	4	1.41	52	2,704	7.21	102	10,404	10.10
3	9	1.73	53	2,809	7.28	103	10,609	10.15
4	16	2.	54	2,916	7.35	104	10,816	10.20
5	25	2.24	55	3,025	7.42	105	11,025	10.25
6	36	2.45	56	3,136	7.48	106	11,236	10.30
7	49	2.65	57	3,249	7.55	107	11,449	10.34
8	64	2.83	58	3,364	7.62	108	11,664	10.39
9	81	3.	59	3,481	7.68	109	11,881	10.44
10	100	3.16	60	3,600	7.75	110	12,100	10.49
11	121	3.32	61	3,721	7.81	111	12,321	10.54
12	144	3.46	62	3,844	7.87	112	12,544	10.58
13	169	3.61	63	3,969	7.94	113	12,769	10.63
14	196	3.74	64	4,096	8.	114	12,996	10.68
15	225	3.87	65	4,225	8.06	115	13,225	10.72
16	256	4.	66	4,356	8.12	116	13,456	10.77
17	289	4.12	67	4,489	8.19	117	13,689	10.82
18	324	4.24	68	4,624	8.25	118	13,924	10.86
19	361	4.36	69	4,761	8.31	119	14,161	10.91
20	400	4.47	70	4,900	8.37	120	14,400	10.95
21	441	4.58	71	5,041	8.43	121	14,641	11.
22	484	4.69	72	5,184	8.49	122	14,884	11.05
23	529	4.80	73	5,329	8.54	123	15,129	11.09
24	576	4.90	74	5,476	8.60	124	15,376	11.14
25	625	5.	75	5,625	8.66	125	15,625	11.18
26	676	5.10	76	5,776	8.72	126	15,876	11.22
27	729	5.20	77	5,929	8.77	127	16,129	11.27
28	784	5.29	78	6,084	8.83	128	16,384	11.31
29	841	5.39	79	6,241	8.89	129	16,641	11.36
30	900	5.48	80	6,400	8.94	130	16,900	11.40
31	961	5.57	81	6,561	9.	131	17,161	11.45
32	1,024	5.66	82	6,724	9.06	132	17,424	11.49
33	1,089	5.74	83	6,889	9.11	133	17,689	11.53
34	1,156	5.83	84	7,056	9.17	134	17,956	11.58
35	1,225	5.92	85	7,225	9.22	135	18,225	11.62
36	1,296	6.	86	7,396	9.27	136	18,496	11.66
37	1,369	6.08	87	7,569	9.33	137	18,769	11.70
38	1,444	6.16	88	7,744	9.38	138	19,044	11.75
39	1,521	6.24	89	7,921	9.43	139	19,321	11.79
40	1,600	6.32	90	8,100	9.49	140	19,600	11.83
41	1,681	6.40	91	8,281	9.54	141	19,881	11.87
42	1,764	6.48	92	8,464	9.59	142	20,164	11.92
43	1,849	6.56	93	8,649	9.64	143	20,449	11.96
44	1,936	6.63	94	8,836	9.70	144	20,736	12.
45	2,025	6.71	95	9,025	9.75	145	21,025	12.04
46	2,116	6.78	96	9,216	9.80	146	21,316	12.08
47	2,209	6.86	97	9,409	9.85	147	21,609	12.12
48	2,304	6.93	98	9,604	9.90	148	21,904	12.17
49	2,401	7.	99	9,801	9.95	149	22,201	12.21
50	2,500	7.07	100	10,000	10.	150	22,500	12.25

Using the Pythagorean Rule

By knowing the Rule of Pythagoras, we can solve many problems of length and distance when right triangles are concerned.

How to Apply the Pythagorean Rule

Problem: Traveling by car from his home to the other end of the city, Roger went 2 miles east and 4 miles north. How much distance would he have saved if he could have traveled in a straight line from his home to his destination ?

Step 1: Find the distance he traveled.

4 miles + 2 miles = 6 miles.

Step 2: Find the distance he would have traveled if the route were straight.

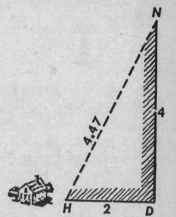

$$c^2 = a^2 + b^2$$
$$c^2 = 4^2 + 2^2 = 16 + 4$$
$$c^2 = 20$$
$$c = \sqrt{20} \text{ or } 4.47 \text{ miles}$$

from home directly to his destination.

Step 3: Find the difference between the two distances.

$$\begin{array}{r} 6.00 \\ -4.47 \\ \hline 1.53 \end{array}$$ Roger would have saved 1.53 miles.

EXERCISES

Using Square Roots

1. Using the table on page 354, find to the nearest hundredth the square root of:

a. 51	d. 79	g. 37	j. 146	m. 775
b. 127	e. 10	h. 122	k. 132	n. 264
c. 40	f. 150	i. 19	l. 106	o. 420

2. Use the Rule of Pythagoras to find the missing value in the dimensions of each of the following right triangles. (Use the table of squares and square roots on page 354.) Then find the perimeter of each triangle.

   a. leg 1 — 6 inches   *d.* hypotenuse — 10 yards
       leg 2 — 4 inches   leg 1 — 6.5 yards
   b. hypotenuse — 22 feet   *e.* leg 1 — 20 feet
       leg 1 — 16 feet   leg 2 — 17 feet
   c. leg 1 — 15 yards   *f.* leg 1 — 8 inches
       leg 2 — 9 yards   leg 2 — 12 inches

3. A 12-foot ladder rests just below a window of a building and touches the ground 4 feet from the building. How far from the ground is the window?

4. Pete and Jim were putting up a pup tent. The pole in the center was 3.5 feet high, and the boys wanted a distance of 2.5 feet on either side of the pole. What must be the length of the canvas to cover the tent?

Areas of Plane Figures

The *area* of any plane figure or surface is the number of square units of a given size that the surface contains. The units of square measure that are commonly used in expressing area are square inches, square feet, square yards, square miles, etc.

Area of a Rectangle

Suppose that this rectangle is 4 inches long and 3 inches wide. It has been divided into squares, each covering 1 square inch. To find the area of the rectangle we count the number of squares. The area of the rectangle is 12 square inches. To find the area more quickly, we can multiply the length by the width.

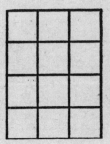

Rule to Remember

The area of a rectangle equals the length times the width.

$$A = lw$$

To find the area of a rectangle, the dimensions (length and width) must both be expressed in the same unit. If they are not, they must be changed to the same unit before multiplying.

Finding the Area of a Rectangle

Problem: Find the area of a rectangle which is 6 feet long and 9 inches wide.

Method: First change 9 inches to feet
$$\frac{9 \text{ in.}}{12 \text{ in.}} = \frac{3}{4} \text{ ft.}$$

Substitute values for literal numbers in the formula
$$A = lw$$
$$= 6 \times \tfrac{3}{4}$$
$$= \tfrac{18}{4}$$
$$A = 4\tfrac{1}{2} \text{ sq. ft.}$$

EXERCISES

Area of Rectangles

1. Write the formula used to find the area of a rectangle whose length is l and whose width is w.

2. Find the area of each of the following rectangles:
   - *a.* $l = 7$ inches, $w = 5$ inches
   - *b.* $l = 3$ yards, $w = 12$ feet
   - *c.* $l = 2.5$ feet, $w = 3.4$ feet
   - *d.* $l = 3.1$ miles, $w = 4.7$ miles
   - *e.* $l = 4\tfrac{1}{4}$ inches, $w = 5\tfrac{3}{4}$ inches
   - *f.* $l = 8$ inches, $w = 3$ feet

3. The dimensions of a rectangular living room are 21 feet by 13 feet. How many square feet of carpet are required to cover the whole floor?

4. How many tiles, each of which is a square foot, are needed to cover the floor of a pool 60 feet wide and 100 feet long?

5. How many tiles which measure one square foot each are needed to cover the floor of a hall which is 2 yards wide and 15 yards long?

6. The living room of a home is 18 feet long and 12 feet wide. If a rug 9 feet by 12 feet is placed on the floor of the room, how many square feet of the floor will remain uncovered?

GEOMETRY

Area of a Square

Since a square is a type of rectangle, we can find the area of a square by using the formula for the area of a rectangle, $A = lw$.

Let s represent the length of the square. Since the sides are equal, s must also represent the width. Substituting s in the formula, we have

$$A = lw$$
$$A = s \cdot s$$

When a number is multiplied by itself, that number is said to be squared. You have learned that the exponent ^{2} near the upper right corner of a number tells us to square that number. Thus, if the area of a square equals s times s, the area may be written s^2 instead of $s \cdot s$.

Rule to Remember

The area of a square equals the square of one side.

$$A = s^2$$

Frequently we must change units of square measure to other units. Memorize the following list of square measure.

144 square inches	= 1 square foot
9 square feet	= 1 square yard
43,560 square feet	= 1 acre
640 acres	= 1 square mile

Essential to Remember

1. To change from a larger unit of measurement to a smaller unit, multiply.

2. To change from a smaller unit to a larger unit, divide.

EXERCISES

Area of a Square

1. Write the formula you would use in finding the area of a square whose side is *a*.

2. Find the area of the squares whose sides are:
   a. 4 feet   c. 3.2 inches   e. 1 yard
   b. 6 feet   d. 8 miles   f. $3\frac{3}{4}$ inches

3. How many tiles one square inch in size are needed to cover a floor which is square in shape if each side of the floor is 9 feet?

4. The perimeter of a square is 20 yards. Find the area of the square.

5. A baseball diamond is a square 90 feet on a side. What is the area enclosed by the base lines?

6. Complete each of the following:
   a. 3 sq. ft. = ... sq. in.   e. 1920 acres = ... sq. mi.
   b. 576 sq. in. = ... sq. ft.   f. 28 sq. mi. = ... acres
   c. 36 sq. ft. = ... sq. yd.   g. 87,120 sq. ft. = ... acres
   d. 4 sq. mi. = ... acre   h. 864 sq. in. = ... sq. ft.

Area of a Parallelogram

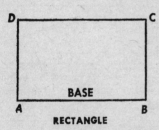

RECTANGLE

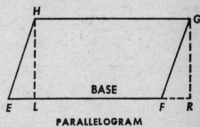

PARALLELOGRAM

The line upon which a plane figure rests is called the *base*. Thus, *AB* is the base of the rectangle, and *EF* is the base of the parallelogram. The *altitude* or height of a plane figure is the perpendicular distance from the highest point in the figure to the base. Thus, *CB* is the altitude of the rectangle and *HL* is the altitude of the parallelogram.

Let us assume that we cut off the triangle *ELH* and placed it so that *EH* fell on *FG* and *HL* on *GR*. We now have a rectangle *LRGH*. Measuring the base *EF* of the parallelogram and base *LR* of the rectangle we find them to be equal. Measuring the altitude *HL* of the parallelogram and the altitude *GR* of the rectangle we find that they too are equal. Since the area of the rectangle is found by multiplying its base by its altitude, the area of the parallelogram, which we have seen to be the same as that of the rectangle, will be found in the same way.

Rule to Remember

The area of a parallelogram equals the product of its base and its altitude.
$$A = bh$$

HOW TO DO THE EXAMPLE

Problem: Find the area of a parallelogram whose base is 20 inches and whose altitude is 12 inches.

Method:

$b = 20$ $A = bh$

$h = 12$ Substitute in the formula:

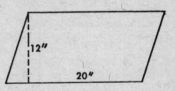

$$A = 20 \times 12$$

Area $= 240$ square inches.

EXERCISES

Area of a Parallelogram

1. Write the formula you would use to find the area of a parallelogram whose base is *b* and whose altitude is *h*.

2. Find the area of each of the following parallelograms:

   a. $b = 4$ feet, $h = 3$ feet   *f.* $b = 2\frac{1}{2}$ feet, $h = 9$ inches

   b. $b = 6$ feet, $h = 1$ yard   *g.* $b = 5$ yards, $h = 9$ yards

   c. $b = 4.5$ inches, $h = 6.3$ inches   *h.* $b = 1$ inch, $h = 3\frac{3}{4}$ inches

   d. $b = 1.5$ feet, $h = 8$ inches   *i.* $b = 2.4$ feet, $h = 6$ inches

   e. $b = 3\frac{1}{2}$ yards, $h = 6\frac{1}{4}$ inches   *j.* $b = 12$ feet, $h = 3$ yards

Area of a Triangle

In parallelogram *ABCD* draw the diagonal *DB*. A *diagonal* is a line between any two non-consecutive vertices of a figure. Now, with a scissors divide the parallelogram into two triangles by cutting along the diagonal. Place one triangle on top of the other. Are these triangles equal? Since they fit on each other, the triangles are equal in area. In addition, we see that triangle *ABD* is one-half of the parallelogram. Since the area of a parallelogram equals the product of its base and altitude, the area of a triangle must equal one-half the product of its base and height.

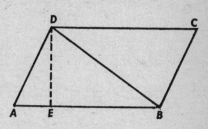

Rule to Remember

The area of a triangle equals one-half the product of its base and height. $A = \frac{1}{2}bh$.

HOW TO DO THE EXAMPLE

Problem: Find the area of a triangle that has a base of 18 inches and a height of 10 inches.

Method:

$$A = \frac{1}{2}bh$$

$b = 18$ Substitute in the formula

$h = 10$ $A = \frac{1}{2} \times 18 \times 10$

$A = \frac{180}{2} = 90$ square inches

EXERCISES
Area of a Triangle

1. Write the formula you would use to find the area of a triangle whose base is *b* and whose height is *h*.

2. Find the area of each of the following triangles:

a. $b=12$ inches, $h=6$ inches   e. $b=2\frac{1}{3}$ yards, $h=4\frac{1}{2}$ yards

b. $b=2$ yards, $h=9$ inches   f. $b=3\frac{1}{2}$ feet, $h=9$ inches

c. $b=4.8$ feet, $h=3.6$ feet   g. $b=1$ foot, $h=\frac{1}{2}$ foot

d. $b=2.5$ yards, $h=14$ inches   h. $b=3$ inches, $h=10$ inches

3. Fill in the dimensions of these triangles.

	Base	Height	Area
a.	14 feet	?	70 sq. ft.
b.	?	13 yards	195 sq. yds.
c.	6 yards	?	1200 sq. ft.
d.	?	60 rods	6 acres

Area of a Trapezoid

The area of a triangle, we have found, is $\frac{1}{2}bh$. If a trapezoid can be divided into two triangles and we know the area of both, we can add them together and find the area of the trapezoid.

We have divided trapezoid $QRST$ into triangles QRT and RST, and we have drawn a perpendicular from base 1 to base 2 to represent the heights of the triangles. The area of triangle RST is $\frac{1}{2}$ *base 1* times the *height*, or $\frac{1}{2}b_1h$. The area of

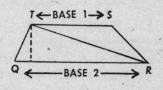

triangle QRT is $\frac{1}{2}$ *base 2* times the *height*, or $\frac{1}{2}b_2h$. The area of the trapezoid would be the sum of the areas of the two triangles that comprise it:

$$A=\tfrac{1}{2}b_1h+\tfrac{1}{2}b_2h$$

In a simplified form, the formula is written:

$$A=\tfrac{1}{2}h(b_1+b_2)$$

Rule to Remember

The area of a trapezoid equals one-half the height times the sum of the bases. $A=\frac{1}{2}h\,(b_1+b_2)$ or $A=\dfrac{h(b_1+b_2)}{2}$.

[Continued on top of page 363]

Problem: Find the area of a trapezoid that has a height of 4 inches, one base of 9 inches, and a second base of 14 inches.

Method:

Substitute in the formula:

$A = \frac{1}{2}h\ (b_1 + b_2)$ (or) $A = \dfrac{h(b_1 + b_2)}{2}$

$A = \frac{1}{2} \cdot 4\ (9 + 14)$

$\quad = 2 \cdot\ (9 + 14)$ $A = \dfrac{4(9 + 14)}{2}$

$\quad = 2 \cdot 23$

$A = 46$ square inches $A = \dfrac{4(23)}{2}$

$A = \frac{92}{2}$

$A = 46$ square inches

Area of the trapezoid is 46 square inches.

EXERCISES

Area of a Trapezoid

1. Write the formula you would use to find the area of a trapezoid whose bases are b_1 and b_2 and whose altitude is h.

2. Find the areas of trapezoids which have the following dimensions:

a. $b_1 = 5$ feet	*c.* $b_1 = 17$ inches	*e.* $b_1 = 3$ inches
$b_2 = 9$ feet	$b_2 = 20$ inches	$b_2 = 5$ inches
$h = 2.5$ feet	$h = 9$ inches	$h = 4\frac{1}{2}$ inches
b. $b_1 = 10$ miles	*d.* $b_1 = 40$ yards	*f.* $b_1 = 16$ feet
$b_2 = 7$ miles	$b_2 = 20$ yards	$b_2 = 21$ feet
$h = 1$ mile	$h = 22$ yards	$h = 9$ feet

GENERAL SKILLS EXERCISE

Try the following test of your skill. If you get any wrong, turn to the pages shown after each question, and learn the correct answer.

1. Plane figures have two dimensions, length and .... (page 336).

2. A triangle has .... sides and .... angles (page 337).

3. A triangle which has two equal sides is called a (an) .... triangle (page 337).

4. The side opposite the right angle in a right triangle is the .... (page 338).

5. A quadrilateral in which two pairs of opposite sides are parallel is called a(an) .... (page 341).

6. A polygon having eight sides is called a(an) .... (page 343).

7. The perimeter of any plane figure can be found by .... the lengths of its sides (page 346).

8. The formula $P = 2a + b$ is used to find the perimeter of a (an) .... triangle (page 348).

9. The number of square units a figure contains is called the .... of the figure (page 356).

10. The formula for the area of a triangle is $A =$ .... (page 361).

11. A closed plane figure formed by straight lines is called a .... (page 336).

12. A quadrilateral is a polygon with .... sides (page 341).

13. To construct a regular hexagon you must divide a .... into six equal parts (page 344).

14. In a right triangle, the square on the .... is equal to the sum of the squares on the other two sides (page 350).

15. To find the square root of a number, we must find a number that, multiplied by ...., equals the original number (page 351).

_____ *My Score*

Circles

Another plane figure is the circle. A *circle* is a curved line all points of which are the same distance away from the *center*, the fixed central point within. A straight line drawn from the center to any point on the circle is called a *radius*. *OD* is a radius (plural: radii) The straight line that passes through the center of the circle and both of whose ends are

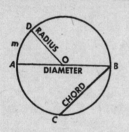

on the circle is called a *diameter*. *AB* is a diameter. A line segment that connects any two points on the curved line of a circle is a *chord*. An example is *BC*.

The length of the curved line, or the distance around the circle, is its *circumference*. Any part of that curved line which makes the circle is an *arc* (see *m*).

The portion of the circle confined in *AOD* is a *sector* of the circle, for two sides are radii and the third side is an arc. Because its vertex is at the center, angle *AOD* is a *central* angle.

Measure the diameter and the radius of the circle. What is the relationship between them?

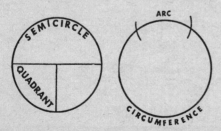

When a circle is cut in half, each of the halves is called a *semicircle*. When a circle is cut into four equal parts, each of the quarters is called a quadrant.

Finding the Circumference of a Circle

Since the circumference is a curved line, it is difficult to find the length by direct measurement. Therefore, mathematicians have found a way to find circumference based on the definite relationship between the circumference and the diameter of a circle.

The circumference of a circle is approximately $3\frac{1}{7}$ times the length of the diameter of the circle.

This relationship between the circumference (C) and the diameter (d) of a circle is represented by the Greek letter π or pi. The approximate value of π is $3\frac{1}{7}(\frac{22}{7})$ or 3.14.

The formula used for finding the circumference of a circle is

$$C = \pi d$$

Since the diameter of a circle equals 2 times the radius, the formula for the circumference is also written

$$C = 2\pi r.$$

Rule to Remember

The circumference of a circle equals pi times the diameter, or pi times twice the radius

$$C = \pi d \text{ or } C = 2\pi r.$$

HOW TO DO THE EXAMPLE

Problem: Find the circumference of a circle whose diameter is 20 in. (Use $\pi = 3\frac{1}{7}$)

Method 1:	Method 2:
$C = \pi d$	$C = 2\pi r$
$C = (\frac{22}{7})20$	$r = \frac{1}{2}d = \frac{1}{2} \cdot 20 = 10$
$C = \frac{440}{7}$	$C = (2)(\frac{22}{7})(10)$
$C = 62\frac{6}{7}$ in.	$C = \frac{440}{7} = 62\frac{6}{7}$ in.

Area of a Circle

If a circle is divided into 4 quadrants and a square is circumscribed about the circle as shown, four small squares are formed.

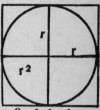

The side of each small square is equal to the radius r. The area of each small square is r^2; the area of the large square is equal to the sum of the four small squares, or $4r^2$.

We can see that the area of the circle is about $\frac{3}{4}$ of the large square. It is approximately equal to $3\frac{1}{7}$ of the small squares, or $3\frac{1}{7}r^2$. This can also be written πr^2.

Rule to Remember

The area of a circle equals pi times the radius squared.

$$A = \pi r^2$$

HOW TO DO THE EXAMPLE

Problem: How many square yards of grass sod are required to cover a circular lawn whose radius is 20 yards?

Method:

$A = \pi r^2$

radius of circle $= 20$

$\pi = 3\frac{1}{7} = \frac{22}{7}$

$A = \frac{22}{7} \times 20^2$

$A = \frac{22}{7} \times 400$

$A = \frac{8800}{7}$

$A = 1257.1$ sq. yards.

EXERCISES

Circles

1. *a.* OA is a.........................
   b. AB is a.........................
   c. O is the.........................
   d. AE is a.........................
   e. t is an.........................
   f. $\angle DOB$ is a.........................

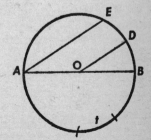

2. What is the ratio of *BO* to any other radius of the circle?

3. What is the relationship between a diameter of a circle and a radius of the circle?

4. Write a formula showing the relationship between the radius of a circle and its diameter.

5. Give two formulas which can be used to find the circumference of a circle.

6. A circular swimming pool has a radius of 13.2 feet. Find the circumference of the pool.

7. A circular lamp shade has a radius of 8½ inches. Find the circumference of the shade.

8. At the equator the circumference of the earth is 25,000 miles. Find the radius of the earth.

9. A globe has a diameter of 1½ feet. What is its circumference?

Geometric Solids

We have been studying plane figures, which have only two dimensions: length and width. Now we shall study figures with three dimensions. Figures that have three dimensions are called *geometric solids* or *solid figures*. The three dimensions of solid figures are length, width, and thickness, or height.

Prisms

A *prism* is a solid, each side of which is a polygon, and the upper base of which is parallel and congruent (exactly the same in size and shape) to the lower base; the corresponding vertices of the top and bottom polygons are joined by parallel edges. In a *right prism*, the lateral faces (sides) are perpendicular to the bases. Right prisms include:

1. The Rectangular Prism. A geometric figure which has 6 sides, all of which are rectangles, is called a *rectangular solid* or *rectangular prism.*

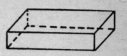

2. The Cube. If the dimensions (length, width and height) of a rectangular solid are equal, the solid is called a *cube.* The faces of a cube are all squares.

3. The Triangular Prism.   *4. The Pentagonal Prism.*

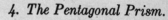

The Right Circular Cylinder

A cylinder is a circular prism, the bases of which are equal circles that are parallel to each other. If the sides of the cylinder are perpendicular to the bases, the cylinder is called a *right* cylinder.

CYLINDER

The Sphere

A sphere is a solid in the shape of a ball. Half of the sphere is a *hemisphere.*

SPHERE   **HEMISPHERE**

The Cone

The cone is a solid figure whose base is a circle and whose sides taper to a point.

CONE

The Pyramid

A pyramid is a solid whose sides are triangles and whose base can be a polygon of 3 or more sides. The kind of pyramid de-

pends on the type of base.
For example, if the base
is a square, the pyramid
is called a *square pyramid*.
If the base is a triangle,
the pyramid is called a
triangular pyramid.

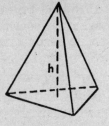 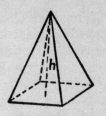

TRIANGULAR PYRAMID   SQUARE PYRAMID

The perpendicular distance from the top of the pyramid to
the base is the *height* of the pyramid. The height is usually
represented by *h*.

EXERCISES

Geometric Solids

1. *Identify each of the following solids.*

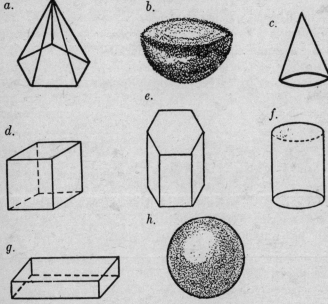

2. What general name applies to *d*, *e* and *g*?
3. What do figures *b*, *c*, *f* and *h* have in common?
4. How is *b* related to *h*?
5. What general name is applied to the base of *a*, *d*, *e* and *g*?

Volume of Solids

Volume. The volume of a geometric solid is the amount of space, expressed in cubic units, that the solid occupies. The unit of measure used to express volume may be the cubic inch, the cubic foot, the cubic yard. A cubic inch is a cube one inch long, one inch wide and one inch deep.

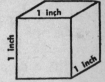

Rule to Remember

The volume of any cylinder or prism equals the area of the base multiplied by the height. $V = Bh$.

Volume of a Rectangular Prism

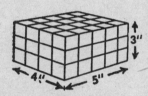

How can we find the volume of this rectangular box whose dimensions are 5 inches by 4 inches by 3 inches? We are actually trying to find the number of 1-inch cubes contained in the box. On examining the box closely, we see that it is composed of three layers. Each layer contains 5×4 cubes or 20 cubes. Three such layers will, therefore, contain 3×20 or 60 cubes. Since the box contains 60 one-inch cubes, we say that the volume of the box is 60 cubic inches.

To find the volume, we multiply the length by the width by the height.

Rule to Remember

The volume of a rectangular solid equals the product of the length, width and height.

$$V = lwh$$

The volume is expressed in cubic units of whatever kind is being used.

HOW TO DO THE EXAMPLE

Problem: Find the volume of a box 5 feet long, 4 feet high and $2\frac{1}{2}$ feet wide. [Continued on top of page 372]

Method:

(1) List given facts	(2) Substitute in formula
$l = 5$ ft.	$V = lwh$
$w = 2\frac{1}{2}$ ft.	$V = 5 \times 2\frac{1}{2} \times 4$
$h = 4$ ft.	$V = 50$

The volume of the box is 50 cubic feet.

Converting Units

You may sometimes have to change from one unit of volume to another. Therefore, it is wise to memorize this table of cubic measures:

$$1728 \text{ cubic inches} = 1 \text{ cubic foot}$$
$$27 \text{ cubic feet} = 1 \text{ cubic yard}$$

EXERCISES

Volume of Solids

1. Write the formula you would use to find the volume of a rectangular solid if the length of the base is l, the width of the base is w, and the height is h.

2. Find the volume of the rectangular solids whose dimensions are:
   a. $l = 2$ inches, $w = 4$ inches, $h = 7$ inches
   b. $l = 7$ feet, $w = 8$ feet, $h = 5.3$ feet
   c. $l = 8$ inches, $w = 3$ feet, $h = 9$ feet
   d. $l = 12\frac{1}{2}$ yards, $w = 3\frac{1}{5}$ yards, $h = 9$ inches

3. Fill in the dimensions of the following rectangular solids.

	Length	Width	Height	Volume
a.	?	4 feet	9 feet	144 cu. ft.
b.	8 inches	?	1 foot	236 cu. in.
c.	1 yard	30 inches	?	27 cu. ft.
d.	3.5 feet	?	2 inches	360 cu. in.

4. How many cubic feet of air are contained in a room which is 20 feet long, 14 feet wide, and 9 feet high?

5. Find the volume of each of these rectangular solids.

6. An excavation for a building is 50 yards long, 20 yards wide and 15 yards deep. How many cubic yards of earth must be removed?

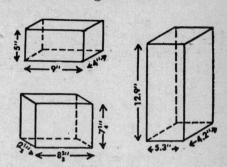

7. A candy box is 2 inches high, 10.3 inches long and 6.7 inches wide. How many cubic inches does it contain?

Volume of a Cube

Since a cube is a rectangular solid, its volume may be found by using the general formula for a rectangular solid:

Volume = length × width × height, or $V = lwh$

However, the sides of a cube are equal and, thus, *length equals width equals height*. Therefore, the volume of a cube may be found by multiplying one edge e by e by e.

When a number is multiplied by itself, we have learned, that number is squared. When a number is used as a factor three times (as $e × e × e$), we say that the number is cubed.

Rule to Remember

The volume of a cube equals one edge cubed.

$$V = e^3$$

The volume is expressed in cubic units.

HOW TO DO THE EXAMPLE

Problem: Find the volume of a cube whose edge is 4 inches.

Method:
$$V = e^3$$
$$V = 4 × 4 × 4$$
$$V = 64 \text{ cubic inches.}$$

EXERCISES

Volume of a Cube

1. Write the formula for the volume of a cube in terms of an edge, *e.*
2. Find the volume of the cube whose edge is:

     a. 4 inches   *c.* 9 feet   *e.* 6.25 ft   *g.* 5 ft.
     b. 6 inches   *d.* 2.5 yards   *f.* $3\frac{1}{2}$ in.   *h.* 2 ft.

3. *a.* Find the area of the base of a cube whose edge is 3 inches.
     b. Find the volume of this cube.
     c. What is the surface area of the cube?

Volume of a Right Circular Cylinder

The volume of a cylinder is found by multiplying the area of the base by the height of the cylinder.

Since the base of a cylinder is a circle, its area is πr^2.

Substituting πr^2 for the area of the base in the formula $V = Bh$, we get: $V = \pi r^2 h$

Rule to Remember

The volume of a cylinder equals pi times the radius squared times the height. $V = \pi r^2 h$.

HOW TO DO THE EXAMPLE

Problem: What is the volume of a cylinder whose height is 14 inches and whose diameter is 4 inches? Use $\pi = \frac{22}{7}$

Method:

Since the diameter is 4 in., the radius is 2 in. Using the formula $V = \pi r^2 h$, we get

$$V = \frac{22}{7} \times 2 \times 2 \times 14$$
$$V = 176 \text{ cu. in.}$$

EXERCISES

Volume of a Right Circular Cylinder

1. *a.* How many bases does a cylinder have?
     b. What is the shape of each base?
     c. How do they compare in size?

2. Write the algebraic formula for the volume of a cylinder if the area of the base is B and the altitude is h.

3. Write the algebraic formula for the volume of a cylinder if the radius of the base is r and the height is h.

4. Find the volume of right cylinders with the following dimensions: (Use $\pi = \frac{22}{7}$)

   a. radius: 4 feet   *d.* radius: $6\frac{1}{4}$ inches
       height: 10 feet   height: $9\frac{1}{2}$ inches

   b. diameter: $2\frac{1}{2}$ yards   *e.* base: 64 square feet
       height: 9 yards   height: $9\frac{1}{2}$ feet

   c. base: 124 square feet   *f.* diameter: 80 feet
       height: 52 feet   height: 120 feet

5. A can of peas has a diameter of 3 inches and a height of 4 inches. What is its volume?

6. A silo is 21 feet high and has a radius of 7 feet. Find its volume.

7. A gas tank is cylindrical in shape. If the diameter of the tank is 40 feet and the height of the tank is 90 feet, find the number of cubic feet of gas it contains.

8. A right cylindrical wastepaper basket is one foot high and has a radius of 5 inches. How many cubic inches of space can be filled with waste paper?

The Volume of the Pyramid and the Cone

Neither the pyramid nor the cone is a prism. But each is related to a prism in a similar way. The pyramid is related to a prism of an equal base and height just as the cone is related to a cylinder of equal base and height.

PRISM   PYRAMID   CYLINDER   CONE

Rules to Remember

The volume of a pyramid equals one-third the volume of a prism which has an equal base and an equal height.

[Continued on top of page 376]

The volume of a pyramid equals one-third the area of the base times the height.

$$V = \tfrac{1}{3}Bh$$

The volume of a cone equals one-third the volume of a cylinder which has an equal base and an equal height. The volume of a cone equals one-third the area of the base times the height.

$$V = \tfrac{1}{3}\,Bh \text{ or } \tfrac{1}{3}\pi r^2 h$$

EXERCISES

Volume of Pyramid and Cone

1. Find the volume of a pyramid whose base is a square 6 inches on a side and whose height is 8 inches.

2. *Complete the following table:*

	Base of Pyramid	*Height*	*Volume*
a.	Triangle: base, 6 in; height, 4 in.	20 in.	?
b.	Rectangle: 10 in. × 12 in.	30 in.	?
c.	Square: 12 in. × 12 in.	15 in.	?

3. Richard and Jim went into a soda shop. Richard ordered an ice cream soda that was served in a glass that had a diameter of 2½ inches and a height of 6 inches. The glass was a right circular cylinder. Jim ordered a soda that was served in a cone-shaped cup, resting in a holder. The cone also had a height of 6 inches and a diameter of 2½ inches. How many times as big was the volume of Richard's drink?

4. *Complete the following table:*

	Diameter of Cone	*Radius*	*Height*	*Volume*
a.	5 feet	?	20 feet	?
b.	?	16 inches	52 inches	?
c.	12 feet	?	28 feet	?
d.	?	6 inches	16 inches	?

Finding the Surface Area of Solids

Sometimes we must know the surface area of a solid. For example, if we want to cover a cylindrical hassock with leather, we will want to know how much leather we will need to cover the hassock on all sides. Then we will find the sum of the areas of the surfaces. This will be the *surface area*.

Surface Area of a Prism

The surface area of a prism equals the area of base$_1$ + the area of base$_2$ + the areas of all the sides.

Thus, to find the surface area of a cube, we would add:

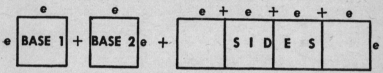

But since all the sides of a cube are equal and there are six sides in all, we need only find the area of one side and multiply this by six.

The area of one side equals e^2. Therefore, the surface area of a cube is:

$$A_s = 6e^2$$

Rule to Remember

The surface area of a cube equals six times one edge squared.

A triangular prism, a rectangular prism or any other kind of prism does not always have equal sides.

Surface Area of Any Right Prism

1. Find twice the area of one base.

Reason: The bases of a right prism are equal.

2. Find the area of the sides by multiplying the perimeter of the base by the height.

[Continued on top of page 378]

Reason: The perimeter of the base is the length of all sides of the base added together. Multiplying this by the height will give you the total area of the sides, for the area of a rectangle equals length × height.

3. Add the area of the bases and the area of the sides.

HOW TO DO THE EXAMPLE

Problem: Gerald wanted to build a wooden chest 3 feet high, 5 feet long and 2 feet deep. Approximately how many board feet would he need to make the chest?

Solution:

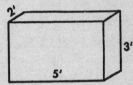

1. Each base is 5 feet long and 2 feet wide. Therefore, the area of each base is *lw* or 5×2 or 10 sq. ft.

The combined area of the two bases is 20 square feet.

2. The perimeter of the base is

$$P = 2(l+w)$$
$$= 2(5+2)$$
$$= 14 \text{ feet}$$

3. The area of the sides (lateral area) is:

$$A_1 = ph$$
$$= 14 \cdot 3$$
$$= 42 \text{ square feet}$$

4. The surface area of the chest will be

$$\begin{array}{r} 42 \text{ square feet} \\ +20 \text{ square feet} \\ \hline 62 \text{ square feet} \end{array}$$

Therefore, Gerald must get at least 62 square feet of boards to build the chest.

Surface Area of a Cylinder

The surface area of a prism can be found by adding the area of the bases and the area of the sides. The cylinder follows the same rule, but its side must first be changed into a rectangle.

You can easily see how this is done if you take any item of canned goods and cut off the label along a line perpendicular to the base. When you spread out the label, you will have a rectangle. The length of that rectangle will equal the circumference of the circle. Can you see why? The length times the height will equal the area.

The surface area of a cylinder equals the sum of the areas of the side and the bases.

Surface Area of a Right Circular Cylinder

1. Find twice the area of one base. $(A = \pi r^2)$
2. Find the area of the side.
   Circumference of base $\times$ height
   $(C = 2\pi r)$
3. Add the area of the side and the area of the bases.

HOW TO DO THE EXAMPLE

Problem: A factory is manufacturing metal cans. If the cans must be 14 inches high and they must have a diameter of 8 inches, how much metal is needed for each can?

Method:

1. The area of one
   base is:

$A = \pi r^2$
$r = 8 \div 2 = 4$
$A = \frac{22}{7} \cdot 4^2$
$\quad = \frac{22}{7} \cdot 16$
$\quad = 50\frac{2}{7}$ square inches

2. The area of the
   two bases equals:

$50\frac{2}{7} \times 2 = 100\frac{4}{7}$ square inches

[Continued on top of page 380]

3. The area of the side equals:

circumference of base $\times$ height

$$C = 2\pi r$$
$$= 2 \cdot \tfrac{22}{7} \cdot 4$$
$$= 25\tfrac{1}{7} \text{ inches}$$
$$h = 14 \text{ inches}$$
$$A_s = 25\tfrac{1}{7} \times 14$$
$$A_s = 352 \text{ square inches}$$

4. Total surface area is:

352 square inches
$\underline{+100\tfrac{4}{7}}$ square inches
$452\tfrac{4}{7}$ square inches

The factory will need $452\tfrac{4}{7}$ square inches of metal to manufacture each can.

EXERCISES

Surface Area

1. Jane wants to wrap a package. The box is 2 feet long, 1 foot wide and 4 inches high. She wants to buy wrapping paper that will cover $1\tfrac{1}{2}$ times the area of the box. How much paper will she have to buy?

2. Susan is going to paint a hat box to use as part of the setting in the school play. If the box has a diameter of 18 inches and a height of 12 inches, how much surface will she have to cover with paint?

3. Find the surface area of each of the following:

    a. a cylinder 20 feet high and 9 feet in diameter.

    b. a cylinder 16 yards high and 5 yards in radius.

    c. a triangular prism 5 inches high. The base is an equilateral triangle, each side of which is 9 inches.

    d. a cube 2.5 feet high.

    e. a rectangular prism 16 inches wide, 19 inches long and 7 inches high.

    f. a cylinder with a circumference of 20 yards and a height of 8 yards.

Symmetry

If the parts of a geometric figure are so arranged that they are in perfect balance, we say that the figure possesses *symmetry*.

If a plane geometric figure possesses balance about a line, the figure has *line symmetry*. If the balance is about a point, it has *point symmetry*.

Line Symmetry

A dotted line has been drawn in the figure shown. The figure is now divided into two parts that have the same size and shape. If the figure is folded on the dotted line, the two parts will coincide. We say that the figure is symmetrical about the dotted line. The dotted line is called the *axis of symmetry*.

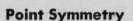

It is possible for a figure to have more than one axis of symmetry.

In this figure, line *RS* is an axis of symmetry. If we fold the figure along *RS*, the two parts will coincide. A point on the left side will fall on only one point on the right side. Any two such points are called *corresponding points*. For example, *A* and *B* are corresponding points.

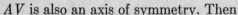

AV is also an axis of symmetry. Then *B* and *R* are corresponding points. What is the third possible axis of symmetry? What two points will correspond when this axis is drawn?

Notice that, if line *AB* is drawn, the axis of symmetry *RS* is perpendicular to, and bisects, *AB*. If a figure has line symmetry, then the axis of symmetry must be perpendicular to the line joining every two corresponding points and must also bisect it.

Point Symmetry

If a dotted line is drawn from any one point on this figure to any corresponding point, the dotted line will be bisected by the point O. The figure has balance about point O and is, therefore, an example of *point symmetry*. Point *O* is called the *center of symmetry*.

If a figure has point symmetry, then the line which connects every two corresponding points must pass through the center of symmetry and be bisected by it.

It is possible for a figure to have both point symmetry and line symmetry. An example is the circle. Any diameter will be an axis of symmetry. Hence the circle possesses line symmetry.

Pick any point A on a circle. Connect this point with center O. Extend this line to a point B, on the other side of the circle. The radius OA is equal to the radius OB. Because this is true of any line drawn through O and bounded at either end by the circle, O is the center of symmetry and the circle possesses point symmetry as well as line symmetry.

Figures that have point symmetry.
   1. Which figures have point symmetry? line symmetry?
   2. Which figures have both point and line symmetry?

EXERCISES

Line Symmetry

1. When does a geometric figure possess line symmetry?
2. What is the axis of symmetry?
3. Give examples of line symmetry in nature.
4. Name three objects in your house that have line symmetry.
5. How many axes of symmetry can you draw in the regular hexagon at the right?
6. Let a drop of ink fall on a paper. Fold the paper on the ink drop and then unfold the paper. Does the design possess line symmetry?

EXERCISES

Point Symmetry

1. When does a geometric figure have point symmetry?
2. What is the center of symmetry?
3. Give some examples of point symmetry in nature.

4. Name three objects in your house which have point symmetry.

5. Draw each of the following figures. If the figure has point symmetry, mark the center of symmetry.

    a. scalene triangle   *f.* rectangle
    b. isosceles triangle   *g.* square
    c. equilateral triangle   *h.* circle
    d. quadrilateral   *i.* sector of a circle
    e. parallelogram

6. Which of the figures below have point symmetry?

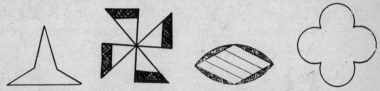

7. Draw two figures each of which possesses both point and line symmetry. Draw in the axis of symmetry and mark the center of symmetry.

Plane Symmetry

If a solid can be divided into two equal solids by a plane, and if every part on one side of the plane has a corresponding part on the other, the original solid has *plane symmetry*. The plane itself is called the *plane of symmetry*.

Suppose that the body of a car is divided lengthwise into two parts by a plane, and that for every part on the left side, there is a part on the right side which corresponds to it. Then the body of the car has plane symmetry. What would prevent all but a dual-controlled car from having plane symmetry?

Similarly, if an apple is a sphere, then a knife or plane cut through the center will divide the apple into two corresponding parts. The apple has plane symmetry.

EXERCISES

Plane Symmetry

1. When does a solid have plane symmetry?

2. What is the name of the plane that divides the solid into two equal parts?

3. Where can plane symmetry be found in nature? Give three examples.

4. Where can plane symmetry be found in your house? Give three examples.

5. Through some of the objects below, a plane of symmetry can be indicated by a line. Draw the plane of symmetry where it is possible.

GENERAL SKILL EXERCISE

How are you doing? Try the following test. If you get any wrong, turn to the pages shown after each question. Practice those problems until you have mastered them.

1. The distance around a circle is called its .... (page 366).

2. The symbol π is used to express the relation between the circumference and the .... of a circle (page 366).

3. The formula for the area of a circle is .... (page 367).

4. Geometric solids have .... dimensions (page 368).

5. A solid whose bases consist of equal parallel circles is called a .... (page 369).

6. The number of cubic units in a solid is called the .... of the solid. (page 371).

7. If the side of a cube is e, the formula you would use to find the volume would be .... (page 373).

8. The formula for finding the volume of a cylinder is .... (page 374).

9. If the parts of a geometric figure are in perfect balance, we say that the figure has .... (page 381).

10. The line around which the parts of a figure are balanced is called the .... (page 381).

11. The volume of a right prism equals the .... of the base times the height (page 371).

12. The surface area of a cube equals .... (page 377).

_____*My Score*

Similar Figures

These two figures look alike, but one is a smaller copy of the other. These are *similar figures:* figures having the same shape but not necessarily the same size.

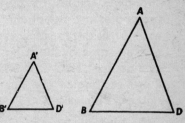

The sides in the same position are the *corresponding sides* of the figures, and the angles in the same position are the *corresponding angles* of the figures. For example, AB and $A'B'$ (read A prime B prime) are corresponding sides in the figures above, and $\angle ABD$ and $\angle A'B'D'$ are corresponding angles. The corresponding angles of similar polygons are equal.

If the ratio of side AB to side $A'B'$ is 2:1, then the ratio of a pair of any other two corresponding sides must also be 2:1. The corresponding sides of similar figures must be proportional. The corresponding sides of similar polygons will be parallel if the polygons are placed in the same position.

Rule to Remember

Two polygons are similar if two conditions are satisfied:
1. Corresponding sides are proportional.
2. Corresponding angles are equal.

HOW TO DO THE EXAMPLE

Problem 1: Are two squares always similar?
Method:
All the corresponding sides are in the ratio of $\frac{a}{b}$. The corresponding angles are equal since all the angles of a square are right angles and all right angles are equal.

Therefore, all squares are similar. [Continued on top of page 386]

Problem **2:** Are all rectangles similar?

Method:

Although the corresponding angles of the rectangles are equal, the ratio of side *a* to side *c* is not the same as the ratio of side *b* to side *d*. Then

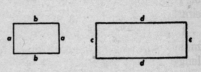

these rectangles are not similar. Therefore, not all rectangles are similar.

Problem **3:** The figures below are similar. Find the values of the unknown sides.

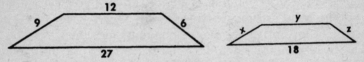

Method: Since these figures are similar, the corresponding sides are in proportion. Therefore:

(1) $\frac{18}{27} = \frac{x}{9}$ or $\frac{18}{27} = \frac{x}{9}$

$27x = 162$ In a proportion the cross-products are equal. $\frac{18 \div 3 = 6}{27 \div 3 = 9}$

$\frac{27x}{27} = \frac{162}{27}$ $x = 6$

$x = 6$

(2) $\frac{18}{27} = \frac{y}{12}$ (3) $\frac{18}{27} = \frac{z}{6}$

$27y = 216$ $27z = 108$

$\frac{27y}{27} = \frac{216}{27}$ $\frac{27z}{27} = \frac{108}{27}$

$y = 8$ $z = 4$

EXERCISES

Similar Figures

1. Raymond was making a poster. The poster paper was 30 inches wide and 42 inches long. Over the original poster paper, Raymond wanted to paste a smaller, similar rectangle of a different color that

measured 36 inches long. What would be the width of the second rectangle?

2. The sides of pentagon A are in the ratio 2:3:3:2:4. The sides of pentagon B are in the ratio $7\frac{1}{2}$:$7\frac{1}{2}$:5:10:5. Are the pentagons similar?

3. An isosceles triangle has a base of 17 inches and a leg of 25 inches. If a similar triangle has a base of $42\frac{1}{2}$ inches, what will be the length of each leg of the second triangle?

4. Triangle A is similar to triangle B. Mark the number of degrees in each angle in triangle B.

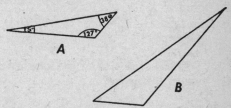

5. In column B are the dimensions of a figure similar to the figure represented in column A. Find the missing dimensions of the similar figure.

	A	B
a.	2,3,2,3	5,?,5,?
b.	5,10,10,5,5	$2\frac{1}{2}$,?,?,$2\frac{1}{2}$,$2\frac{1}{2}$
c.	12,18,10	2,?,?
d.	1,5,1,5	6,?,6,?

Proving Triangles Similar
Method 1

If we can prove that two angles of one triangle are equal respectively to two angles of another triangle, then we can conclude that all the corresponding angles are equal, all the corresponding sides are proportional, and the triangles are similar.

Rule to Remember

Two triangles are similar if two angles of one triangle are equal respectively to two angles of the other triangle.

[Continued on top of page 388]

HOW TO DO THE EXAMPLE

Problem **1.** Are the following triangles similar? Explain.

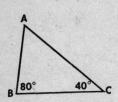
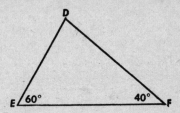

Solution: The sum of the angles of any triangle is 180°. ∡*ABC* + ∡*ACB* = 80° + 40° = 120°. Therefore, ∡*BAC* = 180° − 120° = 60°. Therefore, ∡*BAC* = ∡*DEF* = 60°. Also ∡*ACB* = ∡*EFD* = 40°. △*ABC* is similar to △*DEF* because two angles of △*ABC* are equal respectively to two angles of △*DEF*.

Note: The symbol used in geometry to mean "is similar to" is ∼. In the diagram above △*ABC* ∼ △*DEF*.

Problem **2.** Is △*ABC* similar to △*DEC*? Explain.

Solution: When two lines intersect, four angles are formed. The opposite angles are called *vertical angles*. We have learned that vertical angles are always equal (see p. 325). ∡*ACB* and ∡*DCE* are vertical angles. Therefore they are equal. ∡*BAC* = ∡*DEC* = 48°. Therefore, △*ABC* ∼ △*DEC* because two angles of one triangle are equal respectively to two angles of the other triangle.

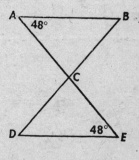

Method 2

Rule to Remember

Two triangles are similar if an angle of one triangle is equal to an angle of the second triangle and the sides including these angles are proportional.

HOW TO DO THE EXAMPLE

Problem **1.** Are the two triangles similar?

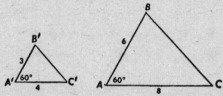

Solution: ∡BAC = ∡B′A′C′ = 60°. The ratio $\frac{8}{4}$ is the same as $\frac{6}{3}$. Therefore the two triangles are similar because ∡BAC = ∡B′A′C′ and the including sides are proportional.

Problem **2.** Are the two triangles similar?

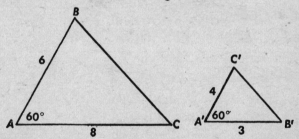

Solution: ∡BAC = ∡B′A′C′ = 60°. $\frac{8}{3}$ is not equal to $\frac{6}{4}$. But $\frac{8}{6}$ is equal to $\frac{4}{3}$. So again ∡BAC = ∡B′A′C′ = 60° and the including sides are proportional. The triangles are similar.

If △A′B′C′ is turned so that side 3 is on the left and 4 becomes the base, the problem is the same as in Problem 1.

Triangles are similar if corresponding angles are equal, or if corresponding sides are proportional.

Locating the Corresponding Sides

In the similar triangles on page 389, problem 2, AB corresponds to $A'B'$, AC to $A'C'$, and BC to $B'C'$. $\angle BAC = \angle B'A'C'$, $\angle ABC = \angle A'B'C'$, and $\angle ACB = \angle A'C'B'$. Notice that AB and $A'B'$ are opposite the equal angles $\angle ACB$ and $\angle A'C'B'$. AC and $A'C'$ are opposite $\angle ABC$ and $\angle A'B'C'$ and BC and $B'C'$ are opposite $\angle BAC$ and $\angle B'A'C'$.

Rule to Remember

If two triangles are similar, corresponding sides are always opposite the corresponding equal angles, and the corresponding equal angles are opposite the corresponding sides.

HOW TO DO THE EXAMPLE

Problem 1. Write a proportion involving the sides of $\triangle ABC$ and $\triangle CDE$.

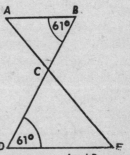

Solution: The vertical angles $\angle ACB$ and $\angle DCE$ are equal. $\angle ABC = \angle CDE = 61°$. The two triangles are similar. AC in $\triangle ABC$ is opposite $61°$ and CE in $\triangle CDE$ is opposite $61°$ in $\triangle CDE$. Hence, AC and CE are corresponding sides. AB in $\triangle ABC$ is opposite $\angle ACB$, and DE in $\triangle DCE$ is opposite $\angle DCE$. Since the vertical angles are equal, AB corresponds to DE. If the two triangles are similar, the corresponding sides are proportional. Then

$$\frac{AC}{CE} = \frac{AB}{DE}$$

Using Similar Triangles to Find Distances

Problem 1. Find the unknown distance *x*.

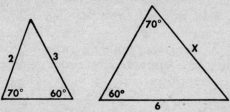

Solution: The two triangles are similar because two angles of the first triangle are equal respectively to two angles of the second triangle. Since the two triangles are similar, the corresponding sides are proportional. 6 and 3 correspond because they are opposite the equal 70° angles. *x* and 2 correspond because they are opposite the equal 60° angles. Therefore, setting up the proportion of the corresponding sides, we get:

$$\frac{x}{2} = \frac{6}{3}$$

$3x = 2(6)$ or 12   In a proportion the cross-products are =

$$\frac{3x}{3} = \frac{12}{3}$$

$$x = 4$$

Problem 2. A 12-foot pole casts a shadow of 16 feet at the same time that a building casts a shadow of 32 feet. Find the height of the building.

Solution:

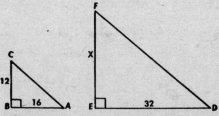

The sun's rays will form the same angle with the ground

[Continued on top of page 392]

at *A* as they do at *D*. The pole and the building form right angles with the ground. Therefore, △*ABC* is similar to △*DEF*.

x and 12 are opposite the equal angles at *A* and *D*. Therefore, they are the corresponding sides of the triangles.

32 and 16 are corresponding sides of the triangles because they are opposite the equal remaining angles at *C* and *F*. Therefore:

$$\frac{x}{12} = \frac{32}{16}$$

$$16x = (12)(32) = 384$$

$$\frac{16x}{16} = \frac{384}{16}$$

$x = 24$ feet, the height of the building

EXERCISES

Similar Triangles

1. Jim wanted to find the length of tunnel *AB*. He measured *BE* and found that it was 20 feet. *ED*, he found, was 2 feet, and *CD* was 7 feet. What was the length of the tunnel?

2. John stands at *C*, a distance of 20 feet from a building *DE* and 7 feet from stick *AB*. The stick is 4 feet long. If ∢*DEC* = ∢*BAC*, find the height of the building.

3. Bob's tent has a base 8 feet long. The length of the canvas on each side of the pole is $5\frac{1}{2}$ feet from the pole to the ground. If the entrance measures $2\frac{1}{4}$ feet on each side, and if angle *c* equals angle *d*, how long is the base of the entrance?

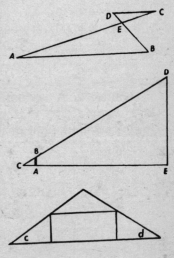

4. A telephone pole 12 feet high casts a shadow 5 feet long. A building near the pole casts a shadow 7 feet long. How high is the building?

Constructing a Triangle Similar to a Given Triangle

HOW TO DO THE EXAMPLE

Construct a triangle similar to a given triangle ABC with corresponding sides in the ratio of 2:1.

Method: Start by drawing DE equal to twice AB. At D measure with the protractor an angle equal to ∡BAC. At E measure an angle equal to ∡ABC. Extend these sides until they meet in F. Then △ABC is similar to △DFE because ∡BAC = ∡EDF and ∡ABC = ∡DEF.

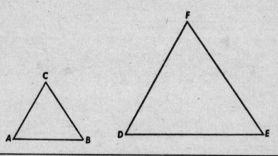

EXERCISES
Constructing Triangles Similar to a Given Triangle

1. Construct a triangle similar to a given triangle *ABC* with corresponding sides in the ratio of:

a. 3:1	*c.* 5:1	*e.* 7:1	*g.* 2:1	*i.* 10:1
b. 4:1	*d.* 6:1	*f.* 8:1	*h.* 9:1	

2. Given △*ABC*. Draw a line *A'B'*. Construct a △*A'B'C'* similar to △*ABC* so that *AB* and *A'B'* will be corresponding sides.

Congruent Triangles

If the corresponding sides of two similar polygons have the ratio of 1:1, these polygons are *congruent*. Similar triangles, you have learned, have the same shape but not the same size. Congruent triangles have exactly the same shape and the same size. Because congruent polygons are exactly alike, they can be made to coincide (fit together), like the pages in this book. The symbol used to mean "is congruent to" is ≅.

Triangles are congruent under these conditions:

Rules to Remember

1. Two triangles are congruent if the three sides of one are equal respectively to the three sides of the other. This statement is abbreviated $S.S.S = S.S.S.$

2. Two triangles are congruent if two sides and the included angle of one are equal respectively to two sides and the included angle of the other $(S.A.S = S.A.S.)$

3. Two triangles are congruent if two angles and the included side of one are equal respectively to two angles and the included side of the other $(A.S.A. = A.S.A.)$

Do you see now why it was possible to construct a triangle when you were given dimensions only of three sides, or of two sides and the included angle, or of two angles and the included side?

HOW TO DO THE EXAMPLE

Problem 1. Is AC equal to DF?

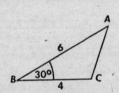 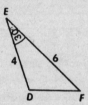

Method:

$\triangle ABC \cong \triangle DEF$ because S.A.S. = S.A.S. Sides AC and DF are the corresponding sides of the triangles because they are opposite the equal angles. Therefore, AC = DF because corresponding sides of congruent triangles are equal.

Problem 2. Show that the following triangles are congruent.

[Continued on top of page 395]

Method:

$\triangle ABE \cong \triangle CFD$ because A.S.A. = A.S.A.

Problem 3. Does angle *BCA* equal angle *ACD* ?

Method:

AC is a side of both tri-
angles. *AB* = *AD* because
both sides equal 4. *BC* = *CD*
because both equal 2. There-
fore, $\triangle ABC \cong \triangle ACD$ because
S.S.S. = S.S.S.

∡*BCA* is opposite 4 and
∡*ACD* is opposite 4. Angles
opposite corresponding sides
are corresponding angles.

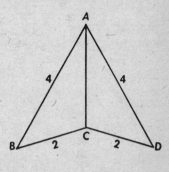

∡*BCA* and ∡*ACD* are opposite corresponding sides;
therefore they are corresponding angles. Corresponding
angles in congruent triangles are equal. Therefore ∡*BCA*
equals ∡*ACD*.

EXERCISES

Congruent Triangles

1. The sides of $\triangle ABC$ are 3, 4 and 5. The sides of $\triangle DEF$ are
5, 4 and 3. Are the triangles congruent?

2. The sides *AB* and *AC* of $\triangle ABC$ are 5 and 8 respectively and
∡$A = 32°$. The sides *DE* and *EF* of $\triangle DEF$ are 8 and 5 respectively
and ∡$E = 32°$. Are the triangles congruent?

3. Side *AB* of $\triangle ABC$ is 6, ∡$BAC = 40°$ and ∡$ABC = 30°$. Side *DE*
of $\triangle DEF = 6$ and ∡$FED = 30°$ and ∡$EDF = 40°$. Are the triangles
congruent?

4. $AD = 10$, $BC = 10$,
$AB = 7$, and $CD = 7$
Is $\triangle ABD$ congruent to $\triangle BCD$?
Explain.

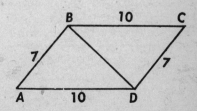

5. *a.* Is △*ABC* congruent to △*CEB*?
Explain.

　b. If *AC* = 8, find *EC*.

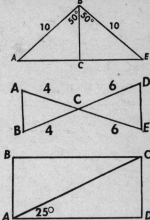

6. Is △*ABC* congruent to △*CDE*?
Explain.

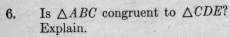

7. In this rectangle,
∡*CAD* = 25°. Find
∡*BCA*.

GENERAL SKILL EXERCISE

Try the following practice examples. If you need help, turn to the pages listed at the end of the example and learn how to do the exercise.

1. If two polygons are similar, their corresponding sides are .... and their corresponding angles are ....(page 385).

2. If two angles of one triangle are equal respectively to two angles of another triangle, the two triangles are .... (page 387).

3. In similar triangles, the sides opposite the equal angles are called the .... (page 390).

4. If a 6-foot pole casts a 2-foot shadow, a 3-foot pole nearby at the same time of day casts a .... -foot shadow (page 391).

5. Polygons which can be placed so that they coincide are called .... polygons (page 393).

6. The symbol ≅ means .... (page 393).

7. Two triangles are congruent if the three sides of one triangle are equal to .... of the other triangle (page 389).

8. Two triangles are .... if an angle of one is equal respectively to an angle of another, and the sides including these angles are proportional (page 389).

9. In geometry, *A.S.A.* = *A.S.A.* means .... (page 394).

_____ *My Score*

PRINCIPLES TO REMEMBER

1. A line indicates length and direction. Level lines are called horizontal lines; lines running straight up and down are vertical lines; straight lines which are neither horizontal nor vertical are slanting lines. Parallel lines are lines which are always the same distance apart and never meet, no matter how far extended.

2. Two straight lines meeting at a point form an angle. The unit of measurement for an angle is the degree. A straight angle contains 180°. A right angle contains 90° and its legs are perpendicular. An acute angle contains less than 90°; an obtuse angle contains more than 90° but less than 180°, and a reflex angle contains more than 180° but less than 360°. The size of an angle depends on the amount one side of the angle has turned away from the other. The size may be measured with a protractor.

3. To bisect means to divide into two equal parts. A line or an angle may be bisected.

4. Plane figures lie on flat surfaces and have two dimensions: length and width. Examples are triangles, quadrilaterals, pentagons, octagons, hexagons and circles. Plane closed figures formed by straight lines are called polygons.

5. The distance around a plane figure is called its perimeter.

6. The number of square units in a plane figure is called its area.

7. A circle is a curved line, all points of which are the same distance from the center. The length of the curved line is called the circumference. The circumference of a circle is $3\frac{1}{7}$ times the length of the diameter of the circle.

8. A triangle is a three-sided polygon. A scalene triangle has no equal sides; an isosceles triangle has two equal sides; an equilateral triangle has three equal sides. In a right triangle, the side opposite the right angle is called the hypotenuse.

9. The square root of a number is that number which, multiplied by itself, will give you the original number.

10. Geometric solids have three dimensions—length, width and height. Cubes, right circular cylinders, spheres and pyramids are examples. A prism is a solid whose bases are congruent and parallel polygons, and whose lateral edges are parallel.

11. A figure has symmetry when its parts are so arranged that the figure has perfect balance. If a line which connects every two corresponding points passes through a central point and is bisected by it, the figure has point symmetry. If a plane figure is symmetrical with respect to a line, the figure has line symmetry. If a solid is divided into two equal parts by a plane, and every part on one side of the plane corresponds with an equal part on the other side, the solid has plane symmetry.

12. Similar figures have the same shape but not necessarily the same size. Their corresponding sides are proportional and their corresponding angles are equal.

13. Triangles are similar if two angles of one triangle are equal to two angles of the other triangle; if an angle of one is equal to an angle of the second and the sides including these angles are proportional; if all corresponding angles are equal, or if all corresponding sides are proportional.

14. Congruent figures have exactly the same shape and the same size. Figures are congruent if all corresponding sides and all corresponding angles are equal.

15. Triangles are congruent if the three sides of one are equal to the three sides of the other; if two sides and the included angle of one are equal to two sides and the included angle of the other; if two angles and the included side of one are equal to two angles and the included side of the other.

FORMULAS

Plane Figures		
	perimeter (distance around)	area
rectangle	$P = 2l + 2w$	$A = lw$
square	$P = 4s$	$A = s^2$
triangle	$P = a + b + c$	$A = \frac{1}{2}bh$
parallelogram	$P = 2l + 2w$	$A = bh$
trapezoid	$P = a + b + c + d$	$A = \frac{1}{2}h(b_1 + b_2)$
circle	$C = \pi d$ or $2\pi r$	$A = \pi r^2$

Volume of Geometric Solids	
all prisms and circular cylinders	$V = Bh$
rectangular prism	$V = lwh$
cube	$V = e^3$
circular cylinder	$V = \pi r^2 h$
pyramid	$V = \frac{1}{3} Bh$
cone	$V = \frac{1}{3} \pi r^2 h$

MASTERY TEST

A

1. Three angles measure 16°, 90° and 95°. Which one or ones of these three are acute angles?

2. Which of the following contains the greatest number of degrees: an acute angle, an obtuse angle or a right angle?

3. The sides of a right angle are .... to each other.

4. Two angles of a triangle measure 75° and 45°. How many degrees are there in the third angle?

5. How many degrees less than a right angle is an angle of 74°?

6. Which of the angles below is an obtuse angle?

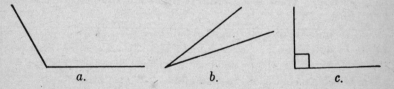

a.   *b.*   *c.*

7. What is the complement of the angle shown in 6c? What is the supplement? What is the relationship between the lines that form the legs of the angle?

8. Copy the angle drawn in 6b above.

9. Using compasses and straightedge, bisect the angle that you have just constructed.

10. A plane figure bounded by four straight lines is called a ....
.... Three examples are ...., and ....

11. A hexagon is a plane figure which has ....
sides. Construct a hexagon with compasses and a straightedge.

12. A rectangle in which all the sides are equal in length is called
a .... Using compasses and a straightedge, construct a figure of this kind.

13. Angles are measured in units called ....
Using a protractor, determine how many of these units are in the
angle shown in 6a above.

14. A certain triangle has a base angle of 55°, a base of 3 inches,
and a leg (which meets the base to include the 55° angle) of 2 inches.
   a. Construct this triangle.
   b. Using compasses and a straightedge, construct a triangle
      congruent to this triangle.
   c. Using compasses and a straightedge, construct a similar
      triangle.

15. Use compasses and a straightedge to construct a plane figure
having:
   a. Point symmetry   b. Line symmetry

B

1. A rectangular garden plot is 12 feet wide. If it contains 288
square feet, how long is it?

2. Find the area of a triangle having an altitude of 10 feet and a
base of 14 feet.

3. Find the volume of a grain bin that is 12 feet long, 9 feet wide
and 8 feet high.

4. If one side of a rectangle is 4 inches, what is the length of the
opposite side?

5. If the sides of a triangle are 4 inches, 7 inches and 10 inches,
what is the perimeter of the triangle?

6. How many inches are there in the diameter of a circle having a
circumference of 44 inches?

7. If the length of one side of a rectangle is 8 inches and the width
is $2\frac{1}{2}$ inches, how many square inches are there in the area of the
rectangle?

8. Mr. Cane has a house on a square-shaped piece of land 190 feet long. He wants to put a fence around his property. How many feet long must the fence be?

9. Mr. Ames is repairing a sidewalk. After removing the old, cracked sidewalk, he must fill a space 3 feet wide, 7 feet long and 4 inches thick. How many cubic feet of concrete must he mix?

10. Which of the following figures would have the greater area?
   a. A square with a side of 6 feet.
   b. A circle with a diameter of 6 feet.

11. A ten-foot ladder rests just below the roof of a garage. The distance between the base of the garage and the point where the ladder touches the ground is 6 feet. How high is the garage?

12. *a.* A ten-foot flag pole casts a shadow $3\frac{1}{2}$ feet long. A tree nearby casts a shadow $2\frac{3}{4}$ feet long. How high is the tree?
   b. Why must you measure the shadow cast by the tree immediately before or after you measure the shadow cast by the flag pole?

13. Find the circumference of a circle whose radius is 14 feet (Use $\pi = \frac{22}{7}$).

14. If one side of a square is 12 inches long, what is the area of the square?

15. Each edge of a cube is 2 centimeters long. What is the volume of the cube?

16. What is the area of triangle *ABE* shown in the diagram if the dimensions of rectangle *ABCD* are 16 inches by 10 inches?

17. *a.* What is the area of the circle inscribed within the square?
   b. What is the area of the square?
   c. What is the perimeter of the square?
   d. What is the circumference of the circle?
   e. What is the area of the part of the square not included within the circle?

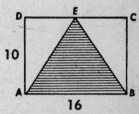

f. How much longer is the perimeter of the square than the circumference of the circle?

18. Mr. Prag wants to manufacture tin cans that have a volume of 68 cubic inches. If the diameter is to be 3 inches,

  a. What will be the height of the can?

  b. What will be the area of the label that must be pasted on the can, supposing that the height of the label is equal to the height of the can?

C

Terms Used in Geometry

Place the number of the phrase in Column B before the proper term or expression in Column A.

Column A	Column B
( ) Vertical angles	1. The number of square units contained in a surface.
( ) Parallel lines	2. The distance around a polygon.
( ) Obtuse triangle	3. The distance around a circle.
( ) Radius	4. An angle less than 90°.
( ) Chord	5. A triangle that contains an angle greater than 90°.
( ) Perimeter	6. A line drawn from the center of a circle to the circumference.
( ) Acute angle	7. Angles formed by two straight lines which meet.
( ) Equilateral triangle	8. Lines which do not meet no matter how far extended.
( ) Circumference	9. A straight line which joins two points on a circle.
( ) Area	10. An instrument used to measure angles.
( ) Volume	11. The space occupied by a solid, expressed in cubic units.
( ) Protractor	12. A triangle that contains three equal angles.

GLOSSARY OF TERMS

absolute value. The numerical value of a number, regardless of the sign of the number.

acute angle. An angle of less than 90° and more than 0°.

acute triangle. A triangle having all acute angles.

altitude. The height measured perpendicular to the base.

amount. In interest problems, the sum to be paid back, such as the principal plus the interest.

angle. A figure formed when two straight lines intersect at a point.

annual. Once a year; *i.e.*, interest paid annually is interest paid once a year

approximate number. A number that is not exact but whose accuracy is sufficient for the purpose desired.

arc. Any part of a section of the circumference of a circle.

area. The number of square units contained in the surface of a plane figure.

assessed value. The value given real estate (property) for the purpose of raising taxes.

balance (bank). The amount of money remaining in the bank after some money is withdrawn.

bank discount. The interest on a bank loan that is taken from the face of the loan by the bank at the time the loan is made.

bank statement. A bank's monthly or quarterly record of a depositor's money in the checking account.

bar graph. A graph made up of parallel bars whose lengths represent given quantities drawn to scale.

base. The line or surface upon which a plane or solid figure rests.

beneficiary. The person who receives the face value of a life insurance policy after the death of the insured.

bisect. To cut into two equal parts.

budget. A plan for spending one's income wisely.

cash account. A record indicating the amount of money received and money spent.

cash surrender value. A fixed sum of money returned to an insured if he returns his insurance policy to the company.

check. A written order instructing a bank to pay money from an individual's account.

circle. A closed curve all points of which are the same distance from a point within called the center.

circle graph. A graph in the form of a circle in which the angles (parts) indicate relations between each other and to the whole.

circumference. The curved line bounding a circle; the length or distance around a circle.

coefficient. A number written in front of an algebraic expression.

commission. A fee paid to an agent for the service of buying or selling property or materials.

common denominator. A number into which all the given denominators divide evenly.

compasses or compass. An instrument for drawing circles and arcs.

403

cone. A solid figure having a circular base and a curved surface which comes to a point at the vertex.

congruent triangles. Triangles that have the same size and shape and can be made to coincide.

consecutive numbers. Numbers that follow one another, such as 1, 2, 3, 4, etc.

corresponding parts. Angles or sides of triangles which are placed in the figures in the same positions.

cube. A rectangular solid with 6 equal square faces; or, the product obtained by multiplying a number by itself three times.

cylinder. A solid figure with bases made of two equal circles and with curved sides.

day of maturity. The date on which a promissory note is to be paid.

decagon. A polygon having ten sides and ten angles.

decimal fraction. A part of a whole expressed by using a decimal point.

degree. A unit used in measuring angles. $360° =$ one complete rotation.

diagonal. A straight line drawn in a plane figure joining two non-consecutive vertices.

diameter. A straight line drawn through the center of a circle and dividing the circle into two equal parts.

digit. Any one of the ten numbers from 0 to 9.

dimension. A linear measurement such as the length, width or height of a figure.

discount. An amount of money subtracted from the list or marked price of an object; a deduction made in advance by a bank as an interest charge for the loan of money.

dividends. A share of profits paid to owners or policyholders of an insurance company.

endorse. To sign one's name on the back of a check or note before payment.

equation. A statement showing the equality of two quantities.

equivalent fractions. Fractions having different forms but equal values.

evaluate. To determine the value of an unknown letter in a formula; to find the value of an algebraic expression by substituting in the arithmetic values of the literal quantities.

exponent. The small number or letter written slightly above and to the right of a number or letter to indicate how many times the number is to be multiplied by itself.

extremes. The first and last quantities of a proportion.

face of an insurance policy. The amount of insurance guaranteed in the policy; *face of a promissory note:* the amount stated in the note.

factor. One of two or more numbers which when multiplied together give a certain product.

formula. A statement of a general rule expressed by means of letters and numbers.

graph. A representation of relationships by means of lines, bars, circles or symbols.

gross income. The entire income without any deductions being taken.

height. The distance from the top to the base of an object.

hemisphere. One half of a sphere.

hexagon. A plane figure having six sides and six angles.

hypotenuse. The side opposite the right angle in a right triangle.

installment buying. Buying in which part of the price is paid at the time of the purchase, and the balance is paid at stated times.

insurance. Financial protection offered by an insurance company (insurer) to the insured who pays a premium for this protection.

interest. Money paid for the use of money.

isosceles triangle. A triangle having two equal sides.

latitude. Distance measured in degrees north or south from the equator along the earth's surface.

like terms. The terms of an algebraic expression containing the same letters.

longitude. Distance measured in degrees east or west from the prime meridian passing through Greenwich, England, along the earth's surface.

lowest terms. When both the numerator and denominator of a fraction are reduced as far as possible.

maker. The person or individual who makes a promissory note.

market value. The price that property, such as real estate, stocks, bonds, will bring when offered for sale on the market.

maximum. The greatest possible value.

metric system. A system of weights and measures based on the decimal system.

minimum. The smallest value of a quantity.

monomial. An algebraic expression consisting of a single term.

mortgage. An assignment of property as collateral for a debt.

negative number. A number whose value is less than zero and is preceded by a minus sign.

obtuse angle. An angle containing more than 90° but less than 180°.

obtuse triangle. A triangle containing an obtuse angle.

octagon. A plane figure containing 8 sides and 8 angles.

overhead. The expenses necessary to run a business.

parallel lines. Lines that extend in the same direction and are the same distance apart no matter how far extended.

parallelogram. A four-sided figure (quadrilateral) whose opposite sides are parallel.

payee. The person or persons to whom a check is payable.

payer. The person who pays the check.

pentagon. A plane figure with 5 sides and 5 angles.

per cent. A value expressed in hundredths using the per cent sign (%) or the words "per cent."

perimeter. The sum of the lengths around a plane figure.

perpendicular. Lines which meet at right angles.

pi (π). The ratio of the circumference to the diameter of a circle is π: 3.14159 or $\frac{22}{7}$.

policy, insurance. An agreement between an insurance company and the insured.

polygon. A closed straight line figure having any number of sides and angles.

positive number. A number whose value is greater than zero and which is sometimes preceded by a plus (+) sign.

premium, insurance. A fixed sum of money paid monthly for protection given by the insurance company.

promissory note. A written promise to pay a certain amount of money on a stated day to a certain person.

protractor. An instrument marked off in degrees used for measuring or marking off angles of a given size.

pyramid. A solid figure having triangles for faces.

quadrilateral. Any four-sided plane figure.

radius. The distance or straight line from the center to the circumference of a circle.

ratio. The comparison, by means of a division, of two like quantities.

rectangle. A quadrilateral whose opposite sides are equal and which has four right angles.

rectangular solid. A solid figure whose six faces are rectangles.

regular figure. A plane figure whose angles are equal and whose sides are equal in length.

right angle. An angle which contains 90°; one-fourth of a rotation.

right triangle. A triangle containing a right angle.

round number. A number that is approximate to a certain extent, not accurate.

scale drawing. A drawing that is the exact shape of an object but which is reduced or enlarged in size in a definite ratio.

scalene triangle. A triangle in which no two sides are equal.

secant. A line drawn through a circle and extending beyond it.

sector. The portion of a circle between two radii and an arc.

semicircle. Half of a circle.

signed numbers. A number with direction, either positive or negative.

solid figure. A figure having three dimensions: length, width, and height.

sphere. A circular solid such that all points on the surface are the same distance from the center.

square. A rectangle all of whose sides are equal.

straight angle. An angle containing 180°.

symbol. A representation by means of a sign or a letter.

symmetry. The correspondence of parts such as lines or points.

term. A member of an expression.

trapezoid. A quadrilateral having two parallel sides.

triangle. A closed plane figure with 3 sides and 3 angles.

triangular prism. A solid figure having 3 rectangular faces and 2 parallel triangles for bases.

unlike terms. The terms of an algebraic expression containing different letters.

vertex. The point of intersection of the sides of an angle.

volume. The number of cubic units in a solid figure.

INCREASE YOUR SKILL

Whole Numbers

(For a review of rules and methods, see Chapter 1, Pages 1-24)

Addition of Whole Numbers

1.

42	24	67	44	14
89	98	19	23	83
76	73	10	92	96
63	81	99	63	72
97	67	87	46	66
18	28	64	51	96
37	11	55	16	43

2.

269	327	273	375	134
152	486	684	827	815
487	975	345	365	913
964	543	164	924	164
111	461	189	461	375
873	971	481	753	436
415	184	133	634	985
819	233	976	589	817
167	118	642	919	617

3.

18925	58960	37659	18429	28419
37641	40916	18469	32765	15113
97631	32718	28032	46832	29103
84296	10029	10976	21968	40910

4.

12.63	674.81	11.26	814.26	976.84
184.19	1341.29	123.75	97.18	1327.26
376.43	16543.17	432.89	346.75	32176.14
4125.12	253.46	1760.46	8732.21	8471.53
976.19	19.19	30170.10	1137.15	19732.16

5.   4672+7946+6802+1106+5837

38451+86417+96432+73541+26501

Subtraction of Whole Numbers

1.

678	846	976	461	231	965
342	127	306	103	116	104

866	787	958	983	846	866
136	786	612	527	757	866

2.

2709	7346	5812	3590	8637
1852	3607	4765	2764	5733

6150	7374	8973	6421	1376
4736	5277	3784	5764	1274

3.

641,387	426,123	973,184	146,271	981,911
576,978	127,846	237,976	137,841	873,989

536,841	748,964	376,542	349,876	487,321
373,989	673,978	267,245	294,678	278,123

4.

$3467.21	$8763.99	$3499.75	$6463.27	$7644.99
2764.19	7631.89	1500.49	3647.73	4689.49

$75869.66	$96532.88	$86475.25	$10763.19	$68964.12
1374.26	76371.99	73296.57	10317.98	53946.78

5.

$396 - 281$	$689 - 129$	$126 - 103$	$979 - 679$
$7984 - 2653$	$1562 - 766$	$1427 - 1230$	$3847 - 2784$

Multiplication of Whole Numbers

1.

823	965	136	656	998
37	26	49	82	46

637	198	826	464	564
25	99	37	77	89

2.

641	365	947	702	976
196	257	376	639	824

985	402	750	684	399
406	204	103	120	269

3.

7321	5824	3194	7137	1372
629	157	209	718	490

6420	7008	7913	5794	2649
852	206	284	342	190

4. 9701×8431   9216×3164   3714×2613

5. 2165×7329   4601×2006   6036×1070

6. $126.14×230 $961.15×125 $840.10×461

7. $456.19×326 $319.25×640 $785.97×175

8. $319.80×115 $619.67×346 $843.15×621

9. $116.99×211 $486.23×316 $819.14×183

10. $564.25×841 $976.46×286 $636.68×421

Division of Whole Numbers

1. 6) 684   5) 2107   3) 9015   4) 2812   8) 4916

    9) 954   7) 3163   8) 4856   6) 5419   9) 8127

2. 26) 3028   49) 3170   61) 6258   37) 2744   53) 4029

    71) 3828   56) 5026   87) 1127   29) 4314   93) 8462

3. 243) 109727   414) 347209   159) 275174   375) 194206

    768) 609712   215) 751256   518) 328412   652) 863271

4.

2,418÷31	4,618÷12	5,345÷76	4,352÷54
1,245÷17	5,897÷33	6,057÷45	8,746÷63
1,468÷80	6,974÷68	1,884÷42	1,859÷22
3,545÷82	2,859÷42	8,142÷33	1,070÷45

5.

28,494÷25	14,888÷25	23,849÷49	16,159÷49
67,215÷53	72,064÷57	32,020÷18	34,043÷36
39,429÷79	17,835÷39	13,419÷25	41,056÷62
320,172÷86	453,486÷45	872,835÷58	718,530÷49

6.

32,989÷239	82,591÷426	31,983÷127	49,139÷459
26,311÷194	45,741÷375	86,496÷396	57,841÷275
169,372÷395	497,312÷416	579,832÷649	787,391÷712

Common Fractions

(For a review of rules and methods, see Chapter 2, Pages 25-69)

1. *Write as improper fractions:*

 $1\frac{1}{2}$ $4\frac{5}{8}$ $5\frac{1}{3}$ $3\frac{5}{6}$ $4\frac{3}{8}$ $2\frac{3}{10}$ $3\frac{1}{8}$

 $1\frac{3}{4}$ $3\frac{1}{4}$ $2\frac{5}{6}$ $7\frac{1}{10}$ $9\frac{5}{16}$ $8\frac{3}{8}$ $3\frac{5}{8}$

2. *Reduce to whole or mixed numbers:*

 $\frac{29}{4}$ $\frac{20}{7}$ $\frac{39}{39}$ $\frac{17}{4}$ $\frac{32}{15}$ $\frac{52}{16}$ $\frac{32}{8}$

 $\frac{11}{2}$ $\frac{15}{6}$ $\frac{13}{5}$ $\frac{18}{12}$ $\frac{34}{16}$ $\frac{40}{40}$ $\frac{38}{4}$

3. *Reduce to lowest terms:*

 $\frac{9}{12}$ $\frac{4}{16}$ $\frac{45}{180}$ $\frac{16}{80}$ $\frac{12}{72}$ $\frac{6}{64}$ $\frac{18}{126}$

 $\frac{32}{64}$ $\frac{14}{56}$ $\frac{9}{108}$ $\frac{32}{256}$ $\frac{9}{81}$ $\frac{19}{76}$ $\frac{64}{512}$

4. *Complete:*

 $\frac{1}{2}=\frac{}{8}$ $4\frac{9}{2}=4\frac{}{16}$ $\frac{4}{3}=\frac{}{24}$ $\frac{5}{8}=\frac{}{16}$

 $\frac{2}{3}=\frac{}{12}$ $7\frac{5}{8}=7\frac{}{32}$ $\frac{9}{12}=\frac{}{60}$ $\frac{19}{16}=\frac{}{32}$

Addition of Fractions

1.

 $\frac{2}{8}$ $\frac{6}{7}$ $\frac{3}{8}$ $\frac{1}{4}$ $\frac{5}{12}$ $\frac{1}{9}$

 $\frac{1}{8}$ $\frac{3}{7}$ $\frac{5}{8}$ $\frac{3}{4}$ $\frac{1}{12}$ $\frac{4}{9}$

2.

 $1\frac{5}{9}$ $12\frac{4}{5}$ $8\frac{3}{16}$ $10\frac{2}{11}$ $38\frac{2}{7}$ $24\frac{3}{8}$

 $2\frac{1}{8}$ $19\frac{1}{8}$ $4\frac{7}{16}$ $13\frac{3}{11}$ $15\frac{5}{7}$ $16\frac{3}{4}$

3.

 $\frac{1}{4}$ $\frac{2}{3}$ $\frac{2}{5}$ $\frac{1}{6}$ $\frac{1}{8}$ $1\frac{1}{2}$

 $\frac{3}{8}$ $\frac{1}{4}$ $\frac{7}{10}$ $\frac{5}{12}$ $\frac{1}{2}$ $\frac{3}{4}$

4.

 $\frac{1}{8}$ $\frac{1}{2}$ $\frac{4}{5}$ $\frac{2}{3}$ $\frac{1}{5}$ $\frac{2}{7}$

 $\frac{2}{3}$ $\frac{3}{4}$ $\frac{7}{10}$ $\frac{1}{6}$ $\frac{5}{6}$ $\frac{9}{28}$

 $\frac{5}{6}$ $\frac{5}{12}$ $\frac{2}{15}$ $\frac{9}{15}$ $\frac{9}{10}$ $\frac{3}{14}$

5.

 $5\frac{1}{2}$ $4\frac{1}{10}$ $12\frac{3}{4}$ $17\frac{5}{12}$ $15\frac{3}{8}$ $18\frac{5}{12}$

 $2\frac{5}{8}$ $3\frac{1}{8}$ $18\frac{1}{8}$ $27\frac{1}{8}$ $19\frac{1}{4}$ $32\frac{3}{4}$

6.

 $12\frac{2}{3}$ $22\frac{3}{5}$ $5\frac{3}{8}$ $4\frac{1}{5}$ $26\frac{1}{4}$ $18\frac{1}{8}$

 $1\frac{1}{2}$ $\frac{9}{10}$ 11 $15\frac{3}{4}$ $32\frac{7}{8}$ 17

 $8\frac{1}{6}$ $15\frac{1}{2}$ $12\frac{7}{16}$ $21\frac{1}{2}$ $19\frac{5}{12}$ $15\frac{2}{3}$

7.

 $\frac{1}{3}+\frac{1}{8}$ $\frac{3}{4}+\frac{5}{6}$ $\frac{1}{8}+\frac{5}{8}$ $\frac{7}{16}+\frac{5}{8}$

 $\frac{2}{3}+\frac{1}{2}+\frac{1}{4}$ $\frac{3}{4}+\frac{5}{8}+\frac{1}{3}$ $\frac{2}{3}+\frac{4}{5}+\frac{1}{10}$ $\frac{1}{8}+\frac{3}{4}+\frac{5}{12}$

 $3\frac{1}{2}+2\frac{1}{4}$ $3\frac{2}{5}+2\frac{1}{4}$ $3\frac{1}{8}+2\frac{3}{4}$ $5\frac{5}{6}+3\frac{3}{8}$

Subtraction of Fractions

1. $\dfrac{7}{10}$ $\dfrac{5}{6}$ $\dfrac{5}{6}$ $\dfrac{3}{4}$ $\dfrac{3}{4}$ $\dfrac{5}{12}$
$\dfrac{3}{10}$ $\dfrac{1}{8}$ $\dfrac{5}{12}$ $\dfrac{1}{2}$ $\dfrac{3}{8}$ $\dfrac{1}{8}$

2. $3\frac{1}{4}$ $5\frac{7}{8}$ $3\frac{7}{8}$ $1\frac{5}{6}$ $6\frac{3}{4}$ $15\frac{1}{4}$
$1\frac{1}{2}$ $2\frac{1}{4}$ $3\frac{1}{8}$ $\frac{1}{2}$ $4\frac{5}{6}$ $3\frac{7}{8}$

3. $8\frac{1}{6}$ $15\frac{3}{10}$ $6\frac{3}{4}$ $3\frac{1}{8}$ $15\frac{2}{5}$ $7\frac{3}{4}$
$3\frac{2}{3}$ $12\frac{4}{5}$ $3\frac{5}{8}$ $1\frac{1}{4}$ $10\frac{9}{10}$ $7\frac{2}{3}$

4. $5\frac{1}{8}$ 6 $6\frac{1}{4}$ $9\frac{1}{2}$ 12 $3\frac{1}{4}$
$3\frac{3}{4}$ $\frac{3}{8}$ $2\frac{7}{12}$ $8\frac{2}{3}$ $\frac{3}{8}$ $\frac{3}{10}$

5. $6\frac{5}{12}$ $8\frac{9}{16}$ $8\frac{3}{10}$ 15 $5\frac{5}{8}$ $27\frac{5}{9}$
$1\frac{1}{2}$ $3\frac{5}{32}$ $1\frac{1}{20}$ $7\frac{6}{19}$ $1\frac{7}{8}$ $11\frac{5}{18}$

6. $\frac{3}{8}-\frac{1}{2}$ $\frac{2}{3}-\frac{1}{2}$ $\frac{5}{12}-\frac{1}{8}$ $\frac{5}{6}-\frac{5}{8}$ $\frac{9}{10}-\frac{3}{8}$
$\frac{3}{4}-\frac{3}{8}$ $\frac{5}{6}-\frac{1}{2}$ $\frac{3}{5}-\frac{1}{3}$ $\frac{7}{10}-\frac{2}{5}$ $\frac{7}{16}-\frac{1}{4}$

7. $2\frac{1}{2}-\frac{3}{4}$ $3-\frac{2}{5}$ $4\frac{3}{8}-2\frac{3}{4}$ $9\frac{2}{3}-3\frac{1}{8}$
$4\frac{1}{2}-1\frac{3}{8}$ $2\frac{1}{4}-\frac{5}{8}$ $5\frac{5}{12}-3\frac{2}{3}$ $8\frac{1}{4}-5\frac{7}{8}$

Multiplication of Fractions

1. $\frac{2}{5}\times 9$ $\frac{1}{6}\times 24$ $\frac{7}{16}\times 28$ $\frac{3}{10}\times 16$ $\frac{2}{3}\times 8$
$36\times\frac{7}{12}$ $15\times\frac{1}{4}$ $16\times\frac{1}{8}$ $\frac{9}{16}\times 3$ $\frac{2}{15}\times 105$

2. $\frac{1}{4}\times\frac{3}{5}$ $\frac{4}{5}\times\frac{3}{5}$ $\frac{5}{12}\times\frac{4}{7}$ $\frac{3}{8}\times\frac{1}{15}$
$\frac{7}{16}\times\frac{1}{4}$ $\frac{3}{8}\times\frac{4}{15}$ $\frac{1}{3}\times\frac{6}{16}$ $\frac{2}{9}\times\frac{9}{20}$

3. $3\frac{1}{2}\times\frac{1}{6}$ $2\frac{1}{4}\times\frac{2}{3}$ $\frac{7}{10}\times 3\frac{2}{3}$ $4\frac{1}{6}\times\frac{3}{8}$ $\frac{3}{4}\times 3\frac{1}{8}$
$5\frac{2}{3}\times\frac{1}{3}$ $\frac{1}{2}\times 5\frac{1}{2}$ $7\frac{1}{2}\times\frac{3}{5}$ $2\frac{3}{10}\times\frac{1}{6}$ $\frac{2}{3}\times 2\frac{2}{5}$

4. $2\frac{1}{2}\times 2\frac{1}{2}$ $1\frac{2}{5}\times 2\frac{1}{2}$ $4\frac{1}{4}\times 2\frac{1}{7}$ $3\frac{3}{8}\times 5\frac{1}{2}$ $7\frac{1}{2}\times 2\frac{1}{3}$
$3\frac{1}{4}\times 1\frac{1}{4}$ $3\frac{3}{8}\times 4\frac{1}{10}$ $3\frac{1}{2}\times 4\frac{3}{4}$ $1\frac{1}{4}\times 1\frac{1}{4}$ $6\frac{1}{8}\times 1\frac{5}{16}$

5. $\frac{1}{3}\times\frac{1}{2}\times\frac{1}{4}$ $\frac{2}{3}\times\frac{1}{3}\times\frac{1}{2}$ $\frac{3}{8}\times\frac{2}{3}\times\frac{1}{9}$ $\frac{5}{6}\times\frac{3}{8}\times\frac{7}{12}$
$\frac{1}{8}\times\frac{4}{5}\times\frac{3}{8}$ $\frac{2}{3}\times\frac{7}{8}\times\frac{1}{4}$ $\frac{1}{7}\times\frac{2}{5}\times\frac{1}{9}$ $\frac{1}{9}\times\frac{2}{5}\times\frac{1}{8}$

6. $1\frac{1}{2}\times 2\frac{1}{4}\times 4\frac{1}{5}$ $1\frac{4}{5}\times 2\frac{1}{6}\times 3\frac{2}{3}$ $7\frac{3}{4}\times 1\frac{1}{8}\times 2\frac{1}{8}$ $1\frac{3}{4}\times 1\frac{1}{8}\times 1\frac{7}{8}$
$3\frac{1}{6}\times 2\frac{1}{2}\times 1\frac{1}{8}$ $3\frac{1}{8}\times 3\frac{1}{3}\times 3\frac{5}{8}$ $3\frac{1}{3}\times 2\frac{2}{5}\times 4\frac{1}{6}$ $4\frac{1}{6}\times 3\frac{2}{3}\times 2\frac{1}{4}$

Division of Fractions

1. $4\div\frac{1}{4}$ $10\div\frac{1}{4}$ $15\div\frac{7}{10}$ $12\div\frac{3}{4}$ $7\div\frac{3}{14}$
$6\div\frac{1}{5}$ $12\div\frac{1}{3}$ $13\div\frac{4}{5}$ $16\div\frac{3}{4}$ $20\div\frac{1}{2}$

2. $\frac{3}{8}\div\frac{1}{4}$ $\frac{3}{5}\div\frac{9}{10}$ $\frac{3}{16}\div\frac{1}{3}$ $\frac{3}{4}\div\frac{5}{12}$ $\frac{13}{16}\div\frac{4}{5}$
$\frac{7}{8}\div\frac{2}{5}$ $\frac{7}{12}\div\frac{1}{8}$ $\frac{5}{6}\div\frac{3}{8}$ $\frac{2}{3}\div\frac{3}{16}$ $\frac{5}{8}\div\frac{1}{4}$

3. $\frac{2}{3} \div 4$ $\frac{1}{10} \div 4$ $\frac{3}{8} \div 20$ $\frac{5}{16} \div 14$ $\frac{1}{4} \div 6$
      $\frac{3}{4} \div 9$ $\frac{1}{14} \div 21$ $\frac{1}{6} \div 3$ $\frac{3}{16} \div 20$ $\frac{7}{10} \div 5$

4. $\frac{3}{4} \div 2\frac{1}{3}$ $\frac{2}{5} \div 2\frac{1}{2}$ $\frac{7}{10} \div 1\frac{3}{4}$ $\frac{5}{8} \div 3\frac{3}{4}$ $\frac{7}{10} \div 1\frac{1}{2}$
      $\frac{3}{16} \div 3\frac{1}{12}$ $\frac{2}{9} \div 1\frac{1}{3}$ $\frac{3}{4} \div 5\frac{3}{8}$ $\frac{3}{16} \div 1\frac{1}{12}$ $\frac{5}{6} \div 4\frac{1}{2}$

5. $5\frac{1}{4} \div 3\frac{1}{2}$ $6\frac{2}{3} \div 3\frac{1}{3}$ $2\frac{2}{5} \div 1\frac{1}{6}$ $8\frac{3}{4} \div 6\frac{2}{3}$ $10\frac{3}{4} \div 2\frac{1}{2}$
      $10\frac{1}{2} \div 4\frac{2}{3}$ $7\frac{1}{2} \div 2\frac{2}{5}$ $6\frac{1}{8} \div 1\frac{3}{4}$ $1\frac{1}{3} \div 10\frac{2}{3}$ $4\frac{1}{2} \div 1\frac{1}{8}$
      $5\frac{5}{8} \div 3\frac{3}{4}$ $4\frac{3}{8} \div 2\frac{1}{2}$ $1\frac{1}{2} \div 3\frac{1}{3}$ $2\frac{1}{4} \div 1\frac{1}{2}$ $1\frac{3}{5} \div 1\frac{7}{9}$

Decimal Fractions

(For a review of rules and methods, see Chapter 3, Pages 70-104)

1.   *Write each of the following decimals in words:*
     .6   .003   6.24   .87532   3.2007
     .85   3.8   3.70   5.40   2050.6

2.   *Round off each of the following decimals to the nearest hundredth:*
     3.490   .6350   .006084   15.607   6.9901
      .47   .0256   115.523   .60321   16.859

3.   *Change the following decimal fractions to common fractions or mixed numbers:*
     1.6 $.66\frac{2}{3}$ .55 $.08\frac{1}{3}$ $.37\frac{1}{2}$
     .5 $.12\frac{1}{2}$ 5.70   6.17   1.25

4.   *Change the following to decimal fractions:*
     $\frac{1}{4}$ $\frac{2}{5}$ $1\frac{1}{5}$ $2\frac{9}{20}$ $3\frac{9}{10}$
     $\frac{2}{3}$ $\frac{5}{6}$ $3\frac{5}{8}$ $\frac{6}{50}$ $16\frac{8}{8}$

5.   *Change to common fractions or mixed numbers:*
     \$9.50 $\$.12\frac{1}{2}$ $\$67\frac{1}{2}$ \$16.75   \$6.63
     \$4.65   \$2.50   \$10.20   \$5.90 $\$10.82\frac{1}{2}$

Addition of Decimal Fractions

1.   4.8   1.9   15.6   3.4   66.2
      3.6   2.4   16.4   0.9   68.7
      0.3   .5   17.8   0.6   1.8
      ——   ——   ———   ——   ——

2.   1.65   2.65   6.30   18.75   3.28
      .94   326.86   8.79   27.38   1.08
      .89   910.12   .24   3.26   .37
     3.43   18.06   1.46   1.04   13.68
     ————   ————   ————   ————   ————

3.   8.97   6.37   27.09   115.09   99.06
     4.65   12.96   18.36   3271.46   110.11
     1.98   56.87   97.27   132.57   75.46
     3.21   21.16   86.43   206.08   23.15
      .89   8.08   69.69   15.75   209.98
     ————   ————   ————   ————   ————

4.

0.356	3.498	6.507	25.169	96.867
0.235	5.283	8.789	49.836	48.184
1.708	6.597	0.396	52.975	1.087

5. *Add the following:*
a. 3.29+2.153+9.36+8.465
b. 6.008+9.043+.055+1.52+3.46
c. 4.1521+.0476+12.976+8.42
d. 19.076+18.6432+75.0912+83.9765
e. .0070+8.9637+29.0964+89.6056

Subtraction of Decimal Fractions

Subtract each of the following:

1.

.49	.34	6.75	2.50	9.76	19.87
.26	.18	.89	.74	5.28	12.15

51.29	29.76	32.27	18.94	37.09	105.86
14.63	19.25	18.19	15.49	16.29	67.91

2.

0.637	.964	7.533	5.073	19.687
0.185	.873	5.697	4.819	12.768

39.637	138.365	436.867	264.481	1491.469
22.458	67.189	93.409	191.189	589.567

3.

$36.65	$19.67	$60.42	$15.96	$87.46
14.48	8.97	46.86	13.99	57.09

$240.72	$160.60	$388.61	$568.42	$897.50
58.99	39.69	69.54	121.79	197.90

Multiplication of Decimals

1. *Multiply each of the following decimals by 10, 100 and 1,000:*

5.6	.005	$.37	18.36	.0053
4.23	2.40	.16$\frac{2}{3}$	.4651	.12$\frac{1}{2}$

Multiply:

2.

.49	.26	.58	2.8	.806	1.94
7	9	11	26	21	42

3.

.8	.06	.9	.07	.6	.15
.3	.4	.2	.6	.9	.3

4.
.65	.35	.53	.04	.52	.78
.12	1.63	7.8	.04	1.97	.75

5.
.356	1.096	2.008	3.284	8.765
4.1	2.6	.06	.96	1.95

6.   *a.*   .719×.06   .25×.516   .97×.463
      b.   64.06×.027   .806×119   19.3×.057

Division of Decimals

1. $2\overline{)\,6.4}$ $3\overline{)\,.84}$ $8\overline{)\,1.704}$ $5\overline{)\,2.565}$

     $9\overline{)\,7.605}$ $6\overline{)\,4.26}$ $7\overline{)\,205.8}$ $6\overline{)\,.192}$

2. $.6\overline{)\,4.26}$ $.5\overline{)\,1.99}$ $1.5\overline{)\,.4530}$ $.7\overline{)\,1.463}$

     $.8\overline{)\,.328}$ $.9\overline{)\,10.89}$ $2.4\overline{)\,1.236}$ $2.5\overline{)\,.05025}$

3. $.25\overline{)\,.850}$ $.21\overline{)\,97.31}$ $.27\overline{)\,8532}$ $.76\overline{)\,215.08}$

     $.74\overline{)\,77.9}$ $.062\overline{)\,1.098}$ $.36\overline{)\,.7236}$ $.47\overline{)\,2.5756}$

4. $3.14\overline{)\,13.6}$ $1.38\overline{)\,3.1162}$ $.18\overline{)\,1.4367}$ $.213\overline{)\,21.604}$

     $.37\overline{)\,92.9}$ $.45\overline{)\,.1597}$ $.84\overline{)\,19.2}$ $.638\overline{)\,126.841}$

Percentage

(For a review of rules and methods, see Chapter 4, Pages 105-125)

A

1.   *Change the following per cents to decimal fractions:*

17%	$33\frac{1}{3}\%$	67%	4.6%	$9\frac{1}{5}\%$
20%	98%	$37\frac{1}{2}\%$	$41\frac{1}{4}\%$	5.9%
45%	$82\frac{1}{2}\%$	19.4%	110%	03%

2.   *Change the following per cents to common fractions:*

15%	29%	14%	$62\frac{1}{2}\%$	18%
$33\frac{1}{3}\%$	$16\frac{2}{3}\%$	$\frac{1}{2}\%$	90%	27%
$12\frac{1}{2}\%$	150%	2.5%	175%	$87\frac{1}{2}\%$

3. *Find the following per cents:*

5% of $340	$3\frac{1}{4}$% of $154	$62\frac{1}{2}$% of $4.68
25% of $280	20% of $450	$16\frac{2}{3}$% of $948
$33\frac{1}{3}$% of $540	$4\frac{1}{2}$% of $180	$20\frac{1}{4}$% of $448

4. *Find what per cent the first number is of the second number.*

7, 35	2, 16	15, 80	8, 40	15, 200	10, 36
5, 80	4, 32	48, 60	19, 76	14, 32	30, 240

B

1. *Finding a number when part of it is known:*

10% of ? = 6	$87\frac{1}{2}$% of ? = 56	60% of ? = 54
50% of ? = $1\frac{1}{2}$	20% of ? = 16	$66\frac{2}{3}$% of ? = 82

2.

150% of ? = 60	132% of ? = 158.4	110% of ? = 110
5% of ? = 7.2	80% of ? = .032	$\frac{1}{10}$% of ? = 40

3. *Find the new amount in each of the following:*

$ .25 increased by 40%	$1,200 increased by $16\frac{2}{3}$%
$600 increased by 10%	$880 increased by $12\frac{1}{2}$%
$65.50 increased by 10%	$300 increased by 25%

4. *Find the new amount in each of the following:*

$1,500 decreased by 30%	$1,600 decreased by $37\frac{1}{2}$%
$900 decreased by 15%	$560 decreased by 11%
$65 decreased by 18%	$99 decreased by 22%

5. *Find the per cent of increase or decrease.*

From $.90 to $.60	From $240 to $480	From $55 to $44
From $80 to $120	From $1,500 to $1,800	From $6 to $9

C

1. *Find the amount of commission in each of the following:*

$1,400 at 4%	$360 at $2\frac{1}{2}$%	$976 at 5%
$740 at 2%	$890 at 6%	$1,156 at $4\frac{1}{2}$%
$550 at 10%	$602 at $3\frac{1}{2}$%	$2,642 at 8%

2. *Find the rate of commission when the commission is:*

$50 on $1,000	$4.80 on $960	$54 on $1,800
$35 on $420	$25 on $152	$20 on $160
$40 on $800	$28 on $1,400	$86.88 on $1,448

3. *Find the amount of discount and the net price for each of the following:*

$150 less 20%	$18.66 less 50%	$144 less 4½%
$90 less 25%	$400 less 12½%	$49.98 less 30%
$66 less 33⅓%	$880 less 37½%	$266 less 15%

4. *Find the rate of discount and amount of discount in each of the following:*

Original Price	Net Price	Original Price	Net Price
$60.00	$10.00	$520.00	$480.00
$75.00	$50.00	$37.50	$30.00
$180.00	$90.00	$100.00	$71.00

D

1. *Find the interest and the amount due in each of the following:*

$200 at 6% for 1 year	$400 at 2½% for 3 years
$550 at 4% for 2 years	$900 at 5½% for 2½ years
$800 at 7% for 3 years	$1,200 at 3½% for 1½ years

2. *Find the interest and the amount due in each of the following:*

$250 at 3% for 6 months	$600 at 4% for 60 days
$950 at 4% for 9 months	$700 at 5% for 45 days
$1,200 at 2½% for 8 months	$1,500 at 4½% for 90 days

3. *Find the bank discount and proceeds in each of the following promissory notes:*

$500 note at 6% interest for 2 years
$900 note at 4% interest for 6 months
$2,500 note at 3% interest for 1 year
$3,000 note at 4% interest for 60 days
$5,000 note at 6% interest for 30 days
$1,500 note at 2½% interest for 45 days

4. *Find the selling price in each of the following:*

Cost $100, Profit $40, Overhead $20
Cost $200, Profit 10% of cost, Overhead 20% of cost
Cost $800, Profit 20% of cost, Overhead $150
Cost $1,400, Profit $250, Overhead 15% of cost
Cost $2,000, Profit 20% of cost, Overhead $400
Cost $3,000, Profit 25% of cost, Overhead 20% of cost

5. *Find the cost of the following bonds:*

3-$1,000 bonds quoted at 103⅓
2-$1,000 bonds quoted at 105⅛
5-$1,000 bonds quoted at 105 brokerage $5 a bond
6-$1,000 bonds quoted at 106½ brokerage $5 a bond

Algebra

(For a review of rules and methods, see Chapter 10, Pages 259-318)

1. *If n represents a certain number, write*
   3 more than the number
   4 less than twice the number
   The number divided by 5
   6 less than three times the number
   5 more than half the number
   One-half the number increased by two

2. *If a and b represent two numbers, write:*
   The sum of the two numbers
   Twice the first number plus the second
   The first number divided by the second
   Three times the second number times the first
   $\frac{1}{8}$ the first number plus the second number
   The second number minus the first

3. *Find the value of each of the following expressions if $a=2$, $b=3$ and $c=5$:*

$a+b+2c$	$c-b+a$	$4a+2b-c$
$2a-b+c$	$2a+2b+3c$	$3a-b+c$

4. *Combine similar terms:*

$5x+2x+y+4y$	$2t+3x+t+x$	$3a-a+b+3b$
$5t+3t+4s+s$	$a+2a+4b-2b$	$4a-2a+2b-b$

5. *Solve and check each of the following equations:*

$3x=15$	$3\frac{1}{2}x=7$	$5x+10=25$
$9x=108$	$2x+2=6$	$8x+2=18$
$35=5a$	$x-7=14$	$7x-2=12$

6 *Solve and check the following:*

$a+1.5=6$	$5x+6=26$	$\frac{1}{2}x+5=10$
$R+5\frac{1}{2}=9$	$3x+4=13$	$\frac{2}{3}y=6$
$x+1\frac{1}{2}=6\frac{1}{2}$	$2x-4=14$	$\frac{3}{4}x=3$

7. *Express the following algebraically:*
   a. Jack weighed m pounds and gained 3 more pounds. He now
      weighs ....
   b. Alice's age 3 years from now if she is a years old is ....
   c. John is b years old. How old was he 5 years ago?
   d. 3 times a number divided by 2 and then increased by 5.

8. *Evaluate the following if* $a=4$, $b=5$, *and* $c=3$:

$a+b+c$	a^2+b-3c	$2a-b+c^3$
$a+b^2$	$2a-b+c^2$	$2a-b+c^2$
$2a+3b^2$	$a-b+c^3$	$a-3a+2c^3$

Skill in Geometry

(For a review of rules and methods, see Chapter 11, pages 319-402)

1. The formulas required in the column at the left are found in the column at the right. Match them by inserting the proper number in the blank space.

( ) The perimeter of a triangle   1. $A=lw$
( ) The perimeter of an equilateral triangle   2. $C=2\pi r$
    3. $V=lwh$
( ) The perimeter of a square   4. $A=bh$
( ) The perimeter of a rectangle   5. $A+B+C=180°$
( ) The area of a triangle   6. $P=4s$
( ) The area of a rectangle   7. $S=6l^2$
( ) The area of a parallelogram   8. $P=2l+2w$
( ) The area of a circle   9. $V=l^3$
( ) The circumference of a circle   10. $P=a+b+c$
( ) The surface of a cube   11. $V=\pi r^2 h$
( ) The volume of a cube   12. $A=\pi r^2$
( ) The volume of a rectangular solid   13. $P=3s$
( ) The volume of a cylinder   14. $A=\frac{1}{2}bh$
( ) The sum of the angles of a triangle is $180°$

2. Match the number of the phrase in Column B with the proper term or expression in Column A.

A	B
( ) The perimeter of a triangle	1. $A=lw$
( ) The perimeter of a square	2. $C=2\pi r$
( ) The perimeter of a rectangle	3. $V=lwh$
( ) The square of the hypotenuse	4. $A=bh$
( ) The area of a triangle	5. $a+b+c=180°$
( ) The area of a rectangle	6. $P=4s$
( ) The surface area of a cube	7. $P=2l+2w$
( ) The area of a parallelogram	8. $P=a+b+c$
( ) The area of a trapezoid	9. $A=\frac{1}{2}bh$
( ) The circumference of a circle	10. $c^2=a^2+b^2$
( ) The volume of a rectangular solid	11. $A_S=6e^2$
( ) The sum of the angles of a triangle	12. $A=\frac{1}{2}h\,(b_1+b_2)$

3. Match the number of the phrase in the column at the right with the proper term or expression in the column at the left.

( ) Vertical angles
( ) Parallel lines
( ) Obtuse triangle
( ) Chord
( ) Tangent
( ) Hypotenuse
( ) Central angle
( ) Radius
( ) Perimeter
( ) Scalene triangle
( ) Equilateral triangle
( ) Bisect
( ) Acute angle
( ) Area
( ) Isosceles triangle
( ) Volume
( ) Perpendicular lines

1. A triangle with three equal sides
2. The number of square units contained in a surface
3. The distance around a figure
4. An angle less than 90°
5. A triangle that contains an angle greater than 90°
6. A triangle with 2 equal sides
7. A line drawn from the center of a circle to the circumference
8. To divide into 2 equal parts
9. A triangle with 3 unequal sides
10. Angles formed by two straight lines which meet
11. Lines on a flat surface which do not meet no matter how far produced
12. A line which touches a circle at only one point
13. An angle formed by 2 radii at the center of a circle
14. A line which joins 2 points on the circumference of a circle
15. The line opposite the right angle in a right triangle
16. The number of cubic units contained in a solid
17. Two lines that intersect at right angles

4. The four fundamental geometric constructions are:
(1) bisecting a straight line
(2) bisecting an angle
(3) dropping a perpendicular from a point to a line
(4) erecting a perpendicular to a line at a point in the line

List the numbers 1 through 4 and after *each* write the letter *A, B, C* or *D* to show which one of the following diagrams illustrates that construction.

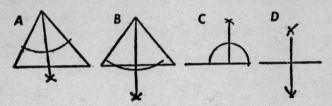

5. Column A contains drawings of geometric figures. Column B lists the names of geometric figures. Write the letters *a* to *j* and opposite *each* letter write the number from Column B that stands for the name of the corresponding figure.

Column A   *Column B*

a   1. lines perpendicular to each other

b   2. horizontal parallel lines

c   3. vertical parallel lines

d   4. acute angle

e   5. obtuse angle

f   6. circle

g   7. cube

h   8. right triangle

i   9. equilateral triangle

j   10. rectangle

                                        11. cylinder

6. In each of the following statements only one of the expressions within the parentheses makes the statement true. List the numbers 1 through 6 and after *each* number write the expression that makes the statement true.

(1) A semicircle is (twice, half, four times) as large as a circle.
(2) In 10 minutes the minute hand of a clock describes an angle of (10°, 60°, 30°).
(3) If two angles of a triangle are 50° and 50°, the triangle will have (two sides equal, three sides equal, no sides equal)
(4) The opposite sides of a rectangle are (parallel, perpendicular, unequal) to each other.
(5) The formula for finding the area of a triangle is $(A = \frac{1}{2}b, A = bh, A = b^2)$.
(6) A hexagon has (5, 6, 8) sides.

7. Answer each of the following:

a. In the diagram at the right, the line *AB* was constructed (*a*) bisecting *CD* (*b*) parallel to *CD* (*c*) perpendicular to *CD* at *A*

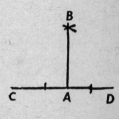

b. Lines *AD* and *AB* of the rectangle pictured at the right are (*a*) equal (*b*) horizontal (*c*) parallel (*d*) perpendicular

c. For which one of the following geometric solids is it possible to find the volume merely by multiplying its base by its height?

    a   *b*   *c*   *d*

d. At a certain time of day a flagpole 60 feet high casts a shadow 80 feet long. At exactly the same time of day, a near-by tree casts a shadow 120 feet long. Find the height of the tree.

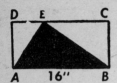

e. What is the area of triangle *ABE* shown in the diagram if the dimensions of rectangle *ABCD* are 16 inches by 10 inches?

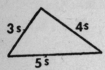

f. Express in terms of *s* the perimeter of the triangle at the left.

g. By what number do you multiply 9 in order to square it?

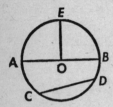

h. Name a line in the drawing at the left that represents a radius of the circle.

i. Write the following statement in the form of an equation: If three times a certain number (x) is increased by 2, the result is 8.

j. Find the value of P in the formula $P = 2l + 2w$ when $l = 8$ inches and $w = 6$ inches.

k. Solve the equation: $3x - 6 = 15$

VERBAL PROBLEM DRILLS

Percentages

(For a review of rules and methods, see Chapter 4, Pages 105-125)

1. An apple is divided equally among 5 children. What percent of the apple will each receive?

2. Judy received 87% on her English test and 73% on her mathematics test. By how much did her English mark exceed her mathematics mark?

3. Jane received a mark of 80% on a test consisting of 20 questions. How many did she answer correctly?

4. A sum of money is divided among four boys. If the first boy receives 10% of the total, the second boy 25%, and the third boy 40%, what percent of the money will the fourth boy receive?

5. In a bowling club of 36 men, 20 of them are 24 years old. What percent of the club is this?

6. Last year there were 52 members in a reading club. This year there are 44 members. What percent of decrease is this?

7. Mr. Jones earns $105 a week. When his salary is raised 5%, how much will he earn per week?

8. Tom has had 5 hits and has been at bat 8 times. What is his batting average?

9. Jane bought a coat at a sale for $32.75. This was 75% of the original price. What was the original price of the coat?

10. Last year the Right Manufacturing Company did $23,000 worth of business. This year their business has increased 125%. How much business are they doing now?

11. Tom bought a bike for $25 and later sold it for $30. What percent of increase is this?

12. Mr. Johnson planned to sell television sets for $225 each. Since they did not sell well, he finally marked them down to $180 each. What percent of decrease is this?

Measurement

(For a review of rules and methods, see Chapter 5, Pages 126-153)

1. Joan is 5 feet, 6 inch tall and Mary is 4 feet, 11 inches tall. How much taller is Joan than Mary?

2. A boy was 4 feet 7 inches tall a year ago. How tall is he now if he has grown 6 inches?

3. What part of a quart is a pint? What percent is this?

4. Which is greater?
   a. 5 pecks *or* 1 bushel.   *c.* 3 yds. *or* 8 ft.   *e.* 45 oz. *or* 3 lb.
   b. 2 quarts *or* 5 pints.   *d.* 4 ft. 6 in. *or* 68 in.   *f.* 2980 ft. *or* ½ mile.

5. Jack placed 7 blocks one on top of the other. If each block was 3½ inches high, how high was the pile in feet and inches?

6. A certain factory has a bolt of cloth containing 33 yards of material. How many dresses can be made from this, if each dress requires 3¾ yards of material, including waste?

7. Tom's train arrived at the station at 1:05 p.m. It was due at 11:55 a.m. How late was the train?

8. Joe starts work at 8:30 a.m. and finishes at 5:45 p.m. How long is he at work? Give your answer in hours and minutes.

9. A man needs to cut five lengths of board, each 2 ft. 3 in. long. What is the length of the shortest board he can use? (Disregard waste).

10. How many quart bottles of milk can be filled from three 10-gallon cans of milk?

11. George Washington was born on February 22, 1732, and died on December 14, 1799. How old was he in years, months, and days when he died?

12. Bill has a board 6 feet long. He cuts pieces from it 1 foot 5 inches, 2 ft. 1 in., and 2 ft. 2 in. long. How much of the board is left over?

Scale Drawings
(For a review of rules and methods, see Chapter 6, Pages 154-165)

1. What is the scale of a drawing if a line 5 inches long represents 30 inches on the object?

2. Find the distance between two cities 3½ inches apart on a map whose scale is 1" = 30 miles.

3. How far apart on a map should two cities be placed if the cities are 150 miles apart and the scale of the map is 1" = 50 miles?

4. On the scale drawing for a tool, one length is marked 2.43" ± .01". What does this mean?

5. Joe wants to reduce his drawing to 5/16 of its present size. A line on his present drawing is 4 inches long. How long should he make it on his new drawing?

6. A snapshot is 3 inches long and 4 inches wide. If it is enlarged to be 8 inches long, how wide will it be?

7. A baseball diamond is really a square 90 feet on a side. Find the shortest distance between second base and home plate by means of a scale drawing.

8. If the scale of a map is 75 miles to the inch, what is the distance between two cities that are 3¾ inches apart on the map?

9. A figure has sides of 1 inch, 3 inches, 2½ inches and 2 inches on a scale drawing. Find the actual perimeter of this figure if the scale is 1 in. = 30 ft.

10. A square piece of property has sides of 4 inches on a map. Find its actual area if the scale of the map is 1 in. = 20 yd.

Ratio and Proportion

(For a review of rules and methods, see Chapter 6, Pages 154-165)

1. What is the ratio of:
   - *a.* 4 to 16
   - *b.* 8 to 10
   - *c.* 3 to 5
   - *d.* 5 to 50
   - *e.* 20 to 100
   - *f.* 5 to 75
   - *g.* 5 to 115
   - *h.* 13 to 65
   - *i.* 26 to 130
   - *j.* 38 to 114
   - *k.* 43 to 129
   - *l.* 96 to 384

2. The chimney on John's house is 9 feet high. His friend Al's chimney is 18 feet high.
   - *a.* Compare the shorter chimney with the longer.
   - *b.* Compare the longer chimney with the shorter.

3. What is the ratio of 12 oz. to 2 lb?

4. What is the ratio of 2 gal. to 1 qt.?

5. A sheet of paper is 8½" by 11". What is the ratio of its width to its length?

6. A flagpole 48 feet tall casts a shadow 36 feet long. Find the ratio of the length of the shadow to that of the pole.

7. Find the ratio of:
   - *a.* a quarter to a dollar
   - *b.* a dime to a dollar
   - *c.* a half dollar to a nickel
   - *d.* 8 dollars to 4 dimes
   - *e.* 4 things to a dozen
   - *f.* 2 doz. to 8 doz.
   - *g.* 10 things to a doz.
   - *h.* 6 in. to 9 in.
   - *i.* 30 in. to 1 yd.
   - *j.* 1 gal. to 1 pt.
   - *k.* 1 hr. 30 min. to 30 min.
   - *l.* 18 mo. to 2 years.

8. In a local school there are 988 students and 38 teachers. What is the ratio of the number of students to the number of teachers?

9. A rectangle is 18 ft. long and 12 ft. wide. What is the ratio of the width to the length?

10. In a triangle having a base of 12 ft. and a height of 9 ft., what is the ratio of the height to the base?

11. Frank is 14 years old and Anne is 12 years old. What is the ratio of Frank's age to Anne's age?

12. Find the value of x in each of the following proportions:

   a. $\dfrac{x}{8} = \dfrac{15}{24}$
      d. $\dfrac{x}{27} = \dfrac{16}{9}$
      g. $\dfrac{x}{6} = \dfrac{7}{12}$

   b. $\dfrac{x}{42} = \dfrac{9}{21}$
      e. $\dfrac{x}{4} = \dfrac{44}{16}$
      h. $\dfrac{x}{15} = \dfrac{9}{27}$

   c. $\dfrac{x}{8} = \dfrac{18}{16}$
      f. $\dfrac{x}{12} = \dfrac{20}{48}$
      i. $\dfrac{x}{39} = \dfrac{28}{16}$

13. If Mary can earn $1.50 in 2 hours baby sitting, how much can she earn in 16 hours?

14. The ratio of the width of a lawn to its length is 4:7. The length is 21 ft. What is the width?

15. In 6 hours a car traveled 240 miles. At this rate, how long would it take to travel 600 miles?

16. In one year a farmer had 56 hogs and used 110 tons of feed for them. In the following year he had 82 hogs. How many tons of feed will he need to feed them?

17. A picture 3¾″ wide and 7½″ long is 3½″ wide after being reduced in size. What is the new length?

18. Find the standings of the following major league teams:
    a. 116 won and 36 lost   c. 91 won and 61 lost
    b. 97 won and 55 lost   d. 86 won and 66 lost

19. A picture of a moth in a dictionary is labeled ⅔. A length of 1¼″ on the picture is equal to what length on the moth?

20. In 3 days The Fair sold $895 worth of goods. If sales continued at that rate, how much would The Fair sell at the end of 18 days?

Business Problems
(For a review of rules and methods, see Chapter 7, Pages 166-215)

1. A boy receives a commission of 15% on all he sells. How much will he make when his sales total $720?

2. Jane sells cards for $1 a box. She receives a commission of 20¢ on each box. What is her rate of commission?

3. Mr. Jones receives a salary of $100 per week plus a commission of 5% on all he sells over $500. One week his sales totaled $850. How much did he earn in all that week?

4. Last summer Jack sold $150 worth of fruits and vegetables for his father. His father paid him $30. What rate of commission did he receive?

5. Bill works for a 20% commission. How much will he make when his sales total $280?

6. Bob works for a commission of 15%. He hopes to earn $500. How much merchandise must he sell in order to earn that sum?

7. Joan was asked to sell cards on a 20% commission basis. What must her sales total each week if she is to earn $8 a week?

8. A man sold a car for $1250 and received a commission of $200. What rate of commission was this?

9. A salesman works on a 15% commission basis. How much merchandise must he sell to earn $300?

10. Mr. Brown receives a commission of 15% on all he sells while Mr. Jones receives a salary of $50 plus a commission of 2% on all sales over $300. One week, each of the two men's sales amounted to $350. Which man made the most money that week? How much more did he make?

11. Find the interest on $640 at 6½% for two years.

12. Find the net price of an article marked $64 and sold at a discount of 10%.

13. Mr. Jones receives $15 for every $50 worth of goods he sells. What is his rate of commission?

14. Janie can buy a bicycle at Mr. Smith's store for $45.98 with a discount of 10%. Mr. Jones will sell her a similar bike for $45 with two successive discounts of 5% and 5%.
    a. Which is the better offer?
    b. How much better?

15. One store offers a discount of 20% on a television set priced at $225. Another store advertises a similar set for $220, with discounts of 10% and 10%.
    a. shoes, regular price, $12; reduced 10%.
    b. How much better?

16. Ann bought a coat at a sale for $45.50 that had been selling for $53.00.
    a. How much did she save?
    b. What was the rate of discount?

17. Find the selling price of a table priced at $89.50 and sold at a discount of 15%.

18. Mr. Brown borrowed $400 at 6% for 6 months. Find the amount of the bank discount and the net proceeds.

19. A man borrowed $850 at 5½% for 2 years. How much interest did he pay?

20. Find the interest of $420 at 2% for 3 months.

21. Mr. Brown had some chairs for sale in his store. They had been priced at $25 each but, because they were damaged, he reduced the price by 20%. How much did he lose on each chair?

22. Jane sold 40 pot holders at 20 cents each. Her materials cost her $4.20. How much did she make? What was her percent of profit?

23. A man bought a car for $600. Repairs cost him $45. What must he sell the car for if he wishes to make a $10 profit?

24. A television set that costs $250 was sold for $200. What was the percent of loss?

25. Find the net amount of a bill received from the May Co. for $180 with discounts of 20% and 5%.

26. The list price of a refrigerator is $525. Find the net price if discounts of 35% and 3% are given.

27. The Marks Co. bought merchandise whose list price was $3800. Because he bought the merchandise out of season he was given a 25% discount. The Marks Co. paid cash, so it received an additional discount of 4%. What was the net price of the merchandise?

28. Joan bought a cocker spaniel from the Pet Corner that was listed at $75. She received a discount of 15% and 3%. Find the net price.

29. Find the net price of each of the following items.
    a. shoes, regular price, $8; reduced 10%.
    b. camera, list price, $74.80; reduced 10% and then 4%.
    c. dining room set, list price, $650; 20%. 6% and 3% off.
    d. lamp, marked at $23.75; reduced 8% and 2%.

30. A catalogue lists a television set at $450. The discount sheet shows successive discounts of 20%, 8% and 2%. What is the net price?

31. One dozen shirts cost $30 less 10%, 3% and 2%. What is the cost of one shirt?

32. What is the net price of an air conditioner, listed at $315 with a trade discount of 15%, additional cash discount of 4% and self-delivery discount of 2%.?

33. Mr. Smith bought 100 dozen packages of seed at $1.80 a dozen, list price. He was allowed a discount of 30% and additional discounts of 8% and 2%.
    a. What was the amount of the purchase before figuring discounts?
    b. What was the amount of the first discount?
    c. The second? The third?
    d. What was the net cost to Mr. Smith?

34. Mr. Paul bought $2860 worth of furniture. He received discounts of 12% and 4%. He paid the bill in 10 days and received an additional discount of 2%. How much did Mr. Paul pay for the furniture?

35. Find the net cost and the total discount on a table lamp listed at $95 with discounts of 15%, 5% and 2%.

36. A grocer buys goods for $980, less 20% and 7%, plus a discount of 2% for cash. How much did he actually pay?

37. A builder needed 3600 feet of redwood. The list price was 13¢ per foot. If he received discounts of 25%, and 6%, plus 3% for cash, how much did he pay for the lumber?

38. What is the net price of a motorboat listed at $1575, with discounts of 30% and 10%, plus a cash discount of 3%?

39. The list price of a bicycle is $130. A dealer receives discounts of 33⅓%, 10% and 2% additional for cash. What does he pay for the bicycle?

40. On a purchase listed at $750 there is a single discount of 50% or successive discounts of 30% and 25%. Which should the buyer take? How much will he save?

41. At a special sale, Phil bought a $28 catcher's mitt and got discounts of 20%, 5% and 2%. How much did he pay for the mitt?

42. Find the net price on each of these purchases:

List Price	Discounts
a. $525.50	15%, 10%
b. $2400.00	25%, 5%, 3%
c. $79.89	50%, 3%
d. $19.90	10%, 3%, 2%
e. $380.00	33⅓%, 10%
f. $1150.00	25%, 10%, 4%

43. What is the net price of a rug marked $1875 if discounts of 25%, 8% and 2% are allowed?

44. The Sellall Dept. Store advertised a huge sale of merchandise. Jane's mother bought a gas range marked 33⅓% off the net price of $289. She also received additional discounts of 15% and 3%. How much did Jane's mother pay for the gas range?

45. Jack bought a bicycle that regularly sells for $48 when it was on sale for $40.
    a. How much did he save?
    b. What was the rate of discount?

46. A desk that usually sells for $38.50 is now on sale for $35. Find the rate of discount.

47. Mr. Adams estimates that his overhead amounts to 30% of the cost of his merchandise. He buys a table for $40 and wishes to make a profit of 10% of the cost on it. What must his selling price be?

48. A town has a tax rate of 28 mills. How many dollars is this per $1000?

49. Newtown has a tax rate of 32 mills. Express this tax rate in two other ways.

50. Find the tax on a house assessed at $12,500 if the tax rate is 35 mills.

51. A man insured his house against fire for $8500. Find his annual premium if the rate is 42¢ per $100.

52. A man sold eight suits for $35 each and received a commission of 20%. How much did he make?

53. Ourtown has a budget of $38,500 and its assessed valuation is $6,284,-000. What is its tax rate? Express this tax rate in two different ways.

54. Mr. Jones' house cost him $12,500. It is assessed for three-fourths of its value. How much must Mr. Jones pay in taxes if the tax rate is $3.50 on $1000?

55. Mr. Davis bought a new home for $14,500. He paid $6,500 down and mortgaged the rest at 4% interest for 15 years.
a. For how much did Mr. Davis mortgage the house?
b. What average monthly payment on the principal must he pay?
c. Find the amount of interest Mr. Davis will pay with his first month's payment.

56. Mr. Brown drives his car to work each day, five days a week. He estimates his daily round trip to be 24 miles. His car averages about 15 miles to a gallon of gasoline. He pays 31.8¢ per gallon with 7¢ of this price per gallon being a gasoline tax.
a. Find the number of miles Mr. Brown drives each month in going to and from work. (Let one month = 4 weeks.)
b. How many gallons does this take each month?
c. How much does the gasoline cost him per month?
d. Find the total amount of tax he pays on the gasoline per month in driving to work.
e. What percent of the price per gallon is tax?

57. Mr. Jones borrowed $300 for one year and paid $15 interest. What rate of interest did he pay?

58. Last year a school purchased 25 English textbooks at $4.75 each, less a discount of 15%; 10 general science textbooks listed at $4.30 each, less a discount of 10%; and 20 social studies books at $4.90 each, less a discount of 10%. Find the total cost of the books.

59. Jack receives a salary of $40 per week plus a commission of 5% on all he sells over $600. His sales for four successive weeks were: $650, $500, $710 and $750.
a. What was his "take home" pay for each one of the four weeks?
b. What was his average weekly pay for these four weeks?

60. Dealer A offers a television set for $280 with discounts of 10% and 5%. Dealer B offers a similar set for $275 with discounts of 5% and 5%.
a. Which dealer offers the better price?
b. How much better is it?

Arithmetic in the Home

(For a review of rules and methods, see Chapter 8, Pages 216-238)

1. Jane keeps a cash account of her money. Her cash on hand at the beginning of May was $3.12. Her allowance for the month was $6.00 and she made $2.70 during the month baby sitting. During the month of May, she spent $4.50 for lunches, $1.60 for movies, 80¢ for contributions, and $1.75 for a present for her mother's birthday. What was her cash on hand at the end of the month?

2. Mr. White earns $5000 a year. He spends $600 a year for rent. What percent of his income is this?

3. Bob saves $5 a week. If this is 8% of what he makes, how much does he make each week?

4. Mr. Davis earns an annual salary of $8,660. His income tax last year amounted to $986 for the year. The family's expenses were $75 per month for rent, $150 per month for food, $70 per month for clothes, $70 per month to operate the house and $50 per month for education and recreation. Life insurance payments amounted to $350 for the year. The family saved the remainder.
   a. Find the amount spent during the year for each item.
   b. How much did the family save last year?
   c. What percent of Mr. Davis' annual salary did they save?

5. Mrs. Clark bought the following items during a recent sale:
   2 cans of peas for 27¢ (regularly 15¢ a can).
   3 lb. of hamburger for $1.00 (regularly 37¢ a lb).
   1 box of macaroni for 13¢ (regularly 15¢ a box).
   2 bottles of ketchup for 27¢ (regularly 14¢ each).
   How much did she save in all?

6. At a recent sale, applesauce that usually sells for 18¢ a can was priced at six cans for $1.00. How much would be saved by buying six cans during the sale?

7. Mr. Jones sells ten pound bags of potatoes for 49¢ a bag or they may be bought by the pound at 5½¢ a pound. How much is saved by buying the ten-pound bag?

8. Mary's mother bought the following items at the store:
   3 yds. toweling @ 35¢   2 spools thread @ 10¢
   4 yds. terry cloth @ 88¢   2 sheets @ $2.19
   2 cards buttons @ 10¢   Find the total amount of her bill.

9. Mrs. Brown had a balance of $119.50 in her checking account. Find her new balance after she wrote a check for $34.98 if the bank charges a service charge of 10¢ for each check she writes.

10. At the end of April, Mrs. Davis had a balance of $42.54 in her checking account. During May, she made two deposits of $68.50 and $102.98. She wrote checks as follows: $65 for rent; $6.50 for television repair; $18 to the dentist; $22.48 for clothes; $12.50 for dry cleaning; $10 to the doctor; and $28.80 for milk. If the bank charges 10¢ for each check she writes, find her balance at the end of May.

11. Mr. Jones can buy a television set for $220 cash or he can pay $50 down plus $20 a month for 9 months. Find the carrying charge he must pay if he buys on the installment plan.

12.   Jane wants to buy a bicycle that sells for $48.75. She can buy it on the installment plan if she pays $15 down plus seven monthly payments of $5 each.
    a. What will be the carrying charge if she buys the bicycle on the installment plan?
    b. Find the percent of the carrying charge.

13.   A store offers a $350 refrigerator for sale on the installment plan for 25% down plus twelve monthly payments of $22.50 each.
    a. Find the amount of the down payment.
    b. What does the refrigerator cost on the installment plan?
    c. How large is the carrying charge?

14.   Change 3892 watt-hours to kilowatt-hours.

15.   Change 675 watt-hours to kilowatt-hours.

16.   How many kilowatt-hours of electricity are used by a 50-watt bulb that is burned for 30 hours?

17.   Find the cost of using a 100-watt bulb in a lamp for four hours each day during the month of June if the electricity costs 4¢ per kilowatt-hour.

18.   Jim listens to his radio about four hours per day. If a radio uses about 30 watts of electricity per hour, find the number of kilowatt-hours of electricity used in four weeks. How much would this cost if electricity cost 4½¢ per kilowatt-hour?

19.   Draw electric meters to show these readings:
    a. 798 kw.-hr.   *c.* 572 kw.-hr.
    b. 1237 kw.-hr.   *d.* 5418 kw.-hr.

20.   Draw gas meters to show these readings:
    a. 5800 cubic feet   *c.* 52,100 cubic feet
    b. 16,200 cubic feet   *d.* 70,800 cubic feet

21.   On March 31, Mr. Brown's electric meter read 6695 kilowatt-hours and on April 30, his meter read 7095 kilowatt-hours. His electrical rate is 4½¢ per kilowatt-hour.
    a. How many kilowatt-hours of electricity did he use during the month?
    b. What was the amount of his bill for the month of April?

22.   A train leaves Cincinnati at 8:45 a.m. (E.S.T.) and arrives in Columbus at 11:38 a.m. (E.S.T.). How long does this trip take?

23.   Jane is making chocolate squares for the girls in her Scout troop. The recipe makes 20 squares and calls for the following ingredients:
    2 squares bitter chocolate   3 eggs
    ½ cup shortening   1 cup sugar
    ¾ cup flour   1 teaspoon vanilla
    1 teaspoon baking powder   1 cup nut meats
There are 15 girls in Jane's troop, including herself, and she wishes to make enough chocolate squares so that each girl may have four.
    a. By what number must each ingredient be multiplied?
    b. Rewrite the recipe as Jane would have to use it.

24. Mary wished to make sugar cookies. She found a recipe that called for:

    2 cups flour   ⅔ cup shortening
    2 teaspoons baking powder   ⅔ cup sugar
    2 eggs   1 teaspoon vanilla
    ½ teaspoon salt

When Mary went to make the cookies, she found there was only one egg in the refrigerator.

a. If Mary uses just the one egg, how much should she use of every other ingredient?

b. If the original recipe would make two and a half dozen cookies, how many cookies should Mary get from the new recipe?

Graphs

(For a review of rules and methods, see Chapter 9, Pages 239-258)

1. The graph at the right shows the number of bonds sold at a bond meeting. Using the graph, answer the following questions:

    a. How many bonds of each type were sold?

    b. Find the total value of the bonds sold.

    c. What was the total number of bonds sold?

    d. What percent of the total number of bonds sold were $50 bonds?

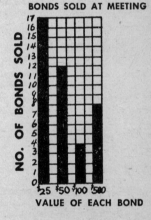

BONDS SOLD AT MEETING

NO. OF BONDS SOLD

VALUE OF EACH BOND

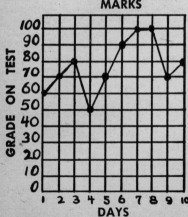

MARY'S SPELLING MARKS

GRADE ON TEST

DAYS

2. The graph at the left shows Mary's daily spelling marks over a two-week period. Using the graph, answer each of the following questions:

    a. What was Mary's mark on each of the ten days?

    b. What was her lowest mark?

    c. Find Mary's average for the ten days.

    d. How many marks did she have that were lower than her average?

    e. Find the difference between her lowest mark and her highest mark.

FRESHMEN 35%	SOPHOMORES 25%	JUNIORS 25%	SENIORS 15%

STUDENTS AT VALLEY HIGH (Total Number of Students—860)

3. The graph above shows the percentage of students in each class at Valley High.
   a. Find the number of students in each class.
   b. How many more freshmen are there than seniors?
   c. What should be the total of your four answers in part a?
   d. If you add the per cents shown on the graph, what should the total be?

4. The circle graph at the right shows how Kathy spends each dollar of her allowance.
   a. What percent of her allowance is spent for each item?
   b. If Kathy receives an allowance of $4 a week, how much does she actually spend on each item?

HOW EACH DOLLAR IS SPENT

5. The pictograph at the left shows the change in the number of schools in one county. Using this graph, answer the following questions:
   a. How many more elementary schools were there in 1955 than in 1925?
   b. Find what percent the number of high schools present in 1925 is of the number in 1955.
   c. Find the total number of schools in the county in 1955.

ELEMENTARY SCHOOLS   HIGH SCHOOLS

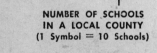

NUMBER OF SCHOOLS
IN A LOCAL COUNTY
(1 Symbol = 10 Schools)

6. Make a bar graph to show the length of these principal rivers in North America:
   Mackenzie River—2,525 miles; Mississippi River—2,546 miles; St. Lawrence River—2,000 miles; Yukon River—2,100 miles; Rio Grande River—1,800 miles; Missouri River—2,470 miles and the Arkansas River—1,500 miles.

7. Make a bar graph to show the distribution of students in Ourtown High School if the enrollments are: freshmen—110 students; sophomores—98 students; juniors—84 students; and seniors—75 students.

8. Mary's arithmetic marks for ten consecutive tests were 98, 83, 88, 90, 85, 80, 86, 90, 94, 88. Make a line graph to show these marks.

9. During July, the daily temperature at noon for one week was 82°, 88°, 94°, 88°, 87°, 82°, 88°. Make a line graph to show the daily noon temperature.

10. Out of a group of 120 students who were graduated from high school last June, 20 entered college, 20 joined the army, 10 joined the navy, 65 went into industry, and 5 remained at home. Make a rectangular distribution graph to show where these students went from high school.

11. Last year, Jane read 50 books, 25 of them were historical novels, 10 were mysteries, 5 were biographies, 7 were westerns, and 3 were books of essays. Make a rectangular distribution graph to show the types of books Jane read last year.

12. A certain company spends each dollar of its income as follows:

Labor 40¢	Rentals 20¢
Materials 25¢	Dividends 6¢
Interest 5¢	Taxes 4¢

Make a circle graph to show these facts.

13. In a certain school, the number of students taking the various grades of mathematics in the school are as follows:

Elementary Algebra	800	Trigonometry	75
10th Year Math	650	Advanced Algebra	30
Intermediate Algebra	250	Solid Geometry	35

Make a circle graph to show these facts. (First find the total number of students taking high school mathematics.)

14. The formula for the wage a boy would earn at 40¢ an hour is $W = 40n$, where $n =$ the number of hours he works and the wage W is in terms of cents. Substituting into this formula, make a table of values with the number of hours ranging from 1 to 5. Plot the points on a line graph.

15. The cost of any number of pencils at 5¢ a pencil is given by the formula $C = 5n$ where C stands for the cost in cents and n is the number of pencils. Substituting into this formula, make a table of values with the number of pencils ranging from 1 to 5. Plot the points on a line graph.

Algebra

(For a review of rules and methods, see Chapter 10, Pages 259-318)

1. Express algebraically:
   a. the number of inches in f feet.
   b. the number of inches in f feet and i inches.
   c. the number of months in y years.
   d. the number of cents in d dimes.
   e. the number of pints in q quarts.

2. Using the formula, $p = 7l + 2w$, find p if
   a. $l = 5$ and $w = 3$ c. $l = 10$ and $w = 3$
   b. $l = 18$ and $w = 4$ d. $l = 6\frac{1}{2}$ and $w = 2\frac{1}{2}$

3. Using the formula $A = 6w$, find A if
    a. $w = 7$ *b.* $w = 2\frac{1}{2}$ *c.* $w = 3$ *d.* $w = 5/6$

4. What are the factors of each of the following?
    a. $2x$ *c.* $3xy^2$ *e.* $12ac$
    b. ax^2 *d.* $8abc$ *f.* $5x^3y$

5. Factor each of the following:
    a. $2x + 2y$ *e.* $5a + 5b$ *i.* $4x - 2y$
    b. $3x - 6y$ *f.* $ax + ab$ *j.* $cd - ce$
    c. $ax + 2a$ *g.* $2x + 2$ *k.* $3m + 3n$
    d. $2a + 6x$ *h.* $by + bz$ *l.* $ax + bx$

6. Add: *a.* $\begin{array}{r} +3 \\ -7 \end{array}$ *c.* $\begin{array}{r} -6 \\ +7 \end{array}$ *e.* $\begin{array}{r} -8 \\ -7 \end{array}$ *g.* $\begin{array}{r} -1 \\ +7 \end{array}$ *i.* $\begin{array}{r} +2 \\ +5 \end{array}$

               b. $\begin{array}{r} -5 \\ -4 \end{array}$ *d.* $\begin{array}{r} +9 \\ -2 \end{array}$ *f.* $\begin{array}{r} +2 \\ -2 \end{array}$ *h.* $\begin{array}{r} -3 \\ -9 \end{array}$ *j.* $\begin{array}{r} +7 \\ +9 \end{array}$

7. Subtract the second number from the first:
    a. $-7, +3$ *d.* $+6, +4$ *g.* $+2, +5$ *j.* $-5, -4$
    b. $+6, -2$ *e.* $-1, +7$ *h.* $-7, +6$ *k.* $+8, -7$
    c. $-8, -4$ *f.* $-3, +9$ *i.* $-8, -3$ *l.* $+2, -$

8. Multiply:
    a. $(-2)(3)$ *e.* $(4a)(2)$ *i.* $(+7a)(-$
    b. $(-3)(-4)$ *f.* $(-3x)(-4)$ *j.* $(-3a)(-$
    c. $(-7)(+8)$ *g.* $(+4)(-2x)$ *k.* $(+11x)(+$
    d. $(+4)(2)$ *h.* $(-7)(-3x)$ *l.* $(-12x)(-$

9. Divide:
    a. $\dfrac{-8}{+2}$ *c.* $\dfrac{12}{3}$ *e.* $\dfrac{+25t}{5}$ *g.* $\dfrac{+42rt}{-7r}$

    b. $\dfrac{-16}{-4}$ *d.* $\dfrac{15}{-3}$ *f.* $\dfrac{-60x}{-12}$ *h.* $\dfrac{-72t}{+12t}$

10. Write equations for each of the following problems:
(Do not solve).
    a. Five apples cost 30¢. What is the cost of one apple?
    b. Three times a number is 69. Find the number.
    c. 12% of a number is 60. Find the number.
    d. Jim bought a pencil and a pad of paper for 30¢. The paper cost 20¢ more than the pencil. Find the cost of each.
    e. Jane went to the store with $15. After buying a dress, she had $5.75 left. Find the cost of the dress.

11. Solve and check the following:
    a. $7x + 2x = 36$ *d.* $3x + 5x - 2x = 30$
    b. $6x - 2x = 16$ *e.* $\frac{1}{2}x + \frac{1}{4}x = 9$
    c. $\frac{3}{4}x - \frac{1}{2}x = 2$ *f.* $\frac{1}{3}t - \frac{1}{4}t = 2$

12. Write a formula for each of the following:
    a. The volume of a box equals its length times its width times its height.
    b. The number of feet in y yards and f feet.
    c. Interest equals principal times rate times time.

13. Study each of the following tables and write a formula to represent the facts.

a.

a	0	1	2	3
b	0	3	6	9

b.

x	0	1	2	3	4
y	2	3	4	5	6

c.

a	5	7	9	12
b	2	4	6	9

d.

x	1	2	3	4	5
y	4	6	8	10	12

14. Represent as signed numbers:
    a. a gain of 3 yards
    b. 2 degrees below zero
    c. 20 miles south
    d. depositing $15 in the bank
    e. a loss of $8
    f. going down 3 floors in an elevator
    g. 10 miles north

15. Solve each of the following using algebraic equations.
    a. A number increased by 6 gives 21.
    b. One number is three times another number. Their sum is 16. Find them.
    c. Jean is 4 years older than Anne. The sum of their ages is 20. How old is each girl?
    d. Three times a number increased by 10 equals 46. Find the number.
    e. Find the side of a square whose perimeter is 24 inches.
    f. Separate 16 into two parts so that one part is three times the other.
    g. A number decreased by 6 equals 10. What is the number?
    h. Find the rate a man must go in order to travel 120 miles in 4 hours.
    i. A man left $12,000 to his wife, daughter, and son. The daughter received twice as much as the son and the wife received seven times as much as the son. How much did each receive?

Geometry

(For a review of rules and methods, see Chapter 11, Pages 319-402)

1. What is the perimeter of a square whose side is:
   a. 4 in.   b. 1½ ft.   c. 3 yd.
2. An isosceles triangle has a perimeter of 24 feet and a base of 8 feet. How long is each of the two legs?
3. One side of an equilateral triangle is 2¾ inches. Find the perimeter.
4. The length of a rectangle is 13 and the width is 5. Find its diagonal.
5. A ladder 15 feet long leans against a building. If the foot of the ladder is 9 feet out from the building, how high up on the building does the ladder reach?
6. A right triangle has legs of 15 inches and 8 inches. How long is its hypotenuse?
7. Find the area of a rectangle if:
   a. $l = 10$ ft. and $w = 2½$ ft.   b. $l = 24$ in. and $w = ½$ ft.
8. Find the area of a square whose sides are:
   a. 5 inches   b. 2½ ft.   c. 1¾ yards
9. Find the area of a parallelogram if:
   a. $b = 5$ ft., $h = 12$ inches.   c. $b = 3$ yards, $h = 2$ ft.
   b. $b = 2½$ feet, $h = ½$ ft.   d. $b = 5$ feet, $h = 3$ yds.

10. Find the area of a triangle if:
    a. $b=5$ feet, $h=4$ feet   c. $b=2\frac{1}{2}$ ft., $h=6$ in.
    b. $b=54$ inches, $h=2$ feet   d. $b=12$ ft., $h=3\frac{3}{4}$ ft.
11. Find the area of a trapezoid with bases of 20 ft. and 15 feet and an altitude of 5 feet.
12. Find the area of a trapezoid whose bases are 16 feet and 12 feet and whose altitude is 4 feet.
13. Find the circumference of a circle whose radius is 21 feet.
14. Find the circumference of a wheel whose diameter is 10 feet.
15. Mr. Brown has a circular swimming pool whose radius is 12 feet. Find the distance around the pool.
16. A pie tin has a diameter of 9 inches. Find its circumference.
17. Find the area of a circle whose radius is 7 feet.
18. A circle has a diameter of 15 inches. What is its area?
19. A semicircle has a radius of 21 inches. Find its area.
20. What is the area of a circle whose diameter is 16 feet?
21. Find the volume of a box whose length is 5 feet, width 3 feet, and whose height is 2 feet.
22. A fish tank is 14 inches long, 4 inches wide and 5 inches high. What is its volume?
23. A cube has an edge of 3 feet.
    a. What is its volume?   b. What is its surface area?
24. A wooden block is a cube with edges of 2 inches.
    a. Find its volume.   b. Find its surface area.
25. Find the volume of a tin can, cylindrical in shape, if the bottom has a radius of 3 inches and it is 5 inches high.
26. A silo is 18 feet high and has a diameter of 10 feet. Find its volume.
27. Find the volume of a cone whose height is 3 inches and whose diameter is 1½ inches.
28. A cone has a radius of 2 inches and a height of 5 inches. What is its volume?
29. Find the volume of a pyramid if the area of its base is 25 sq. ft. and it has a height of 2 ft.
30. A pyramid has a triangular base whose area is 32 sq. inches and it has a height of 18 inches. Find the volume.
31. The base of a pyramid is a square 4 feet on a side. The height of the pyramid is 5 feet. Find its volume.
32. The base of a pyramid is a triangle whose base is 5 inches and whose height is 2 inches. The altitude of the pyramid is 3 inches. What is its volume?
33. Find the height of a tree that casts a shadow 5 feet long when a two-foot pole casts a shadow one-foot long.
34. A pole casts a shadow 8 feet long at the same time that a yardstick casts a 2-foot-long shadow. Find the height of the pole.
35. 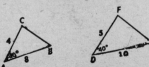 Complete: $\triangle ABC$ is———
    $\triangle DEF$

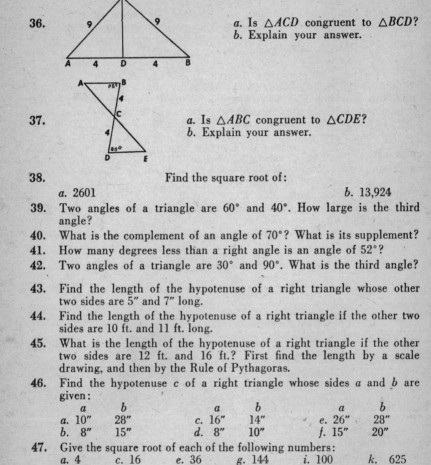

36. *a.* Is △*ACD* congruent to △*BCD*?
    b. Explain your answer.

37. *a.* Is △*ABC* congruent to △*CDE*?
    b. Explain your answer.

38.   Find the square root of:
    a. 2601   *b.* 13,924

39. Two angles of a triangle are 60° and 40°. How large is the third angle?

40. What is the complement of an angle of 70°? What is its supplement?

41. How many degrees less than a right angle is an angle of 52°?

42. Two angles of a triangle are 30° and 90°. What is the third angle?

43. Find the length of the hypotenuse of a right triangle whose other two sides are 5″ and 7″ long.

44. Find the length of the hypotenuse of a right triangle if the other two sides are 10 ft. and 11 ft. long.

45. What is the length of the hypotenuse of a right triangle if the other two sides are 12 ft. and 16 ft.? First find the length by a scale drawing, and then by the Rule of Pythagoras.

46. Find the hypotenuse *c* of a right triangle whose sides *a* and *b* are given:

	a	*b*		*a*	*b*		*a*	*b*
a.	10″	28″	*c.*	16″	14″	*e.*	26″	28″
b.	8″	15″	*d.*	8″	10″	*f.*	15″	20″

47. Give the square root of each of the following numbers:

a. 4	*c.* 16	*e.* 36	*g.* 144	*i.* 100	*k.* 625
b. 9	*d.* 25	*f.* 49	*h.* 81	*j.* 225	*l.* 1849

48. What are the factors of

a. 21	*c.* 48	*e.* 60	*g.* 108	*i.* 288
b. 25	*d.* 56	*f.* 88	*h.* 130	*j.* 314

49. What is the value of

a. 4^2	*c.* 1^2	*e.* 12^2	*g.* 11^2	*i.* 6^2
b. 15^2	*d.* 20^2	*f.* 9^2	*h.* 25^2	*j.* 8^2

50. Find the side of a square whose area is

a. 49 sq. in.	*d.* 9 sq. yd.	*g.* 16 sq. ft.
b. 25 sq. in.	*e.* 100 sq. mi.	*h.* 64 sq. yd.
c. 36 sq. ft.	*f.* 144 sq. in.	*i.* 81 sq. rd.

INDEX

INDEX

INDEX

INDEX

INDEX